Courts and Judicial Activism under Crisis Conditions

This collection examines topical issues related to the impact of courts on constitutional politics during extreme conditions.

The book explores the impact of activist courts on democracy, separation of powers and rule of law in times of emergency constitutionalism. It starts with a theoretical explanation of the concept, features and main manifestations of judicial activism and its impact in shaping the relationship between constitutional, international and supranational law. It then focuses on judicial activism in extreme conditions, for example, in times of emergencies and pandemics, or in the context of democratic backsliding, authoritarian constitutionalism and illiberal constitutionalism. Thus, the book may be considered as a contribution to the debates on judicial activism, including the discussion of the impact of courts on certainty, proportionality and balancing of rights, as well as on revolutionary courts challenging authoritarian context and generally over the role of courts in the context of illiberalism and democratic backsliding. The volume thus offers an explanation of the concept of judicial activism, its impact on both the legal system and the political order and the role of courts in shaping the structures of the legal order. These issues are explored in theoretical and comparative constitutional perspectives.

The book will be a valuable resource for academics and researchers working in the areas of courts, constitutional law and constitutional politics.

Martin Belov is Professor of Constitutional and Comparative Constitutional Law at the University of Sofia 'St. Kliment Ohridski', Bulgaria.

Comparative Constitutional Change

Series editors:

Xenophon Contiades is Professor of Public Law, Panteion University, Athens, Greece and Managing Director, Centre for European Constitutional Law, Athens, Greece.

Thomas Fleiner is Emeritus Professor of Law at the University of Fribourg, Switzerland. He teaches and researches in the areas of Federalism, Rule of Law, Multicultural State; Comparative Administrative and Constitutional Law; Political Theory and Philosophy; Swiss Constitutional and Administrative Law; and Legislative Drafting. He has published widely in these and related areas.

Alkmene Fotiadou is Research Associate at the Centre for European Constitutional Law, Athens.

Richard Albert is Professor of Law at the University of Texas at Austin.

Comparative Constitutional Change has developed into a distinct field of constitutional law. It encompasses the study of constitutions through the way they change and covers a wide scope of topics and methodologies. Books in this series include work on developments in the functions of the constitution, the organization of powers and the protection of rights, as well as research that focuses on formal amendment rules and the relation between constituent and constituted power. The series includes comparative approaches along with books that focus on single jurisdictions, and brings together research monographs and edited collections which allow the expression of different schools of thought. While the focus is primarily on law, where relevant the series may also include political science, historical, philosophical and empirical approaches that explore constitutional change.

Also in the series:

Accountability and the Law
Rights, Authority and Transparency of Public Power
Edited By Piotr Mikuli and Grzegorz Kuca

Illiberal Constitutionalism in Poland and Hungary
The Deterioration of Democracy, Misuse of Human Rights and Abuse of the Rule of Law
Tímea Drinóczi and Agnieszka Bień-Kacała

Courts and Judicial Activism under Crisis Conditions
Policy Making in a Time of Illiberalism and Emergency Constitutionalism
Edited by Martin Belov

For more information about this series, please visit: www.routledge.com/Comparative-Constitutional-Change/book-series/COMPCONST

Courts and Judicial Activism under Crisis Conditions

Policy Making in a Time of Illiberalism and Emergency Constitutionalism

Edited by
Martin Belov

Routledge
Taylor & Francis Group
LONDON AND NEW YORK

First published 2022
by Routledge
2 Park Square, Milton Park, Abingdon, Oxon OX14 4RN

and by Routledge
605 Third Avenue, New York, NY 10158

Routledge is an imprint of the Taylor & Francis Group, an informa business

British Library Cataloguing-in-Publication Data
A catalogue record for this book is available from the British Library

Library of Congress Cataloging-in-Publication Data
Names: Belov, Martin, editor.
Title: Courts and judicial activism under crisis conditions : policy making in a time of illiberalism and emergency constitutionalism / edited by Martin Belov.
Description: Abingdon, Oxon ; New York, NY : Routledge, 2022. | Series: Comparative constitutional change | Includes bibliographical references and index.
Identifiers: LCCN 2021012351 (print) | LCCN 2021012352 (ebook) | ISBN 9781032060828 (hardback) | ISBN 9781032060927 (paperback) | ISBN 9781003200666 (ebook)
Subjects: LCSH: War and emergency legislation--Europe. | Political questions and judicial power--Europe. | Constitutional courts–Europe.
Classification: LCC KJC7520 .C68 2022 (print) | LCC KJC7520 (ebook) | DDC 347.4/03504--dc23
LC record available at https://lccn.loc.gov/2021012351
LC ebook record available at https://lccn.loc.gov/2021012352

ISBN: 978-1-032-06082-8 (hbk)
ISBN: 978-1-032-06092-7 (pbk)
ISBN: 978-1-003-20066-6 (ebk)

DOI: 10.4324/9781003200666

Typeset in Galliard
by Taylor & Francis Books

To my beloved children: my daughter Albena and my son Boyan

Contents

List of contributors ix

Introduction 1
MARTIN BELOV

PART I
Judicial activism: Conceptual and comparative constitutional issues 19

1 Law, politics, and the constitutional courts' activism: Setting the starting point 21
MAURO ZAMBONI

2 Activism as defence: The role of courts in shaping the relationship between constitutions and international law: A comparison of the apex courts of Switzerland, Germany and Austria 43
STEFAN SCHLEGEL

PART II
Judicial activism of international and supranational courts and its impact on national constitutional orders 61

3 The revolutionary impact of European Court of Human Rights case law on the idea of *res judicata* in criminal justice: The Italian experience 63
MARIA LUCIA DI BITONTO

4 Thinking outside the politics box: Framing a judicial role in shaping militant democracy in the European Union 74
VIOLETA BEŠIREVIĆ

PART III
Judicial activism and illiberal constitutionalism 99

5 An illiberal turn or a counter-constitutional revolution?: About the Polish Constitutional Tribunal before and after 2015 101
ALEKSANDRA KUSTRA-ROGATKA

6 When activism takes the wrong turn: The case of the Romanian Constitutional Court 125
BIANCA SELEJAN-GUȚAN

7 The revolutionary role of constitutional courts in Morocco and Jordan as a contemporary example from the MENA region 145
HADEEL S. ABU HUSSEIN

PART IV
Judicial activism and emergency constitutionalism 169

8 Mastering emergency situations: The activist role of the Bulgarian Constitutional Court in redefining the constitutional design of war, state of siege and state of emergency 171
MARTIN BELOV

9 Activism of the Croatian Constitutional Court and Covid-19: A Bridge Too Far 194
DJORDJE GARDASEVIC

Conclusion 213
MARTIN BELOV

Index 217

List of contributors

Professor Dr Martin Belov (editor) (University of Sofia 'St. Kliment Ohridski')

Martin Belov is Professor in Constitutional and Comparative Constitutional Law at the University of Sofia 'St. Kliment Ohridski'. He is Vice Dean of the University of Sofia 'St. Kliment Ohridski', Faculty of Law, responsible for the international relations and digitalisation. Martin has been visiting professor at Harry Radzyner Law School, IDC Herzliya, Israel (2021), University Paris II Pantheon-Assas (2019), University Roma Tre, Rome, Italy (2019), Goethe-University Frankfurt am Main, Germany (2019), University of Girona, Spain (2019), University 'Pompeu Fabra', Barcelona, Spain (2019), Europa-University Viadrina, Frankfurt/Oder, Germany (2017 and 2018), University of Bari, Italy (2018), European Law and Governance School, Athens (2017–2018 and 2020–2021), University of Södertorn, Stockholm, Sweden (2017), Scuolla Superiore Sant'Anna, Pisa, Italy (2016), University of Warsaw, Poland (2015), University of Lisbon, Portugal (2012), State University of Milan, Italy (2011), University of Cologne, Germany (2007–2009), etc. Martin has been project researcher at the Max-Planck Institute for European Legal History, Frankfurt am Main, Germany (2010–2012) and visiting researcher at the Institute for Federalism, Fribourg, Switzerland (2014). He has specialised at the University of Oxford (UK) (2017), Max-Planck Institute for Comparative Public Law and International Law, Heidelberg, Germany (2009), and many other academic institutions. Martin is a member of the European Group of Public Law, International Association of Legislation, the Advisory Board of the Central and Eastern European Forum of Young Legal, Political and Social Theorists, and other scientific and academic organisations. Martin is a member of the scientific boards of many academic journals. He has published 20 books and more than 90 scientific papers.

Professor Dr Violeta Beširević (Union University, Belgrade, Serbia)

Violeta Beširević is a tenured Professor of Law at Union University Law School Belgrade, a Research Associate at Central European University in Budapest, an Affiliate Professor at the University of Milano-Bicocca, Center for Law and Pluralism, and Editor-in-Chief of *Pravni Zapisi, Union University Law School Review*. She serves as a member of the Board of Directors of the European

Public Law Organization and Fund for Open Society, Belgrade. Violeta Beširević holds an L.L.M. and an S.J.D. in Comparative Constitutional Law from the Central European University, Budapest, and a B.A. from Belgrade University Law School. Professor Beširević was awarded a Fulbright stipend in 2012. She was a visiting scholar at NYU Law School, George Washington University Law School, Brigham Young University Law School, and ASSER Institute in The Hague. Professor Beširević works in the field of Constitutional Law, EU Constitutional Law, European Human Rights Law, and Bioethics. Her recent works include 'Making Sense of the Political Question Doctrine: The Case of Kosovo,' *Review of Central and East European Law* (2020, forthcoming) and *New Politics of Decisionism* (ed.), Eleven International Publishing, The Hague, 2019.

Professor Dr Maria Lucia Di Bitonto (LUISS 'Guido Carli', Rome, Italy)

Maria Lucia Di Bitonto is full Professor of Criminal Procedure Law. She is Associate Professor at the School of Law in the University of Camerino. She is Adjunct Professor of Criminal Procedure Law at the Department of Law of the Luiss Guido Carli University, where she is also Adjunct Professor of Corporate Criminal Law and Procedure. She wrote extensively on the subject of criminal procedure. Her studies are focused on criminal evidence, public prosecutor, human rights and criminal procedure, pretrial detention, defensive investigations, a defendant's right to be silent, criminal proceedings against corporations, due process of law and corporate criminal liability. On those issues she published four monographs, several articles or papers, and participated in seminars, conferences and research groups.

Professor Dr Djordje Gardasevic (University of Zagreb, Croatia)

Djordje Gardasevic is an Associate Professor of Constitutional Law at the Zagreb Faculty of Law (Croatia). He earned his L.L.M. degree at the Central European University in Budapest (thesis title: 'Independence and Impartiality of Courts – Article 6 of the ECHR') and his Ph.D. at the Zagreb Faculty of Law (thesis title: 'Restrictions of Human Rights and Fundamental Freedoms in States of Emergency'). He participated, among other events, at the 7th and 9th World Congresses of the International Association for Constitutional Law (Athens, 2007, Oslo 2014), the 22nd and 23rd Congresses of the International Political Science Association – IPSA (Madrid, 2012, Montreal, 2014), the APSA Annual Meeting (San Francisco, 2015) and the ASN World Conventions (New York, 2017, 2018 and 2019). His research interests include: states of emergency, fundamental rights and freedoms, constitutional theory and comparative constitutional law.

Professor Dr Bianca Selejan-Guțan (University of Sibiu, Romania)

Bianca Selejan-Guțan – Ph.D. (Bucharest), L.L.M (Nottingham) – is a Professor of Constitutional Law and of Human Rights Law at the Lucian Blaga University of Sibiu, Romania, Faculty of Law. Her main areas of research are judicial review, comparative constitutional law and European law of human rights. She is a member of the advisory board of the ICON-S CEE Chapter, vice-president of the Romanian Association of Constitutional Law and a member of the editorial board of the Romanian Journal of Comparative Law. She is the author of the book The Constitution of Romania: A Contextual Analysis (Hart Publishing, 2016) and of numerous other books, articles and chapters in the above-mentioned fields.

Dr Hadeel S. Abu Hussein (University of Oxford, UK)

Hadeel S. Abu Hussein is a research fellow at the Middle East Centre, St Antony's College, University of Oxford and Early Career Fellow at Bonavero Institute of Human Rights, Law School, Mansfield College at the University of Oxford. She holds a Ph.D. in law from the National University of Ireland, Galway. Hadeel's research focuses on public international law, human rights law and comparative constitutionalism, international legal discourse in the Middle East, and Israeli/Palestinian conflict. Her work is enlightened by and engages with Third World Approaches to International Law. Previously she was a senior research fellow and consultancy advisor at the Max Plank Foundation for International Peace and the Rule of Law, Heidelberg, Germany. Also, she was a research visitor at the Bonavero Institute of Human Rights, Law School at Oxford. She completed her LL.B. and LL.M. degrees at Tel Aviv University; and she is a member of the Israeli Bar Association. Moreover, she completed an executive education programme, 'Leadership Program for Legal and Business Women Fellowship', at the Wharton Business School and Penn Law at the University of Pennsylvania in the United States of America.

Professor Dr Aleksandra Kustra-Rogatka ('Nicolas Copernicus' University of Torun, Poland)

Aleksandra Kustra-Rogatka is Associate Professor at Nicolaus Copernicus University in Toruń. Previously she worked as a legal clerk at the Constitutional Court of Poland (2008–2017). She was visiting researcher at Georg-August-Universität Göttingen (2006), Freie Universität Berlin (2010) and Libera Università Internazionale degli Studi Sociali Guido Carli in Rome (2020). She was re:constitution fellow 2019/20. Her research interest covers comparative constitutional law, European constitutionalism and legal philosophy. She has published on topics such as the impact of the European integration on constitutional law of the EU Member States, judicial review, transitional justice and rule of law in Europe. She is a Member of the International Association for Philosophy of Law and Social Philosophy (IVR) and the International Society of Public Law (Central and Eastern European Chapter).

Dr Stefan Schlegel (University of Bern, Switzerland)

Stefan Schlegel is a postdoctoral researcher and lecturer in Public Law at the University of Bern (Switzerland), where he is working on his second book on the constitutional guarantee of property. He obtained his master's degree from the University of Zurich and his Ph.D. in law from the University of Bern.

Previously to his current position, Stefan was a Visiting Researcher at the University of Toronto and Senior Postdoctoral Research Fellow at the Max Planck Institute for the Study of Multiethnic and Multireligious Societies in Göttingen (Germany). Among Stefan's main research interests are immigration law, the relationship of international and domestic law, and the distributional effects of public law.

Professor Dr Mauro Zamboni (University of Stockholm, Sweden)

Mauro Zamboni is Professor of legal theory at Stockholm University, Senior Associate Research Fellow at the Institute of Advanced Legal Studies, University of London (UK), and Korea Legislation Research Institute Global Research Fellow (South Korea). His fields of interest are legislative studies and the relationships between law and politics (mostly from a legal theoretical perspective).

Introduction

Martin Belov

Courts are cornerstone institutions of liberal-democratic constitutionalism. They are at the core of liberal-democratic constitutional design and are considered as the most important safeguards for liberal constitutional values. Thus, courts are safeguards for liberal-democratic constitutional axiology and teleology and as such are integrated in the institutional scheme of representative democracy. In fact, courts are important for all forms of constitutional governance but are indispensable especially for liberal-democratic constitutionalism. This is true for ordinary and specialised courts as well as for constitutional courts.

Courts are cherished as neutral arbiters and politically independent guardians of constitutional rights and freedoms detached from political pressures, party political schemes of power and populist temptations. They are supposed to be islands of technocratic wisdom within the sea of politics. Courts, together with administration, are promoted and safeguarded as realms of political impartiality and competence within the overall political power grid of constitutional democracy. They are esteemed as preserves of legal purity, political detachment and purely technocratic expertise.

It is not always the case that the courts are, have been or will be just neutral arbiters and politically independent institutions. Indeed, liberal-democratic constitutionalism is inconceivable without independent courts. Powerful constitutional and administrative courts are indispensable elements of this form of constitutionalism which has been the unchallenged and dominant version of constitutionalism in the Global North until the deep crises that have hit it in the last decade – the financial crisis, the migration crisis, and most recently the Covid-19 crisis. Courts have been promoters of rights and constitutionally based and legally framed freedom even at the expense of confronting institutions that have larger democratic backgrounds and possess higher democratic legitimacy, such as the parliaments and the executive power institutions. Courts have gained the position of safeguards of the constitutional framework of the political process and the legal framework of the substantial policy-making. They also have positioned themselves as authoritative interpreters of the constitution and the constitutional order.

DOI: 10.4324/9781003200666-1

The interpreters became central players of the evolving constitutional and political order. This became more visible since the death of the author[1] in the context of accelerating legal post-modernity based on interpretative negotiation of meaning of constitutional texture and the concepts enshrined in it. Moreover, the demise of democracy is paralleled by the rise of technocracy. In this context, we are witnessing the emergence of national – and in Europe also of supranational – judicial empire.[2] The courts – more precisely the constitutional and supreme courts – are increasingly engaging in interpretative activities based on the 'open texture of law'.[3] This way they are participating in norm-setting activities and in policy-making. Thus, they are more and more assuming the role of authoritative speakers of the community and strategic policy-makers in central policy domains and in crucial moments of the political process. In contrast, they are withdrawing from the position of neutral arbiters and safeguards for the observation of the rules of the game.

Hence, constitutional and supreme courts as well as international and supranational courts are increasingly assertive in promoting political objectives, thus disproportionally engaging not only in technocratic policy-making but also in politics. This might be the case for both constitutional politics and sector-specific politics in different policy domains. Courts may prove to be powerful sources of policy visions without any proper democratic justification. They may be triggers and promoters of legal and political revolutions[4] in ways that are not controllable by virtue of the institutional checks and balances provided by the contemporary constitutional orders.

Thus, judicial activism needs theoretical conceptualisation and critical exploration of its effects and side effects. This is especially true for judicial activism producing outcomes with revolutionary impact for national, sub-national and supranational constitutionalism. This is due to the fact that courts are increasingly involved in legal interpretation on the edge between national, international, supranational and at times also sub-national legal orders.

The proper assessment of courts' activist engagement in constitutional policy-making by virtue of judicial politics is one of the keys to the understanding of contemporary constitutionalism. Judicial activism[5] is a central phenomenon for

1 See Barthes, R., La mort de l'auteur, https://monoskop.org/images/3/38/Barthes_Roland_1968_1984_La_mort_de_l_auteur.pdf.

2 See Belov, M. 'Global Rule of Law Instead of Global Democracy? Legitimacy of Global Judicial Empire on the Edge between Westphalian and post-Westphalian Constitutionalism'. In: Belov, M. (ed.) *The Role of Courts in Contemporary Legal Orders*, The Hague, Eleven, 2019.

3 For the open texture of law, see Hart, H.L.A. *The Concept of Law*, Oxford, Oxford University Press, 1997, pp. 124–136.

4 For the problems of legal revolution see Belov, M. and A. Abat I Ninet (eds) *Revolution, Transition, Memory, and Oblivion. Reflections on Constitutional Change.* Edward Elgar, 2020; Ackerman, B. *Revolutionary Constitutions, Charismatic Leadership and the Rule of Law*, Harvard University Press, 2019; Jacobsohn, G. and Y. Roznai, *Constitutional Revolution*, Yale University Press, 2020; Albert, R. (ed.) *Revolutionary Constitutionalism, Law, Legitimacy, Power*, Hart Publishing, 2020.

5 See Tridimas, T. 'The Court of Justice and Judicial Activism', *European Law Review*, Vol. 21, No. 3, 1996, pp. 199–210; Constantinesco, V. 'The ECJ as a Law-maker

understanding the role of courts in contemporary legal orders. Thus, when courts are engaged in activist judicial politics (or when they deliberately refrain to do so), this is an important reason for critical theoretical reflection. Judicial politics is a challenge to the traditional neutral role of courts as technocratic expert bodies entrenched in rule of law and restricted from activist engagement in sovereignty, democracy and policy-making. Hence, judicial activism is an appealing occasion for reconsideration, critical deconstruction and subsequent context adequate reconstruction of key principles of constitutionalism, such as rule of law, separation of powers and democracy. These principles need deconstruction and subsequent reconstruction in the light of judicial activism. In that regard, this book is an invitation for reflection on the role of courts in liberal-democratic constitutional orders and their functioning as engines for rule of law and democracy or for their 'constructive deconstruction'.

The courts produce 'constructive deconstruction' of rule of law and democracy in a paradoxical way. They are important contributors to the establishment of liberal democracy based on rule of law being defenders of the supremacy of the constitution, the primacy of international law, and human rights. Thus, they construct constitutional order together with the official political players – the parliaments, the governments, the institutions of the constituent power. At the same time, they deconstruct our traditional understanding of democracy by promoting technocratic governance based on judicial activism.

Hence, courts are deconstructing and constructing, promoting and hampering constitutional democracy in a rather asymmetric and dubious manner. This is visible also with regard to horizontal and especially vertical judicial dialogue.[6] In fact, judicial dialogue with international and supranational courts puts the constitutional jurisdictions in the role of ultimate players in multilevel constitutional games.[7] That is why judicial activism, sometimes amounting to judicial imperialism, on national, international and supranational levels, shifts the courts from the purely legal order to the realm of the political. It makes them overt political players capable of inflicting even revolutionary changes in both the legal and the political orders. In fact, we are witnessing the emergence of networked 'empire of courts' – a global judicial empire – which plays pivotal role in mastering and

praeter aut contra legem?' In: O'Keeffe, D. (ed.) *Judicial Review in European Union Law: Liber Amicorum in Honour of Lord Slynn of Hadley*, The Hague, Kluwer, 2000, pp. 73–79; Weatherill, S. 'Activism and Restraint in the European Court of Justice', in Capps, P. et al. (eds) *Asserting Jurisdiction. International and European Legal Perspectives*, Oxford, Hart, 2003, pp. 255–281; Muir, E., Dawson, M. and de Witte, B. 'Introduction: The European Court of Justice as a Political Actor'. In: Dawson, M. et al. (eds) *Judicial Activism at the European Court of Justice*, Cheltenham, Edward Elgar, 2013, pp. 1–10; Arnull, A. 'Judicial Activism and the European Court of Justice: How Should Academics Respond?', ibid., pp. 211–232.

6 See Belov, M. (ed.) *Judicial Dialogue*, The Hague, Eleven, 2019.

7 See Belov, M. 'Constitutional Courts as Ultimate Players in Multilevel Constituent Power Games: The Bulgarian Case'. In: Belov, M. (ed.) *Courts, Politics and Constitutional Law. Judicialization of Politics and Politicization of the Judiciary*, Abingdon, Routledge, 2019.

shaping globalism, or vice versa – in triggering and promoting neo-nationalism. Courts may be agents of liberalism and neoliberalism, but also of nationalism and neo-nationalism. They may be promoters of globalism, regionalism or nationalism. In any case, their increasing role in policy shaping and policy-making should not be neglected. The role of courts in contemporary legal and political orders must be thoroughly explored and the concepts of judicial activism and revolutionary courts may serve as important viewpoints for such research.

This edited volume is a multidiscoursive contribution to the existing debate on judicial activism, judicialisation of politics and politicisation of the judiciary.[8] In fact, it is a follow-up of a previous volume that I have published with Routledge, namely the book *Courts, Politics and Constitutional Law. Judicialization of Politics and Politicization of the Judiciary*. Thus, the current volume will be embedded in a solid academic discourse on topical issues related to the impact of courts on constitutional politics – a debate that has already attracted the attention of the academic community and the readership.

However, this book has something more to offer. It provides the reader with critical contributions dedicated to several important and still less researched aspects of judicial activism. The majority of the book chapters are devoted to the impact and the interrelations of judicial activism on illiberal constitutionalism and emergency constitutionalism.[9] Hence, the book provides research of the role of courts in times of emergency constitutionalism, and the rising populist constitutionalism and illiberal constitutionalism.[10]

This book is a collective effort for exploring the phenomenon of judicial activism under crisis conditions and its impact on democracy and rule of law. It is structured around the concept of (re)evolutionary courts intensively engaging in judicial policy-making – a phenomenon which is especially problematic in times of illiberalism and emergency constitutionalism. Several interrelated phenomena underline this main approach. These are judicial activism, judicial intervention in politics, judicial policy-making, and judicial expansionism in the sphere of constitutional and ordinary politics. Courts are considered to be revolutionary and activist especially when their activity leads to radical changes in the constitutional and legal order or when they have revolutionary impact on the social life and the political process. Hence, this is a book about blurring the demarcation lines provided by the normative theories for separation of powers. It is a book that targets

8 See Stone Sweet, A. *Governing with Judges*, Oxford, Oxford University Press, 2000.

9 Albert, R. and Y. Roznai (eds) *Constitutionalism Under Extreme Conditions: Law, Emergency, Exception* (Ius Gentium: Comparative Perspectives on Law and Justice), Springer, 2020; Greene, A. *Permanent States of Emergency and the Rule of Law. Constitutions in the Age of Crisis*, Hart, 2018.

10 See *German Law Journal*, Populist Constitutionalism: Varieties, Complexities and Contradictions, Volume 20, Special Issue 3, April 2019; Belov, M. (ed.) *Populist Constitutionalism and Illiberal Democracies*, Intersentia, 2021; Drinoczi, T. and A. Bien-Kacala, 'Illiberal Constitutionalism: The Case of Hungary and Poland', *German Law Journal*, Volume 20, Issue 8, December 2019, pp. 1140–1166.

judicial expansion in the sphere of politics and the way the courts challenge established concepts that are essentially important for rule of law and democracy.

All chapters of the book are united by the idea of exploration of judicial activism and its impact on rule of law and its concrete elements – certainty and proportionality. The book explores the different manifestations of judicial activism that allow courts to play a central political role in mastering socio-political relations. The concept of revolutionary courts is both an innovative feature of the book and another unifying threat allowing the book chapters to engage in intellectual dialogue with each other. Last but not least, the coherency of the book is assured by the socio-legal approach of most of the chapters and their focus on constitutionalism under extreme conditions[11] consisting of democratic backsliding, rising anti-constitutionalism and spreading of emergency and more precisely of pandemic constitutionalism.

To sum up, there are several factors that unite the contributions of this volume. These are the research methodology, the core concepts and theoretical concerns, some of the main assumptions and the underlying topic of revolutionary courts as judicial engines of constitutional and political order which are especially powerful in times of crisis. In that regard, the book is based on clear logic. It starts with conceptual and comparative issues, continues with the role of judicial activism on the edge of national, international and supranational law, explores the interplay between judicial activism and illiberal constitutionalism and concludes with an analysis of the interrelation between judicial activism and authoritarian trends in times of emergency constitutionalism based on pandemic measures.

The last two chapters explore exactly what is the impact of pandemic and emergency constitutionalism on rule of law and democracy and what is the contribution of the courts to the trend for emergence of a new 'health Leviathan'.[12] Thus, Chapters 8 and 9 are an intellectual response to the role of courts as preventive players or as contributors and precursors of democracy and rule of law infringements and trends towards paternalistic and authoritarian constitutionalism.

In that regard, the last two chapters of the book included in Part IV are a must for a book on judicial activism in the current socio-legal circumstances and context. This is due to the fact that judicial activism in times of pandemic and emergency constitutionalism is a topical issue which should attract the attention of the academic audience. More precisely, we should upgrade the traditional debate on the impact of judicial activism on sovereignty, representative democracy and separation of power with research and deliberation focused on judicial activism in the context of emergency and pandemic constitutionalism, failures of rule of law systems, and the interplay between militant democracy and democratic backsliding. This should be a discussion of the topical issues which allow novel viewpoints on the role of courts in a socio-political context that is detrimental to rule

11 See Albert, R. and Y. Roznai (eds) op. cit.

12 For the concept of 'health Leviathan', see Belov, M. 'The Role of Fear Politics in Global Constitutional "Ernstfall": Images of Fear under COVID-19 Health Paternalism'. In: Belov, M. (ed.) *Populist Constitutionalism and Illiberal Democracies. Between Constitutional Imagination, Normative Entrenchment and Political Reality*, Cambridge, Intersentia, 2021, pp. 187–220 and the literature cited there.

of law and democracy. One of the tasks of this book is to launch arguments and insights for researching judicial activism under extraordinary and extreme conditions that put the liberal-democratic constitutional order and constitutionalism under a kind of stress test.

Usually judicial activism is revolutionary. This is due to the fact that it produces radical changes in the constitutional and legal order, with a massive impact on the socio-political order. Conceptually activism relates to revolution, not to evolution. Both revolution and evolution are associated with profound change with legal, political and social dimensions. Activism and revolution produce shifts of reality and ruptures of established patterns and are promoters of socio-political and legal dynamics and change.

However, there are situations when judicial activism may also be evolutionary. This is the case when courts follow already established jurisprudential patterns produced by previous revolutionary case law while still engaging in policy-making and thus in constitutional politics. The confirmation and continuation of existent judicial politics is still politics. Thus, it constitutes a form of judicial activism.

Hence, judicial activism can be both revolutionary and evolutionary. It can both produce radical novelties and open new patterns of development, or produce ruptures in constitutional orders. But it can also confirm established jurisprudence that has already triggered legal revolution or has had revolutionary impact on constitutionalism and the social and political life. Thus, activist courts may also be producing affirmative case law serving as a continuation of previous revolutions, or it can even be entrenched in jurisprudential path-dependency. That is why activist courts are typically revolutionary, but may be evolutionary as well, although as an exception. Consequently, the book explores judicial activism of both revolutionary and evolutionary courts, focusing mainly on constitutional courts as well as on international and supranational courts.

The book assesses the impact of expansive, activist and even imperial courts on rule of law, separation of powers and democracy, taking into account both the advantages and disadvantages of such institutional behaviour. Most of the chapters of the book focus of activist courts which had revolutionised some policy domains, or may, could or should do this in the future. Thus, the book looks at the revolutionary impact of judicial policy-making that has already occurred as a fact (Di Bitonto) or as a phenomenon producing a negative turn in constitutional politics (Belov, Gardasevic, Kustra-Rogatka, Selejan-Guţan). The book also explores the eventual need for judicial activism that may or should be accomplished (Abu Hussein, Beširević). One of the contributors (Abu Hussein) explores the revolutionary impact of the mere introduction of constitutional courts in countries with authoritarian constitutional design and a traditionally conservative socio-political context. Thus, to an extent, paradoxically, the existence of constitutional courts, their introduction in the institutional design of the constitutional orders of late-comer rule of law states is considered to have a revolutionary impact on their social, political and constitutional orders. Moreover, some of the chapters (e.g. Schlegel, but also in a different context Beširević) conceptualise judicial activism as a defence strategy.

In that regard, judicial activism is viewed as both shield and sword. It is understood as an instrument for expansive judicial policy-making that may endanger democracy and rule of law, impede legitimate norm-setting through parliamentary process, and introduce '*gouvernement des juges*'.[13] It is conceived as a defence strategy for democracy against populist political regimes and authoritarian constitutionalism. And it is conceptualised as a tool for organising the constitutional order in a technocratic manner on the edge between democracy, technocracy and authoritarianism, and on the border between rule of law and rule of men.

In other words, the book is an attempt to expose both the advantages and disadvantages of judicial activism. It shows the perils of power-hungry courts and the threats of extensive constitutional interpretation by activist courts to constitutional democracy, separation of powers and the rule of law. It demonstrates the possible alliances between courts and governments in seizing power from parliaments and the people, especially in times of constitutional emergency. However, it also shows the impact of judicial activism on 'ordering constitutional orders'[14] in times of 'constitutionalism beyond statehood'.[15] The book defines the promises of judicial activism for safeguarding democracy and rule of law in times of illiberalism, populist constitutionalism, illiberal democracies, authoritarian constitutionalism and democratic backsliding. Hence, the book aims to explore the impact of activist courts on democracy and rule of law under extreme conditions.

The book is settled on the borderline between law and politics in a twofold manner. First, it explores the way the courts – especially the constitutional courts – are blurring the line between law and politics. It has already been mentioned that the book analyses judicial policy-making, judicialisation of politics, politicisation of the judiciary, and their impact on constitutionalism and the constitutional order. In this context constitutionalism is conceived as a socio-legal phenomenon with implications in the ideal, written and factual constitution, while the constitutional order denominates the valid law and the way it is structured, maintained and evolved. Hence, the book explores the impact of courts on both constitutionalism as a socio-political phenomenon and empirical process and on the constitutional order conceived as systems of legal rules structured and organised in a particular way.

Second, some of the contributions to this volume explore the impact of politics and political actors on courts. Thus, it problematises the politicisation of the judiciary and the perils to judicial independence stemming from political factors and power centres. The debate here is structured around several main groups of issues – the threats to judicial independence in times of populist constitutionalism

13 See Montesquieu, 'De l'esprit des lois', Ellipses Marketing, 2015.

14 For the concept of 'ordering of constitutional orders', see Tanchev, E. 'The Contemporary Supranational Constitutional Pluralism or the Ordering of Constitutional Orders'. In: Kirov, P. (ed.) *Constitutional Studies 2012–2013*, Sofia, 'St. Kliment Ohridski' University Press, 2014, pp. 171–198 (in Bulgarian).

15 For the 'constitutionalism beyond statehood', see Dobner, P. and M. Loughlin (eds) *Twilight of Constitutionalism?* Oxford, Oxford University Press, 2010; Walker, N. 'Taking Constitutionalism beyond the State', *Political Studies*, Vol. 56, No. 3, 2008, pp. 519–543.

and illiberal democracies (Kustra-Rogatka, Selejan-Guţan and Beširević), the use of courts as triggers of political reforms (Abu Hussein, Beširević) or the concerted action between courts and political players, e.g. the governments, to promote emergency constitutionalism limiting in a disproportional and imbalanced manner constitutional rights and endangering parliamentarism, legal certainty, proportionality and the rule of law (Belov, Gardasevic).

The book starts with a theoretical explanation of the concept, features and main manifestations of judicial activism and on its impact on shaping the relationship between constitutional and international and supranational law. However, the book focuses mainly on judicial activism in extreme conditions (e.g. in times of emergencies and pandemics) or in the context of democratic backsliding, authoritarian constitutionalism and illiberal constitutionalism. Thus, the book may be considered a contribution not only to the debates on judicial activism (including the discussion of the impact of courts on certainty, proportionality and balancing of rights), but also on revolutionary courts either challenging authoritarian context or contributing for its expansion. Thus, this is a book on the role of courts in the context of illiberalism and democratic backsliding.

Part I of the book explores the concept of judicial activism, its impact on both the legal system and the political order and the role of courts in shaping the structures of the legal order. These issues are explored in theoretical and comparative constitutional perspective. Hence, Part I offers theory, comparative analysis and important case law study.

In Chapter 1 Mauro Zamboni explores the stretching of the courts between law and politics from an institutionalist and functionalist perspective. The author critically assesses the standing and role of courts as institutions performing important political as well as legal functions. Zamboni outlines the main reasons for justification of the institutional performance of the courts from the competing perspectives of the legal and the political order.

Zamboni explores judicial activism from different perspectives, such as institutionalism and functionalism, legality and legitimacy. He analyses judicial activism as a socio-legal phenomenon and compares it with other related phenomena. That is why the author provides the reader with a 'definitional framework' comparing judicial activism with 'constitutional politics', 'government of judges' and 'judicialisation of politics'. Furthermore, he also defines the use of the concepts of courts, legal actors and political actors in this chapter. This is due to the fact that the chapter explores the judicial activism of all the highest courts in their dual capacity as both legal and political actors.

Mauro Zamboni offers an insightful analysis of the position of the constitutional courts between law and politics. He explores the relevance of the 'political vs. legal nature' discussion with regard to the constitutional courts. Finally, he provides a possible solution to the problem of judicial activism as a twofold (legal and political) phenomenon stretching the courts between the legal and the political order from the perspective of legal theory.

The main claim of Zamboni is that 'constitutional courts, though playing a bridging role between the political and legal worlds, are – from an institutional and functional perspective – primarily legal actors'. Thus, according to the author, 'the constitutional courts' primary responsibility is towards the legal community and the paradigms governing its discourse'.

The second chapter in Part I of the book is written by Stefan Schlegel. It explores the strategies of the apex courts – the constitutional and supreme courts – in domesticating international and supranational law. Thus, the chapter explores the role of these courts for 'ordering of constitutional orders'. Schlegel confronts us with an original intellectual provocation defining the judicial activism of the courts on the edge of constitutionalism 'within' and 'beyond' statehood as a national judicial self-defence.

Schlegel explores the role of courts for adjustment of plurality of legal orders in the zone of interaction between national, international and supranational law. His chapter is a particular and specific continuation of Mauro Zamboni's chapter in the sense that they both focus on the institutional reasoning on their common problem – the judicial activism of constitutional and supreme courts. Apart from this commonality these two chapters that jointly form the first part of the book have several differences. Two of them are of special importance. First, Zamboni compares the impact of courts on legal and political order, while Schlegel differentiates between cultural and institutional embeddedness of the reasoning for the role of courts as activist moderators between different legal orders. Second, Zamboni offers conceptual analysis of judicial activism from the viewpoint of legal theory, while Schlegel explores a particular manifestation of this phenomenon from a comparative perspective.

In that regard, Schlegel provides a comparative chapter that sets three case studies within a broader conceptual framework determined by the problems of judicial activism. More precisely, he compares the attitude of three courts – the Swiss Supreme Court and the German and Austrian Constitutional Courts. Schlegel explores the interdependence between the role of courts, the flexibility of constitutions and the constitutionally provided rank of international law in the domestic legal order. He shows the intensity and patterns of judicial activism related to that specific issue of adjustment of constitutional orders and their sources of law. The very topic of such judicial activity demonstrates the key role of courts in the world with increasing legal pluralism. Their role as masters of adjustment of international and supranational to national law shows the huge importance of conceptual and comparative research of judicial activism on the border between legal orders and its impact on democracy, separation of powers, and rule of law, which is the overall theoretical concern of this volume.

Part II of the book is devoted to the judicial activism of international and supranational courts and its impact on national constitutional orders. More precisely, the two chapters published in this part focus on the effects of judicial activism of the two most important 'courts beyond statehood', namely the European Court of Human Rights and the Court of Justice of the EU. The chapters are united by the common problem of judicial activism of these courts and its impact on the national constitutional orders. Thus, both Di Bitonto and Beširević explore the increased political influence of the international and supranational courts, their role in contemporary democracies and their standing with the evolving concept of rule of law at the beginning of the twenty-first century.

Both chapters investigate the effects of the jurisprudence of these courts on rule of law and democracy on a national level. However, while Di Bitonto focuses on the influence of case law of the European Court of Human Rights on rule of law, outlining the eventual threats of such an impact on domestic legal order and the principle of legal certainty, Beširević explores the role of the Court of Justice of the EU as activist promoter of democracy and rule of law in EU Member States, leaning towards populist constitutionalism and illiberal democracies. Hence, a common issue – judicial activism of international and supranational courts – is examined from different standpoints. Some of the authors are rather critical of the judicial activism of the European Court of Human Rights, while others appeal for more activism to the extent of promoting 'militant' jurisprudence imposing rule of law and democracy standards on national legal and political orders. Hence, Part II exemplifies the dubious nature of judicial activism as both poison and medicine for constitutional democracy and rule of law. It demonstrates that judicial activism is both shield and sword, cause and remedy for the 'twilight of constitutionalism'[16] in the form it has spread as a universal phenomenon during the last century.

This is actually the main value of this part of the book. It offers a critical assessment of the impact of case law in international and supranational courts on domestic constitutional systems, expressing concerns about too much activism or, alternatively, demanding more activism. In that regard, activist, imperial and militant international and supranational courts are praised and criticised at the same time. Such controversial analysis allows for a proper assessment of the role of international and supranational courts in contemporary constitutionalism.

In Chapter 3 Maria Lucia Di Bitonto critically assesses the impact of case law of the European Court of Human Rights on legal certainty as a key element of the principle of rule of law. More precisely, the chapter explores one important aspect of legal certainty, namely the idea and concept of *res iudicata* in criminal justice in the light of the Italian experience. The starting point of the author's analysis is the idea of *res iudicata* as rooted in both traditions of civil law and common law. Di Bitonto's central claim is that 'the traditional approach of the criminal justice system regarding *res iudicata* had been deeply revolutionised after the establishment of the European Court of Human Rights – especially after its most recent case law'.

The author offers an informative outline of the normative basis of the problem and the case law of the European Court of Human Rights related to *res iudicata*. She devotes special attention to the impact of this case law on the reopening of criminal cases and on imprisonment, as well as to the adoption of some normative ideas stemming from it in the jurisprudence of the Italian courts. The chapter concludes by posing the question whether we are exposed to the emergence of a new conception of the principle *ne bis in idem*.

In Chapter 4 Violeta Beširević raises a radical claim. It consists of establishing militant democracy in the EU by virtue of fostering a deliberately activist Court of Justice of the EU, possessing the role and features of a militant court. In that

16 See Dobner, P. and M. Loughlin, op. cit.

regard, judicial activism is viewed by the author as a positive phenomenon able to promote rule of law and democracy even beyond the framework of traditional conceptualisation of representative democracy. Hence, Beširević is inviting us to think outside of the box. She is proposing militant democracy and activist courts focusing especially on the Court of Justice of the EU as devices for protection of the 'democratic minimum core'.

Beširević explains the concept of militant democracy, engaging in the debates on the EU's democratic credentials, the democratic deficit of the EU, the democratic backsliding and the tendency towards illiberalism and populist democracies. Then, the author explores what she defines as 'CJEU's revolutionary case law on democracy'. Violeta Beširević believes that the EU is militant democracy per se. In order to justify her thesis, the author briefly presents the concept of militant democracy. Afterwards, she outlines the EU's features as a militant democracy while also demonstrating its limits.

Furthermore, Beširević critically assesses the judicial means for enhancement of EU militant democracy. She focuses on two main instruments for safeguarding rule of law and democracy in the multilevel constitutionalism of the EU, thus also analysing the activist stance of the Court of Justice of the EU in them. In that regard, Beširević explores the means for enforcing EU democratic values through infringement proceedings as well as by virtue of preliminary rulings.

Violeta Beširević's contribution is the natural intellectual bond between Part II of the book which addresses the problems of the effects of the judicial activism of international and supranational courts on certainty and proportionality and Part III which explores the impact of illiberalism and populism on the role of courts at the beginning of the twenty-first century. Beširević pleads for enhanced engagement of courts in the promotion of rule of law and democracy, while the next two chapters explore the impact of the illiberal turn on courts. In that regard, the chapters belonging to Part III and written by Kustra-Rogatka and Selejan-Guţan are a logical consequence of Beširević's Chapter 4, demonstrating some of its important concerns. And, vice versa, Beširević's chapter offers possible solutions, not undisputable, for the problems exposed by Aleksandra Kustra-Rogatka and Bianca Selejan-Guţan. Thus, all three chapters should be considered an invitation for further discussion on the performance, task and future of courts in the context of illiberal constitutionalism that has gained momentum in recent years.

Indeed, populist constitutionalism and illiberal constitutionalism are massively challenging the central role of courts in constitutional politics. Judicial activism and the political role of courts is largely criticised as incompatible with democracy, separation of powers and popular sovereignty. Indeed, such criticism is justified also from the viewpoint of liberal-democratic constitutionalism. However, the populist and illiberal constitutionalism are targeting not only the excess of judicial activity. They are also questioning the overall legitimacy of the human rights-centred approach to democracy, granting an active protectionist role for courts even at the expense of majoritarian democracy.

In that regard, Part III of the book explores two interrelated groups of issues. These are the attempts of populist governments at curtailing the institutional autonomy of courts and more precisely of constitutional courts, and the illiberal and populist turn of these courts following the general trend towards the establishment of illiberal democracy in some EU Member States. Hence, the chapters written by Aleksandra Kustra-Rogatka and Bianca Selejan-Guțan offer important case studies of the Polish and the Romanian Constitutional Courts and their recent experience with rising illiberalism in the EU on a national level.

In Chapter 5 Aleksandra Kustra-Rogatka explores the status, role and functioning of the constitutional court in the context of increasing clashes between liberal and illiberal democracy in Poland. Her main research target is the 'gradual dismantling of the existing system of checks and balances and the subordination of judiciary power to executive power', which in her account has been visible since 2015 in Poland. She engages in the debates on the role of courts in the context of constitutional breakdown, constitutional crisis, rule of law crisis, democratic backsliding, populist backsliding and statutory anti-constitutionalism.[17]

Kustra-Rogatka explores the shifting role of the Polish Constitutional Court in the context of a process which she defines as 'illiberal turn' and 'counter-constitutional revolution'. This is done on the basis of theoretical engagement with arguments related to Bruce Ackerman's theory of constitutional moments and other normative theories on constitutional revolution. According to the author, 'the changes that have occurred in Poland since 2015 should really be conceptualised as illiberal, counter-constitutional revolution. Its aim, despite maintaining the nominal continuity of the system, is to destroy the essence of the current constitution.'

Kustra-Rogatka presents the status and functioning of the Polish Constitutional Court before and after 2015. She provides an important overview of the history of judicial activism of this court starting as early as the last years of the communist regime. She briefly explains the political background of the rule of law crisis in Poland with its impact on the Polish Constitutional Court. Then, she focuses on the political battles over the composition of the Polish Constitutional Court in 2015–2016, which were of key importance for the illiberal turn. Furthermore, the author presents what she calls the 'final stage of the Constitutional Tribunal takeover' that occurred in 2017–2018 and the 'counter-constitutional case law of the Constitutional Tribunal in 2019–2020'. Kustra-Rogatka comes to an important conclusion. In her view, the constitutional dynamics since 2015 have impacted the Polish Constitutional Court in such a way, so that 'this typically counter-majoritarian institution has radically changed its role. From a fairly activist court, one of the main actors of the political transition of the 1990s, it became a body which post-factum legitimises the systemic changes violating the Constitution of 1997.'

The discussion on the illiberal turn of constitutional courts provided by Violeta Beširević and Aleksandra Kustra-Rogatka is continued by Bianca Selejan-Guțan. In Chapter 6 she offers an insightful case study on the impact of democratic backsliding and illiberal and populist constitutionalism on the Romanian Constitutional Court.

17 For references for these concepts, see the citations provided by Kustra-Rogatka in her chapter.

Bianca Selejan-Guţan starts with a brief overview of the status, role and functions of constitutional courts in modern European constitutionalism. She emphasises the central role of constitutional courts for the maintenance of rule of law by providing a short introduction to their most important competences and the safeguards for their institutional independence. Selejan-Guţan focuses her attention on the risks of politicisation of constitutional courts. She outlines the most important strategies for their politicisation or, alternatively, for keeping their political independence.

The author engages in the debate on judicial activism. She provides some important insights for the proper scientific qualification of this phenomenon. Prominently, Selejan-Guţan critically assesses the risks of judicial activism in non-consolidated democracies, likening them to a 'constitutional tsunami'. This is especially problematic in the case of fragile systems of rule of law with a tendency towards judicial activism when the court acts as 'positive legislator'. In fact, the similar concerns of excessive political engagement of constitutional courts, especially in times of crisis and emergency, are expressed also in Djordje Gardasevic's chapter, as well as in my own.

Selejan-Guţan raises the question whether one can properly qualify the Romanian Constitutional Court as an activist constitutional jurisdiction. She observes that during the first period of its existence – 1992–2012 – the Court had been predominantly passive. Then, since 2012, a period of judicial activism emerged during which time the Court was activist and also produced rather inconsistent case law, conceived by the author as a challenge to legal certainty and thus to rule of law. She explores the reasons and the main manifestations of the tendency towards politicisation of the Constitutional Court in Romania in recent years.

Selejan-Guţan explores what she defines as 'pathology of judicial review'. She focuses on several types of judicial activism performed by the Romanian Constitutional Court: activism in the constitutional review of legislation and of constitutional amendments in Romania; activism in solving conflicts between authorities; and the role of the Court as 'activist judge of its own powers'. Thus, Selejan-Guţan offers an insightful case study contributing to the problems of judicial activism, judicialisation of politics, politicisation of the judiciary and legal certainty.

Part III concludes with Chapter 7, which is devoted to the revolutionary role of constitutional courts in Morocco and Jordan. Its author – Hadeel S. Abu Hussein – explores the impact of the introduction of constitutional justice and the constitutional courts as novel institutions on democracy and rule of law in the Middle East and North Africa region. Actually, she demonstrates the revolutionary impact of the very fact of the introduction of this institutional novelty of the constitutional design on the prospects of furthering the constitutional democracy.

Chapter 7 combines theoretical and comparative reflections with two important case studies of Morocco and Jordan. The author compares the impact of the introduction of constitutional courts in the constitutional systems of these two countries. She focuses on the revolutionary role of the constitutional court in Morocco and Jordan as well as in the whole Middle East and North Africa region as protector of freedom, individual rights and human rights. The analysis is put in the context of the post-Arab Spring developments. Abu Hussein explores the political continuity and rupture of the Arab Spring and its impact on the introduction of constitutional justice in the focus countries. She analyses the reasons of the leaning of these two constitutional courts towards judicial self-restraint and the perspective for their engagement in judicial activism in the future. The chapter concludes with some reflections on the future of the Arab constitutional courts.

The novelty of the chapter is predetermined by the fact that the problems of constitutional justice in these two countries are rather under-researched. Thus, Abu Hussein's chapter is a valuable contribution in the overall discussion in transitology and transplantology regarding the effects and efficiency of transplanting Western institutional design – in this case the centralised model of constitutional justice concentrated in constitutional courts – in a non-Western context: the constitutional monarchies of Morocco and Jordan. Her chapter is embedded also in the discourse on the role of courts in authoritarian and illiberal constitutional orders, thus spreading the discussion beyond the EU context.

The book concludes with Part IV, which is devoted to the topical issues of judicial activism in times of pandemic. This part of the book explores the performance of constitutional courts in extraordinary and emergency situations. Indeed, the focus is on pandemic constitutionalism and the case law of the courts on issues stemming from the Covid-19 regimes established in 2020. However, they set the problems of judicial activism as a response to pandemics in the broader context of judicial activism related to all types of emergencies.

Chapter 8 explores the activist role of the Bulgarian Constitutional Court in mastering emergency situations. In this chapter I critically assess the judicial activism of the Court in shaping and further developing by virtue of activist interpretation the constitutional provisions related to emergency situations: war, state of siege and state of emergency. Hence, the chapter explores the contribution of the Constitutional Court in emergency constitutionalism and emergency constitutional politics. It provides a case study which is focused on Bulgaria and the activity of the Bulgarian Constitutional Court.

The activist case law of the Court in the spheres of constitutional emergency showing its appetite for emergency constitutional politics, frequently in cooperation with the government, is contrasted with its reluctance in engagement in judicial dialogue with international and supranational courts. The chapter demonstrates that the Bulgarian Constitutional Court is a key player in shaping and further developing the constitutional model of separation of powers. This practice contravenes the principles of popular sovereignty, democracy and separation of powers.

The focus of the chapter is on the activist engagement of the Bulgarian Constitutional Court in reshaping the constitutional competences of key state institutions via activist interpretation of constitutional provisions related to emergency situations (war, state of siege, state of emergency) and to the institutional design of the national defence. The chapter opens with an outline of the constitutional model for crisis management provided by the 1991 Bulgarian Constitution. It offers structured information regarding the regimes for crisis management enshrined in the Bulgarian Constitution as instruments for mastering of emergency situations. Hence, I am outlining the emergency constitutional politics and emergency constitutional regimes serving as a playground for judicial activism and, alternatively, being themselves framed and shaped by activist case law of the Bulgarian Constitutional Court. I outline the reasons for the judicial activism of the Bulgarian Constitutional Court, its activist role in shaping and mastering military emergency situations and health-related emergency situations. Against this background I substantiate the claim of unconstitutionality of other emergency regimes created by virtue of the ordinary legislation and subsequently legitimated by activist jurisprudence of the Constitutional Court.

Special emphasis is placed on the judicial activism of the Bulgarian Constitutional Court related to mastering of emergency situations. The activist stance of the Court regarding issues of war, state of siege, state of emergency and other – in fact unconstitutional – regimes of emergency measures such as the 'extraordinary epidemic situation' and the 'state of disaster' is explained. The focus of the chapter is on the introduction of the 'extraordinary epidemic situation' by virtue of legislative amendments which are declared to be in compliance with the Constitution by the Bulgarian Constitutional Court. In the chapter I demonstrate why this is not the case.

Finally, in Chapter 9 Djordje Gardasevic explores the judicial activism of the Croatian Constitutional Court during the Covid-19 pandemic. Hence, the chapter addresses the issues of emergency constitutionalism and health emergency-related case law of constitutional jurisdictions challenging rule of law, separation of powers and democracy. It explores the impact of the Covid-19 crisis on the Croatian constitutional order as a stress test for the engagement of the constitutional court in constitutional politics. It demonstrates the risks to democracy and rule of law of unbalanced case law of the courts, especially in times of emergency.

The analysis commences with an outline of the constitutional framework of the state of emergency. Gardasevic makes the reader acquainted with the approach of the Croatian authorities in tackling the Covid-19 pandemic and its effects on constitutionalism and constitutional law.

Gardasevic thoroughly explores the pandemic case law of the Croatian Constitutional Court. He critically assesses the approach of the Court to the problems of emergency constitutionalism through the prism of judicial activism and on the basis of arguments based on democracy and rule of law defence. The author outlines the main arguments presented in the opinion of dissenting judges, which gives a multifaceted and balanced approach to this topical issue.

Gardasevic offers critical reflections on the rule of law and its 'emergency exceptions'. He engages with theories of emergency and discretionary powers provided by key authors in the constitutionalist and political philosophy discourse, such as J. Rousseau, J. Locke, C. Schmitt, A. Hamilton, C.L. Rossiter and C.J. Friedrich. Thus, Gardasevic provides a solid conceptual basis for assessing the constitutional provision, legislative developments and constitutional court's jurisprudence on state of emergency, evaluated against the background of emergency constitutionalism, political discretion, state of exception and 'constitutional dictatorship'.

The crisis conditions seem to endure and determine the socio-political conditionality of constitutionalism at least for the recent future. Thus, they will also put our constitutional orders to systemically stress-test the results, which will show whether liberal constitutional democracy will continue to be the main normative and conceptual model for ordering Western societies. In that regard, constitutional responses will be needed and they will most likely be given not only by genuinely political players, but also by expert institutions, including the courts.

In fact, we have been living in an almost permanent crisis situation since the beginning of the twenty-first century. The century commenced with a horrible opening – the 9/11 terror attacks – that has served as justification of the 'war on terror', which has triggered a range of anti-terrorist emergencies and extraordinary measures. Then, in 2009, the financial crisis hit the world, having a severe impact on Southern Europe. In such a context, the financial austerity measures have been imposed, structured mostly around the 'balanced (or golden) budget rule'. Hence, a second wave of emergency – the financial emergency – followed the first wave of anti-terrorism emergency. The next wave of emergency started spreading in the Global North (and especially in Europe), mainly after 2011. This third consecutive emergency measures were triggered and justified on the basis of the migration crisis. Finally, at least for now, we have witnessed a fourth big wave of emergency measures produced by the global Covid-19 pandemic.

The four emergency waves came one after the other. However, they also coincided with each other, thus having a mutually reinforcing negative impact on liberal-democratic constitutionalism. They served as reasons for the introduction of emergency measures that have contributed to the rise and spread of four main types of emergency constitutionalism: anti-terrorist emergency constitutionalism, financial emergency constitutionalism, migration emergency constitutionalism and health emergency constitutionalism. At the same time, during the last decade the world has witnessed the (re-)emergence and spread of illiberal and authoritarian constitutionalism paralleled by processes of democratic backsliding.

In such turbulent times, when emergency is the 'new normal' and the 'sea of life' is constantly hitting us with a series of emergency waves, the 'sand castles of liberal democracy' – the courts – may, should and do play a central and even crucial role. This is especially visible with regard to the 'apex courts' (the constitutional and supreme courts), but is also important for the ordinary courts, although their activity lies beneath the constitutional surface.

The impact of courts on contemporary constitutionalism is multilayered and varying. Judicial activism is sometimes, to an extent paradoxically, masquerading as judicial self-restraint. Judicial activism has both supported the rule of law and promoted human rights. Nevertheless, it has also impacted in dubious ways democracy, separation of powers and human rights. Courts were both guardians of liberal-democratic constitutionalism and bastions against populism, but also promoters of illiberalism and contributors to democratic backsliding, especially in times of crisis and emergency. They were both key safeguards for human rights in times of pandemics and the illiberal turn that they triggered and enhanced, but also promoters of illiberal trends towards pandemic illiberalism and emergency anti-constitutionalism.

Consequently, it seems that the debates on judicial activism and its impact on rule of law, separation of powers, democracy and human rights will remain topical for years to come. Special attention should be devoted to the impact of judicial activism on the rule of law and its core elements: legal certainty, legal predictability, and the proportionality of the limitations of human rights. The rather traditional debate on judicial activism should be embedded in the context of emergency constitutionalism and has to critically assess challenges stemming from the new forms of illiberalism and authoritarianism it promotes. The debate will be of crucial importance for both theory and practice because it is related to the key dimensions of the endurance of constitutionalism, rule of law and democracy. This book should be considered as a modest attempt at engaging with some of the topical issues related to the role of courts in policy-making in a time of illiberalism and emergency constitutionalism exploring judicial activism under crisis conditions.

Part I

Judicial activism

Conceptual and comparative constitutional issues

1 Law, politics, and the constitutional courts' activism

Setting the starting point

Mauro Zamboni

1 Introduction

'Judicial activism' or 'judicialisation of politics' indicates the leaning towards the political game on the part of judges, in particular those sitting in the highest courts. Though not being a novelty of our times, the role that the judicial bodies play in the political arena has become one of the hottest topics of debate in the legal world in the last decades.[1] For reasons which will not be explored in this chapter, many Constitutional Courts in the Western or Western-like democracies have become increasingly 'active' by furthering their activities in a law-making direction and offering authoritative interpretations of the valid law, different from that of other actors at the top of the constitutional structure which are institutionally devoted to law-making (*e.g.*, the national assemblies or the executive branch).[2] In other words, many Constitutional Courts have shifted their 'recognised' role of being the authoritative interpreter of the law, in light of the

1 *See* Ran Hirschl, *The Judicialization of Politics, in* R. E. GOODIN (ED.), THE OXFORD HANDBOOK OF POLITICAL SCIENCE, 2011, Oxford: Oxford University Press, 253. *See, e.g.*, EUROPEAN COMMISSION FOR DEMOCRACY THROUGH LAW (VENICE COMMISSION), THE BINDING EFFECT OF FEDERAL CONSTITUTIONAL COURT DECISIONS UPON POLITICAL INSTITUTIONS (available at www.venice.coe.int/docs/2003/CDL-JU(2003)018-e.pdf); or Sandra Day O'Connor, *Importance of an Independent Judiciary*, in WEBCAST – CONFERENCE ON THE STATE OF THE JUDICIARY – IMPORTANCE OF AN INDEPENDENT JUDICIARY (available at www.law.georgetown.edu/webcast/eventDetail.cfm?eventID=178) ('Directing anger toward judges has had a long tradition in our nation … While scorn for some judges is not altogether new, I do think that the breadth of the unhappiness being currently expressed, not only by public officials but in public opinion polls in the nation, shows that there is a level of unhappiness today that perhaps is greater than in the past and is certainly cause for great concern.'). As to judicial activism in history, *see, e.g.*, the French LOI DES 16–24 AOÛT 1790 SUR L'ORGANISATION JUDICIAIRE, 1790, tit. II, art. 12 (available at https://www.legifrance.gouv.fr/affichTexte.do?cidTexte=JORFTEXT000000704777); or the famous MARBURY V MADISON, 5 U.S. (1 CRANCH) 137 (1803) (available at http://cdn.loc.gov/service/ll/usrep/usrep005/usrep005137/usrep005137.pdf).

2 *See, e.g.*, Richard A. Posner, *The Supreme Court 2004 Term-Foreword: A Political Court*, 119 HARVARD LAW REVIEW 35–39 (2005); or Michael Hein, *The Least Dangerous Branch? Constitutional Review of Constitutional Amendments in Europe*, in M. BELOV (ED.), COURTS, POLITICS AND CONSTITUTIONAL LAW: JUDICIALIZATION OF POLITICS AND POLITICIZATION OF THE JUDICIARY, 2020, Abingdon: Routledge, 187–206.

DOI: 10.4324/9781003200666-3

constitutional documents, towards the middle of the institutional map of a democracy based on the rule of law. Thus, they have grown more distant from the legal arena (as the ultimate authority on what constitutes valid law) and closer to the political one (by limiting and/or expanding the operating space of the political actors and their legislative tools).[3]

As can be understood from this concise introduction, judicial activism (in particular on the part of the highest courts) focuses primarily on the relations between law and politics. Therefore, the main purpose of this chapter is to evaluate whether Constitutional Courts should be considered legal actors simply enforcing what is written by political actors in statutes and constitutions, or institutional actors with a predominantly political nature, determining what the law should say. In order to achieve this, the investigation will not only focus upon the function that Constitutional Courts play, between law and politics, but also on their institutional positioning.

The basic thesis of this chapter is that Constitutional Courts, though playing a bridging role between the political and legal worlds, are – from an institutional and functional perspective – primarily legal actors. Without a doubt, these Courts play a role in the political game; however, their position as an institutional actor should be based upon the direct effects of their decisions ('outputs') on the legal arena, rather than on the indirect consequences ('outcomes') on the political arena. As a consequence, the Constitutional Courts' primary responsibility is towards the legal community and the paradigms governing its discourse.

This chapter makes no pretensions on providing any final words either in the discussion on judicial activism or in respect of the relations between the legal and political worlds in general. First, the focus here is solely on Western (or Western-like) legal systems. Second, this work has a more limited objective of contributing to clarifying the terms of the discussion, in particular by finding a solid basis (at least from a legal perspective) upon which to begin the discussion on whether judicial activism is good or bad. In other words, this investigation is primarily to clarify what is meant when the legal discussion deals with the 'political' in the work of Constitutional Courts.

While in section 2 certain key concepts used in this chapter are defined, the focus in section 3 is on a feature of Constitutional Courts in well-established Western democracies, namely their positioning in between the legal and political arenas. The final sections 4 and 5 then identify why the characterisation of Constitutional Courts, as either legal or political actors, is relevant from a legal perspective, both in descriptive and normative terms. These parts also explore how it is possible to resolve the dilemma of 'legal vs. political actors' by defining Constitutional Courts as legal actors performing a political function.

3 *See* Joseph Raz, *On the Nature of Law, in* J. RAZ, BETWEEN AUTHORITY AND INTERPRETATION – ON THE THEORY OF LAW AND PRACTICAL REASON, 2009, Oxford: Oxford University Press, 99–100. *See, e.g.*, Julien Mouchette, *The French Constitutional Council as a Law-Maker: From Dialogue with the Legislator to the Rewriting of the Law, in*M. FLORCZAK-WĄTOR (ED.), JUDICIAL LAW-MAKING IN EUROPEAN CONSTITUTIONAL COURTS, 2020, London: Routledge, 9–27; or Harvie J. Wilkinson, *Of Guns, Abortions, and the Unraveling Rule of Law*, 95 VIRGINIA LAW REVIEW 275–288 (2009).

2 A definitional framework

Before we delve into the topic at hand, some key concepts used in this text must be clarified. First, *judicial activism*, sometimes referred to by other words (*e.g.*, 'constitutional politics', 'government of judges', or 'judicialisation of politics'), identifies the general phenomenon – typical of (but not limited to) well-established Western democracies – when 'courts impose a judicial solution over an issue erstwhile subject to political resolution' by intervening against and striking down a part of properly enacted legislation, or by 'legislating' in an area in the absence of legislation.[4] Judicial activism thus identifies a judicial activity directed at stretching the formal structures and the letter of the law in order to fill gaps (or what are perceived as gaps) left by politicians. The judges take a more 'active' stance towards law-making (in particular in its legislative form), in order to implement values that the political actors are unable to sense in the community or are unable to transform into legislative measures, or that are part of the political baggage of certain judges.[5] Usually, the courts find support for their new course in the foundational structures of the legal system, *e.g.*, the constitution or international treaties. In other words, judicial activism refers to the complex of judicial activities through which the judges consciously and explicitly take upon themselves a power that has traditionally been left to other institutional actors, *e.g.*, the political actors sitting in the national assemblies or (to a lesser extent) the public administration. In doing so, the courts are guided by the idea that their primary role is neither to find the true intention of the legislative bodies nor to review the work done by the public agencies. Instead, they intend to act as guardians of the legal system as a whole, by positioning themselves as a third party and solving disputes in the light of fundamental legal principles which have not been contemplated by the legislative bodies and/or which have been neglected in administrative practice.

Second, when referring to *Constitutional Courts*, this includes all the highest courts that – under varying names (*e.g.*, High Council or Supreme Court) – have among their primary legal duties the jurisdiction to evaluate the constitutionality of the law, *i.e.*, the consistency or conflict of legally relevant documents produced

4 David L. Anderson, *When Restraint Requires Activism: Partisan Gerrymandering and the Status Quo Ante*, 42 STANFORD LAW REVIEW 1570 (1990). *See also* Keenan D. Kmiec, *The Origin and Current Meanings of Judicial Activism*, 92 CALIFORNIA LAW REVIEW 1463–1476 (2004); ALEC STONE SWEET, GOVERNING WITH JUDGES: CONSTITUTIONAL POLITICS IN EUROPE, 2000, Oxford: Oxford University Press, 61–66; and CHARLES S. LOPEMAN, THE ACTIVIST ADVOCATE: POLICY MAKING IN STATE SUPREME COURTS, 1999, London: Preager, 3. *But see* Frank H. Easterbrook, *Do Liberals and Conservatives Differ in Judicial Activism?*, 73 UNIVERSITY OF COLORADO LAW REVIEW 1403 (2002) or William P. Marshall, *Conservatives and the Seven Sins of Judicial Activism*, 73 UNIVERSITY OF COLORADO LAW REVIEW 1220–1221 (2002) (pointing out to the difficulties of identifying a single meaning of 'judicial activism').

5 *See, e.g.*, AHARON BARAK, THE JUDGE IN A DEMOCRACY, 2006, Princeton: Princeton University Press, 8–10. *See also*NIELS PETERSEN, PROPORTIONALITY AND JUDICIAL ACTIVISM – FUNDAMENTAL RIGHTS ADJUDICATION IN CANADA, GERMANY AND SOUTH AFRICA, 2017, Cambridge: Cambridge University Press, 18–33 (pointing out judicial activism as aimed to correct the failures of the political market).

within a certain legal system in relation to the basic legal documents of that community. Such courts are also characterised, at least with respect to conducting constitutional reviews, by being positioned outside the ordinary court system, in a sense, and by their work being completely independent (at least in its modality) from the other branches of the state.[6] It is worth noting that several types of Constitutional Courts can find a place under this definitional umbrella. In particular, this definition allows placing under scrutiny both Constitutional Courts that have an abstract review competence (*i.e.*, when a Constitutional Court is asked to determine the compatibility of statutory law with the Constitution at the request of non-judicial public bodies, *e.g.*, a law-drafting committee of the national assembly or a regional government), and those that have a more concrete review power (*i.e.*, when a Constitutional Court's review jurisdiction is activated by a party to litigation, or by a lower judge, stating that a law violates the constitutional texts).[7]

Third, the definition of *political actors* adopted here is fairly different from that used by the other discipline that also investigates the role of Constitutional Courts in and in relation to the political system, namely political science. While for the latter, political actors are more or less identified as all institutional actors that 'make the law', the term in this chapter is intended from a more legal perspective and refers to a narrower range of institutional entities whose primary goal is to see their values implemented into a community by making use of the legal apparatus and system, *e.g.*, political parties or interest groups. Political actors can (and usually do) have a primary goal of a non-legal nature (*e.g.*, an economic or social nature) and therefore, in their operations, mainly take into consideration the environments surrounding the legal arena, *e.g.*, the political or socio-economic ones. Moreover, their primary intention is to influence people into adopting a certain model of behaviour by convincing the addressees of the 'inner goodness' of their model.[8]

6 *See* Ralf Rogowski and Thomas Gawron, *Constitutional Litigation as Dispute Processing, in*R. ROGOWSKI AND T. GAWRON (EDS.), CONSTITUTIONAL COURTS IN COMPARISON: THE US SUPREME COURT AND THE GERMAN FEDERAL CONSTITUTIONAL COURT, 2nd edn., 2016, Oxford: Berghahn, 1. Due to this very 'external' position in relation to the ordinary judiciary, Western legal systems usually assign to Constitutional Courts other fundamental 'above the parties' types of jurisdiction. *See*VÍCTOR FERRERES COMELLA, CONSTITUTIONAL COURTS AND DEMOCRATIC VALUES: A EUROPEAN PERSPECTIVE, 2009, Yale: Yale University Press, 6.

7 *See* Alec Stone Sweet, *Constitutional Courts, in*M. ROSENFELD AND A. SAJÓ (EDS.), THE OXFORD HANDBOOK OF COMPARATIVE CONSTITUTIONAL LAW, 2012, Oxford: Oxford University Press, 823; and WOJCIECH SADURSKI, RIGHTS BEFORE COURTS: A STUDY OF CONSTITUTIONAL COURTS IN POSTCOMMUNIST STATES OF CENTRAL AND EASTERN EUROPE, 2005, Dordrecht: Springer, 65–74. *See also* Albert H. Y. Chen and Miguel Poiares Maduro, *The Judiciary and Constitutional Review, in*M. TUSHNET, T. FLEINER, AND C. SAUNDERS (EDS.), ROUTLEDGE HANDBOOK OF CONSTITUTIONAL LAW, 2015, Abingdon: Routledge, 97–98 (as to the distinction between an American 'decentralised' model and a continental European one of a more 'centralised' character).

8 *See* Raz, *On the Nature of Law, supra* at 101; NIKLAS LUHMANN, LAW AS A SOCIAL SYSTEM, 1994, Oxford: Oxford University Press, 370; and Gunther Teubner, *Substantive and Reflexive Elements in Modern Law*, 17 LAW AND SOCIETY REVIEW 259 (1983). *See also*

Lastly, particularly in Western legal systems, *legal actors* can be defined as institutional actors primarily aiming at influencing the legal system, and therefore mainly focusing on the latter's logical structure. As for political actors, the main goal of legal actors is to exercise power, *i.e.*, to force people to do things that they otherwise are not willing to do. As pointed out by Hans Kelsen, both law and politics try to make people do something, the law being 'a social order, that is to say an order regulating the mutual behavior of human beings'.[9] However, legal actors, when dealing with a statute or legal precedent, consider these normative documents as exercising their (binding) power on the addressees only as (and as long as they are) part of a larger hierarchical system of norms with a similar (legal) nature, and with specific (legal) rules to be used for interpretation, application, and creation (legal reasoning).[10]

3 Constitutional Courts between law and politics

When dealing with the issue of Constitutional Courts in relation to politics, the first question is where these institutional actors should be positioned on an imaginary map of two ideal-typical continents, namely the legal world and the political world. This question is legitimate, since it is easy to see the importance of the role played by the courts in general and the Constitutional Courts in particular, within both the legal and political systems.

As far as the legal system is concerned, Constitutional Courts are ranked at the top, being the supreme and ultimate interpreters of the constitution, and consequently of the constitutionality of different law-making measures, in particular (but not exclusively) statutes. In other words, constitutional review is the legal competence allowing such courts to enjoy an exclusive decision-making power and a legal superiority in relation to the other branches of power, to an extent which is often unknown to most of the other judicial bodies within a national community. In addition to this lofty position within the legal structure, Constitutional Courts also tend to occupy a dominant place in the political building characterising a democratic form of state. Constitutional Courts are entrusted by the political system (and, through it, by the community as such) to act as the ultimate guardians of the basic values that inspired the founding fathers and mothers when

JÜRGEN HABERMAS, BETWEEN FACTS AND NORMS: CONTRIBUTIONS TO A DISCOURSE THEORY OF LAW AND DEMOCRACY, 1998, Cambridge: The MIT Press, 266. *Compare to* Frederick W. Frey, *The Problem of Actor Designation in Political Analysis*, 17 COMPARATIVE POLITICS 127–129 (1985).

9 Hans Kelsen, *Law, State, and Justice in the Pure Theory of Law, in* H. KELSEN, WHAT IS JUSTICE? JUSTICE, LAW AND POLITICS IN THE MIRROR OF SCIENCE, 1957, Berkeley: University of California Press, 289. *See also*MAX WEBER, THE THEORY OF SOCIAL AND ECONOMIC ORGANIZATION, 1964, Glencoe: Free Press, 152.

10 *See*HABERMAS, BETWEEN FACTS AND NORMS, *supra* at 233–234; KAARLO TUORI, CRITICAL LEGAL POSITIVISM, 2002, Aldershot: Ashgate Publishing, 36–39; and LUHMANN, LAW AS A SOCIAL SYSTEM, *supra* at 188 (and his idea of 'juridical rationality'). *See also*MAX WEBER, ECONOMY AND SOCIETY: AN OUTLINE OF INTERPRETIVE SOCIOLOGY, 1978, Berkeley: University of California Press, 657.

writing the fundamental documents (or in establishing the fundamental customs) underpinning and regulating the life of the political community.[11]

However, if the Constitutional Courts are seen from the perspective of the relations of law and politics, one can assert that they actually occupy a third position, at a much deeper level, functioning as a sort of transfer point between the legal and political worlds. If one considers the primary position occupied by Constitutional Courts (which is often implicit in the building of a modern democracy), this location can be identified as a bridge between values produced in the political world and in legal thinking. As stated by a political scientist:

> *constitutional courts act systematically both in the legal and the political systems.* Almost every judgment has some consequences on the legal system (e.g. the abrogation of an unconstitutional law) and the political system (e.g. the retroactive defeat of the parliamentary majority that enacted this law).[12]

As previously seen, the primary function of a Constitutional Court is constitutional review, *i.e.*, to continuously monitor the compatibility of legislation and other normative measures with the basic values as announced in the constitution or other fundamental laws. While this role assigned to the Courts is largely undisputed, it carries an underlying problem of conflicting logic. At one end, the legal message of the Constitution, namely the models of behaviours prescribed, is heavily affected by the fact that constitutions are not only written by political actors (as are most legal measures), but are also often the product of extremely complex political compromises or very general political statements. Their being a political product, the constitution or fundamental law tends to be written less in legal terms, *i.e.*, as (at least in their intention) 'if x then y' or 'either/or' statements, and more as political messages, *i.e.*, in terms that resemble political propaganda, where the fundamental goals are models of behaviour that the political actors want to be 'realised' in the community itself.[13] At the other end, constitutional documents are for historical reasons regarded as the highest sources of law

11 *See* CONRADO HÜBNER MENDES, CONSTITUTIONAL COURTS AND DELIBERATIVE DEMOCRACY, 2015, Oxford: Oxford University Press, 73–82. *See also*CASS R. SUNSTEIN, LEGAL REASONING AND POLITICAL CONFLICT, 1998, Oxford: Oxford University Press, 82–83; and (as to this dualistic position of the legal discourse in general) Robert Alexy, *The Dual Nature of Law*, 23 RATIO JURIS 167–182 (2010).

12 Michael Hein, C*onstitutional Conflicts between Politics and Law in Transition Societies: A Systems-Theoretical Approach*, 3 STUDIES OF TRANSITION STATES AND SOCIETIES 17 (2011) [italics in the original]. *See, e.g.*, MARTIN SHAPIRO AND ALEX SWEET STONE, ON LAW, POLITICS, AND JUDICIALIZATION, 2002, Oxford: Oxford University Press, 81; Ralf Michaels, *American Law (United States), in*J. M. SMITS (ED.), ELGAR ENCYCLOPEDIA OF COMPARATIVE LAW, 2nd edn., Cheltenham: Edward Elgar Publishing, 2012, 75–76; or Nevil Johnson, *The Interdependence of Law and Politics: Judges and the Constitution in Western Germany*, 5 WEST EUROPEAN POLITICS 239–244 (1982).

13 *See, e.g.*, Rudolf Streinz, *The Role of the German Federal Constitutional Court – Law and Politics*, 31 RITSUMEIKAN LAW REVIEW 103–104 (2014); or JEREMY WALDRON, LAW AND DISAGREEMENT, 2001, Oxford: Oxford University Press, 220–222.

in Western legal systems or, in other words – at least from a legal perspective – the constitution is legal in nature, *i.e.*, it is binding towards the addressees. As the constitutions are designed as legal documents, they are treated as legal sources, having the strongest binding force on all the national law-making and law-applying agencies and on the community as well.[14] In other words, constitutions or fundamental laws in general have contents that tend to be dominated by the logics of the political discourse, but that are inserted into shells which have the form of laws and legal logics and shaping – somehow setting the agenda (at least as a direct effect) for the entire legal arena of a certain community.[15] As recently stated by a legal scholar: 'Constitutions structure the relationship of law and politics. They politicize the production of law, by connecting the legal system to a political process, and they legalize this political process through its obligation to superior legal rules.'[16]

Since the primary goal of a Constitutional Court is to 'protect' such documents, it is easy to understand how this institutional actor tends to end up being a legal player, but inclined towards the political world. Three different features affect Constitutional Courts, making them actors that, though having their feet in the legal world, tend to lean heavily towards the political arena. First, Constitutional Courts are legal actors leaning into politics from an *institutional perspective, i.e.*, from the perspective of where these courts are positioned among the different organisations in a certain community which has as its primary goal governing the behaviour of individuals, and are characterised as being permanent as well as making and enforcing rules governing human behaviour. A Constitutional Court maintains its role as a legal institution, *i.e.*, an organisation constructed to safeguard certain important legal issues from a legal perspective, not the political opportunities that statutes create.[17]

At the same time, a Constitutional Court indirectly places the activities and operations of political actors, such as national or local assemblies, under scrutiny.

14 *See, e.g.*, ANDRÁS SAJÓ AND RENÁTA UITZ, THE CONSTITUTION OF FREEDOM: AN INTRODUCTION TO LEGAL CONSTITUTIONALISM, 2017, Oxford: Oxford University Press, 23–25; or JOHN O. MCGINNIS AND MICHAEL B. RAPPAPORT, ORIGINALISM AND THE GOOD CONSTITUTION, 2013, Cambridge: Harvard University Press, 130–132.

15 *See*ROBERT ALEXY, A THEORY OF CONSTITUTIONAL RIGHTS, 2002, Oxford: Oxford University Press, 349–351; and Martin Loughlin, *Fundamental Law, in*M. NOGUEIRA DE BRITO AND L. PEREIRA COUTINHO (EDS.), THE POLITICAL DIMENSION OF CONSTITUTIONAL LAW, 2020, Cham: Springer, 8–19.

16 Christoph Möllers, *Legality, Legitimacy, and Legitimation of the Federal Constitutional Court, in*M. JESTAEDT, O. LEPSIUS, C. MÖLLERS, AND C. SCHÖNBERGER (EDS.), THE GERMAN FEDERAL CONSTITUTIONAL COURT: THE COURT WITHOUT LIMITS, 2020, Oxford: Oxford University Press, 143.

17 *See* Dieter Grimm, *What Exactly Is Political about Constitutional Adjudication?, in*C. LANDFRIED (ED.), JUDICIAL POWER: HOW CONSTITUTIONAL COURTS AFFECT POLITICAL TRANSFORMATIONS, 2019, Cambridge: Cambridge University Press, 310–311. *But see* Robert A. Dahl, *Decision Making in Democracy: The Supreme Court as National Policy-Maker?*, 6 JOURNAL OF PUBLIC LAW 279 (1957); and Kevin T. McGuire, *The Institutionalization of the U.S. Supreme Court*, 12 POLITICAL ANALYSIS 129–135 (2004) (as to the traditional political science perspective on the issue).

It is true that its evaluation is directly legal in nature, but it is also true that the law is the main voice of political actors – at least in a democratic form of a state that has adopted the rule of law. Each time Constitutional Courts modify, approve, or even remain silent as to that which political actors have expressed through the law, the courts operate in the political institutional arena, particularly by allowing or disallowing certain political actors to produce statements that are directly relevant to and binding for the entire community from which such actors have (directly or indirectly) been chosen.[18] In other words, Constitutional Courts are legal institutional actors because of their being a court, but, at the same time, they are gatekeepers in relation to the political world, allowing the actors in the latter to be heard (or not) in the legal world.

Alongside this institutional factor, concerning the location of Constitutional Courts among the different actors, a second factor operates from a *structural perspective* in such a way as to render Constitutional Courts as legal actors heavily leaning into the political arenas. It has been mentioned how Constitutional Courts reside outside of the ordinary court system and are independent from other branches of the public authorities. However, Constitutional Courts always tend to present a certain 'structural cohesion' with the actors belonging to the political arena. This means that almost all Western legal systems have foreseen that political actors, either as legislators or within the executive branch, can have partial (as in Italy) or total (as in the US) control as far as concerns the individuals who are to sit as justices in the Constitutional Courts. As a consequence, the political arena and the ideologies prevailing within it affect and to a certain extent overlap with the structure of the courts and their fundamental components, by means of the legal power to decide who will be justices.[19]

Despite this important political influence in deciding the structure of Constitutional Courts, these courts cannot be considered as having a purely and exclusively 'political structure'. Though the justices sitting in such courts can (and often are) politicised individuals, they nevertheless come from the legal world, *i.e.*, the predominant feature of individuals sitting in Constitutional Courts is normally that they are chosen among lawyers or individuals with a formal education in law. In other words, even when all justices are chosen based on political considerations and personal political ideologies and affiliations, the selection process is limited

18 *See* Grimm, *What Exactly Is Political about Constitutional Adjudication?*, *supra* at 308–309; and Nuno Garoupa and Tom Ginsburg, *Building Reputation in Constitutional Courts: Political and Judicial Audiences*, 28 ARIZONA JOURNAL OF INTERNATIONAL & COMPARATIVE LAW 541 (2011).

19 *See* CARLO GUARNIERI AND PATRIZIA PEDERZOLI, THE POWER OF JUDGES: A COMPARATIVE STUDY OF COURTS AND DEMOCRACY, 2003, Oxford: Oxford University Press, 138–141; WALTER F. MURPHY AND CHARLES HERMAN PRITCHETT, COURTS, JUDGES, AND POLITICS: AN INTRODUCTION TO THE JUDICIAL PROCESS, 4th edn., 1986, New York: Random House, 139; and NICOLA CH. CORKIN, EUROPEANIZATION OF JUDICIAL REVIEW, 2014, Abingdon: Routledge, 115–116. *See, e.g.*, Donald P. Kommers, *American Courts and Democracy: A Comparative Perspective, in* K. L. HALL AND K. T. MCGUIRE (EDS.), THE JUDICIAL BRANCH, 2005, Oxford: Oxford University Press, 207.

(either by law or by constitutional customs) to individuals trained at least formally in the art of law, *e.g.*, holding a law degree. Moreover, most (but not all) of the time, the recruitment procedures require that the candidates have some experience from the judiciary branch at a high level.[20]

Lastly, Constitutional Courts can be seen as legal actors inclined towards the political world from a *functional perspective, i.e.*, by observing the function these courts have in the relations between lawyers and politicians.[21] Viewed from this functional perspective, one can note how Constitutional Courts perform an intermediary function between these two arenas. As briefly sketched above, one of the major contributions of a Constitutional Court to its community is mediating between the highly political statements present in the constitution. The articles of a constitution tend to be dominated, from a legal perspective, by the rationality of the political discourse; at the same time, they are 'legally relevant' concepts and categories, *i.e.*, concepts binding public officials and the community in general through their observance of the parameters of the rationality required by a legal system.[22]

This mediating role played by Constitutional Courts is not only directed at the legal world, where the Courts define for its actors in legal terms what the general statements of goals in the constitutional documents or practices mean, *e.g.*, by guiding a justice in the interpretation of constitutionally questionable statutes. The mediating function is also aimed at the political arena, as the decisions of Constitutional Courts set the legal frameworks that the political actors ought to respect in their law-making.[23]

Since a constitution is the product of the will of a community (through their political representatives), at least in theory, a Constitutional Court in a democratic state has the function of mediating to the community and, in particular, to its political representatives, the value message that this same community and its political actors

20 *See* STONE SWEET, GOVERNING WITH JUDGES, *supra* at 45–49; and Klaus Stüwe, *The U.S. Supreme Court and the German Federal Constitutional Court: Selection, Nomination, and Election of Justices, in*ROGOWSKI AND GAWRON (EDS.), CONSTITUTIONAL COURTS IN COMPARISON, *supra* at 242–244. *But see* Peter H. Russell, *Conclusion: Judicial Independence in Comparative Perspective, in*P. H. RUSSELL AND D. M. O'BRIEN (EDS.), JUDICIAL INDEPENDENCE IN THE AGE OF DEMOCRACY: CRITICAL PERSPECTIVES FROM AROUND THE WORLD, 2001, Charlottesville: University of Virginia Press, 303–304.

21 In this chapter, 'function' refers to the 'function as effects' (as different from 'function as purpose') of a certain institution on a certain environment, or, as in this case, the concrete outcomes that the work of Constitutional Courts have on both legal and political structures. *See*BRIAN Z. TAMANAHA, LAW AS A MEANS TO AN END: THREAT TO THE RULE OF LAW, 2006, Cambridge: Cambridge University Press, 245–249.

22 *See* Joseph Raz, *On the Authority and Interpretation of Constitutions: Some Preliminaries, in*RAZ, BETWEEN AUTHORITY AND INTERPRETATION, *supra* at 369–370; and JIŘÍ PŘIBÁ[illegible], LEGAL SYMBOLISM: ON LAW, TIME AND EUROPEAN IDENTITY, 2007, Abingdon: Routledge, 21. *See, e.g.*, RONALD DWORKIN, LAW'S EMPIRE, 1986, Cambridge: Belknap Press, 370–371.

23 *See* Torbjörn Vallinder, *When the Courts Go Marching In, in*C. NEAL TATE, T. VALLINDER (EDS.) THE GLOBAL EXPANSION OF JUDICIAL POWER, 1995, New York: New York University Press, 13–24. *See, e.g.*, Ulrich K. Preuß, *Die Wahl der Mitglieder des BVerfG als verfassungsrechtliches und -politisches Problem*, 19 ZEITSCHRIFT FÜR PARLAMENTSFRAGEN 389–391 (1988); or MARK TUSHNET, TAKING THE CONSTITUTION AWAY FROM THE COURTS, 1999, Princeton: Princeton University Press, 7–9.

originally adopted, but now in terms of a legal message, *i.e.*, a message primarily directed at the actors given the duty of implementing the legal rules as interpreted (or accepted) by the Constitutional Court. As, in particular, the American legal realists and Alf Ross have pointed out, judges in general play a decisive role as the point of passage where the 'law-in-books' becomes the 'law-in-action', *i.e.*, the normative apparatus of rules felt as binding by the population or by the public officers.[24]

In this case, Constitutional Courts have the primary function of translating into binding norms for the political actors and the community, the law-in-books that the political actors have enacted. Constitutions tend to be documents where the political origins of the law, a typical feature of contemporary law, surface more clearly than in other legal documents (*e.g.*, a statute regulating taxation law). Constitutions are often used not only as a legal document grounding a new legal system, but also as a primary form of 'political symbol', *i.e.*, a message to the community from the political actors as to which fundamental values the state/community is based upon.[25] Moreover, and as a consequence of this partially political nature, legal language in the Constitution tends to be interspersed with political language.[26] A classic example of this is the article of the Italian constitution stating that property ownership is guaranteed by the law as long as it fulfils its social function.[27]

This being the situation, where judges are the intermediaries between the 'paper law' and 'real law', with the 'paper law' being the constitution – a mixture of political statements and legal concepts – it is not surprising that Constitutional Courts, more than other branches of the judiciary, become the law-making actors by being the interpreters of the law. As already pointed out by many legal scholars, the interpretation of the law that is typical for a court in general can become a law-making power.[28] In the case of the Constitutional Courts, this phenomenon is more evident, because

24 *See* KARL N. LLEWELLYN, BRAMBLE BUSH: ON OUR LAW AND ITS STUDY, 1951, New York: Oceana Publications, 150; Roscoe Pound, *Law in Books and Law in Action*, 44 AMERICAN LAW REVIEW 35–36 (1910); and ALF ROSS, ON LAW AND JUSTICE, 1959, Berkeley: University of California Press, 75–77. *See also*RONALD DWORKIN, FREEDOM'S LAW: THE MORAL READING OF THE AMERICAN CONSTITUTION, 1996, Cambridge: Harvard University Press, 7–15; and WALDRON, LAW AND DISAGREEMENT, *supra* at 262.

25 *See* Raz, *On the Authority and Interpretation of Constitutions, supra* at 343–344.

26 *See* Raz, *On the Authority and Interpretation of Constitutions, supra* at 365–366; and HABERMAS, BETWEEN FACTS AND NORMS, *supra* at 388–389. *See also* Mark Tushnet, *Abolishing Judicial Review*, 27 CONSTITUTIONAL COMMENTARY 585–586 (2011).

27 ITALIAN CONSTITUTION, ART. 42: 'Private property is recognised and guaranteed by the law, which prescribes … its limitations so as to ensure its *social function* and make it accessible to all' [*italics added*]. *See also* GIUSEPPE PORTONERA, THE PROBLEM OF SQUATTING IN ITALY: A NEW APPROACH BY THE COURTS, 2019, 4–5, available at https://papers.ssrn.com/sol3/Delivery.cfm/SSRN_ID3472293_code3097842.pdf?abstractid=3472293&mirid=1.

28 *See, e.g.*, Frederick Schauer, *Opinions as Rules*, 53 UNIVERSITY OF CHICAGO LAW REVIEW 684 (1986); HERBERT L. A. HART, THE CONCEPT OF LAW, 3rd edn., 2012, Oxford: Oxford University Press, 132–136; or NEIL MACCORMICK, H. L. A. HART, 2nd edn., 2008, Stanford: Stanford University Press, 157–159. *See also* Aharon Barak, *A Judge on Judging: The Role of a Supreme Court in a Democracy*, 116 HARVARD LAW REVIEW 62 (2002); and JOHN HART ELY, DEMOCRACY AND DISTRUST: A THEORY OF JUDICIAL REVIEW, 1980, Cambridge: Cambridge University Press, 1–9.

the legal text against which the interpretation of the statutes has to take place (namely the constitutional document) is so vague that the clarification of its content and of its borders becomes law-making (at least if seen from a legal perspective) directly applicable in concrete cases (as regards the concrete constitutional review) or in general (as regards the abstract constitutional review).[29] In summary, Constitutional Courts, for all the reasons mentioned above, are a special type of institutional actor that, though positioning themselves among the legal actors, *i.e.*, the actors aiming at interpreting and applying the law, tend to lean heavily into the political world of law-making, since Constitutional Courts through interpretation shape the legal panorama regulating a certain community.[30]

4 'Political vs. legal nature' as to the Constitutional Courts

Shifting attention to the topic central to this work, namely whether Constitutional Courts should be defined as primarily legal or political actors, a first reaction could be to question the importance of this issue. It appears to be a purely terminological matter, as the competence and jurisdiction accorded to Constitutional Courts, at least in well-established Western democracies, tend to be the same from a legal perspective, regardless of whether they are considered more political or more legal actors operating inside a certain system of powers. Whether they are seen primarily as legal or political actors, justices sitting on the highest benches will always be in charge of determining the constitutionality of statutes and, by doing this, will always be influenced by the political environment and prevailing political ideologies.[31]

However, the question presented here is not simply a definitional or academic problem. As often happens in legal matters, defining something or someone means attributing it with certain legal areas of competence and jurisdiction and, at the same time, limiting its capacity to operate in other legal areas. In other words, when it comes to legal issues, the classification of either a problem or a subject matter means shaping it and, at the same time, restricting it.[32]

29 *See* Gunther Teubner, *And God Laughed … Indeterminacy, Self- Reference and Paradox in Law, in* J.-P. DUPUY AND G. TEUBNER (EDS.), PARADOXES OF SELF-REFERENCE IN THE HUMANITIES, LAW AND THE SOCIAL SCIENCE, 1991, Stanford: Anma Libri, 31. *See also* Stone Sweet, *Constitutional Courts, supra* at 827–828; and Anna Gamper, *Constitutional Courts and Judicial Law-Making: Why Democratic Legitimacy Matters*, 4 CAMBRIDGE JOURNAL OF INTERNATIONAL AND COMPARATIVE LAW 824–834 (2015).

30 *See* LUHMANN, LAW AS A SOCIAL SYSTEM, *supra* at 235.

31 *See* HANS KELSEN, THE PURE THEORY OF LAW, 1970, Berkeley: University of California Press, 3–5; and Waldron, *Law and Disagreement, supra* at 144. *See, e.g.*, ALEXY, A THEORY OF CONSTITUTIONAL RIGHTS, *supra* at 366; or LAWRENCE BAUM, AMERICAN COURTS: PROCESS AND POLICY, 7th edn., 2013, Boston: Wadsworth, 270–272.

32 *See* Timothy A. O. Endicott, *Law and Language, in*J. L. COLEMAN AND S. SHAPIRO (EDS.), HANDBOOK OF JURISPRUDENCE AND LEGAL PHILOSOPHY, 2002, OXFORD: Oxford University Press, 935–968. *See also*WALDRON, LAW AND DISAGREEMENT, *supra* at 229; and PETER GOODRICH, LEGAL DISCOURSE: STUDIES IN LINGUISTICS, RHETORIC, AND LEGAL ANALYSIS, 1988, London: Palgrave Macmillan, 2–3. *See, e.g.*, Linda L. Berger, *Applying the New Rhetoric to Legal Discourse: The Ebb and Flow of Reader and Writer, Text and Context*, 49 JOURNAL OF LEGAL EDUCATION 155 (1999).

If one considers in particular Constitutional Courts and the definition of their nature as actors working in a certain environment, it has previously been seen that among their central tasks is 'checking' that the transformations of ideologies or values into law are done in accordance with (or at least not in gross contradiction of) the basic and often politically formulated principles enumerated in the constitution or fundamental laws of a certain community. The characterisation of Constitutional Courts as being either legal or political actors brings with it the identification of fundamental criteria, or in Max Weber's terminology, 'rationalities', that ought to govern this control over the constitutionality of the lawmaking that takes place in a certain legal system.[33] By normatively defining the nature and function of Constitutional Courts (*i.e.*, what they 'ought' to be and to do), it becomes possible to answer the following normative question that is fundamental for every democratic legal system: What is the fundamental criterion that ought to guide a Constitutional Court when performing its task of constitutional review?

Considering that Constitutional Courts operate between the legal and political worlds, it is possible to identify two fundamental criteria, or rationalities, which could shape Constitutional Courts in their work. First, at least when seen from a legal perspective, Constitutional Courts have the option to primarily embrace a Weberian substantive rationality in order to resolve issues of constitutionality.[34] This choice would mean that, in order to reach the 'best' solution, justices would regard the legal system as primarily instrumental to the fulfilment of certain goals external to the system itself. In other words, Constitutional Courts ought to be ready to 'sacrifice' the internal rationality and rules traditionally superseding Western legal systems and reasoning, if and as long as this capitulation is directly functional to achieving the political, social and economic values the courts intend, on various grounds, to insert into a certain community.

However, there is another possible ideal-type rationality or criterion that may guide Constitutional Courts in their work. As pointed out by Weber, in modern capitalist societies, the fundamental criterion inspiring the work of legal actors is formal rationality: they reach a decision or a legal solution based on the logical criteria internal to the legal system and with the purpose of maintaining its consistency, regardless of the actual effects in the surrounding environments.[35] This respect for formal rationality (or 'legality') is and ought to be, as Weber stated, because it is directly functional and fundamental for legal actors (and judges in particular) in order to gain and maintain their legitimacy, *i.e.*, a high degree of

33 *See* WEBER, ECONOMY AND SOCIETY, *supra* at 650–658; and MAX WEBER, MAX WEBER ON LAW IN ECONOMY AND SOCIETY, 1954, New York: Simon and Schuster, 63–64.

34 *See* WEBER, ECONOMY AND SOCIETY, *supra* at 656–658. *See also*REZA BANAKAR, NORMATIVITY IN LEGAL SOCIOLOGY – METHODOLOGICAL REFLECTIONS ON LAW AND REGULATION IN LATE MODERNITY, 2015, Cham: Springer, 219.

35 *See* WEBER, ECONOMY AND SOCIETY, *supra* at 655. *See also* David M. Trubek, *Max Weber on Law and the Rise of Capitalism*, 3 WISCONSIN LAW REVIEW 733 (1972); and ANTHONY T. KRONMAN, MAX WEBER, 1983, Palo Alto: Stanford University Press, 90.

probability that their decisions will be observed by the majority of addressees because they are considered 'correct' and therefore binding.[36]

The characterisation of a certain actor as legal or political is then always fundamental, at least from a legal perspective, in order to attach to a certain actor a certain criterion (or type of rationality, as in this chapter) that should guide it in its operations. This definition, however, is even more important in the case of Constitutional Courts, due to the position such courts occupy in modern democratic forms of political organisation. Constitutional Courts are certainly not the only actors whose nature can be and is widely disputed. For example, the legal nature of in-house attorneys is often heavily questioned; they are sometimes treated as simply facilitating a legal cover-up of economic and political programmes.[37] However, the theoretical issue of normatively defining Constitutional Courts is fundamental: the decisions of these courts (and consequently the criteria inspiring them) are those that can shape the fundamental legal, but also political and social, features of an entire community, sometimes even more than the decisions made in the democratically elected assembly. For example, in deciding *Brown v. Board of Education* (1954), the Supreme Court of the United States shaped (at least as much as Congress did ten years later with the 1964 Civil Rights Act) the future of an entire national community as far as concerned unlawful structural discrimination based on ethnicity.[38]

It is also true – using Ronald Dworkin's famous metaphor – that Constitutional Courts write just one chapter in the chain novel that constitutes the valid law, since, after their decisions, their words will be interpreted by all the other actors, *e. g.*, legal scholars, lower judges and law-makers.[39] However, even if the subsequent actors write a 'different' continuation of the novel, it is the Constitutional Courts

36 *See* WEBER, ECONOMY AND SOCIETY, *supra* at 654–658. *See also* Sally Ewing, *Formal Justice and the Spirit of Capitalism: Max Weber's Sociology of Law*, 21 LAW & SOCIETY REVIEW 497–502 (1987). *But see* Arthur L. Stinchcombe, *Reason and Rationality*, 4 SOCIOLOGICAL THEORY 151 (1986) (as to the substantive rationality being a *conditio sine qua non* for every formal rationality).

37 *See, e.g.*, Robert L. Nelson and Laura Beth Nielsen, *Cops, Counsel, and Entrepreneurs: Constructing the Role of Inside Counsel in Large Corporations*, 34 LAW & SOCIETY REVIEW 464–468 (2000); or PRASHANT DUBEY AND EVA KRIPALANI, THE GENERALIST COUNSEL: HOW LEADING GENERAL COUNSEL ARE SHAPING TOMORROW'S COMPANIES, 2013, Oxford: Oxford University Press, 66–67.

38 *See Brown v. Board of Education of Topeka*, 347 U.S. 485 (1954); and MICHAEL J. KLARMAN, BROWN V. BOARD OF EDUCATION AND THE CIVIL RIGHTS MOVEMENT: THE SUPREME COURT AND THE STRUGGLE FOR RACIAL EQUALITY, 2007, Oxford: Oxford University Press, 302–338. As to a more European context, *see also*GUARNIERI AND PEDERZOLI, THE POWER OF JUDGES, *supra* at 1–4; and STONE SWEET, GOVERNING WITH JUDGES,*supra* at 66–70.

39 *See* DWORKIN, LAW'S EMPIRE, *supra* at 228–238. *See also* Mark J. Richards and Herbert M. Kritzer, *Jurisprudential Regimes in Supreme Court Decision Making*, 96 THE AMERICAN POLITICAL SCIENCE REVIEW 306 (2002) ('[L]aw at the Supreme Court level is to be found in the structures the justices create to guide future decision making: their own, that of lower courts, and that of non-judicial political actors'); and MARTIN SHAPIRO, THE SUPREME COURT AND ADMINISTRATIVE AGENCIES, 1968, New York: Free Press, 39.

that have the privilege of setting the agenda for future discussion.[40] For example, with *Brown v. Board of Education*, the US Supreme Court definitively opened the door to de-segregation, *i.e.*, it gave a strong push to put into the trash can all the attempts to retain in American society the racist principle 'separate but equal'.

Many other aspects, of both political and legal character, underscore the necessity of coming forward with a clear definition of what kind of actors Constitutional Courts should be. From a political perspective, the definition of a Constitutional Court is important as it clarifies, and therefore partially prevents, possible points of collision between the highest powers in a community. Pointing out the basic features and criteria that should inspire the work taking place in the courts allows for a better and more precise control of the activity of the courts by political authorities, *e.g.*, in the form of offering a clear matrix to parliamentary committees or investigators against which to evaluate certain constitutional judicial decisions. In other words, this definition more clearly pinpoints a fundamental actor on the political map, either as primarily promoting certain ideologies that vary over time (if defined as a political actor) or as primarily attempting to maintain one single and established legal ideology, namely the rule of law (if defined as a legal actor).

Characterising the nature of Constitutional Courts is also important from a legal perspective, as this allows normative fixing of what type of rationality Constitutional Courts ought to apply in their work. At one end, justices sitting on the highest benches may be defined primarily as legal actors. Accordingly, from a legal perspective, the legality of their decisions in 'hard cases' can and should be questioned, even by lower courts, when their legal reasoning is mainly grounded on the goal of implementing values they consider as immanent in a community, although such values do not explicitly appear in the constitutional documents or fundamental laws. This critique of the legality of their decisions can and ought to be performed, in particular when the realisation of values is done at the expense of the traditional criteria superseding the legal reasoning (*e.g.*, consistency or respect for previous decisions on similar matters), *i.e.*, the only type of reasoning on which legal actors in modern democracy have a legitimate domain. For example, if a court decides within a quite narrow timeframe in diametrically opposite directions in similar cases or issues, it can be directly criticised from a legal perspective for violating a fundamental principle of Western legal systems, namely equal treatment of individuals under identical circumstances.

At the other end, in the event that Constitutional Courts are defined primarily as political actors, the possibility of holding them responsible from a legal perspective for doing something 'illegal' is more restricted. If they are considered political actors, it is not possible to 'force' the courts to decide in accordance, or at least in consistency, with previous decisions, although it is always possible to legally criticise Constitutional Courts for violating certain basic rights guaranteed in

40 *See* LUHMANN, LAW AS A SOCIAL SYSTEM, *supra* at 406 (indicating how the main feature of modern constitutions is their 'openness to the future'). *See also* Raz, *On the Authority and Interpretation of Constitutions*, *supra* at 338–343.

the constitution. One privilege accorded to political actors in general is that they can change their value system without being held responsible (at least legally) for this. If a political party or national assembly decides to pursue values other than those previously planned, it cannot be criticised or held responsible from a legal perspective.[41]

Lastly, another element highlights the importance of normatively setting the nature of Constitutional Courts in Western legal systems. These courts symbolise (and stretch to the limits) an underlying feature typical of most legal actors operating in contemporary Western legal systems: their position in between the political world, where values (or models of society) are created, and the legal world, through which those values have to pass in order to be implemented into a community.

Each of the individuals forming the skeletal structure of the legal actors is educated in the law and such an education is almost always a formal requirement to becoming a part of this group of actors. The individuals composing the legal actors are, in other words, all educated in the idea that law, although highly politicised, has certain features that distinguish it from purely political statements.[42] For justices working in Constitutional Courts, it is the same as for most legal actors: they operate within the legal system, but with the knowledge that law is instrumental in order to introduce into a community models of behaviours or values embraced by their political source (*e.g.*, legal experts working in political parties) or their economic source (*e.g.*, in-house attorneys for large corporations). This feature of the law in the Western legal systems, *i.e.*, always being functional to something else, then forces legal actors in general to always take into consideration the value systems (and the underpinning ways of reasoning) affecting the origins, development and environment in which the making or application of the law is taking place.[43]

In short, the importance of defining Constitutional Courts as either legal or political actors lies also in the fact that such institutional actors represent, better

41 *See* STONE SWEET, GOVERNING WITH JUDGES,*supra* at 62. *See also* John Ferejohn and Pasquale Pasquino, *Constitutional Courts as Deliberative Institutions: Towards an Institutional Theory of Constitutional Justice, in*W. SADURSKI (ED.), CONSTITUTIONAL JUSTICE, EAST AND WEST: DEMOCRATIC LEGITIMACY AND CONSTITUTIONAL COURTS IN POST-COMMUNIST EUROPE IN A COMPARATIVE PERSPECTIVE, 2002, The Hague: Kluwer Law International, 23.

42 *See* TUORI, CRITICAL LEGAL POSITIVISM, *supra* at 161; and ROGER COTTERRELL, LAW'S COMMUNITY: LEGAL THEORY IN SOCIOLOGICAL PERSPECTIVE, 1995, Oxford: Clarendon Press, 108–110. *See also*GUNTHER TEUBNER, LAW AS AN AUTOPOIETIC SYSTEM, 1993, Oxford: Blackwell Publishers, 33; ANDREW D. ABBOT, THE SYSTEM OF PROFESSIONS: AN ESSAY ON THE DIVISION OF EXPERT LABOR, 1988, Chicago, University of Chicago Press, 52–57; and NEIL MACCORMICK, LEGAL REASONING AND LEGAL THEORY, 1978, Oxford: Clarendon Press, 188.

43 *See* COTTERRELL, LAW'S COMMUNITY, *supra* at 281–284; Richard Posner, *The Decline of Law as an Autonomous Discipline: 1962–1987*, 100 HARVARD LAW REVIEW 773–774 (1987); and Francis J. Mootz III, *'Die Sache': The Foundationless Ground of Legal Meaning, in*J. M. BROEKMAN AND F. J. MOOTZ III (EDS.), THE SEMIOTICS OF LAW IN LEGAL EDUCATION, 2011, Dordrecht: Springer, 48–49. *See also* Raz, *On the Nature of Law*, *supra* at 99–100; and Jeremy Waldron, *Legislation, Authority, and Voting*, 84 GEORGETOWN LAW JOURNAL 2198 (1996).

than many others, the difficult situation in which lawyers in general operate nowadays. While they are educated in the law and employed to build, interpret and apply the law, legal actors operate under a constant and extreme pressure that pushes them towards a disregard for what are considered the characterising elements of a Western or Western-like legal system (predictability, certainty, rule of law and so on), in order to instead fulfil political (or non-legal) goals.[44]

5 A possible solution

Section 4 (*Constitutional Courts between law and politics*) showed how Constitutional Courts can be considered as actually belonging to the legal world, but strongly leaning towards the political arena. Section 5 (*'Political vs. legal nature' as to the Constitutional Courts*) pointed out that it is important, for several reasons, to normatively 'insert' the Constitutional Courts into either of these two ideal-typical boxes, *i.e.*, to establish which of the two natures (political vs. legal) should dominate their work and should be used as a starting point for investigating and (if warranted) criticising their decision-making.

It is helpful here to start by taking a slight detour to a sociological distinction between the *institutional* (or *organisational) position* (or *status*) of a certain actor (or agent) and the *function-effects* of that actor's work.[45] By the "institutional position" I mean the position occupied by a certain actor operating inside a larger environment (or organisational structure).[46] This positioning, as far as concerns judicial bodies, is mainly a combination of the operation of two (often overlapping) factors: the degree of legitimacy that judicial bodies enjoy, indicating where along the spectrum of power judges are inserted (vertical positioning), and the distribution of power as sanctioned in the law, which indicates where, at the stage assigned by the legitimacy, the judicial body is located (horizontal positioning). The function-effects of an actor's work simply refers to the impact that the work of the actor has on the environment.[47] These effects can be of different

44 *See* Gunther Teubner, *The Transformation of Law in the Welfare State, in*G. TEUBNER (ED.), DILEMMAS OF LAW IN THE WELFARE STATE, 1986, Berlin: Walter de Gruyter, 6–7; Lawrence Friedman, *Introduction*, 4 THEORETICAL INQUIRIES IN LAW 446 (2003); and Kaarlo Tuori, *Legislation between Politics and Law, in*L. J. WINTGENS (ED.), LEGISPRUDENCE: A NEW THEORETICAL APPROACH TO LEGISLATION, 2002, Oxford, Hart Publishing, 100–101.

45 *See* TALCOTT PARSONS, THE SOCIAL SYSTEM, 1951, New York: Free Press, 25. As to an application of this distinction within the legal discourse (specifically to the judiciary), *see, e.g.*, Robert F. Williams, *In the Supreme Court's Shadow: Legitimacy of State Rejection of Supreme Court Reasoning and Result*, 35 SOUTH CAROLINA LAW REVIEW 397–402 (1984).

46 *See* PHILIP SELZNICK, LEADERSHIP IN ADMINISTRATION: A SOCIOLOGICAL INTERPRETATION, 1957, Berkeley: University of California Press, 17–22. *But see*OTA WEINBERGER, LAW, INSTITUTION AND LEGAL POLITICS: FUNDAMENTAL PROBLEMS OF LEGAL THEORY AND SOCIAL PHILOSOPHY, 1991, Dordrecht: Springer, 18–24 and Neil MacCormick, *Norms, Institutions, and Institutional Facts*, 17 LAW AND PHILOSOPHY 324–331 (1998) (where 'institutions' within a traditional legal context instead refers to the regulatory tools, *e.g.*, contract or ownership).

47 *See* ROGER COTTERRELL, THE SOCIOLOGY OF LAW: AN INTRODUCTION, 2nd edn., 1992, London: Butterworths, 72–73.

ideal-typical natures. They can be ***intended***, where they correspond to the original goal that the actor had in mind when starting the work, or ***unintended***, where they do not (fully or partially) correspond to the original motive of the action.[48] Effects can also be in the form of either ***outputs*** or ***outcomes***.[49] Outputs are the impacts (intended or unintended) a certain action has inside the ideal-typical arena in which the action has taken place (*e.g.*, the effect of a court decision on the legal right of the convicted party to appeal). Outcomes, by contrast, mark the effects (intended or unintended) such impacts have on the surrounding environment (*e.g.*, the effect of a court decision on the economic situation of the convicted party's family).[50]

If one considers Constitutional Courts in light of these distinctions between institutional positions and function-effects (and the different types of effects), one can see that the dominant features of the courts are of a legal nature. Starting from the ***institutional position***, Constitutional Courts are, first and foremost, 'courts'. This label means that their rulings are considered binding by the vast majority of the addressees, not because of the content of the decisions, *i.e.*, the models of behaviours they aim to impose on a community, but because they are legal normative decisions. This means that they are rulings that ought to be obeyed because they are produced by a legally formed body, which is entrusted, in the forms prescribed by the law, with the legal power to produce such binding decisions. In contrast to political actors, such as political parties or lobby groups, the consideration and respect for the work of Constitutional Courts is not mainly based on the intrinsic values promoted by its decisions, such as the 'popularity' of a certain political program, for example. The respect, or legitimacy, is given to the decisions due to the legal form such rulings take, and the forms that have been observed while

48 *See* Robert K. Merton, *The Unanticipated Consequences of Purposive Social Action*, 1 AMERICAN SOCIOLOGICAL REVIEW 894–904 (1936).

49 This separation of outputs from outcomes is an adaptation of the results reached by a long series of studies developed in political science. *See*DAVID EASTON, A SYSTEMS ANALYSIS OF POLITICAL LIFE, 1965, New York: Wiley, 3531–3552; GABRIEL ABRAHAM ALMOND, G. BINGHAM POWELL, AND ROBERT J. MUNDT, COMPARATIVE POLITICS: A THEORETICAL FRAMEWORK, 1993, New York: Harper Collins, 20; and JAN-ERIK LANE AND SVANTE T ERSSON, THE NEW INSTITUTIONAL POLITICS: OUTCOMES AND CONSEQUENCES, 2000, London: Routledge, 60–62. *See, e.g.*, Selden Biggs, LELIA B. HELMS, THE PRACTICE OF AMERICAN PUBLIC POLICY-MAKING, 2015, London: Routledge, 370–371.

50 *See* the distinction between 'consequences' and 'juridical consequences' as developed by Neil MacCormick, *On Legal Decisions and Their Consequences – From Dewey to Dworkin*, 58 NEW YORK UNIVERSITY LAW REVIEW 247–251 (1983). *See, e.g.*, Tomas M. Koontz and Craig W. Thomas, *Measuring the Performance of Public-Private Partnerships. A Systematic Method for Distinguishing Outputs from Outcomes*, 35 PUBLIC PERFORMANCE & MANAGEMENT REVIEW 772 (2012) (under Figure 1). In reality, these different ideal-types (*intended outputs, unintended outputs, intended outcomes, unintended outcomes*) almost always tend to be mixed with each other, *e.g.*, in the form of court decisions that have intended and unintended outputs and outcomes simultaneously. Despite this overlapping in the real world, such ideal-types can be useful analytical tools to reveal specific tendencies of an actor to operate in one environment instead of another to gain certain effects, and then normatively choosing the type of rationality more suitable for that purpose, *i.e.*, indicating the line that the actors, as belonging to a certain arena, ought to pursue.

producing the decisions and choosing the individuals (*i.e.*, judges) in charge of making such decisions. In other words, Constitutional Courts keep their position and 'job' in the community as the highest dispute-resolving actor as long as they are able to maintain their legal legitimacy, *i.e.*, a legitimacy gained in Western legal systems mostly by observing the paradigms of formal legal rationality (or 'legality').[51]

Naturally, this pushing of the Constitutional Courts into the 'legal box' cannot ignore the fact that justices have political sympathies. However, even when justices are strongly politicised, they still ought to operate with an eye to (and being forced to comply with the barriers of and limits as set by) the legal system. In other words, despite being connected to the political world, the judges sitting in the Constitutional Courts ought to observe the principles or paradigms established by the dominating legal culture (*e.g.*, rule of law, bill of rights, separation of powers, due process and so on) in order not to lose their legitimacy among the addressees (and the community at large).[52]

As to their *function*, if one starts by considering the *intended* and *unintended outputs* of a certain decision by a Constitutional Court, the primary arena of operation of Constitutional Courts is the legal one. A Constitutional Court, per definition, evaluates legal issues, in particular the potential unconstitutionality of statutes or acts from law-making agencies. The outputs of the courts' deliberation are to decide whether certain legal rules of a lower dignity can still be considered as 'binding and therefore existing' legal rules. In particular, Constitutional Courts 'prove' the existence of these rules by evaluating whether they are compatible with the fundamental rules and principles enumerated in (or somehow derived from) constitutions and fundamental laws. This test, as pointed out before, is a typically legal problem since it can operate if, and only as far as, one axiomatically accepts the existence of an ascending structure of rules, where the lower rules, in order to exist as legal (and therefore binding) rules, cannot be in conflict with the higher ones.[53]

51 *See* JOHN HART ELY, DEMOCRACY AND DISTRUST – A THEORY OF JUDICIAL REVIEW, 1980, Cambridge: Harvard University Press, ch. 4; and HABERMAS, BETWEEN FACTS AND NORMS, *supra* at 278–279. *See also* Hein, *Constitutional Conflicts between Politics and Law in Transition Societies, supra* at 17 ('Constitutional courts, per se, have some leeway for making decisions based on political criteria. However, if this margin is too wide, and if the court is dependent on the political interests of other state powers, constitutional conflicts will be provoked'); and HANS KELSEN, GENERAL THEORY OF LAW AND STATE, 2005 [1949], London: Routledge, 117. *But see*SADURSKI, RIGHTS BEFORE COURTS, *supra* at 53–61 (pointing out, in order to be transformed into legitimacy, the necessity of formal rationality, or 'legality' in his words, to be finalised to the realisation of certain values external to the legal discourse, *i.e.*, substantive rationality).

52 *See* Niklas Luhmann, *Operational Closure and Structural Coupling: The Differentiation of the Legal System*, 13 CARDOZO LAW REVIEW 1435 (1991). *See, e.g.*, ALEXY, A THEORY OF CONSTITUTIONAL RIGHTS,*supra* at 367. *See also*FERRERES COMELLA CONSTITUTIONAL COURTS AND DEMOCRATIC VALUES, *supra* at 19 ('We cannot automatically claim that if a given institution strikes down statutes, it is really a 'legislative' body, whereas if it merely sets them aside for purposes of resolving disputes, it acts as a real 'court'. What matters is the sort of grounds – political or legal – on which the institution rests its decisions').

53 *See* HART, THE CONCEPT OF LAW,*supra* at 100–110; and HANS KELSEN, INTRODUCTION TO THE PROBLEMS OF LEGAL THEORY, 1996 [1934], Oxford: Clarendon Press, 11 ('To

As pointed out by Kelsen and other legal scholars, this presupposition is typical of the legal arena.[54] By contrast, the hierarchical structure in the political arena, though present (*e.g.*, basic values vs. tactical choices), is not fundamental to give 'validity' to the lower types of decision. Tactical decisions taken by a congressional party are still considered 'valid' for the political line of a certain party (*e.g.*, because such tactical decisions can strengthen the party's positions in an upcoming election), even if they are contrary to the fundamental values contained in the party programme.

In contrast to political actors, Constitutional Courts are not totally free from what can be defined as the external borders of legal reasoning. 'External borders' are identified in particular as the no-cross limits of the legal culture of a certain community, limits which have to exist in order for the legal system as such to survive.[55] In a democratic free-market regime, for example, these no-cross borders can be defined as the fundamental legal principles (*e.g.*, protection of private property) expressing the bedrock of political, cultural and economic forces upon which the regime itself is created and to which it is functional.[56]

Political actors do not necessarily have to respect such external borders of legal reasoning. Actually, for many political parties, the primary and fully politically legitimised goal for their existence is to change or shift such external borders, for example by eliminating the legal protection accorded to private property. The situation changes if one moves the focus to the *outcomes* of the decisions taken by Constitutional Courts, *i.e.*, the effects (intended or unintended) that their decisions have on the (non-legal) environments surrounding the (legal) one in which the courts operate. It is easy to see how the legal feature characterising the function played by the Constitutional Courts here tends to disappear. Decisions by Constitutional Courts almost always have effects outside the legal world, *e.g.*, in the cultural, economic or political spheres.[57] In other words, as far as concerns the

comprehend something legally can only be to comprehend it as law'). *See also-* LUHMANN, LAW AS A SOCIAL SYSTEM, *supra* at 406–407.

54 *See* KELSEN, GENERAL THEORY OF LAW AND STATE,*supra* at 110–113. *See* also KELSEN, THE PURE THEORY OF LAW, *supra* at 3–4 and 19; ROBERT S. SUMMERS, FORM AND FUNCTION IN A LEGAL SYSTEM: A GENERAL STUDY, 2006, Cambridge: Cambridge University Press, 313; and Neil MacCormick, *Natural Law Reconsidered*, 1 OXFORD JOURNAL OF LEGAL STUDIES 108 (1981).

55 *See* HART, THE CONCEPT OF LAW, *supra* at 193-200; and Herbert L. A. Hart, *Problems of the Philosophy of Law, in* H. L. A. HART, ESSAYS IN JURISPRUDENCE AND PHILOSOPHY, 1983, Oxford: Clarendon Press, 112 (as to his idea of 'minimum content of natural law'). *See also*TUORI, CRITICAL LEGAL POSITIVISM, *supra* at 177–183 (as to his idea of the 'general legal principles' of the legal culture).

56 *See, e.g.*, JEREMY WALDRON, THE RULE OF LAW AND THE MEASURE OF PROPERTY, 2012, Cambridge: Cambridge University Press, 103; or Neil MacCormick, *MacCormick on MacCormick, in*A. J. MENÉNDEZ AND J. E. FOSSUM (EDS.), LAW AND DEMOCRACY IN NEIL MACCORMICK'S LEGAL AND POLITICAL THEORY – THE POST-SOVEREIGN CONSTELLATION, 2011, Dordrecht: Springer, 23.

57 From a legal theoretical perspective, this different kind of effect (output as legal and outcome as non-legal) can be considered a consequence of the more general distinction between the normative and social functions of the law. *See* Joseph Raz, *On the*

outcomes of their decisions, Constitutional Courts have certain similarities with political actors, such as the government or national assemblies. What is more, Constitutional Courts with their decisions ultimately attempt (consciously or unconsciously) to impose certain models of behaviours or values upon a community.

Despite this leaning into the political arena, Constitutional Courts should be considered to have a legal nature, *i.e.*, as legal actors (and act as though they are). First, the grouping of an actor under a certain terminological roof has to be done primarily based on its *institutional location* and the function-effects of its work, in particular the *intended outputs* that its actions produce.[58] If one were to look at the outcomes, the analytical possibility of grouping actors in ideal-typical arenas, and the resulting possibility of identifying some normative criteria upon which to evaluate and criticise their work, would disappear. Outcomes of decisions almost always tend to spread in different directions and, especially for unintended outcomes, it is often not possible to determine in which area a certain action has had its major impact, particularly after a long period of time. For example, a decision made by a large corporation can have relevant outcomes in the religious or cultural fields, but it would be quite strange to define such corporations as primarily religious or cultural actors, and consequently impose upon the CEO or the board of directors religious or cultural criteria according to which their work is evaluated.

It goes without saying that the positioning of Constitutional Courts among legal actors (and the subsequent imposition of legal criteria in order to evaluate their work) does not rule out the possibility that they can (and often do) play a political function. As already stated, all legal decisions have certain outcomes, but Constitutional Courts, due to the task assigned to them in the constitutional architecture, make their decisions by looking to the legal outputs, namely the constitutionality or not of certain provisions. As stated by a legal scholar, '[c]ourts legislate, but that does not make them legislatures'.[59]

*Functions of Law, in*A. W. B. SIMPSON (ED.), OXFORD ESSAYS IN JURISPRUDENCE (SECOND SERIES), 1973, Oxford: Clarendon Press, 280.

58 *See, e.g.*, LOPEMAN, THE ACTIVIST ADVOCATE, *supra* at 3–5 (as to the idea that judicial activism is primarily 'intentional activism'). *But see* Christopher H. Schroeder, *Causes of the Recent Turn in Constitutional Interpretation*, 51 DUKE LAW JOURNAL 352–353 (2001) (as to the difficulty to disconnect the legal reasoning leading to the legal outputs from the desired non-legal outcomes when it comes to constitutional interpretation).

59 Herbert M. Kritzer, *Martin Shapiro: Anticipating the New Institutionalism, in*N. MAVEETY (ED.), THE PIONEERS OF JUDICIAL BEHAVIOR, 2003, Ann Arbor: University of Michigan Press, 409. *See also*NEIL MACCORMICK, QUESTIONING SOVEREIGNTY, 1999, Oxford: Oxford University Press, 11–15 (as to the fundamental ontological difference between the legal and political discourses); and LUHMANN, LAW AS A SOCIAL SYSTEM, *supra* at 162–165. *But see*STONE SWEET, GOVERNING WITH JUDGES, *supra* at 61. *Compare*JEROLD WALTMAN, PRINCIPLED JUDICIAL RESTRAINT: A CASE AGAINST ACTIVISM, 2015, Basingstoke: Palgrave Pivot, 58–61 (with a critical perspective as to the negative effects of introducing the legal paradigms employed by the judiciary into the political discourse).

Justices sitting on the highest benches certainly can (and often do) have a political agenda, but they are still forced to confront it with the legal system and its dominating principles. An inverted example can be seen among the members of parliament. They are unquestionably political actors with a clear political agenda, but they still sometimes play a very relevant legal function, and this is done in accordance with a specific legal agenda, *i.e.*, in accordance with legal criteria as to how the legal system or part of it should look. For example, this functional leaning into the legal world may happen when members of parliament in a special committee evaluate the legal limits of criminal liability attached to the highest position of the state, such as the President of the Republic or the Prime Minister.

Moreover, and connected to the latter, the legal features of Constitutional Courts are traceable to the fundamental ideology shaping their work. Justices working in Constitutional Courts operate in an environment which, though with many political passersby, has a primary legal task: to be the guardian ensuring that the law-making taking place in a certain state is done (or that a conflict among the highest public authorities is settled) in accordance with the highest rules fixed in the constitutional documents or fundamental laws. This task of Constitutional Courts is legal, in the sense that it consists of dealing with legal rules. When justices sit on the bench, they are assigned the primary task of checking the 'constitutionality' of certain legal rules: they ought to evaluate whether, from a legal discourse perspective (*i.e.*, with the traditional rules regulating the legal reasoning), such legal rules can fit (or not) into the legal system as designed in the constitutional documents or fundamental laws. Obviously, justices are often well aware of the indirect political effects of their decisions (outcomes), an awareness that sometimes affects their settling on a certain solution instead of another. However, regardless of any hidden agenda behind a certain decision, justices are always forced to 'squeeze' their politically motivated decisions into boxes of legal justification, to whose fundamental principles and ways of reasoning the justices ought then to sacrifice (in case of conflicts) their political programs.[60]

In other words, in order to keep their legitimacy in the community, Constitutional Courts are always forced to speak the language of the law, not the one of politics, even in the cases when they aim to send political messages. As pointed out by Michel Foucault, language in modern society is power, and this feature persists even in the most 'politicised' legal terminology: simply by classifying a political problem and a political solution into legal language, the justices are (consciously

60 *See* Gonçalo de Almeida Ribeiro, *Judicial Activism and Fidelity to Law, in* L. COUTINHO, M. LA TORRE AND S. SMITH (EDS) JUDICIAL ACTIVISM – AN INTERDISCIPLINARY APPROACH TO THE AMERICAN AND EUROPEAN EXPERIENCES, 2015, Cham: Springer, 36–40; and DIETER GRIMM, CONSTITUTIONALISM: PAST, PRESENT, AND FUTURE, 2016, Oxford: Oxford University Press, 208. *But see* Alec Stone Sweet, *The Politics of Constitutional Review in France and Europe*, 5 INTERNATIONAL JOURNAL OF CONSTITUTIONAL LAW 72 (2007). *See, e.g.*, Lawrence B. Solum, *The Supreme Court in Bondage: Constitutional Stare Decisis, Legal Formalism, and the Future of Unenumerated Rights*, 9 UNIVERSITY OF PENNSYLVANIA JOURNAL OF CONSTITUTIONAL LAW 160–176 (2006); and RONALD DWORKIN, JUSTICE IN ROBES, 2006, Cambridge: Belknap Press, 147–150.

or unconsciously) choosing to impose on the issue the domain and limits set by the legal discourse.[61] Therefore, the work of the Constitutional Courts should be evaluated accordingly, *i.e.*, by using legal criteria and, at the same time, by excluding from the evaluation process all features and limits set by other types of discourses – and, among them, the political one.

6 Conclusion

In light of the debate on judicial activism at the constitutional level, *i.e.*, the involvement of Constitutional Courts in political law-making, this chapter has investigated the issue of whether such courts should be considered primarily legal or political actors. After having pointed out the reasons why Constitutional Courts in established Western democracies can be seen as being legal actors, but with strong ties to the political arena, the central argument of this chapter has been on why one should normatively impose upon these courts the label of 'legal actors', though they play a political function. Based on this location within the legal world, one can then draw two general indications on how to approach the activisms of such highest courts. First, the (natural) political activism of the Constitutional Courts in their functions ought always to be under the scrutiny of exclusively legal criteria (and not, for instance, of political opportunity). Second, the entrance of the political world into the Constitutional Courts should always be tolerated as to their function and not as to their structure, by limiting for instance the further politicisation of the selection process of the justices.

61 *See* MICHEL FOUCAULT, THE ARCHAEOLOGY OF KNOWLEDGE AND THE DISCOURSE ON LANGUAGE, 1972, New York: Pantheon books, ch. 2. *See also* ALAN HUNT AND GARY WICKHAM, FOUCAULT AND LAW: TOWARDS A SOCIOLOGY OF LAW AS GOVERNANCE, 1994, Chicago: Pluto Press, 7–12 and 41–43.

2 Activism as defence

The role of courts in shaping the relationship between constitutions and international law: A comparison of the apex courts of Switzerland, Germany and Austria

Stefan Schlegel

1 Introduction

What determines the relationship between constitutional law and international treaties, and what role do courts play in shaping this relationship? The literature oscillates between cultural and institutional explanations. Cultural explanations pertain to the legal and political culture of a country, whether it has a tradition of nationalism or internationalism, a culture of cooperation or not,[1] and whether it is international or the domestic law that is seen as the 'original' legal order from which the other derives.[2] Institutional explanations draw upon factors such as the 'flexibility' and the degree of detail in a constitution and – closely related – the role of judicial review.[3] The easier a constitution can be amended and the more difficult it is for courts to review the constitutionality of treaties, the more it becomes necessary to grant primacy to international treaty law (even over the

1 See D Thurnherr, 'The Reception Process in Austria and Switzerland' in Helen Keller and Alec Stone Sweet (eds), *A Europe of Rights: The Impact of the ECHR on National Legal Systems* (Oxford, Oxford University Press, 2012), 335 for such a cultural explanation. She is of the opinion that the incorporation of the ECHR was swifter in the francophone Cantons of Switzerland as compared to the German speaking Cantons due to the 'more cosmopolitan attitude' of the former. See also R Wahl, 'Das Bundesverfassungsgericht im europäischen und internationalen Umfeld' in Robert C van Ooyen and Martin H W Möllers (eds), *Handbuch Bundesverfassungsgericht im politischen System*, 2. Aufl. (Wiesbaden, Springer VS, 2015), 831.

2 S Hobe and O Kimminich, *Einführung in das Völkerrecht*, 10th edn (Tübingen, Francke, 2014), 240; A Verdross and B Simma, *Universelles Völkerrecht*: Theorie und Praxis, Unveränderter Nachdruck der 3. völlig neu überarbeiteten Aufl. von 1984 (Berlin, Duncker & Humblot, 2010), 54.

3 See M Schlögl, 'Strategen in Roben: Einflussfaktoren auf die Rechtsprechung des U.S. Supreme Court und deren Implikation für das Bundesverfassungsgericht' in Robert C van Ooyen and Martin H W Möllers (eds), *Handbuch Bundesverfassungsgericht im politischen System*, 2. Aufl. (Wiesbaden, Springer VS, 2015), 897. Overall, see also L Epstein and J Knight, 'The Economic Analysis of Judicial Behavior' in Lee Epstein, Stefanie A Lindquist and Jack Knight (eds), *The Oxford Handbook of U.S. Judicial Behavior* (Oxford University Press, 2017).

DOI: 10.4324/9781003200666-4

constitution) since this is the only way to entrench its binding character.[4] The common denominator of these factors is that they shape the extent of the 'friction surface', the potential of real conflict between international and constitutional law.

The concept of a 'friction surface' that I would like to introduce in this chapter is aware that a pyramidal concept of law, where international public law sits on top, with national constitutional law as a second layer and national statutory law as a third layer, etc., is overly simplistic.[5] It cannot account for the degree to which international law is self-executing and it cannot distinguish between a supremacy within the realm of international law and a possibly differing rank of legal norms in the realm of domestic law.[6] What is more, it cannot account for the fact that the risk of conflict between national and international law heavily depends on the degree to which different countries are involved in international cooperation and namely whether they are member states of supranational organisations or not. Finally, it cannot distinguish between supremacy of one legal order over the other in the application of law as opposed to the supremacy of norms as a constraint to law making. Nevertheless, national and international law create frictions with each other, both in the creation and in the application of law, between international law and constitutional law on the one hand and international law and statutory or lower ranking law on the other hand, and both with self-executing international norms and international norms in need of specification in domestic law. This friction surface is hard to map or picture in a spatial way. It is much more complex than the imagined surface between two layers of a legal edifice.[7] However, if a multitude of factors is taken into account, its extent can be described, at least in relative terms, in the sense that it can be meaningfully compared to friction surface between another state's domestic law and international law. Thus, it helps to substantiate the analytical power of institutional explanations for the varying relationships of constitutional norms with international law in different countries.

This chapter aims to add to such an institutional explanation. It argues that courts play an important role in shaping the relationship between constitutions and international law but that their role is structurally conditioned. The (growing) flexibility of a constitution is the main structural factor that courts must take into account when determining a constitution's rank with regard to international treaties. The easier it is to amend a constitution – and the more details it therefore contains – the larger the friction surface gets and the harder it becomes to avoid

4 A Cassese, *International Law*, Second Edition (Oxford, Oxford University Press, 2005), 222–223.

5 In the Swiss doctrine, however, there is a certain tendency to insist on this pyramidal view. See e.g. W Kälin, 'Der Geltungsgrund des Grundsatzes "Völkerrecht bricht Landesrecht"' in Guido Jenny and Walter Kälin (eds), *Die schweizerische Rechtsordnung in ihren internationalen Bezügen: Festgabe zum Schweizer. Juristentag 1988* (Bern, Stämpfli, 1988), 65. See further O Diggelmann, *Völkerrecht*: Geschichte und Grundlagen. Mit Seitenblicken auf die Schweiz, 1st ed. (Baden, hier+jetzt, 2018), 182.

6 See O Ammann, *Domestic courts and the interpretation of international law: Methods and reasoning based on the Swiss example* (2020), 75.

7 See Diggelmann (n 5), 178–179 who uses the metaphor of a 'joggled' ('*verzahnt*') Relationship between domestic and international law.

irresolvable conflicts with treaty law if – in the application to concrete cases – there is no supremacy of the latter over the former. In addition, the possibility of constitutional review is linked to the flexibility of the constitution and represents another structural factor for the role of courts. The pressure grows for an apex court to seek a 'domestication of the supremacy of international law',[8] i.e. to recognise a supremacy of treaty law not just in the international, but also in the domestic realm. For the domestic context, recognising the supremacy of international law over domestic law remains an exceptional practice (outside of the context of EU law). This holds true especially with regard to the supremacy of international law over the constitution.[9] However, the structural factors mentioned above nudge courts towards judicial activism to establish supremacy of international treaty law.

What is meant by *judicial activism* in the following is the willingness of courts to interfere with the decisions of other branches of government on the ground that those decisions allegedly are in conflict with higher-ranking law. Activism may also manifest itself in a procedural guise, namely, when issues are treated by a court, which are unnecessary to the disposition of the case.[10]

The case study I use to illustrate the influence of structural factors on apex courts is Switzerland, where a series of recent amendments to the constitution – in conflict with treaty law – has led to a jurisprudence that assures the primacy of (some) international treaty norms even over more recent constitutional norms. This, in turn, led to an initiative, which sought to amend the constitution anew in order to enforce the primacy of the constitution over international law,[11] a project that failed at the ballots in 2018.

I compare the case of Switzerland to Austria and Germany. These three mainly German-speaking countries share – especially in the field of constitutional law – a lot of common legal culture and common legal doctrine.[12] Yet, although all three of them are federal democracies, they differ starkly in terms of their institutional architecture regarding the role and the revision of their constitutions, the role of

8 A Nollkaemper, 'Rethinking the Supremacy of International Law' (2010) *ZÖR* 65, 68. See also A Peters, 'Supremacy Lost: International Law Meets Domestic Constitutional Law' (2009) 3(3) *Vienna Online Journal on International Constitutional Law* 170, 174, 184.

9 Nollkaemper (n 8), 68. See also Ammann (n 6), 76.

10 K Roosevelt, 'Judicial activism' (2019) <www.britannica.com/topic/judicial-activism> accessed 23 November 2020.

11 A Glaser and A Brunner, 'Politik in der Defensive: Zwischen Vorrang des FZA und dynamischer Rezeption der EuGH-Rechtsprechung: Anmerkungen zum Urteil 2C_716/2014 vom 26. November 2015' (2016) (18 April 2016) *Jusletter*, No. 48. The German, French and Italian version of the text of this initiative can be found here: https://www.admin.ch/ch/d/pore/vi/vis460t.html.

12 Hans Kelsen himself underlined the importance of both the then German and the Swiss constitutions as models for his Austrian constitution. See K von Beyme, 'Modell für neue Demokratien? Die Vorbildrolle des Bundesverfassungsgerichts' in Robert C van Ooyen and Martin H W Möllers (eds), *Handbuch Bundesverfassungsgericht im politischen System*, 2. Aufl. (Wiesbaden, Springer VS, 2015), 928.

constitutional review and their relationship to European and international law. These differences affect factors that determine the extent of the friction surface between treaties and the constitution.

Methodologically, this comparison follows the 'most similar case' principle:[13] it compares cases, which are similar in many aspects that are potentially decisive factors for the phenomenon under scrutiny, except for one of the possible explanations for the *dependent variable.*[14] The possible explanation that differs here is size of the friction surface between treaties and constitutions. The dependent variable is the rank of treaties relative to constitutions. The case selection should be helpful, therefore, to understand the role of institutional as opposed to cultural explanations of the role of international law in its relation to the constitution and for the role of top courts in shaping and developing this relation.

2 The case of Switzerland: A uniquely malleable constitution

At the risk of applying simplistic labels that require subsequent nuancing,[15] Switzerland follows a moderate form of monism[16] and has an integrated Supreme Court (the Federal Supreme Court). However, the Court's competence for judicial review is restricted. It may not review federal statute law and international law. Art. 190 Federal Constitution (FC)[17] reads: 'The Federal Supreme Court and the other judicial authorities apply the federal acts and international law'. This implies that federal acts and international law have to be applied even when found to be in conflict with the constitution. Switzerland is not a member of the European Union (EU) but participates in its single market through a set of bilateral treaties, which are – in principle – governed by regular international treaty law.

13 See R Hirschl, *Comparative Matters*: The Renaissance of Comparative Constitutional Law, (Oxford, Oxford University Press, 2016), pp. 245–253.

14 See A Stone Sweet and H Keller, 'Introduction: The Reception of the ECHR in National Legal Orders' in Helen Keller and Alec Stone Sweet (eds), *A Europe of Rights: The Impact of the ECHR on National Legal Systems* (Oxford, Oxford University Press, 2012), 18; Hirschl (n 13), 250–251.

15 Peters (n 8), 170.

16 The two archetypes of creating effect of international law in the domestic realm are monism and dualism. Monism is the concept by which the two bodies of rules are part of one single legal order in which rules of international law gain effect in the domestic realm (to the degree that they are self-executing) at the moment that they bind a state. Dualism refers to the concept of domestic law and international law, as two independent, disentangled bodies of law. Rules of international law require *transformation* into domestic law in order to gain effect in the domestic realm. Nowhere can either monism or dualism be found in a pure form. In the case of Switzerland its monism is moderate mainly due to a high threshold to assume a self-executing character of treaty norms (e.g. the UN Covenant on Economic, Social and Cultural Rights is generally not qualified as self-executing in Switzerland). This limits the set of rules that are applicable without an act of transformation into domestic law: Diggelmann (n 5), 182.

17 A Griffel, 'Rechtsschutz' in Oliver Diggelmann, Maya Hertig Randall and Benjamin Schindler (eds), *Verfassungsrecht der Schweiz/Droit Constitutionnel Suisse* (Zürich, Schulthess, 2020), n. 30.

2.1 The institution of the popular initiative

On a purely positivist account, the procedure applicable to constitutional revision is a qualified one in Switzerland (as it is in Germany and Austria). Unlike what applies to the amendment of simple federal statutes, constitutional amendments require a compulsory referendum and a double majority – both of the voting electorate and of the 26 Cantons (States), which compose the Confederation (Art. 140(I)(a) FC).[18] Therefore, if the absence of a qualified legislative procedure were decisive to consider a constitution as malleable as opposed to rigid, the Swiss constitution would not qualify. The reason why it is among the most frequently amended constitutions in the world, and why it contains relatively detailed norms with a comparatively high risk of being in conflict with international law, is a specific tool of its direct democracy, the 'popular initiative'. It allows citizens to gather 100,000 signatures for the purpose of a specific amendment (i.e. a partial revision of the constitution, Art. 139 FC), and to trigger a popular vote on this proposal.[19] If the proposed amendment passes the double majority, it becomes part of the constitution. There is no option for a popular initiative to sponsor or amend statutory law. Therefore, all proposals of citizen committees, as specific and minor as they may be,[20] will become – if successful – part of the constitution. The tool of the popular initiative underwent a fundamental shift in popularity and in its usage in the last quarter century. While just 12 popular initiatives were successful in the 108 years between 1891 (when they were first introduced) and 1999 (when the Federal Constitution underwent total revision), ten of them were successful in the 22 years between 1999 and 2021.[21] Taking other partial revisions into account, (stemming not from popular initiatives but from amendments sponsored

18 An English translation of the Federal Constitution can be found here: https://www.admin.ch/opc/en/classified-compilation/19995395/index.html.

19 There is also a possibility to demand a total revision (Art. 138 FC). However, this provision does not play an important role in practice.

20 In 2018 the Swiss electorate was called to vote on an amendment to the constitution that would have banned cutting of the horns of cows. The initiative was rejected. For a long time, the Swiss constitution contained a ban of the beverage Absinth, the result of a popular initiative of 1910. For a more extensive discussion of this specific issue, see L Rühli and T Alder, 'Die Volksinitiative: Durch Fokussierung zu mehr Demokratie' (Zürich 2015) <cdn.avenir-suisse.ch/production/uploads/2001/01/Die-Volksinitiative.pdf> accessed 29 September 2020, 34–36.

21 B Degen, 'Volksinitiativen' (2016) <www.hls-dhs-dss.ch/textes/d/D10386.php>. However, it is very possible that the boom in popular initiatives, as it occurred between 2004 and 2014, may well be over. No popular initiative has been successful from 2014 to 2021: C Longchamp, 'The decade of ballot box upsets is over' (2018) <www.swissinfo.ch/eng/directdemocracy/political-campaigns-2019_the-decade-of-popular-votes-is-over/44374878> accessed 29 September 2020. In March 2021, a popular initiative was successful at the ballots for the first time since 2014. It prohibits the wearing of a full face veil (e.g. Niqab or Burqa). It was accepted with 51.2% of the popular vote and by 16 4/2 of the Cantons (some small Cantons are counted with just having a vote in assessing the necessary majority of the States). See also the statistics provided by F Caroni and A Vatter, 'Vom Ventil zum Wahlkampfinstrument? Eine empirische Analyse zum Funktionswandel der Volksinitiative' (2016) (2) *LEGES* 189, 196.

by the parliament or the government), the constitution has been amended 36 times since 1999.[22]

One reason for this acceleration in amendments is that the mark of 100,000 signatures becomes ever easier to achieve with a growing citizenry[23] and digital means to mobilise citizens. More important, however, is the fact that popular initiatives have evolved: from an instrument for fringe groups with allegedly popular political proposals but a lack of established support in the federal parliament to a campaigning and agenda-setting tool[24] for well-established political parties, most notably the right-wing populist 'People's Party', currently the strongest party in the country.

Some of these initiatives represented progressive causes. One of the successful popular initiatives made Switzerland a member of the UN in 2002. However, given their structure as extra-parliamentary means, popular initiatives tend to be populist,[25] hostile towards established political processes, towards legal principles that mitigate effects of the dominance of the majority, like the principle of proportionality, and hostile towards the separation of powers, especially to the mitigating power of courts.[26] Finally, yet importantly, they tend to be hostile to and in contradiction with international treaty law, most typically international human rights protection or the set of treaties that govern the complex relationship of the country with the EU.[27] Out of the eleven popular initiatives adopted since 1999, at least six create tensions in their conformity with international human rights law or the bilateral treaties between Switzerland and the EU.[28] One further popular initiative proved difficult to reconcile with other constitutional norms.[29] There is only one substantive limit to the content of partial amendments to the constitution. They must not be in conflict with rules of mandatory provisions of international law (Art. 194 II FC). 'Mandatory' must not be

22 See the list online at https://www.admin.ch/opc/de/classified-compilation/19995395/changes.html. Some of these very numerous revisions up to 2003, however, are afterglow effects of the total revision of the constitution that was revised in a multi-step process; see W Haller, U Häfelin and H Keller, *Schweizerisches Bundesstaatsrecht*, 10. Auflage (Zürich, Schulthess, 2020), n. 70.

23 L Leemann, 'Political Conflict and Direct Democracy: Explaining Initiative Use 1920–2011' (2015) 21(4) *Swiss Political Science Review* 596, 603.

24 Rühli and Alder (n 20), 30. Sceptical on the empirical validity of this claim: Caroni and Vatter (n 21), 205.

25 Populist in the sense that they claim to be the voice of the one true and plain people, as opposed to cosmopolitan elites on the one hand and foreigners or foreigners at heart on the other hand. See J-W Müller, *Was ist Populismus?: Ein Essay* (Berlin, Suhrkamp Verlag, 2016), 19.

26 Of the popular initiatives launched between 2004 and 2014, six came from the political right, two from left-wing alliances, and one did not have a clear political tilt: Longchamp (n 21).

27 Caroni and Vatter (n 21), 190.

28 These are: the initiative 'against mass immigration', adopted in 2014; the initiative 'Pedophiles should no longer be allowed to work with children', adopted in 2014; the initiative 'for the expulsion of criminal foreigners' of 2010; the initiative 'against the construction of Minarets' of 2009; the initiative 'for the imprescriptibility of pornographic offences', adopted in 2008, and the initiative 'for the life-long custody of extremely dangerous offenders' of 2004.

29 The initiative 'against rip-off artists' of 2013.

confused with 'binding', in this context. What is meant by the term (although much about it remains unclear) is the short list of generally acknowledged norms of *ius cogens*, extended by a set of norms that are seen as regional *ius cogens* (such as the prohibition of the death penalty) and '*ius cogens* in the making'.[30] To the degree that popular initiatives violate mandatory provisions of international law, they have to be declared inadmissible (Art. 139 III FC). This implies that mandatory provisions of international law enjoy supremacy over constitutional norms.[31] It also implies, however, that norms of international law other than mandatory provisions of international law do *not* rank higher than the constitution.[32]

2.2 The Federal Court ratcheting-up the rank of treaties relative to the constitution

It is in this fraught institutional context that in 2012 the Federal Court had to decide on the expulsion of a one-time drug dealer, a citizen of Macedonia, who grew up in Switzerland and had not committed any crimes since his initial sentence. It was clear that on the one hand, his expulsion would have infringed his right to family life and private life under Art. 8 ECHR. On the other hand, a recent amendment to the constitution – the result of a recent popular initiative[33] – demanded his automatic expulsion (Art 121. (III) FC). There was no way of mitigating the conflict through consistent interpretation of the constitutional norm. Although there would have been procedural ways for the Court to dodge the question and to invalidate the expulsion of the culprit and thereby to prevent a breach of international treaty law, the Court had to take a bold move. In an *obiter dictum* (a procedural way of judicial activism), it stated that even more recent constitutional amendments must give way to the ECHR.[34]

Three years later, in a case that concerned a conflict between another popular initiative (that demanded that all immigration to Switzerland ought to be limited via immigration caps, Art. 121a FC)[35] and the treaty that guarantees free movement of persons between Switzerland and the EU, the Court extended this jurisprudence –

30 G Biaggini, *BV Kommentar*: Bundesverfassung der Schweizerischen Eidgenossenschaft (Zürich, Orell Füssli, 2017), No. 13 on Art. 139 FC.

31 Peters (n 8), 185. Conflicts between popular initiatives and *ius cogens* actually occurred in Switzerland in the context of expulsion of foreigners regardless of a possible infringement of non-refoulement rules.

32 BGE 139 I 16, E. 5.2.1.

33 The initiative 'for the expulsion of criminal foreigners' of 2010.

34 BGE 139 I 16, E. 5.3; A Epiney, 'Das Verhältnis von Völkerrecht und Landesrecht aus der Sicht des Bundesgerichts: Anmerkung zum BGE 2C_828/2011 vom 12. Oktober 2012' (2013) (Jusletter 18 March 2013) *Jusletter*, No. 30. Writing in 2012, the year of the judgment, Thurnherr (n 1), 330, still holds that the hierarchical relationship of the constitution and the Convention is 'not fully clarified'.

35 The initiative 'against mass immigration', adopted in 2014.

again in an *obiter dictum*[36] – on this specific treaty.[37] An earlier decision already stated that the fundamental liberties as guaranteed in the treaties with the EU override more recently enacted, conflicting statutory law.[38]

This case law is important in two respects: first, because it departs from the ECHR-exceptionalism of earlier cases.[39] The ECHR enjoys a special status in relation to the domestic law of many of its States parties,[40] including Austria and Germany. This is so because of its Court, its effective enforcement procedure and because the Convention requires 'the High Contracting Parties [...] to abide by the final judgment of the Court in any case to which they are parties' (Art. 46 I ECHR). This norm applies regardless of the legal tradition of a specific member country.[41] The 'domestication of the supremacy of international law'[42] is strongly predetermined by this rule. Secondly, this case law underlines the close relationship of popular initiatives and the pressure to assure the primacy of treaties over the constitution. Unlike the ECHR, which was ratified before a referendum for international treaties existed in Switzerland, the treaties linking the country to the European Union (dating from 1999) were affirmed in a (simple majority) popular referendum. This vested the Court with a new argument: the democratic legitimacy of the treaty in question.[43] This argument is, however, limited to more recent and more substantial treaties that already fell under the relatively young referenda for treaties.[44] It therefore entails the risk of a subsequent jurisprudence that downgrades treaties that were ratified in accordance with the law applicable at the time, but not subject to a referendum. The argument, therefore, is rather construed and serves to camouflage the facts that some treaties have counterparts too powerful to upset them. The democratic involvement of the people in the ratification project adds further complication to the issue ('who do the courts/diplomats think they are, ignoring the will of the people?'). On the other hand, a treaty on free movement is structurally comparable to a human rights treaty. It guarantees individual rights in a self-executing manner and its value implodes when judges distinguish between its rank in

36 Glaser and Brunner (n 11), No. 36. For a different opinion, see A Epiney, 'Auslegung und Verhältnis des Freizügigkeitsabkommens zum nationalen Recht: Zum Urteil des Bundesgerichts 2C_716/2014 vom 26. November 2015' (2016) (14 March 2016) *Jusletter*, no. 16.

37 BGE 142 II 35, E. 3.3.

38 BGE 133 V 367, E. 11.6. See also Epiney, 'Auslegung und Verhältnis des Freizügigkeitsabkommens zum nationalen Recht' (n 36), No. 7.

39 For a more general discussion of the special place that human rights hold in the in questions of hierarchy between domestic and international law, see Nollkaemper (n 8), 82.

40 For the case of Switzerland, see Glaser and Brunner (n 11), No. 11.

41 J Meyer-Ladewig, M Nettesheim and S von Raumer, *EMRK; Handkommentar*: Europäische Menschenrechtskonvention, 4. Aufl. (Baden-Baden, Nomos, 2016), No. 39 on Art. 46 ECHR; Wahl (n 1), 841.

42 In the sense of Nollkaemper (n 8), 68.

43 BGE 133 V 367, E. 11.4.

44 S Schürer, 'Die punktuelle Neutralisierung der EMRK in der Praxis des Bundesgerichts. Zur verkürzten Grundrechtsprüfung bei der Anwendung von Bundesgesetzen' (2016) 117 *Schweizerisches Zentralblatt für Staats- und Verwaltungsrecht* 171, 126.

international law and its rank within domestic law.[45] Such treaties are, therefore, another example of the growing need of the 'domestication of the supremacy of international law'.[46]

As things stand currently in Switzerland, its apex court grants an exceptionally elevated rank to treaty law (at least to those treaties with which its constitution so far conflicted): treaties (at least some treaties) trump constitutional legal norms that were enacted after its ratification. That said, it is important to keep in mind that the relevant passages in both decisions are found in *obiter dicta,* and that not just one chamber, but the Court as a whole, would have to decide if this question could not be addressed in an *obiter dicta* but would be the one that decides the outcome of a case.[47] The federal administration, in any case, is of the view that the Federal Supreme Court has not settled the issue definitively so far.[48] Subsequent decisions by different chambers of the Federal Supreme Court went to great lengths to dodge the question of the relationship between the Treaty on the Free Movement of Persons with the EU and domestic law (in this case federal statutory law)[49] in the context of the expulsion of EU citizens who committed criminal offences in Switzerland.[50] The court's activism, therefore, is but a provisional, tentative and defensive one, met with fierce (if so far unsuccessful) resistance by the defenders of a supremacy of the people over the courts and over international treaty law.

2.3 The change of position of the government and the administration

One of the arguments of those proponents of a strong popular sovereignty is that this case law, as it stands now, is at odds with previously stated opinions of the government, which favours a primacy of constitutional norms over treaties.[51] When a popular initiative that clearly violated an international treaty was successful, the government was for a long time willing to interpret such an event as the popular demand, and as a constitutional mandate to withdraw from said treaties as an *ultima ratio.*[52] However,

45 BGE 142 II 35, E. 3.2.
46 In the sense of Nollkaemper (n 8), 68.
47 Glaser and Brunner (n 11), No. 41.
48 Schweizer Bundesrat, 'Klares Verhältnis zwischen Völkerrecht und Landesrecht: Bericht des Bundesrates in Erfüllung des Postulates 13.3805 vom 12. Juni 2015' (2015), 8.
49 However, this statute is the direct consequence of the adoption of the Initiative 'for the expulsion of criminal foreigners' of 2010.
50 BGE 145 IV 55, E. 3 and 4; Bger-E 6B_1152/2017 (28.11.2018), E. 2; Bger-E 6B_1136/2019 (2.7.2020), E. 4.1. See also N Burri, 'Landesverweisung und Freizügigkeitsabkommen – Bundesgericht vertagt Entscheid über Normenkonflikt' (2019) *sui generis*; B Fargahi, V Priuli and Fd Weck, 'Die ersten Urteile des Bundesgerichts zur Landesverweisung (Art. 66a ff. StGB): Erste Erkenntnisse – erste Widersprüche' (2019) (15.04.2019) *Jusletter.*
51 Schweizer Bundesrat, 'Das Verhältnis von Völkerrecht und Landesrecht: in Erfüllung des Postulats 07.3764 der Kommission für Rechtsfragen des Ständerates vom 16. Oktober 2007 und des Postulats 08.3765 der Staatspolitischen Kommission des Nationalrates vom 20. November 2008' (5 March 2010), 2310.
52 Ibid., 2317, 2323. See also, with regard to this position of the Federal Government in the context of the initiative 'against mass immigration', BBl 2013 291 317.

this position was relatively new itself. In a report published in 1989, the two relevant bodies of the administration concluded that international law should be granted primacy over domestic law.[53] That the administration then changed its opinion is all the more astonishing in the light of the initiative to ban minarets, an amendment that most probably conflicts with the ECHR[54] and would, according to this doctrine, entail an obligation to withdraw from the Convention. The government was therefore quick to point out that it seems impossible, either for legal or political reasons, to withdraw from *some* treaties, among them the ECHR, the ICCPR and the WTO agreement.[55] On top of that, it considered the possibility of a new hierarchy between the constitutional law and treaties, along the line of either their democratic legitimacy or their political importance.[56]

This relatively young change of view by the government has since been reversed anew. In statements that occurred *after* the successful initiative 'against mass immigration' (Art. 121a FC, voted on in 2014), the federal government has avoided repeating the view that a successful popular initiative in obvious contradiction with a treaty must be interpreted as an obligation to withdraw from said treaty. The initiative would, after the theory formerly held by government, force Switzerland to withdraw from the most substantial sets of treaties that links it to the EU. In those statements, the withdrawal obligation is no longer mentioned, as it was in previous reports on the matter.[57] In a later report on the ultimately unsuccessful popular initiative 'against foreign judges' (on which citizens voted in 2018), the government went a step further: it rejected – this time explicitly – the idea that a constitutional amendment in contradiction with international treaties involves a mandate for the government to withdraw from said treaty. This change

53 Bundesamt für Justiz and Direktion für Völkerrecht, 'Verhältnis zwischen Völkerrecht und Landesrecht im Rahmen der schweizerischen Rechtsordnung. Rechtliche Grundlagen und Konsequenzen des Vorrangs des Völkerrechts: Gemeinsame Stellungnahme des Bundesamtes für Justiz und der Direktion für Völkerrecht' (26 April 1989). VPB 53.54; No. 15.

54 L Langer, 'Panacea or Pathetic Fallacy? The Swiss Ban on Minarets' (2010) 43(43) *Vanderbilt Journal of Transnational Law* 863, 890.

55 Schweizer Bundesrat, 'Das Verhältnis von Völkerrecht und Landesrecht' (n 51), 2317; BBl 2004 3290.

56 Ibid., 2319. A reform of the constitution that would have required international treaties to be ratified by the same procedure as domestic law of the same material importance would have to be deliberated. Therefore, treaties with content of constitutional importance was proposed by one chamber of the federal parliament but – in spring 2021 – rejected by the other chamber. Such a reform would have had implications for the ranking of treaties relative to the constitution, that are as of yet little understood. See E Schmid, 'Procédure de consultation concernant l'avant-projet de référendum obligatoire pour les traités internationaux ayant un caractère constitutionnel' (2018) <serval.unil.ch/en/notice/serval:BIB_5E3D512733D6> accessed 30 September 2020, 5). A criterion that remains unconsidered for the ranking of treaties (although it apparently plays an important role in practice) is the effectiveness of the political or legal enforcement mechanism. See S Schürer, 'Hat die PKK-Rechtsprechung die Schubert-Praxis relativiert?' (2015) 116–132 *Schweizerisches Zentralblatt für Staats- und Verwaltungsrecht*, 132.

57 Schweizer Bundesrat (n 48), 20.

of position is justified with reference to recent manoeuvres, both by the Federal Parliament and the Federal Supreme Court to avoid conflicts between more recent constitutional norms and treaty law.[58] With that clarification, the government circled back to a position it held at the end of the 1980s, before the surge in treaty-threatening popular initiatives occurred. The government resisted that change of mind (with regard to law making) for a long time after the apex court of the country had taken that step (with regard to the application of law). This hesitation supports the view that court activism in this instance was an act of defence, a necessary move to avoid a conflict that the government, for a long time, was reluctant to avoid.

2.4 The role of constitutional review

There is – aside from the malleability of the constitution – a second factor at play that nudged the Federal Supreme Court towards creating for itself[59] a competence that enhances the visibility and the rank of treaty law, namely that of the ECHR. This factor consists of the duty to apply federal statute law, even when the Court finds it in breach of the constitution (Art. 190 FC).[60] In some cases, however, a federal statute is not only in breach of the constitution, but also of an international treaty vested with a court of its own judgments of which are predictable and binding (as in the case of the ECHR). In such cases, the Federal Supreme Court considered it futile to send a defendant to Strasbourg first, only for Switzerland to be condemned by the ECtHR. It therefore held that Art. 190 FC does not oblige it to apply federal statutory law if a statute breaches the ECHR.[61] This contrasts with the case law concerning the more general question of the hierarchy of international law and federal statutory law, the so-called Schubert Praxis. The Schubert jurisprudence granted (and still grants) the parliament the possibility to override treaties, provided that it is done consciously and by means of statutory law.[62] With the so-called PKK judgment,[63] the ECHR was exempted from this jurisprudence. This exception placed the Convention above statutory law long before the question of its rank relative to the constitution arose. While it does not, in itself, place the ECHR above the constitution, it nevertheless emphasises the importance of the Convention through the Courts' activism. The Convention is instrumentalised

58 BBl 2017 5355 5373. See also S Schlegel, 'Völkerrecht und Verfassungsrecht: Wie eine Volksinitiative in der Schweiz herbeiführte, was sie abzuschaffen vorgibt' (2017) <verfassungsblog.de/voelkerrecht-und-verfassungsrecht-wie-eine-volksinitiative-in-der-schweiz-herbeifuehrte-was-sie-abzuschaffen-vorgibt/>.

59 Schürer, 'Die punktuelle Neutralisierung der EMRK in der Praxis des Bundesgerichts. Zur verkürzten Grundrechtsprüfung bei der Anwendung von Bundesgesetzen' (n 44), 184.

60 See Wahl (n 1), 833, 835.

61 Schürer, 'Die punktuelle Neutralisierung der EMRK in der Praxis des Bundesgerichts. Zur verkürzten Grundrechtsprüfung bei der Anwendung von Bundesgesetzen' (n 44), 171–172.

62 Schürer, 'Hat die PKK-Rechtsprechung die Schubert-Praxis relativiert?' (n 56), 116.

63 BGE 125 II 417 E. 4d.

to widen the Court's elbow room that the constitution severely restricts, namely the space of constitutional review.[64]

3 The case of Germany: Low enough risk to insist on the last word

Germany is a moderately dualist country[65] with a comparatively very robust system of constitutional review.[66] Its constitution is not strictly speaking rigid, but much less malleable than the Swiss constitution. Some of the most central aspects of the constitution are unalterable, even by the most qualified majority. Germany is a member of the EU and recognised – subject to specific conditions – the supremacy of EU law early on.

The case law of the German Federal Constitutional Court concerning the relation of the *Grundgesetz* to treaty law is markedly different from the Swiss Federal Court's willingness to grant treaties supremacy even over the constitution. The German apex court may insist that the ECHR and the decisions of the ECtHR bind all the organs of the German state, not just the state as a subject of international law, and that lower courts therefore have an obligation to incorporate the case law of the ECtHR. But although the obligation to incorporate stems from the principle of the rule of law enshrined in the *Grundgesetz* (Art. 20 III GG), the Convention stands in the rank of a federal statute only and in lower rank than the *Grundgesetz*. One could have argued that the constitutional obligation to respect treaties factually elevates the content of these treaties to the rank of the constitution, but the BVerfG explicitly rejected this interpretation.[67] The Court underlined this position in a recent decision that implied the possibility that the ECHR might be overridden by statutory law.[68] The openness of the German constitution towards international law does not go so far as to waive the possibility of the *last word* that remains for the legislative power.[69] Lower courts are, therefore, obliged to incorporate international treaty law, but only as long as this does not infringe on the constitutional order.[70]

64 Griffel (n 17), n. 31. See also Peters (n 7), 182, describing comparable developments in France and in the Netherlands.

65 Germany's dualism is moderated by Art. 25 GG, which provides that the general principles of international law are part of the federal law. Through this norm, international customary law and general principles of international law gain effect, without need of transformation into domestic law. Diggelmann (n 5), 183.

66 Wahl (n 1), 829.

67 K Goldberg, 'BverfG entscheidet gegen Völkerrechtsfreundlichkeit – manchmal' (2016) <www.juwiss.de/22-2016-2/>.

68 2 BvR 1738/12 (*Beamtenstreikrecht*), Urteil des Zweiten Senats vom 12. Juni 2018, BVerfGE 148, 296, No. 132–133.

69 2 BVR 1481/04, No. 35; Wahl (n 1), 840; E Lambert Abdelgawad and A Weber, 'The Reception Process in France and Germany' in Helen Keller and Alec Stone Sweet (eds), *A Europe of Rights: The Impact of the ECHR on National Legal Systems* (Oxford, Oxford University Press, 2012), 118.

70 2 BVR 1481/04, No. 62; E Benda, 'Die Bindungswirkung von Entscheidungen des Europäischen Geritchshofs für Menschenrechte' (2005) 10 *Anwalts Blatt* 602, 608.

In a recent decision, the German Federal Constitutional Court took a stance regarding the possibility of treaty override that bears remarkable similarities with the Schubert-jurisprudence of the Swiss Federal Court.[71] This doctrine, however, is mitigated by an important exception (that the court only implies) and which the Swiss Federal Court only added to its Schubert jurisprudence in the 1999 'PKK' case – the exception to override human rights treaties.[72]

How is this doctrine related to the degree of flexibility of the *Grundgesetz*? The German *Grundgesetz* is harder to revise than the Swiss Federal Constitution. It requires not just a double majority like in Switzerland, but a qualified majority of two-thirds of both the *Bundestag* and the *Bundesrat*. Still, the *Grundgesetz* is revised rather often compared to other constitutions. Since its entry into force in 1949, it has been revised 60 times. This is too frequently, in the opinion of some, which is why an adaptation of its revision mechanism has been suggested.[73] Much more important is, therefore, what is – unlike in Switzerland – outside the scope of constitutional revision. Art. 79 III GG declares some provisions of the *Grundgesetz* as inalienable and protects notably Art. 1 and 20 GG (the protection of human dignity and the democratic, social and federal nature of the Republic) from revision. This markedly reduces the friction surface between international treaties and the constitution. The Federal Court invokes this fact to argue that the principles it developed in the context of fundamental and human rights issues cannot simply be transferred to problems regarding more mundane conflicts of international and domestic law, e.g. in the area of tax law.[74]

The popular initiative in Switzerland that led to the most immediate problems with treaty law, the initiative 'for the expulsion of criminal foreigners', had – until 2015 – a remarkably similar counterpart in Germany, introduced by the Kohl Administration (§§ 53–56 of the then *Aufenthaltsgesetz*). Yet this counterpart was simple statutory law, not constitutional law as in Switzerland. The mitigation of its effects in order to protect individual rights could, therefore, be done with reference to *both* constitutional guarantees and the ECHR (in this case Art. 6 GG and Art. 8 ECHR).[75] A conflict between constitutional and treaty law, as in Switzerland, was avoidable in the case of Germany. The need to harmonise the rules regarding the expulsion of foreigners with both constitutional and treaty law was the impulse to reform this field of law.[76]

In the German context, too, the decisive question is not so much, whether international treaties are violated, but *which ones* and how effective the mechanisms of

71 This decision even goes somewhat further since the threshold of intentionality of breach of the legislative power seems not to be very high. No special requirements or legitimisation is needed for a breach, 2 BvL 1/12, Dissenting opinion König, no. 7.

72 BvL 1/12, no. 76 and Dissenting opinion König, no. 1.

73 D Grimm, 'Ist das Verfahren der Verfassungsänderung selbst änderungsbedürftig?' (2007) (20) *Humbolt Forum Recht* 213.

74 2 BvL 1/12, no. 76.

75 See BVerwG, Urteil vom 2. September 2009, 1 C 2/09, n. 22 and Urteil vom 23. Oktober 2007, 1 C 10/07, n. 25.

76 Deutscher Bundestag Drucksache 18/4097, 23, 29 and 49.

enforcement of these treaties are. The better the structure of a constitution can avoid the violation of treaties with a biting enforcement mechanism, the easier it is to insist on the primacy of domestic constitutional law over treaty law. In this situation, the German Federal Supreme Court may be rather energetic in defending its own power against the potential power grab of international and European courts. Unlike in Switzerland, however, there is no need for the Court to get into conflict with the legislative or the executive branch of government. Defending the supremacy of domestic law means defending the power of all three branches of government. No activism is needed in that respect. On the contrary, the Court achieves the goal of reducing conflict between international and national law through a very legalistic jurisprudence.

4 The Austrian case: More room for judicial activism but a merely theoretical risk of friction

Like Switzerland, Austria endorses a moderate version of monism.[77] As in Germany, however, the relationship of the Austrian constitution to international law is marked by the dogmatic dichotomy between general principles of international law and international treaties. The Austrian Constitutional Court is recognised as the earliest model of a stand-alone constitutional court.[78] It is the sole court in the country competent for constitutional review. Yet it is less powerful than its German counterpart in the sense that it cannot revise judgments of civil or criminal courts.[79] The constitution can be amended by a two-thirds majority of the two chambers of parliament, and elevating a legal rule to the level of the constitution would immunise it from constitutional review. Austria is a member of the European Union and amended its constitution to enable membership.

The rank of treaties is determined by the importance of their content. 'Which rank an international treaty rule holds depends on the form that it would need to have if it were domestic law.'[80] The similarities to the recent attempt to reform the Swiss constitution (Art. 140 FC, see *supra*) aiming at improving the democratic legitimacy and the clarity of the rank of treaty law are remarkable. At the time of the referendum on EU membership in 1994, Austrian legal scholars disagreed as to whether a referendum can and ought to be held on an international treaty that is of such importance that if it were domestic law, its adoption would require a referendum. This uncertainty was circumvented by creating a domestic statute of constitutional rank that authorised the government to ratify the accession treaty.[81] The same technique was

77 Austria's monism is moderated by ranking international treaties. Only those treaties that had to pass parliament stand in the same rank as statutes. Diggelmann (n 5), 183.

78 Wahl (n 1), 828, 834; von Beyme (n 12), 929; W Haller, A Kölz and T Gächter, *Allgemeines Staatsrecht: Eine juristische Einführung in die Allgemeine Staatslehre*, 5. vollständig überarb. und aktualisierte Aufl. (Zürich, Schulthess; Nomos, 2013), n. 1012.

79 Wahl (n 1), 835.

80 R Walter and H Mayer, *Grundriss des österreichischen Bundesverfassungsrecht* (Wien, Manzsche Verlags- und Universitätsbuchhandlung, 1985), 78, my translation.

81 T Öhlinger, 'Art 50 B-VG: Die neue Integrationsbestimmung des österreichischen Bundesverfassungsrechts' in Waldemar Hummer (ed.), *Neueste Entwicklungen im*

applied for the ratification of subsequent EU primary law.[82] In a general reform of the Austrian constitutional law in 2007/2008, the constitutional rank of a series of international treaties was reaffirmed (by way of not downgrading them and including them into the newly ordered corpus of laws of constitutional rank).[83] Importantly, among those treaties is the ECHR. Thus, the ECHR – along with its additional protocols and a series of other treaties – enjoys constitutional rank in Austria, while it enjoys the rank of regular statutory law in Germany and (as things stand currently) a supra-constitutional rank in Switzerland.

Compared to Switzerland, the friction surface between domestic constitutional law and international law is decisively smaller in Austria due to the country's EU membership. One of the structural characteristics of EU law compared to ordinary international treaty law (the mechanism by which Switzerland is linked to the EU) is that EU law itself sets out its rank in relation to the domestic law. EU law claims supremacy even over domestic constitutional law, which is reflected in Austrian legal doctrine and jurisprudence[84] (with the exception of changes in EU law that are so fundamental that their application in Austria would amount to a total revision of its constitution, which would require a popular referendum).[85] If frictions occur along this (extended) line of potential conflicts, the rules of conflict are settled. Not so for Switzerland. In international treaty law, it remains for the domestic legal order to determine its rank.[86] So for Austria the friction surface is markedly smaller than for Switzerland, since the question of rank is already settled by the legislative process for the vital rules, linking the country to the EU and the ECHR.

The possibility to grant a treaty constitutional status through a qualified process of ratification by the parliament used to immunise treaty norms against constitutional review. Under the former Austrian constitution (in force until 2008), this created an incentive for parliament to lift treaty norms (like domestic statutory law) to the constitutional level, thereby limiting possible activism by the Constitutional Court.[87] Since the reform of the Austrian constitution in 2008, this option no longer exists.[88] This development enlarges both the friction surface between international and constitutional law and the room for activism for the court. However, as already shown, those sets of treaties that cause most of the friction with domestic law in Switzerland – the treaties relating the country to the EU and the ECHR – do enjoy constitutional rank in Austria.

Zusammenspiel von Europarecht und nationalem Recht der Mitgliedstaaten: Ein Handbuch für Theorie und Praxis, (Vienna, Springer Vienna, 2010), 626.

82 Ibid., 629.

83 Lindermuth, p. 301.

84 Öhlinger (n 83), 639.

85 Ibid., 640.

86 Ibid., 638.

87 P Lindermuth, 'Das Recht der Staatsverträge nach der Verfassungsbereinigung' (2009) 64(3) *ZÖR* 299, 307.

88 Ibid., 310. Also see Peters (n 8), 185–186.

A constitutional amendment that is in contradiction with the ECHR is – in the absence of popular initiatives to amend the constitution – rather hypothetical in Austria, which is why the ECHR can hold mere constitutional rank in the Austrian context.[89] Still, this leaves open the possibility for more recent constitutional law to override the ECHR – as the Austrian Constitutional Court implied in its *Miltner* Judgment of 1987.[90] In Switzerland, where a large portion of constitutional law is more recent than the Convention, such a case law would entail a real risk of a severe stand-off between the Federal Supreme Court and the ECtHR. This is why the *Miltner* solution would be very risky for Switzerland. As soon as such contradictions are not only a theoretical problem, and occur with treaties equipped with a mechanism of enforcement (like the ECHR) or backed by overwhelming political power (like the bilateral treaties between the EU and Switzerland), granting supremacy to treaties even over more recent constitutional law becomes – practically speaking – the only viable option.[91] The Austrian example, therefore, corroborates the claim that ranking specific international treaties below the constitution is only a tenable position for a country as long as potential conflicts between the constitution and such treaties remain a largely theoretical possibility.[92] This conclusion may be extended to treaties other than the ECHR with a biting enforcement mechanism.

The fact that the Federal Constitutional Court in Germany developed techniques to circumvent the *lex posterior* rule in the relationship between the ECHR (and its act of transition into German Law) and the *Grundgesetz*[93] further corroborates this hypothesis.

5 Concluding remarks

More and more creativity is needed to argue away the fact that international law is increasingly of a binding and enforceable nature, even when it conflicts with constitutional norms. In some cases, where the friction surface between those bodies of norms is especially extended, like in Switzerland, courts had to admit this straightforwardly.

Against that background, this chapter attempted a critical approach[94] to the relationship between constitutional law and treaties. This approach distrusts the

89 Thurnherr (n 1), 326.

90 Verfassungsgerichtshof, B 267/86, Erkenntnis vom 14. Oktober 1987, VfSlg 11.500/1987; 11. See also R Kunz, *Richter über internationale Gerichte?: Die Rolle innerstaatlicher Gerichte bei der Umsetzung der Entscheidungen von EGMR und IAGMR*, 1st ed. 2020 (2020), 212; Peters (n 8), 190.

91 See also Benda (n 72), 608.

92 One of the criticisms against this case law is that it is inward-looking, not considering the possible damage it does outside the German context, where conflicts between the Convention and the Constitution may be more than just a theoretical possibility. See Wahl (n 1), 841.

93 Lambert Abdelgawad and Weber (n 71), 121.

94 For a less dogmatically and more strategically informed approach to the jurisprudence of apex courts, see Schlögl (n 3), 890.

sophisticated arguments given by apex courts for granting primacy to treaties in specific cases while insisting on the principle of the supremacy of the constitution over treaty law in principle. My approach sets out from the presumption that courts have to give in to political realities and improved mechanisms of enforcement of international treaties and organise their jurisprudence around these constraints. The constraints work from three directions:

- from powerful treaty partners (like the EU in the case of Switzerland) or comparatively effective enforcement mechanisms (like the one that backs the ECHR);
- from constitutions that are – due to their malleability – prone to create conflicts with treaty law;
- from a restriction of constitutional review that creates both a risk of the violation of a treaty holding an analogous rule as the constitution and an incentive for an apex court to circumvent the restriction by elevating the analogous treaty law above the constitution.

Counterintuitively, the practice of the Swiss Federal Court to deal with these constraints is *activism as defence*. It is activism, in the sense that it interferes with the decisions of other branches of government, namely with the constitutional power, the people and the Cantons. However, it is defensive activism in the sense that its aim is not (only) to enhance the power of the judiciary relative to other state powers, but to reduce the otherwise large friction surface between constitutional and international treaty law by granting supremacy to the treaty law.

What does the Swiss government actually mean when it insists that a fixed and inflexible ranking of domestic and international law is to be avoided?[95] It means that some treaties can be violated without major consequences (and that it wants to reserve itself the possibility to violate those treaties) whilst violating others has become very risky.[96] It has been argued that keeping the possibility of an emergency break open is a precondition for constitutions to be opened up towards international law in the first place.[97] In some cases, the 'nuclear option'[98] is too explosive, but in others, it can be risked and therefore the possibility of treaty violation has to be kept open. Which treaties fall into the group 'too nuclear', and which ones in the group 'breakable', is left for an activist apex court to decide. In this particular sense, therefore, it is overly reductionist to state that supremacy is a 'formal principle – blind for substance and effect'.[99] While the *substance* is, in the Swiss cases, the legitimacy given for the supremacy of some treaties, the *effect* of their otherwise possible violation is at least as strong an explanatory factor.

The problem can be stated as one of the relative importance of two constitutional principles, the principle of the rule of law and the principle of democracy.[100] In this

95 BBl 2017 5355 5397. See further Ammann (n 6), 79.
96 Schürer, 'Hat die PKK-Rechtsprechung die Schubert-Praxis relativiert?' (n 56), 132.
97 Peters (n 8), 194.
98 Kunz (n 93), 216.
99 Nollkaemper (n 8), 73.
100 Goldberg (n 69). See also 2 BvL 1/12, Dissenting opinon König, No. 2–3.

light, it becomes clear that courts, when applying the constitution, have to compensate with an overreliance on the principle of the rule of law where the political process limits itself almost entirely on (a questionable understanding of)[101] the principle of democracy. Put differently: the more the constitution stresses the supremacy of its constituent power, the more the mitigating activism of an apex court – who must deal with the frictions thus produced – is needed.

101 It is a questionable understanding because it reduces democracy to majoritarian process of decision-making, neglecting the background conditions for such a process to function, such as basic rights, viable protection of minorities and an independent judiciary.

Part II

Judicial activism of international and supranational courts and its impact on national constitutional orders

3 The revolutionary impact of European Court of Human Rights case law on the idea of *res judicata* in criminal justice

The Italian experience

Maria Lucia Di Bitonto[1]

1 Introduction

The idea of *res judicata* is a concept rooted in both traditions of the civil law and the common law. If the defendant has been convicted, in the common law the judicial pronouncement becomes the conclusive judgment – *id est*, comes into force – immediately after the verdict and the sentencing. In the civil law tradition, the conviction comes into force when the criminal proceeding is definitively concluded after the deadline for appealing, or after the conclusion of the appeal judgments.

Both in the continental and common law systems this idea is accepted: when a criminal proceeding is definitively concluded no one can change the decision, which was made at the conclusion of that proceeding.

Furthermore, if the criminal proceeding ended with a guilty verdict, the detention of the defendant found guilty is considered a legal detention because the judicial control on the detention is incorporated into the original conviction and sentence.

The traditional approach of the criminal justice system regarding *res judicata* had been deeply revolutionised after the establishment of the European Court of Human Rights (ECtHR) – especially after its most recent case law – because the convicted defendant can present the application to this judge only when his proceeding has definitively ended.

The ECtHR's jurisprudence has influenced a lot the national law of the contracting Parties. The impact of Court of Strasbourg case law on the several national law systems can be found not only in those States having been a party to a particular case (*inter partes* effects), but also in those willing to bring its legislation or national case law into line with the principles flowing from the Strasbourg case law (*erga omnes* effects). The ECtHR has its own internal logic and its authoritative interpretation of the human rights treaty contributed to the framing of the domestic human rights protection systems.[2]

1 Associate Professor of Criminal Procedure at University of Camerino School of Law and Adjunct Professor at Luiss Guido Carli University of Rome Department of Law.

2 M. Oetheimer – G. Cano Palomares, *European Court of human rights*, in *Oxford public international law*, 2013, 17.

DOI: 10.4324/9781003200666-6

This framework has changed the role and powers of criminal judges: in the ECHR system, national judges are the first guarantors of human rights granted by the same Convention. They have to apply the ECHR provisions directly, taking into account the case law of the Strasbourg Court. Therefore, the outlook of *res judicata* in criminal matter has been shaped by the need of national criminal systems to comply with the fundamental rights guarantees.

2 The close connection between the Court of Strasbourg's judgments and *res judicata*

According to Art. 35 of the European Convention on Human Rights, people (and also entities or social organisations) can lodge complaints to the Court of Strasbourg against a State Party by claiming that one of their conventional rights has been violated just after the previous exhaustion of 'all domestic remedies'. The exhaustion of 'all domestic remedies' is the condition to bring an action before the European Court of Human Rights, because Art. 13 ECHR provides that 'everyone whose rights and freedoms as outlined in this Convention are violated shall have an effective remedy before a national authority'.

Hence, there are two key points of the ECHR system. The first one is that each national legal system must comply with the regulation established by the European Convention of Human Rights. The second one is that national judges represent the first guarantors of human rights.

Consequently, the control of the ECtHR is external and its jurisdiction is subsidiary. The subsidiarity of the Court of Strasbourg consists in the fact that it might be possible to resort to it only if the domestic remedies have been unsuccessful, on both 'vertical' perspective (*id est*, all instances must be exhausted) and 'horizontal' perspective (*id est*, before appealing to the Strasbourg Court the same claims presented to this judge must have been presented at the national level, and all the means available to promote a successful claim must have been employed at that level, as the respect of the national procedural rules and the production of evidence).[3]

When the ECtHR declares the violation of a human right granted by the ECHR and claimed by the person who promoted the action in front of the same Court, the State in which the right has been violated has to implement this judgment. The enforcement of the Strasbourg Court's pronouncement is a State's duty, according to Art. 46 ECHR, which provides that 'the High Contracting Parties undertake to abide by the final judgment of the Court in any case to which they are parties'. In other words, if a State Party was found to have breached the ECHR, it will be under the obligation not only to pay the just satisfaction but also to take individual and/or general measures in its domestic legal order to put an end to the violation and to redress its consequences; the aim being to put the applicant, as far as possible, in the position in which he or she would have been had the requirements of the ECHR not been disregarded (*restitutio in integrum*).

3 KOSTORIS, *European Law and Criminal Justice*, in KOSTORIS (ed.), *Handbook of European Criminal Procedure*, Springer, 2018, 52.

States are, in principle, free to choose how to comply with the judgment because this freedom of the States is established by the principles of international law on responsibility of States for internationally wrongful acts (see Art. 35 UN ILC 'Draft Articles on Responsibility of States for Internationally Wrongful Acts'). Indeed, the ECHR does not contain a provision similar to Art. 63 American Convention on Human Rights ('ACHR', signed 22 November 1969, entered into force 18 July 1978), which enables the Inter-American Court of Human Rights (IACtHR) to order that the injured party be ensured the enjoyment of the particular right that was violated, and to rule that the consequences of the ACHR violation be remedied.

That's the reason why, in special circumstances, the ECtHR has found it useful to indicate to a State the type of measures that might be taken to put an end to the violation found in its judgment and to redress its consequences. Individual measures may include the re-trial or the re-opening of a case where an individual has been convicted following proceedings that have not met the requirements of Art. 6 ECHR (Öcalan *vs* Turkey [ECtHR] Reports 2005-IV 131 par. 210), and also the immediate release of the applicant (Ilaşcu *vs* Moldova [ECtHR] Reports 2004-VII 179 par. 22[4]).

In the light of the above, it is clear what the close connection between the protection of human rights granted by the ECtHR and *res judicata* is: the effects of the Court of Strasbourg's statements are bound to affect the internal *res judicata* because domestic criminal judges cannot ignore what the ECtHR has decided concerning the specific criminal proceeding in which the violation was put into being. In other words, the need to enforce the European judgments on human rights has consequently imposed that national legal systems have to establish new rules of *res judicata* in order to adjust definitive criminal verdicts with the ECtHR statements.

The implementation of Strasbourg Court's pronouncements in criminal matters operates on multiple levels: the first step is verifying the detention legitimacy of the convicted person who appealed the ECtHR; the second one is activating any remedies to remove the judgment which ended the criminal procedure where the Court of Strasbourg found the violation of a fundamental right. Both levels concern *res judicata* and involve criminal procedure rules established to discipline the stages of the procedure following the final judgment.

3 Court of Strasbourg's judgments and imprisonment

If the applicant is a person who has been convicted by a criminal court, the violation denounced to the Court of Strasbourg concerns in most cases the violation of human rights regarding criminal justice as those granted by Articles 3, 5, 6 or 7 ECHR. But in the same way, it's obvious that the applicants denouncing the violation of human rights in criminal proceedings are, in almost all cases, people against whom a conviction has been pronounced and has come into force. This

4 N. Wenzel, Ilaşcu Case, in *Oxford public international law*, 2007.

means that in many cases the person appealing to the ECtHR is almost always detained in prison because he or she has been sentenced to imprisonment. That's the reason why the Court of Strasbourg's judgments in criminal matters can determine the conditions of legal detention of the person who appealed to the European judge, according to art. 5 ECHR.

On the basis of this art. 5 ECHR, the imprisonment can be considered unlawful when it appears that the conviction has involved a flagrant denial of justice (ECtHR, 26 June 1992, Drozd and Januseck *vs* France and Spain, § 110; ECtHR, 19 January 1994, Iribarne Perez *vs* France). In this perspective, the Stoichov *vs* Bulgaria case has been the landmark in the evolution of jurisprudence guaranteeing the right to liberty. This case claims the idea that people cannot remain in prison if the trial in which they were sentenced to imprisonment had been declared unfair by a pronouncement of the Court of Strasbourg (ECtHR, 3 March 2005, Stoichkov *vs* Bulgaria; however, in a less peremptory way, see ECtHR, 11 July 2017, Moreira Ferreira *vs* Portugal). This idea overcomes the conception of criminal definitive decision as an untouchable verdict, and there is no doubt that this new concept of *res judicata* in criminal law procedure is revolutionary.

The Court has held that if a 'conviction' is the result of proceedings which were a 'flagrant denial of justice', *id est*, was 'manifestly contrary to the provisions of Article 6 or the principles embodied therein', the resulting deprivation of liberty would not be justified under Article 5 § 1. Consequently, if a criminal procedure is found to have been 'manifestly contrary to the provisions of Article 6 or the principles embodied therein', that will unavoidably lead to the conclusion that the applicant's ensuing deprivation of liberty to serve the sentence imposed in these proceedings cannot be considered justified under Article 5 § 1 (a).

On the other hand, if the conviction is not enough to justify the applicant's detention in all the cases in which the ECtHR finds a violation of human rights in the criminal proceeding ended with that conviction, this underlines the absolute primacy of rule of law in the specific field of criminal proceedings. Since criminal proceedings have a strong impact on the personal sphere and the freedom of the accused, they can be initiated only if they strictly comply with the law. This means that a proceeding cannot be considered to be performed according to the law if the rights granted by art. 6 ECHR have not been observed.

4 Court of Strasbourg's judgments and imprisonment in the Italian jurisprudence

In the evolution of the Italian jurisprudence aimed to enforce the pronouncements of the European Court of Human Rights regarding criminal matters, the Stoichov *vs* Bulgaria case has had crucial importance because that decision gave rise to an innovative interpretation of some rules established in the Italian criminal procedure code. The European claim that detention is not legal if it follows an unfair criminal proceeding has forced Italian judges to apply the rules established in the Italian Criminal Procedure Code in such a way to prevent or remedy the illegal detention due a conviction stated after an unfair trial. In this field, the indications coming from ECtHR have been enforced by the judges appointed to deal with this stage of criminal proceedings subsequent to the enforcement of the conviction (so-called 'giudice dell'esecuzione', according to the Italian legal system). Such judges, in accordance with art. 670 c.p.p., have the power to suspend the detention if it is doubtful that the deadline for appealing has been expired or if the defendant's right to appeal the judgment has to be restored (*id est*, if it results or it is doubtful that the defendant did not attack the conviction because he did not know that this pronouncement had been stated before). After the Court of Strasbourg ruled in the Stoichov *vs* Bulgaria case, the Italian Court of Cassazione established that the imprisonment has to be suspended when the person in prison obtained a pronouncement of the ECtHR which declared the violation of art. 6 ECHR or the principles embodied therein regarding the trial in which the applicant has been convicted.

This application of art. 670 c.p.p. has been discussed and it is still under discussion today in Italy. Most of the doctrine criticised the pronouncements with whom the Italian Court of Cassazione allowed the suspension of the imprisonment of those convicted people who presented their application to the Strasbourg Court and won their appeal. Many criminal procedure scholars said that criminal judges haven't got the power of suspension in this case and that those judgments do not comply with the law.[5] According this opinion, the Italian jurisprudence just examined is the umpteenth piece of proof that nowadays Italian courts create criminal procedural rules, despite art. 101 paragraph II of the Italian Constitution, which establishes that judges are subject to statutory law only: they should solely ensure that the law enacted by the parliament is respected and should not become the new lawmakers.

On the other hand, there are other scholars agreeing with the possibility of suspending imprisonment of convicted people based on the need that Italian judges have been bound by Strasbourg Court judgments. This opinion is founded on the idea that in the Italian system judges' power protects people's freedom – according to art. 13 paragraph II of the Italian Constitution, which establishes that the right to liberty shouldn't be violated and according to the law only judges may restrict someone's freedom and they must give their reasons for doing so. Therefore, when judges issue a pronouncement to expand the freedom after it has been restricted, it is an unneeded and superfluous express provision of the law because the judges can always rule in favour of freedom.[6]

5 NEGRI – CARNEVALE, *Corte europea e iniquità del giudicato penale*, in *Diritto penale e processo*, 2007, 1229 ss.; PIERRO, *Equità del processo e principio di legalità processuale*, in *Diritto penale e processo*, 2009, 1515 ss. V. anche EPIDENDIO, *Forza vincolante delle sentenze della Corte europea dei diritti dell'uomo e giudicato penale*, in *Diritto penale e processo*, 2009, 94 ss.

6 DI BITONTO, *Giudice dell'esecuzione e art. 13 C.e.d.u. (argomenti a sostegno delle conclusioni del p.m. d'udienza disattese da Sez. un., 19 aprile 2012, n. 34472, Ercolano)*, in *Cassazione penale*, 2013, 2511 ss.

Between these two interpretations, the second one appears the most plausible and consistent with the role attributed by the Italian Constitution to judges as a guarantor institution protecting freedom and other fundamental rights. Moreover, the second interpretation has to be preferred also because the suspension of the imprisonment – decided by the Sentence Enforcement Court – allows the Italian legal system to find a domestic remedy to prevent the violation of art. 5 ECHR, when the ECtHR recognised that a conviction has followed a criminal proceeding in which procedural rights granted by art. 6 ECHR have been breached.

5 Court of Strasbourg's judgments and the reopening of the criminal proceedings

The case law of the European Court of Human Rights has increasingly identified the reopening of the criminal proceedings as the privileged form of satisfaction for violations of guarantees concerned with procedural fairness[7] (ECtHR, 23 October 2003, Gençel *vs* Turkey, no. 53431/99, § 27; ECtHR, 18 May 2004, Somogyi *vs* Italy, no. 67972/01, § 86; ECtHR, 24 March 2005, Stoichkov *vs* Bulgaria, no. 9808/02, §§ 81, 82; ECtHR, 12 May 2005, Öcalan *vs* Turkey [*GC*], no. 46221/99, § 210 in fine; ECtHR, 1 March 2006, Sejdovic *vs* Italy, no. 56581/00, § 86; See also ECtHR, 17 January 2008, Abbasov *vs* Azerbaijan, no. 24271/05, § 42; ECtHR, 20 April 2010, Laska and Lika *vs* Albania, nos. 12315/04 and 17605/04, § 76). The so-called 'retrial clause' was first claimed in a case against Turkey, regarding the independence and impartiality of the national security courts. The ECtHR established under Article 41 of the Convention that, 'in principle, the most appropriate form of redress would be for the applicant to be given a retrial without delay' (Gençel *vs* Turkey, no. 53431/99, § 27, 23 October 2003). In the same way, the ECtHR ruled in a case against Italy where the violation of art. 6 ECHR consisted of the infringement of the defendant's right to participate in his trial (Somogyi *vs* Italy, no. 67972/01, § 86, 18 May 2004). That's the reason why this statement is usually known as the *Gençel-Somogyi* clause.

In the Öçalan *vs* Turkey case, the Grand Chamber of the ECtHR endorsed this approach, but changed the ECHR article on which to base its pronouncement; according to art. 46 ECHR, the Strasbourg Court claimed that 'a retrial or a reopening of the case, if requested, represents in principle an appropriate way of redressing the violation'.[8]

The States have complied with this approach in different ways. Sometimes, the legislator intervened; other times, judicial practices occurred. The situation is especially sensitive given the need to overcome a domestic final decision in criminal matters (a decision that is the result of the required previous exhaustion of all domestic remedies). Therefore, the legislative solutions adopted in the various contracting Parties have concerned special forms of review of such a judgment, like revision.

7 KOSTORIS, *European Law and Criminal Justice*, cit., 55.
8 ECtHR, 12 May 2005, Öcalan *vs* Turkey [*GC*], no. 46221/99, § 210.

It should be added that in many cases the violation of a human right concerning criminal justice consists of an invalid procedural act. That means that those invalid procedural acts, which could not be reported to an internal criminal court because of *res judicata*, can indeed be reported to the European Court of Human Rights to check if there has been a human rights violation or not. The fact that an applicant could denounce invalid acts of the criminal proceeding to the ECtHR – because those invalidities also consist of a violation of the fundamental rights established by art. 6 ECHR – has produced a revolutionary effect on an essential aspect of the concept of *res judicata*, particularly rooted in the experience of continental law. In these systems, it is usually stated that *res judicata* covers the possible invalid procedural acts which have been made during the criminal proceeding.

The case law of ECtHR breaks this long-standing tradition. Now, the people convicted reporting any violations of the European Convention on Human Rights in front of the Strasbourg Court could challenge the invalid acts that have had been in their proceeding because of the violation of internal rules concerning art. 6 ECHR guarantees, without remaining bound by the deadline of *res judicata*.

The Italian experience highlights that the enforcement of the Strasbourg Court pronouncements in the criminal field has been realised without the intervention of the parliament, but with the mediation of criminal courts, and with one very important pronouncement of the Italian Constitutional Court.

In the previous paragraph we wrote about Italian jurisprudence regarding the suspension of the imprisonment following ECtHR judgments finding the violation of art. 6 ECHR. This interpretation of the domestic criminal procedure rules allowed the Italian system to comply with the ECHR system only partially. Those assessments of criminal courts were necessary to prevent the violation of art. 5 ECHR that it could have been done without the release of the prisoner who applied the Strasburg Court's judgment successfully. But, this suspension of imprisonment did not solve the contrast between the conviction pronounced by Italian criminal courts and the judgment pronounced in Strasbourg. Despite such suspension, according to the Italian legal system, the convicted person remained as he or she was before the ECtHR decision: this person continued to be considered by the Italian law as a guilty person; nevertheless the claim of the violation of art. 6 ECHR in the proceeding ended with the conviction. In all these cases, the suspension of the imprisonment was not an adequate measure to comply with the ECHR system: such action was necessary but not enough to restore the violated applicants' human rights, because only the reopening of the trial could have represented the indispensable action to repair the individual prejudice suffered by the convicted person who appealed the ECtHR decision.

That is the reason why since the early twenty-first century in the Italian parliament there were some legislative drafts to introduce new procedural rules allowing the reopening of criminal proceedings as a remedy for violations of guarantees concerned with procedural fairness. Nevertheless, the Italian parliament has never approved any draft in this matter, probably because the political conditions to introduce the reopening of criminal proceedings have never been met.

The Italian Constitutional Court overcame the parliament's inertia when it established that the lack of a case of revision to remedy the violation of art. 6 ECHR stated by the Strasbourg Court was in contrast to the Constitution. More precisely, in its 7 April 2011 judgment, no. 113, the Italian Constitutional Court ruled that Article 630 of the Code of Criminal Procedure was illegitimate, insofar as it did not include, among the cases of revision of a judgment or of a decree, the reopening of the criminal proceedings subsequent to a finding of a violation of the Convention by a final judgment of the Court. It is clear that the Italian Constitutional Court has introduced a new kind of revision. Thus, when a Strasbourg Court's judgment has been pronounced which demands the reopening of the trial, because the irremediable violation of fair trial guarantees cannot be repaired otherwise, the person whose procedural rights have been breached could promote the revision.

Consequently, Italian criminal justice complies with ECtHR, leveraging two different legal instruments. First of all, it is allowed a specific appeal for the conviction to be reversed (revision) all the times the Strasbourg Court recognised the violation of art. 6 ECHR and stated that the trial had to be reopened. This revision can be granted only when a European judgment has been pronounced and only if the ECtHR demands the reopening of the trial because of the irremediable violation of fair trial guarantees.[9] Furthermore, this revision cannot be promoted by a person who did not apply the Court on Human Rights, even if this person has been harmed by the same violation which has already been decided in another case by the Court of Strasbourg.[10] This statement has been much discussed in Italy, because it is not suitable for fundamental rights violations depending on a common dysfunction at the national level. When the Court of Strasbourg's decision finds a violation which is not connected with the internal proceeding involved by a specific European judgment only, because this breach relates to internal structural problems, people whose same fundamental right has been harmed by a national common dysfunction should be able to apply to an internal judge for revision: even if they did not apply to the Court of Strasbourg, their guarantees concerned with procedural fairness have been infringed because of general structural problems and this, in my opinion, gives them the right to reopen their proceeding in which they have been harmed.

On the other hand, the judge appointed to deal with this stage of the criminal proceedings subsequent to the enforcement of the conviction (so-call 'Giudice dell'esecuzione') can reshape the contents of the original domestic conviction when the contrast between the European and Italian pronouncements can easily be overcome by replacing the internal judicial rulings with the European ones, without any discretionary evaluation.[11] Moreover, this domestic judge retains the power to suspend the imprisonment whenever the judgment in which the detention has been sentenced had been declared unfair by the Strasbourg Court.[12]

9 Cass., 2015, 6 May, Palau Giovannetti, in *C.E.D. Cass.*, n. 264955; Cass., 2017, 20 June, Cariolo, in *C.E.D. Cass.*, n. 271197.

10 Cass., 2019, 24 October, Genco, in *C.E.D. Cass.*, n. 278054.

11 Cass., 2016, 16 October, Dell'Utri, in *C.E.D. Cass.*, n. 267861.

12 Cass., 2015, 6 May, Palau Giovannetti, in *C.E.D. Cass.*, n. 264955.

6 A new conception of *ne bis in idem*?

The idea of *res judicata* in criminal matters has been revolutionised by the ECtHR also because it introduced a new way to apply double jeopardy (or *ne bis in idem*, according to continental traditional terminology). Double jeopardy is a procedural defence that prevents an accused person from being tried again on the same (or similar) charges following a valid acquittal or conviction. Taking into account the latest case law of the Court of Strasbourg (ECtHR, 5 March 2014, Grande Stevens and others *vs* Italy; ECtHR, 20 May 2014, Nykänen *vs* Finland; ECtHR, 20 May 2014, Nykänen *vs* Finland; ECtHR, 20 May 2014, Glantz *vs* Finland; ECtHR, 27 November 2014, Lucky Dev *vs* Sweden), this judge encouraged the progressive extension of *ne bis in idem* to non-criminal areas, primarily to administrative punitive proceedings.

Unlike what has been reported in the past paragraphs, where we examined the evolution of European and Italian case law aimed at expanding the enforcement and the effectiveness of human rights in criminal justice, the European jurisprudence concerning *ne bis in idem* risks jeopardising the maintenance of an essential pillar of the criminal justice guarantees.

The implications of those Strasbourg Court pronouncements are one of the most disputable issues of the ECtHR jurisprudence. In this field, the logic of the internal legal orders does not overlap with that of the conventional system. Therefore, it is not possible to transfer ECtHR claims about *ne bis in idem* to the national context of criminal procedure rules, because in this background the same statement becomes the denial of guarantees rationale of the *ne bis in idem*.

The problem arises from the controversial relationship between the enforcement of regulatory and/or financial sanctions provided by administrative law related to conducts already punished by criminal law. Obviously, in the perspective of the fundamental rights protection system, the Court of Strasbourg cannot be limited by political choices of national parliaments. Everybody knows that the understanding of what constitutes a 'criminal' for the purpose of the European Convention is not restricted to the conception of it under the law of any State bound by this instrument. Like many other provisions in the European Convention, a 'crime' is something that has been given an autonomous meaning by the European Court and the former European Commission.

This has a very important consequence. In the light of domestic jurisdictions, the classification of something as 'criminal' under national law will be decisive in attracting the application of the various requirements of the European Convention to the relevant proceedings. On the contrary, the fact that certain proceedings are not so classified under national law will not preclude those requirements from being considered applicable to them by ECtHR.

According to the Strasbourg Court, the elements to qualify a judicial proceeding as 'criminal' are: 1) the punitive nature of the sanction and its repressive and preventive function; 2) its severity; 3) its connection to a criminal violation (so-called Engel's criteria).[13] On this basis, the ECtHR has recognised the punitive nature of several

13 ECtHR, 8 June 1976, (nos. 5100/71, 5101/71, 5102/71, 5354/72 and 5370/72) Engels and others *vs* Netherlands, § 82.

administrative sanctions in many cases, convicting State parties not only for the violation of art. 6 ECHR – because the administrative proceeding did not comply with rules granted by it – but also for the violation of art. 4 Prot. no. 7 ECHR – because the applicants have been convicted twice, by administrative authorities and by criminal courts.

Although such statements are unquestionable, the second one regarding the violation of art. 4 Prot. no. 7 ECHR cannot be slavishly applied in the national legal system. If it was applied in the domestic level in the same way it has been described in the ECtHR case law, it would follow that the criminal proceeding could not be open after the end of the administrative proceeding.

But if this solution was the right one, the person convicted by the administrative authority would lose the guarantees prescribed by the ECHR in criminal matters. In this way, the result would be the weakening of rights and guarantees and not their increase. The administrative proceeding is in fact faster than the criminal one, just because it is less guaranteed then the other. Consequently, if the national legal systems intended to comply with the mentioned judgments concerning *ne bis in idem* precluding criminal trial after the administrative conviction, the result would be that people suspected of having committed a criminal offence could be punished by administrative authorities all the times the conduct had been sanctioned by both criminal and administrative national law; which means that the person lost his guarantees fixed in art. 6 and 7 ECHR and, exactly for this reason, it cannot be denied that he is legitimised to present an application to the Court of Strasbourg to denounce the violation of criminal guarantees.

Therefore, it's necessary to transfer Strasbourg's *principia iuris* concerning *ne bis in idem* to the domestic level in a different way. National legal systems have to rationalise their punitive frameworks, preventing the double punishment of the same fact, especially when the administrative sanction can be considered criminal according to Strasbourg Court indications to qualify the criminal matter. At the same time, internal criminal procedure rules cannot extend double jeopardy (*ne bis in idem*) to administrative convictions to avoid people convicted by administrative authorities suffering the violation of guarantees granted to criminal matters by ECHR. Indeed, a person must be judged only once according to the criminal guarantees established by criminal procedure law: the need to comply with ECtHR jurisprudence about art. 4 Prot. no. 7 ECHR cannot legitimate national systems in violation of art. 6 ECHR every time the punished conduct has been sanctioned by the administrative authorities.

7 The Italian implementation of the Strasbourg Court's rulings in the case Grande Stevens and others *vs* Italy

The Italian enforcement of Strasbourg Court pronouncements about *ne bis in idem*, administrative sanctions and criminal matters has been influenced by the European Court of Justice jurisprudence. This judge has minimised the impact of ECtHR rulings, taking into account the widespread practice in the EU Member States concerning the imposition of penalties under both administrative law and criminal law in respect of the same offence, especially in fields such as taxation, environmental policies and public safety. In the perspective of the Court of Luxembourg, the double punishment is not prohibited in all the cases, but it is prohibited only when the overall penalty is not proportionate.[14] Following this approach, the Italian case law has repeatedly excluded the violation of art. 4 Prot. no. 7 ECHR when a person has been punished by both criminal and administrative law for the conduct of market abuse.[15] In the same way, it has been denied that violation in the case of the administrative sanction (demolition) decided by the criminal judge pronouncing on a charge of construction abuse,[16] or in the case of the double punishment of a tax offence by criminal and administrative law,[17] or when a legal entity and an individual are both punished by criminal and administrative law for the same VAT violation.[18]

The arguments supporting the double punishment by criminal and administrative law are untenable even if they are according to the European Court of Justice case law, followed by the Italian jurisprudence and by the latest Strasbourg Court ruling, in the case A and B *vs* Norway. The best way to criticise them can be based on the excellent, indisputable and very clear dissenting opinion of the judge Pinto de Albuquerque just in that case. This ECtHR member wrote that *ne bis in idem* is one of the most important principles in the European legal culture and that it has been neglected by the Strasbourg Court in the case above-mentioned. *Ne bis in idem* is a *pro persona* guarantee and the latter ECtHR case law, similar to the European Court of Justice jurisprudence, denaturalised it, changing this principle in a 'tool' which allows defendants' 'manipulation and impunity'.

We can read in the dissenting opinion of the judge Pinto de Albuquerque that: 'After turning the rationale of the *ne bis in idem* principle upside down, the present judgment opens the door to an unprecedented, Leviathan-like punitive policy based on multiple State-pursued proceedings, strategically connected and put in place in order to achieve the *maximum* possible repressive effect'. Unfortunately, Pinto de Albuquerque is right. Therefore, we just have to hope for future pronouncements of the Strasbourg Court, in which it will overrule the statements of A and B *vs* Norway, following the direction highlighted in the dissenting opinion just mentioned.

14 ECtJ, 26 February 2013, *Åklagaren c. Hans Åkerberg Fransson*, C-617/10
15 Cass., 15 April 2019, Respigo, in *C.E.D.* Cass., n. 276863; Cass., 11 November 2018, Erbetta, in *C.E.D.* Cass., n. 276863.
16 Cass., 10 October 2018, M., in *C.E.D.* Cass., n. 274128.
17 Cass., 22 September 2017, Servello, in *C.E.D.* Cass., n. 272588; Cass., 12 September 2019, M., in *C.E.D.* Cass., n. 275833.
18 Cass., 7 November 2017, Passaro, in *C.E.D.* Cass., n. 273107; Cass., 8 August 2018, C., in *C.E.D.* Cass., n. 273939.

4 Thinking outside the politics box

Framing a judicial role in shaping militant democracy in the European Union

Violeta Beširević[1]

1 Introduction

The current global wave of populism did not miss certain Member States of the European Union, most notably Hungary and Poland, now perceived as the first non-democratic Member States in the history of the European Union (the EU).[2] There is a growing concern that the populist governments in both countries have been persistently and successfully eroding what Rosalyn Dixon and David Landau call 'democratic minimum core': commitments to free and fair elections, the separation of powers, fundamental rights and governmental accountability.[3] As populists managed to dismantle constitutional self-defence mechanisms, the

1 Professor of Law, Union University Law School Belgrade. *S.J.D.* Central European University. This paper was written as part of the 2021 Research Program of the Institute of Social Sciences with the support of the Ministry of Education, Science, and Technological Development of the Republic of Serbia.

2 Freedom House describes Hungary as a hybrid rather than a democratic regime and anticipates that Poland will soon join the hybrid regimes. See Freedom House, *Nations in Transition 2020*, available at https://freedomhouse.org/sites/default/files/2020-04/05062020_FH_NIT2020_vfinal.pdf.

3 See D. Landau and R. Dixon, 'Abusive Judicial Review: Courts against Democracy', *U.C. Davis Law Review*, Vol.53, No.3, 2020, p.1323. For scholarly works analysing the situation in Hungary and Poland, see, *e.g.* A. Bozoki, 'Beyond "Illiberal Democracy": The Case of Hungary', in V. Beširević (ed.) *New Politics of Decisionism*, The Hague, Eleven International Publishing, 2019, pp.93–105; M. Matczak, 'Poland: From Paradigm to Pariah? Facts and Interpretations of Polish Constitutional Crisis', in V. Beširević (ed.) *New Politics of Decisionism*, The Hague, Eleven International Publishing, 2019, pp. 141–160; W. Sadurski, *Poland's Constitutional Breakdown*, Oxford, OUP, 2019; L. Sólyom, 'The Rise and Decline of Constitutional Culture in Hungary', in A. von Bogdandy and P. Sonnevend (eds.), *Constitutional Crisis in the European Constitutional Area: Theory, Law and Politics in Hungary and Romania*, Oxford, Hart Publishing, 2015, pp.5–32; D. Kochenov, K. L. Scheppele, B. Grabowska-Moroz, 'Enforcing EU Values through Systemic Infringement Actions by the European Commission and the Members States of the European Union', *Yearbook of European Law*, 2020, forthcoming; K. Kovács and K.L. Scheppele, 'The Fragility of an Independent Judiciary: Lessons from Hungary and Poland – and the European Union', in P.H. Solomon and K. Gadowska (eds.), *Legal Change in Post-Communist States: Progress, Reversions, Explanations*, Stuttgart, Ibidem Verlag, 2019.

DOI: 10.4324/9781003200666-7

European Union's intervention, which would make democracy in Hungary and Poland work, soon appeared necessary. But necessity does not equal legitimacy. Apart from the ruling populists, some sceptics have doubted whether such an intervention makes sense from the standpoint of the EU obligation to respect Member States' national identities (which implies diversity) under Article 4 of the Treaty on European Union (TEU).[4] Others claim that moral or political wisdom speaks against the EU interventions because the EU itself is not democratic.[5]

What I will urge here is that democracy, as the EU's fundamental value, protected under Article 2 TEU, is not just declarative but legally operative value, shared by all Member States.[6] An argument from intervention should not surprise anyone as the obligation of the Union to defend domestic democracy is already fixed in Article 7 TEU. Therefore, the EU defence of domestic democracy, within the limits of EU law, is normatively justified, despite the European Union's own troubling democracy deficit.[7]

Although normatively justified, the issue is whether it is effective. Until now, the EU political responses to populists' erosion of democratic values in Hungary and Poland, either activated as the initiatives to strengthen the rule of law, protect fundamental rights or defend the EU identity values under Article 7 TEU sanction procedure, have not been very effective.[8] Consider, for example, the most recent

4 A. von Bogdandy, 'Fundamentals on Defending European Values', *VerfBlog*, 2019/11/12, p.5.

5 Weiler, for example, finds the democratic deficit, from which the Union suffers, to be a moral obstacle for the Union to employ militant measures and warns that before 'throwing stones', the EU should first 'put its own democratic house in order'. J.H.H. Weiler, 'Epilogue: Living in a Glass House: Europe, Democracy and the Rule of Law', in C. Closa and D. Kochenov (eds.), *Reinforcing the Rule of Law Oversight in the European Union*, Cambridge, CUP, 2016, p.326.

6 The various values common to the Member States, including human dignity, freedom, *democracy*, equality, the rule of law and human rights, including the minority rights, constitute the Union's identity and are protected in Article 2 TEU.

7 The recent scholarship has identified three key principles that normatively justify the EU interventions: the all-affected principle, the supranational federal nature of the EU, and the principle of congruence. These principles, in my view, *mutatis mutandis* justify the Union's measures to confront threats to democracy in the Member States. For a substantive discussion, see C. Closa, D. Kochenov and J.H.H. Weiler, 'Reinforcing Rule of Law Oversight in the European Union', European University Institute, Working Paper RSCAS 2014/25, pp.3–7.

8 See, *e.g.*, Communication from the Commission to the European Parliament and the Council, 'A new EU Framework to Strengthen the Rule of Law', COM/2014/0158 final; European Parliament, Resolution of 3 July 2013 on the Situation of Fundamental Rights: Standards and Practices in Hungary (2012/2130(INI)); European Parliament, Resolution of 25 October 2016 with Recommendations to the Commission on the Establishment of an EU Mechanism on Democracy, the Rule of Law and Fundamental Rights (2015/2254(INL)); European Parliament, Resolution of 12 September 2018 on a Proposal Calling on the Council to Determine, Pursuant to Article 7(1) of the Treaty on European Union, the Existence of a Clear Risk of a Serious Breach by Hungary of the Values on which the Union is Founded (2017/2131(INL)); European Commission, Reasoned Proposal in Accordance with Article 7

EU action, the 2020 European Commission's annual Rule of Law Report.[9] The subject of the Commission's inquiry was the rule of law situation in each of the 27 Member States, but the most critical findings the Commission expressed on the rule of law situation in Hungary and Poland.[10] However, the Report, introduced as a preventive tool to complement the Article 7 TEU sanction procedure, does not contain any recommendations regarding the identified problematic issues, and therefore its effects are questionable. Neither the European Parliament's earlier efforts to prevent the weakening of the fundamental rights in Hungary nor the 2014 Commission Framework to Strengthen the Rule of Law brought the change.[11]

To respond to threats to domestic democracy, for the first time in its history, the EU activated the sanction mechanism as well: for breaching the EU foundational values, in 2017, the Commission initiated Article 7 TEU proceedings against Poland,[12] and then, in 2018, the European Parliament triggered Article 7 TEU mechanism against Hungary.[13] For Hungary, the subject of EU concerns was the judicial independence, freedom of expression, corruption, rights of minorities, and migrants and refugees' situation, while the EU institutions found the rule of law to be at risk in Poland.[14] Both proceedings are still pending and could, eventually, end up with the suspension of Hungary's and Poland's voting rights assigned under the Treaties and EU secondary legislation. But the road to suspension is quite long and the very idea of sanctions appears not to work due to the Article 7 TEU dialogical approach to the threshold for sanctioning breaches of the EU fundamental values.[15] Moreover, for non-compliance with the EU values, no

(1) of the Treaty on European Union Regarding the Rule of Law in Poland, Brussels, 20.12.2017 COM(2017) 835 final.

9 European Commission, 2020 Rule of Law Report: The Rule of Law Situation in the European Union, Brussels, 30.9.2020 COM(2020) 580 final.

10 *Ibid.* See chapters on Hungary and Poland, available at https://ec.europa.eu/info/publications/2020-rule-law-report-communication-and-country-chapters_en.

11 European Parliament, Resolution of 3 July 2013, *supra* note 8.

12 European Commission, Reasoned Proposal in Accordance with Article 7(1) of the Treaty on European Union regarding the Rule of Law in Poland, *supra* note 8.

13 European Parliament, Resolution of 12 September 2018, *supra* note 8.

14 For more, see https://www.europarl.europa.eu/news/en/agenda/briefing/2020-01-13/4/hungary-and-poland-parliament-to-assess-progress-of-article-7-proceedings.

15 For a discussion on Article 7 TEU, see, *e.g.*, W. Sadurski, 'Adding Bite to a Bark: The Story of Article 7, EU Enlargement, and Jörg Haider', *Columbia Journal of European Law*, Vol.16, No.3, 2010, pp.385–426; L. Besselink, 'The Bite, the Bark and the Howl: Article 7 TEU and the Rule of Law Initiatives', in A. Jakab and D. Kochenov (eds.), *The Enforcement of EU Law and Values*, Oxford, OUP, 2017, pp.128–144; B. Bugarič, 'Protecting Democracy inside the EU: On Article 7 TEU and the Hungarian Turn to Authoritarianism', in C. Closa and D. Kochenov (eds.), *Reinforcing the Rule of Law Oversight in the European Union*, Cambridge, CUP, 2016, pp.82–101; C. Hillion, 'Overseeing the Rule of Law in the EU: Legal Mandate and Means', *ibid.*, pp.59–81; D. Kochenov, 'Article 7', in M. Kellerbauer, M. Klamert and J. Tomkin (eds.), *The Treaties and the Charter of Fundamental Rights – A Commentary*, Oxford, OUP, 2019, p.88–98.

expulsion of a Member State from the European Union is envisaged under the Treaties. Accordingly, as the most draconic political tool, this option cannot be activated in cases of democratic backsliding in the Member States. What follows, then, is that the Article 7 TEU option, once called 'nuclear', is anything but nuclear.[16]

There is a good reason to believe that framing the EU responses in legal as additional to political terms would make the Union a proper democracy guardian. Recall here that defending democracy, or turning it into 'militant democracy', is not just political but also a judicial task. Very briefly, 'militant democracy is a political or legal structure aimed at preserving democracy against those who want to overturn it from within or who openly want to destroy it from outside by utilizing democratic institutions as well as support within the population'.[17] Recall also that the Court of Justice of the European Union (CJEU) is a bold and revolutionary adjudicator that managed to ground the European integrations in democracy at a time when that was unthinkable under the Treaties. As I will demonstrate in this chapter, its recent decisions concerning court-packing in Poland are a hint of the CJEU's same revolutionary role in defending domestic democracy in the Member States.

In this chapter, I will argue that the CJEU can be a robust mechanism for declaring the limits of lawfulness in the Union and confronting democratic backsliding in the Member States. To meet the aims, in section 2, I shortly present the EU democratic credentials and the CJEU's politics on turning democracy into the only acceptable form of governance in the Union. In section 3, the notion of militant democracy and its application in a democratic backsliding cases will be explained. In section 4, the excerption from the CJEU's case law serves to frame a more decisive judicial role in shaping militant democracy in the European Union. In conclusion, I advocate for deploying legal techniques that will allow the CJEU to prevent the Member States from reducing democracy only to the election of leaders.

A general objection to the EU protecting domestic democracy derives from the Union's democratic deficit. This article starts with some reflections on the EU's democratic credentials and the judicial efforts to tie the Union with democracy.

2 EU democracy on trial

2.1 The EU democratic credentials: The state of affairs

For different reasons, the founding fathers did not ground the European integrations in democracy.[18] To some extent, this explains why it is still hard to connect the

16 Former European Commission President José Manuel Barroso in 'State of the Union Address 2013' called Article 7 TEU a 'nuclear option'. See https://ec.europa.eu/commission/presscorner/detail/en/SPEECH_13_684.

17 O. Pfersmann, 'Shaping Militant Democracy: Legal Limits to Democratic Stability', in A. Sajó (ed.), *Militant Democracy*, The Hague, Eleven International Publishing, 2004, p.47.

18 For the elaboration of these reasons, see F. Mancini and D. Keeling, 'Democracy and the European Court of Justice', *The Modern Law Review*, Vol.57, No.2, 1994, pp.176–177.

political core of the European integrations with democratic principles, although, in the meantime, the nature of the Union's community has changed considerably.

What can be said on behalf of EU democracy? Consider first what is deemed to be consistent with democratic rule.

Despite a striking diversity of views within the scholarship on democracy, the contemporary understating identifies democracy mostly with the nation-state.[19] However, democracy is not about the state, but about the exercise and the limitation of public power.[20] It is about rulers and the public realm, where the former come to power according to the established norms and are accountable for their actions in the public realm formed by citizens who act indirectly through their representatives.[21] But democracy cannot be reduced to elections and the majority rule. To be considered democratic, any polity must also be set up in respect of the rule of law, provide respect for fundamental rights and judicial review for cherishing freedom and equality. Or, to return to Dixon and Landau, 'minimum substantive core of democracy' includes a commitment to free and fair elections, the separation of powers, fundamental rights and governmental accountability.

Following Dixon and Landau, it is clear that EU democracy is not an exact showcase. This does not mean that the EU is not based on what de Búrca terms 'the democratic-striving approach'.[22] Below, I explain why.

It has been a truism to say that democracy was not in the DNA of the European integration project when it was launched.[23] Instead, it was the Political Messianism which linked up the former enemies with the dream of a federal Europe.[24] Nevertheless, the life of the Political Messianism in the EU integrations (now mostly over) has been predominantly directed at making democracy the only legitimate form of governance in the EU public order, without parallel in transnational or international law.[25]

Historically, democratic principle as a foundational EU value was for the first time introduced in the Maastricht Treaty, which created a political community and signalled that a limited project of functional integration based on market interests had reached its limits.[26] The Lisbon Treaty repeats that democracy is an EU

19 G. de Búrca, 'Developing Democracy Beyond the State', *Columbia Journal of Transnational Law*, Vol.46, No.2, 2008, p.225.

20 Weiler, *supra* note 5, p.320.

21 For a broad discussion of the notion of democracy, see, *e.g.*, P.C. Schmitter and T.L. Karl, 'What Democracy is … and is not', *Journal of Democracy*, Vol.2, No.3, 199, pp.75–88; D. Landau and R. Dixon, *supra* note 3.

22 De Búrca, *supra* note 19, p.222.

23 J.H.H. Weiler, 'The Political and Legal Culture of European Integration: An Exploratory Essay', *International Constitutional Law Review*, Vol.9, No.3–4, 2011, p.694; Mancini and Keeling, *supra* note 18. p.175.

24 J.H.H. Weiler 'Europe in Crisis – On "Political Messianism", "Legitimacy" and the "Rule of Law"', *Singapore Journal of Legal Studies*, 2012, pp.248–268.

25 V. Beširević, 'The Constitution in the European Union: The State of Affairs', in A. Dupeyrix, G. Raulet (eds.), *European Constitutionalism. Historical and Contemporary Perspectives*, Brussels, Peter Lang, coll. 'Euroclio', 2014, pp.16–17.

26 See Article F of the Maastricht Treaty.

foundational value, shared by the Member States. As a foundational value, it is essential for reaching 'ever closer Union among the people of Europe' on two grounds: on one hand, a new state's accession to the EU is conditional on its respect of democracy and a commitment to its promotion (Article 49 TEU); on the other hand, the Member States are obliged to abide by democracy during their membership, while any clear risk, or a serious and persistent breach of democratic values within the Member States, may activate a preventive EU mechanism to defend democracy (Article 7 TEU).

Next, the Lisbon Treaty is drafted to follow the usual qualities of representative democracy and some elements of participatory democracy. Article 10 TEU determines that at the Union level citizens are directly represented in the European Parliament and indirectly represented in the European Council and the Council through their Member State representatives (who are democratically accountable either to their national parliaments or their citizens). Its legislative, supervisory and budgetary powers have increased over time, as has its power over the appointment of the Commission.[27] Besides the representatives, the Lisbon Treaty also speaks about participatory democracy: EU citizens may use the citizens' initiative and invite the European Commission to submit a legislative proposal for adoption.[28] Moreover, the national parliaments are given an opportunity to exercise more efficient control over adopting the EU secondary legislation by supervising the subsidiarity principle's implementation.[29] This so-called 'early warning mechanism' is one of the clearest examples by which the Union deviates from the classical international organisation model and makes EU democracy unique. Finally, the rule of law figures prominently among the EU identity values, while the EU Charter on Fundamental Rights (the Charter), attached to the Lisbon Treaty, has become legally binding for all Member States and does not represent any more a set of empty rights.[30]

Measured by usual democratic standards, the Union now stands closer to democracy than ever before, but it cannot be repeated often enough that it still suffers from a democratic deficit.[31] Weiler cannot be more right when he claims

27 For a similar view, see R. Corbett, F. Jacobs and M. Shackleton, *The European Parliament* (7th ed.), London, John Harper Publishing, 2007, p.245. Note that the Lisbon Treaty secures its participation as an equal partner in the ordinary legislative proceedings (subject to the Commission's initiations), covering approximately 44 areas, including agriculture, services, immigration, structural funds, etc. For a detailed overview, see P. Craig and G. de Búrca, *EU Law: Text, Cases, and Materials* (6th ed.), Oxford, Oxford University Press, 2015, pp.51–58.

28 See Article 11(4) TEU, Article 24 (1) of the Treaty on the Functioning of the European Union (TFEU), Regulations (EU) No. 211/2011 and 2019/788, and Rules 222 and 230 of EU Parliament's Rules of Procedure.

29 The issue is regulated by the Protocol on the Application of the Principles of Subsidiarity and Proportionality (Protocol on Subsidiarity) and the Protocol on the Role of National Parliaments in the EU (Protocol on National Parliaments). Both protocols are annexed to the Lisbon Treaty.

30 Beširević, *supra* note 25, p.24.

31 Thus, the voters still cannot change the executives, nor can determine, by their vote, the composition of the EU institutions – among three institutions performing a legislative function – the only one directly elected is the European Parliament. However,

that two distinguished principles of any functional democracy are missing in the European Union – the principles of representation and accountability.[32] But recall here that there was a time when the European integration project had no centre of gravity to democracy, democratically elected parliament with the power to legislate, or individuals with citizenship status and protected rights and freedoms, which both exist today in the Union, albeit still with imperfections. Much of this improvement is the work of the CJEU. By 'parliamentising' the EU decision-making, delineating the boundaries of institutional balance, encouraging participatory democracy and installing fundamental rights protection together with direct effect doctrine in the DNA of the European integrations, the CJEU turned out to be a major democracy promoter in the Union.

2.2 The CJEU's revolutionary case-law on democracy

Representative democracy, and in particular the parliamentary-type model to which the EU is now apparently streaming, was anunforeseeable model of governance 60 years ago, when it all began. Originally, the Assembly, composed of the members of national parliaments, was the weakest link in the decision-making chain: it had no power to legislate but only power to be informed and consulted in areas mandated by the Rome Treaty. Legislative prerogatives belonged to the Council of Ministers, an executive authority *par excellence*. An important advance came first with the 1970 and 1975 Budget Treaties, when the Assembly received greater powers in the Communities' budgetary process,[33] and then with transition to direct elections in 1979. But the real democratic impetus came in 1980 when the European Court of Justice in the Roquette Frères case, interpreted the Assembly's limited consultative power in the decision-making process as a reflection of 'the fundamental democratic principle that the people should take part in the exercise of power through the intermediary of a representative assembly'.[34] The Court, thus, introduced and endorsed the principle of representative democracy in the decision-making process despite the fact that the Rome Treaty

the European Parliament is not a sovereign legislator whose word is final; it is not a parliament that supports the governing majority, nor it has a majority coalition. Other political institutions are still not fully responsible to the Parliament for all acts they adopt, nor the adaption of all crucial decisions requests the European Parliament's approval. See in Beširević, *supra* note 25, pp. 27–28. Besides, starting from Pildes' premise that the idea of democracy makes sense only to the extent to which political parties are allowed to fight over power, the absence of genuine European parties makes already fragile democratic credentials more obvious. See R. Pildes, 'Political Parties and Constitutionalism', in T. Ginsburg and R. Dixon (eds.), *Comparative Constitutional Law*, Cheltenham, Edward Edgar Publishing, 2011, p.254.

32 Weiler, *supra* note 5, p.320.

33 For more see A.C. L. Knudsen, 'The 1970 and 1975 Budget Treaties: Enhancing the Democratic Architecture of the Community', in F. Laursen (ed.), *Designing the European Union: From Paris to Lisbon*, London, Palgrave Macmillan, 2012, pp.98–123.

34 Case 138/79, *Roquette Frères v. Council of the European Communities*, [1980] ECR 3333, para.33.

equipped the Assembly only with a weak consultative power and provided scant support for democracy in the first place.

The Court continued to bolster democracy in Communities by firming a system of checks and balances in the decision-making progress: it first allowed action for annulment to be brought against the European Parliament,[35] and then empowered the Parliament to challenge acts adopted by other institutions (the Council and the Commission) in order to save its prerogatives (the Chernobyl case).[36] This was a real revolutionary move keeping in mind that at that time the Council dominated in the legislative process, while the Parliament had power to participate in the decision-making process only in limited cases enshrined in the Single European Act. To ensure that under such circumstances each institution does not trespass on the prerogatives of the other institutions was a big step forward in strengthening the democratic legitimacy of the Communities.[37] Besides, the drafters of the Maastricht Treaty followed the Chernobyl ruling[38] and made the system of checks and balances an indispensable tenet of the institutional balance, which in the Union serves as an autonomous version of the separation of powers principle. Today, the European Parliament is a privileged applicant in action for annulment cases, meaning that it can always bring an action, and its acts are amenable to judicial review. The given examples should not lead to the conclusion that the Court has consolidated the powers of the European Parliament at the expense of the institutional balance envisaged in the Treaties. On the contrary, in the 2012 Listing Procedure case, it basically excluded the Parliament from the legislative proceedings in the Common Foreign and Security Policy Area, in which the Treaties gave the Parliament a minor role.[39] The Court reasoning coincides with the political question doctrine, developed mostly by US courts; in line with representative democracy, this is the area predominately reserved for the national executive rule-making.[40]

Even before it became a law, some elements of participatory democracy were endorsed by the CJEU, especially the procedural protection of the individuals affected by the EU regulatory measures.[41] Yet, from the democracy perspective, probably the most significant Court decisions that moved the Communities closer

35 Case 294/83, *Les Verts. v. Parliament* [1986] ECR 1339.

36 Case C-70/88, *Parliament v. Council* (the '*Chernobyl*' case) [1990] ECR I-2041.

37 Mancini and Keeling, *supra* note 18, p.181.

38 *Ibid.*

39 Case C-130/10, *Parliament v. Council*, [2012] ECLI:EU:C:2012:472.

40 For a recent discussion about the political question doctrine see, *e.g.*, T.L. Grove, 'The Lost History of the Political Question Doctrine', *New York University Law Review*, Vol.90, No.6, 2015, pp.1908–1974; M.O. Mhango, *Justiciability of Political Questions in South Africa: A Comparative Analysis*, The Hague, Eleven International Publishing, 2019; V. Beširević, 'Making Sense of the Political Question Doctrine: The Case of Kosovo', *Review of Central and East European Law*, Vol.46, No.1, 2021, pp. 91–130.

41 See, *e.g.*, case C- 49/88, *Al-Jubail Fertilizer Company (Samad) and Saudi Arabian Fertilizer Company (Safco) v. Council of the European Communities*, [1991] ECR I-03187; for a discussion, see J. Mendes, 'Participation and Participation Rights in EU Law and Governance', in H.C.H. Hofmann and A.H. Tuerk (eds.), *Legal Challenges*

to democracy regard the involvement of individuals in the enforcement of Community law and the 'discovery' of fundamental rights in the European legal order. The former is exemplified in the Court's direct effect doctrine, which empowered individuals with rights enforceable by the national courts whenever they applied the Community/EU law.[42] Besides, when announcing the direct effect doctrine, the Court also reminded that Member States' nationals were an important pillar in the decision-making process through the European Parliament and the Economic and Social Committee.[43] Lastly, in a series of three initial rulings, the Court proclaimed that citizens of the Member States had fundamental rights and thus filled the most significant lacuna in the Rome Treaty – the lack of fundamental rights protection.[44] Although the Court was later criticised that it did not distinguish market freedoms from fundamental rights,[45] the fact is that the CJEU's revolutionary case law safeguarded individual rights and freedoms despite underprovided terms in Treaties and placed them at the forefront of the EU legal order.

To conclude, the CJEU has not eliminated the democratic malaise of the Union, but it has managed to enhance its democratic structure considerably despite lacking normative foundations in Treaties. In addition, pitting the EU democratic credentials against the democratic credentials of today's constitutional democracies may soften criticisms about the Union's democratic deficit. Constitutionalism and democracy are not about to triumph across the globe. Executives tend to dominate most modern domestic politics, and populism has recently become a new secular religion. Examined through these lenses, the usual generalisation of EU democracy appears less compelling.

To return to the main issue, the Polish and the Hungarian cases testify that democratic deficit is also visible *within* the Member States. The EU mandate to defend domestic democracy is compatible with the nature of its democracy, which is militant. This claim requires a previous scrutiny of related underlying assumptions.

3 EU democracy is militant

3.1 A brief note on the militant democracy

In its original conception, militant democracy is a concept of legally restrained democracy aimed at preventing the exploitation of democratic opportunities to

in EU Administrative Law: Towards an Integrated Administration, Cheltenham, Edward Elgar, 2009, pp.257–287.

42 Case 26/62, *NV Algemene Transport- en Expeditie Onderneming van Gend & Loos v. Netherlands Inland Revenue Administration* [1963] ECR 1.

43 *Ibid.*, p.12.

44 See Case 29/69, *Stauder v. Ulm*, [1969] ECR 419; Case 11/70, *Internationale Handelsgesellschaft v. Einfuhr-und Vorratsstelle fur Getreide und Futtermittel*, [1970] ECR 1125; Case 4/73, *Nold v. Commission*, [1974] ECR 491.

45 See, *e.g.*, J. Kühling, 'Fundamental Rights', in A. Bogdandy and J. Bast (eds.), *Principles of European Constitutional Law*, Oxford, Oxford University Press, 2011, pp.479–514.

destroy the democracy itself. In view of its first promoter, Karl Loewenstein, who coined the term and introduced the notion into constitutional law, militant democracy was a missing feature of many post-World War I constitutions.[46] Loewenstein claimed that the lack of the lawfully entrenched militancy, in particular restrictions of political rights and freedoms (freedom of speech, freedom of assembly and freedom to form political parties) or its inefficient use, allowed the fascist movement to rise, legally acquire power and eventually kill democracy in Europe and some other parts of the world.[47] Loewenstein suggested that democracy should have gone militant and adopt rights-restrictive legislation and ban subversive movements to prevent such a scenario.[48]

The tragedy of World War II inspired many countries to follow Loewenstein. Militancy of constitutional democracies includes restricting free speech, outlawing hate speech, banning political parties and associations, disqualifying parties from electoral lists, or employing militant language in the emergency powers clause.[49] Thus, notwithstanding different protective techniques that lead to varieties of militancy, contemporary democracies are by default legally structured as more or less militant democracies.[50] Moreover, in contemporary Europe, militant democracy is internationally promoted by the European Court of Human Rights, whose jurisprudence serves as the principal guide on permissible legal obstacles to democracy-endangering actions.[51]

However, because it allows excluding some citizens and their voices from political life, *i.e.*, it departs from a fundamental premise of liberal democracy under which all citizens and all voices should be accorded free expression and participation, from the moment of its conceptualisation, militant democracy has been subject to various critics. Loewenstein himself was aware of the democratic dilemma or so-called 'paradox' of democracy: 'Democracy stands for fundamental rights, for the fair play of all opinions, for free speech, assembly, press. How could

46 See K. Loewenstein, 'Militant Democracy and Fundamental Rights I', *The American Political Science Review*, Vol.31, No.3, 1937, pp.417–432, and K. Loewenstein, 'Militant Democracy and Fundamental Rights II', *The American Political Science Review*, Vol.31, No.4, 1937, pp.638–658, both reprinted in Sajó (ed.), *supra* note 17, pp. 231–262. Further, in this chapter, all mentioned references indicate the pagination in the reprint.

47 Loewenstein, 'Militant Democracy and Fundamental Rights I', *supra* note 46, pp.236–239.

48 Loewenstein, 'Militant Democracy and Fundamental Rights II', *supra* note 46, pp.261–262.

49 For a discussion, see, *e.g.*, M. Thiel, 'Comparative Aspects', in M. Thiel (ed.), *The Militant Democracy Principle in Modern Democracies*, Farnham & Burlington, Ashgate Publishing Limited, 2009, pp.379–424; V. Beširević, Predgovor [Introduction], in V. Beširević, Miltantna demokratija – nekada i sada [Militant Democracy – Then and Now], Belgrade, PFUUB & Službeni Glasnik, 2013, pp.9–29.

50 Pfersmann, *supra* note 17, p.53.

51 See, *e.g.*, V. Beširević, 'A Short Guide to Militant Democracy: Some Remarks on the Strasbourg Jurisprudence', in W. Benedek, F. Benoît-Rohmer, W. Karl and M. Nowak (eds.), *European Yearbook of Human Rights 2012*, Antwerp and Vienna, Intersentia and NW Verlag, 2012, pp.243–258.

it address itself to curtailing these without destroying the very basis of its existence and justification?'[52] Accordingly, the fundamental question is how to synchronise autonomy, lying in the heart of political rights and freedoms, and measures aimed at restricting that autonomy, without turning democracy against itself. Or in the words of Dyzenhaus, 'how far can a democracy go in protecting itself without comprising its democratic nature?'[53]

Now, this is not a place for a substantive discussion on whether it is possible or not to pacify the inherent arbitrariness of militant democracy and prevent democracies from turning abusive in the long run.[54] Here, it is sufficient to say that, today, most scholars agree that a constitution is not a suicidal pact, and therefore are ready to accept that protective measures to preserve democracy, although undesirable, are legitimate.[55] Rawls, for example, claims that '[...] just citizens should strive to preserve the constitution with all its equal liberties as long as liberty itself in their own freedom is not in danger'; otherwise, 'they can properly force the intolerant to respect the liberty of others'.[56] The European Court of Human Rights confirmed this approach by concluding that 'where the presence of such a danger has been established by the national courts [...] a State may reasonably forestall the execution of such a policy, which is incompatible with the Convention's provisions, before an attempt is made to implement it through concrete steps that might prejudice civil peace and the country's democratic regime'.[57] It should be clear, however, that the basic convergence on the idea that democracies have the right to defend themselves does not remove militant democracy from its inherent controversies and arbitrariness, which continue to be the subject of vivid academic arguments.[58]

3.2 EU militant democracy

The EU democracy, despite all its deficiencies, is antagonistic to its enemies. For the first time, the democracy protective mechanism was included in the Amsterdam Treaty, adopted in 1999, and amended by the Treaty of Nice in 2001. The

52 Loewenstein, 'Militant Democracy and Fundamental Rights I', *supra* note 46, p.243.

53 D. Dyzenhaus, 'Constituting the Enemy: A Response to Carl Schmitt', in Sajó (ed.), *supra* note 17, p.15.

54 For recent critical voices see, *e.g.*, C. Invernizzi Accetti and I. Zuckerman, 'What's Wrong with Militant Democracy?', *Political Studies*, Vol.65, No.1, 2017, pp.182–199; T. Ginsburg and A. Huq, *How to Save a Constitutional Democracy*, Chicago, University of Chicago Press, 2018. See also M. Jovanović, 'How to Justify Militant Democracy: Meta-ethics and the Game-like Character of Democracy', *Philosophy & Social Criticism*, Vol.42, No.8, 2016, pp.745–762.

55 See in G. Capoccia, 'Militant Democracy: The Institutional Bases of Democratic Self-Preservation', *Annual Review of Law and Social Science*, Vol.9, 2013, pp. 207–226.

56 J. Rawls, *A Theory of Justice*, Oxford, Oxford University Press, 1972, p.219.

57 *Refah Partisi (The Welfare Party) and Others v. Turkey*, App. No. 41340/98, 41342/98, 41343/98 and 41344/98, Judgment of 13 February 2003, para.102.

58 This is the case particularly with attempts to stretch the application of militant democracy principles to the fight against religious fanaticism and international terrorism. For a discussion, see *e.g.*, Beširević, *supra* note 51, pp.245–246.

amendments were inspired by the sanctions imposed on Austria in 2000 due to the formation of the coalition government that included the far-right Haider's Freedom Party, coupled with the National Socialist past.[59] However, the Austrian case did not involve the EU action, but the 14 EU Member States' joint action.[60] Recall here that the transnational militant democracy mechanism as a response to democratic backsliding in the Member States was for the first time activated only in 2017 against Poland, and soon after, against Hungary in 2018.

The key EU militant democracy tool, the sanction mechanism, is entrenched in Article 7 TEU. Its pronouncements provide a special EU competence to defend democracy insofar as it is one of the EU identity values referred to in Article 2 TEU. EU transnational militant democracy rests on the political rather than the legal tools. The EU political institutions, the Commission, the Council and the European Council, with the European Parliament's involvement, dominate in the democracy defending proceedings. This does not mean that Member States play no role in this context; on the contrary, they also may initiate the proceedings under Article 7 TEU. The proceedings, which may end up in political sanctions, are divided into two stages, the preventive and the remedial. A possible scenario to anchor democracy 'from above' entails the following.

It all begins with recognising the threat to democracy in a Member State. A transnational protective mechanism can be activated by the proposal of one-third of the Member States (acting together), the European Parliament or the European Commission. Upon the proposal, after obtaining the European Parliament's consent, the Council determines whether a clear risk of a serious breach by a Member State of Article 2 values (the democracy) exists. At this stage, before the Council decides, the Member State in question may respond to the allegations and adopt recommendations of the Council, including the recommendation to refrain from political activities perceived to endanger democracy. The Council will regularly monitor whether the grounds on which its determination is made continue to apply.[61]

If this preventive mechanism fails, another EU political institution, the European Council, is empowered to take further democracy protective steps: after inviting the Member State in question to submit its observations, acting by unanimity on a proposal by one-third of the Member States or by the Commission, and after obtaining the consent of the European Parliament, it may establish that a serious and persistent breach by a Member State of democracy values exists.[62] If it determines so, the Council, acting alone, may impose sanctions, which are reduced to the suspension of the rights deriving from the application of the Treaties to the Member State in question, including its voting rights in the

59 For a broad discussion, see Sadurski, *supra* note 15, pp.396–409.

60 The problem was the formation of the coalition government that included a far-right Haider's Freedom Party, coupled with the National Socialist past. The Member States imposed diplomatic sanctions on Austria although the coalition government did not violate any part of EU law. Article 7 (1) prevention stage was inspired by this action. Bugarič, *supra* note 15, p.87.

61 The preventive stage is regulated in Article 7(1) TEU.

62 Article 7(2) TEU.

Council and the rights derived from secondary EU law.[63] As said before, the sanction which is missing is the termination of EU membership.

This purely political mechanism includes a rather limited CJEU role: it has jurisdiction to supervise the conformity of the EU political institutions' actions with Article 7 TEU procedural rules, solely at the request of the Member State concerned.[64]

3.3 The limits of EU militancy

Those who favour the militant democracy model to fight democratic backsliding in the Members State may face two objections. The first objection is general: militant democracy is not applicable in cases of democracy erosion. The second objection is based on the fact that Member States are bound to respect EU law only when they implement it, which does not extend to the functioning of domestic democracy.

As to the first objection, Ginsburg and Huq, for example, argue that militant democracy techniques are not capable to prevent and stop the erosion of democracy.[65] This might be valid, particularly having in mind that traditional militant democracy measures, like banning political parties and associations or disqualifying parties from electoral lists, are not applicable at the Union level. For Weiler, the militant democracy paradigm makes little sense in confronting the anti-democratic risk in the EU Member States because democratic backsliding 'is often done in the name of democracy and popular will'.[66]

Arguments of this kind require broader responses beyond the purpose of this chapter. But to underline my key arguments, I deal with them briefly here. The basic response is that the Union is already structured as militant democracy: its obligation to defend European values, including democracy, even from the threats that come within the Member States, is specified in Article 7 TEU. But, as the Union is not a state, the EU militant democracy is reasonably different from its form in the democratic states.[67] Transnational EU militant democracy is not

63 Article 7(3) TEU. See Besselink, *supra* note 15, pp.129–130. See, also, D. Kochenov, 'Busting the Myths Nuclear: A Commentary on Article 7 TEU', *EUI Working Paper LAW*, 2017/10, available at https://cadmus.eui.eu/bitstream/handle/1814/46345/LAW_2017_10.pdf?sequence=1; T.V. Olsen, 'Liberal Democratic Sanctions in the EU', in A. Malkopoulou and A. Kirshner (eds.), *Militant Democracy and Its Crisis: Populism, Parties, Extremism*, Edinburg, Edinburg University Press, 2019, pp.150–168.

64 Article 269 TEU.

65 T. Ginsburg and A. Huq, *Democratic Erosion and Militant Democracy*, International Journal of Constitutional Law Blog, 18 October 2018, available at http://www.iconnectblog.com/2018/10/democratic-erosion-and-militant-democracy.

66 Weiler, *supra* note 5, p.314.

67 For more details, see, *e.g.*, J. Müller, 'The EU as a Militant Democracy, or: Are there Limits to Constitutional Mutations within EU Member States?', *Revista de Estudios Políticos*, No.165, 2014, pp.141–162; S. Ninatti and M. Arcari, 'Patterns of Democracy in the Case Law of the EU Court of Justice and the European Court of Human Rights', *Polish Yearbook of International Law*, Vol. 5, 2015, pp.171–192; U. Wagrandl, 'Transnational Militant Democracy', *Global Constitutionalism*, Vol.7, No.2, pp.143–172.

individualistic, targeting an individual's political rights and freedoms for putting democracy at risk. At present, it is about preventing a Member State's right to participate in the EU decision-making due to its 'illiberal' turn, which endangers democracy established within the Union. Ultimately, EU militant democracy protects the common democracy from populist capture. At the same time, it preserves the European citizens' sovereignty, as it entails the suspension of the Member State's voting rights and not its people's voting rights in the European Parliament.[68] Accordingly, the EU and militant democracy are not at odds. As to Weiler's approach, his argument that 'the aggression against EU values is often done in the name of domestic democracy'[69] and that therefore EU militant responses conflict with the basis of democratic theory, is acceptable only if one treats Hungary and Poland as democratic states (which is no longer the case), and accepts a rather Schmittian picture of democracy.[70]

The second objection that makes the EU militant democracy mechanism controversial beyond its traditional paradoxes is the scope of its application from the perspective of EU law. The real complexity here is the issue of whether Article 7 TEU can be applied only when a Member State's Article 2 TEU violation falls within the scope of EU law or the EU may intervene when the Article 2 TEU violation does not relate to the specific material EU competence. In other words, can the Union confront democratic backsliding in a Member State as it occurs beyond the application of EU law?

One possible and conventional answer is that the EU cannot override its Member States on matters not connected to the EU law application, or, more precisely, on a subject matter for which the EU has no competence deriving from the Treaties.[71] The opposite answer, offered by the Council Legal Service, implies 'Union competence to supervise the application of the Rule of Law, as a value of the Union, in the context that is not related to a specific material competence or that exceeds its scope'.[72] This answer is more rooted in the philosophy of EU integrations and the fact that the Member States and the Union share the same identity values.[73] From the perspective of public power exercised by the Member States, I agree with Besselink, who claims that it would be untenable that a

68 Wagrandl further develops this argument. See Wagrandl, supra *note* 67, pp.158–159.

69 Weiler, *supra* note 5, p.314.

70 For a similar view, see R.D. Kelemen, T. Pavone and C. Emmons, 'The perils of Passivity in the Rule of Law Crisis: A Response to von Bogdandy', *VerfBlog*, 2019/11/26, p.3. For Schmittian picture of democracy, see V. Beširević, 'Introduction', in Beširević (ed.), *supra* note 3, pp.2–5.

71 The Council, acting on the alleged violations of the rule of law in Hungary, supported this approach, acknowledging that 'the Rule of Law applies as a value of the EU in the areas in which the EU has competence'. The Council Document 16862/14, 12 December 2014, para.12. Besselink rightly notes, the Council has misinterpreted the opinion of its own Legal Service. Besselink, *supra* note 15, pp. 141–142.

72 Council Legal Service, Opinion on Commission's Communication on 'A New EU Framework to Strengthen the Rule of Law – Compatibility with the Treaties, Brussels, 27 May 2014, doc. 10296/14.

73 Besselink, *supra* note 15, pp.142–143: Hillion, *supra* note 15, pp.65–66.

Member State is obliged to respect democracy, human dignity, human rights, the rule of law and other Article 2 TEU values *only* when they act within the confines of EU law and not when their actions fall beyond the scope of EU law.[74] Moreover, if respect for democracy is a prerequisite for a new Member State's Union membership, it must also be a condition for the continued Union membership because, as stated in Article 2 TEU, the EU existence is predicated on the respect for democracy. Accordingly, it can be claimed that Article 7 TEU presents a toolkit for the Union to protect democracy within the Member States even when its violation is not related to the application of EU law.

Accordingly, the problem with the application of militant democracy principles in cases of democratic backsliding within the Member States does not reside in their practical inapplicability, incompatibility with democratic theory or EU law, but in the fact that the political structure of EU militancy proved ineffective enough to confront anti-democratic risk in the Member States. Thus, it has already been noted that the Article 7 TEU sanction mechanism is a much weaker threat to a Member State than the EU threat of withholding EU membership during the pre-accession stage.[75] The Polish and Hungarian cases testify about enormous difficulties in activating Article 7 TEU as no fact-finding and assessment stages are available under the Treaties. Moreover, while the Union was occupied with filling this gap and establishing a 'pre-Article 7 TEU procedure', the ruling governments managed to damage the democratic fabric in Poland and Hungary.[76] For this discussion, it is not relevant that the EU institutions' autonomy in imposing sanctions on a Member State is more limited than the jurisdiction of the CJEU in the infringement cases.[77] Therefore, what might seem to be the missing feature of the present EU militant democracy is judicial remedies for breaches of Article 2 TEU values, including breaches amounting to democracy erosion.[78] However, in the rest of the chapter, I will show emerging evidence that some judicial avenues to confront democratic backsliding in the Member States are already at the CJEU's disposal.

4 Judicial avenues to fortify EU militancy: Emerging tendencies

Increasingly authoritarian regimes in Hungary and Poland have managed to dismantle most of Article 2 TEU protected values, including democracy itself, heavily relying on, to borrow from Weiler, 'democratic majoritarian decisions'.[79] However, the Commission has long insisted that Article 2 TEU values were not legally enforceable, so its

74 Besselink, *supra* note 15, p.143.

75 U. Sedelmeier, 'Anchoring Democracy from Above? The European Union and Democratic Backsliding in Hungary and Romania after Accession', *Journal of Common Market Studies*, Vol.52, No.1, 2014, p.105.

76 For more on Article 7 TEU defects, see Kochenov, Scheppele and Grabowska-Moroz, *supra* note 3, pp.30–35.

77 Sedelmeier, *supra* note 75, p.105.

78 See, *e.g.*, Kochenov, Scheppele and Grabowska-Moroz, *supra* note 3; Besselink, *supra* note 15; Hillion, *supra* note 15.

79 Weiler, *supra* note 5, p.314.

infringement actions against Hungary and Poland were grounded in other EU primary and secondary law provisions and tied to the material scope of the *acquis.*[80] The Commission's approach had tied the CJEU's hands a considerable degree as it was forced to deliver judgments on narrow grounds defined in the Commission's applications.[81] In the meantime, many have questioned Article 2's alleged legal non-enforcement, arguing that no such limitation existed in the Treaties,[82] and that in cases of serious violations, its legal enforcement would justify imposing Article 7 TEU political sanctions.[83] While the cases against Hungary have not yet risen above mentioned, piecemeal level,[84] two recently decided Polish cases, both connected with court-packing, mirror a possible shift in the Commission's approach and shed light on a promising novel approach to already existing judicial avenues for enforcing Article 2 TEU values – infringement actions and a preliminary ruling.[85]

Note that in both cases, the claim, the preliminary references and consequently the CJEU's judgments were constructed in the rule of law terms rather than the democracy term itself. But the separation between the rule of law and democracy is untenable.[86] The rule of law is a part of the ontology of democracy, in the sense of what Frankenberg calls 'the conjunction of the democratic sovereign with the rule of law' according to the formula 'government of laws and not of man'.[87] Having that in mind, I will argue with some confidence that these cases represent emerging CJEU jurisprudence against democratic backsliding in the Member States and frame well the judicial role in shaping militant democracy in the Union.

4.1 Enforcing EU democratic values through infringement proceedings

One of the techniques the populist governments use to bypass checks and balances, an essential device against abuse of power, is court-packing. As democracy is not reduced to the elections and majority rule but also entails judicial review established to preclude tyranny, the court-packing to obtain favourable rulings is a

80 Kochenov, Scheppele and Grabowska-Moroz, *supra* note 3, p.56.

81 Weiler, *supra* note 5, p.316.

82 Editorial Comments, 'Safeguarding EU Values in the Member States – Is Something Finally Happening?', *Common Market Law Review*, Vol.52, No.3, 2015, p.622.

83 Hillion, *supra* note 15; Kochenov, Scheppele and Grabowska-Moroz, *supra* note 3, p.80.

84 See, *e.g.*, the newly decided infringement case concerning academic freedom in Hungary, Case C-66/18, *Commission v. Hungary*, [2020] ECLI:EU:C:2020:792. The decision against Hungary was grounded on its failure to comply with market freedoms, the Charter and the GATT, rather than with human rights values under Article 2 TEU.

85 See case C-619/18, *Commission v. Poland* (Independence of the Supreme Court), 24 June 2019 [2019] ECLI:EU:C:2019:531 and Joined cases C-585/18, C-624/18 and C-625/18, *A.K. and Others v. Sąd Najwyższy (Supreme Court)* (Independence of the Disciplinary Chamber), 19 November 2019 [2019] EU:C:2019:982.

86 Weiler, *supra* note 5, pp.316–318; Müller, *supra* note 67, p.223.

87 G. Frankenberg, 'Democracy', in M. Rosenfeld and A. Sajó (eds.) *The Oxford Handbook of Comparative Constitutional Law*, Oxford, Oxford University Press, 2012, p.254.

clear threat to democracy. Some courts, like the Romanian Constitutional Court, effectively defended itself, admittedly, after the European Commission warned the government that the judicial reform was on the wrong track.[88] However, the courts in Hungary and Poland did not manage to sustain the populist attacks and were soon packed by illiberal forces.

The CJEU ruled on court-packing cases in Hungary and Poland, but it turned really militant only in the Polish case. The Polish case has finally clarified that among the judicial toolkits to protect Article 2 TEU values, including democracy itself, infringement proceedings, initiated before the CJEU either by the Commission or a Member State, for a failure to comply with EU law (Articles 258–259 TFEU), are the most effective.

Nevertheless, this argument is not without its own problems. Activating infringement proceedings in cases concerning democratic backsliding in a Member State may appear disputable on two grounds: first, like in Article 7 TEU cases, one may assert that infringement proceedings can be used only when Member States implement EU law, and not to deal with purely domestic situations such as democratic backsliding in a Member State; and second, it is possible to argue that Article 7 TEU application precludes the institution of infringement proceedings. In what can be described as revolutionary decisions, the CJEU resolved both dilemmas.

As to the first issue, in the Portuguese Judges case that does not concern democratic backsliding but remuneration of judges under domestic rules, the CJEU ruled that the requirements of judicial independence and effective implementation of EU law by national courts under Article 19 (1) subpar. (2) TEU and Article 47 of the Charter, must be secured in all circumstances, regardless of whether or not the concrete case involves the implementation of Union law.[89] In other words, as national courts are entrusted with effective implementation of Union law, they must meet the requirements of the judicial independence. Consequently, the CJEU has sufficient grounds for its jurisdiction, whether or not the case at stake involves EU law implementation. In *Commission v. Poland*, in which it confronted the Supreme Court's reform at the expense of democratic principles, the CJEU relied heavily on this conclusion.[90]

Advocate General Tanchev responded to the second problem in the same Polish case.[91] The fact that Article 7 TEU is activated to combat a Member State's serious and persistent breach of Article 2 TEU values does not preclude a judicial action to enforce the application of EU law by the Member States, concluded the Advocate General, suggesting that the proceedings are complementary and may be applied in

88 For the Romanian case, see S. Tanasescu, 'Romania: From Constitutional Democracy to Constitutional Decay?', in Beširević (ed.), *supra* note 3, pp.177–191; T. Ginsburg, 'The Jurisprudence of Anti-Erosion', *Drake Law Review*, Vol.66, No.4, 2018, pp.823–854; see also Sedelmeier, *supra* note 75.

89 Case C-64/16, *Associação Sindical dos Juízes Portugueses (Portuguese Judges)* [2018] ECLI:EU:C:2018:117, para.29.

90 *Commission v. Poland* (Independence of the Supreme Court), paras.43–57.

91 *Ibid.*, Opinion of Advocate General Tanchev, 11 April 2019, paras.48–51.

parallel.[92] The CJEU did not refer to the relationship between Article 258 TFEU and Article 7 TEU procedures in the judgment, but it reviewed the Supreme Court-packing, and thus confirmed what the Advocate General suggested. Hence, a long-debated issue on whether the EU responses to populist capture in the Member States are reduced to the political sanctions mechanism under Article 7 TEU, or some legal instruments could also turn the Union militant, has been resolved.[93] This point has broad implications for how EU militant democracy should be understood.

That being said, in *Commission v. Poland* (Independence of the Supreme Court), the CJEU announced that it would step in to confront democratic backsliding in the Member States on the grounds of the jurisdiction it has under Article 258 TFEU infringement procedures.

Facts first. The Commission initiated the case alleging that:

> first, by lowering the retirement age of the judges appointed to the Sąd Najwyższy (Supreme Court) and by applying that measure to the judges in post appointed to that court […] and, secondly, by granting the President of the Republic the discretion to extend the period of judicial activity of judges of that court beyond the newly fixed retirement age, the Republic of Poland has failed to fulfil its obligations under the combined provisions of the second subparagraph of Article 19(1) TEU and Article 47 of the Charter.[94]

Clearly, the case involved the organisation of justice in the Member State, falling within the Member States' competence, and not the EU scope of competences in any way.

The CJEU went militant even before it decided the case. Upon the Commission's application, it granted an interim measure and requested Poland to suspend the disputable legislation, revive the former law, and make its provisions applicable until its final judgment.[95] The interim measure was effective, and the President of the Supreme Court ordered the retired judges back to work solely based on the order of the CJEU.[96] The Court also militantly defended its jurisdiction: it confirmed that the organisation of justice is the Member States' competence. But it added that when the Member States exercise this competence, they must comply with their obligations deriving from the EU law, and therefore the CJEU review was justified.[97]

92 *Ibid.*, para.50.
93 See in Editorial Comments, *supra* note 82, pp.626–627; Hillion, *supra* note 15, pp.71–74.
94 *Commission v. Poland* (Independence of the Supreme Court), para.1.
95 *Ibid.*, Order of the Court, 17 December 2018, para.95.
96 P. Bogdanowicz and M. Taborowski, 'How to Save a Supreme Court in a Rule of Law Crisis: The Polish Experience: ECJ (Grand Chamber) 24 June 2019, Case C-619/18, *European Commission* v *Republic of Poland*', *European Constitutional Law Review*, Vol.16, No.2, 2020, p.310, f.20.
97 *Commission v. Poland* (Independence of the Supreme Court), para.52.

What were these obligations in the present case? Relying heavily on the Portuguese Judges case, the CJEU approached the court-packing issue from the Article 2 TEU perspective and human rights concerns, particularly the right to an effective remedy and a fair trial entrenched in the Charter. The CJEU repeated that the rule of law is protected under Article 2 TEU and that its essential tenant is judicial independence.[98] As the Polish Supreme Court is also an EU court and may come into position to rule on questions concerning the application or interpretation of EU law, the CJEU recalls that maintaining its independence is vital, notwithstanding whether or not potential cases involve the application and interpretation of Union law.[99] In this vein, judicial independence, the CJEU underlines, requires, *inter alia*, guarantees against removal from office, which are not absolute but subject to limitations under the principle of proportionality in each particular case.[100] Applying these requirements to the facts of the case, the CJEU found that the Polish law that forced the judges to retire at the lower age than envisaged in the former law, unless they were granted an extension by the President, violated the principle of judicial independence and irremovability of judges.[101] Accordingly, the CJEU ruled that court-packing violated the rule of law principle under Article 2 TEU. As a result, Poland reinstated the Supreme Court judges whom it had forced into early retirement.

Compared with the previously decided Hungarian court-packing case, there is an obvious twist in the Polish case. Although deciding on identical facts, the CJEU's earlier decision in the Hungarian case did not manage to bring any change to the troubling attempts of the Hungarian government to adjust the organisation of justice to its political needs. The case involved a national scheme requiring compulsory retirement of judges, prosecutors and notaries when they reach the age of 62.[102] The Commission tailored the action for failure to fulfil obligations on narrow grounds – age discrimination prohibited under Directive 2000/78/EC.[103] As it did not insist on a larger point – a serious breach of Article 2 TEU values, as it did in the Polish case – the CJEU delivered the ruling on the narrow grounds and confirmed the breach, but its effects were rather modest: the judgement did not restore judicial independence in Hungary; the ruling populists got the judges they wanted.[104] The Commission learned their lesson, and in the Polish case approached identical facts differently. Admittedly, the CJEU, in the meantime, delivered a decision in the Portuguese Judges case, which paved the way for the Commission to argue the case from the EU fundamental values perspective rather than the perspective of EU secondary law.

98 *Ibid.*, para.58.
99 *Ibid.*, paras.55–57.
100 *Ibid.*, para.76.
101 *Ibid.*, para.124.
102 Case C-286/12, *Commission v. Hungary*, 6 November 2012, [2012] EU:C:2018:117.
103 *Ibid.*, para.1.
104 *Ibid.*, para.81.

The Polish case confirms the fact that in democratic backsliding cases, timing also matters. In the pre-litigation procedure, Poland was given the one-month deadline to reply to a letter of formal notice and, subsequently, to the reasoned opinion, which was twice as short as usual.[105] Additionally, upon the Commission request, the CJEU decided the case under the expedited procedure: the judgment that stopped court-packing for illiberal democracy purposes was delivered in just eight months.[106] Having in mind that the Court's interim measure also proved useful, it is not hard to conclude that the infringement proceedings before the CJEU were more effective in confronting the ruling populists in Poland than were the EU political institutions acting under Article 7 TEU – the sanction procedure is still pending in the Council.

The CJEU's approach in the Polish Supreme Court-packing case illuminates potentials of the infringement proceedings in enforcing Article 2 values, which, to remind us, was drafted on the belief that the values, including democracy, are and will be shared by all Member States. In line with this reasoning, to reflect a systemic breach of EU identity values rather than an incidental episode, Kochenov, Scheppele and Grabowska-Moroz have recently proposed a 'path breaking'[107] approach to succeed in infringement proceedings cases.[108] The approach would be based on the series of Article 2 breaches to indicate a general pattern of a Member State conduct.[109] To restore EU values, a systemic approach also requires the use of Article 260 TFEU, particularly imposing fines deducted from EU funds.[110]

Building a systemic approach on breaches of Article 2 values, including democracy, would not be an entirely novel approach in the Court's practice. In environmental cases, the Commission has used it successfully: for example, in the Waste Directive case against Ireland, it used a selective number of infringement cases to argue that they illustrate breaches of a more general nature, which the CJEU accepted, and found Ireland to be in 'general and persistent breach' of the Waste Directive.[111] Similarly, a systemic approach could be used to pursue serious violations by the Member States in cases concerning different modalities of democratic backsliding. The presence of the CJEU's finding that a Member State has systemically and persistently violated democratic values would strengthen the legitimacy of Article 7 TEU proceedings and make it more effective.

105 Bogdanowicz and Taborowski, *supra* note 96, p.311, f.21.

106 *Ibid.*, pp.310–311.

107 Borrowed from Craig and de Búrca, *supra* note 27, p.449.

108 Kochenov, Scheppele and Grabowska-Moroz, *supra* note 3; see, also, K. Scheppele, 'Enforcing the Basic Principles of EU Law through Systemic Infringements Action', in Closa and Kochenov (eds.), *supra* note 5, 105–132.

109 *Ibid.*, pp.61–71.

110 *Ibid.*, p.101.

111 Case C-494/01, *Commission v. Ireland* [2005] ECR I-3331, discussed in Craig and de Búrca, *supra* note 27, p.449.

4.2 Enforcing EU democratic values through preliminary rulings

Another judicial tool at hand to fight populism in the Union is the preliminary ruling proceedings (Article 267 TFEU), although the current developments signal they are *prima facie* less suitable than the infringement proceedings. However, there are many complexities connected with preliminary rulings. Recall first that the CJEU does not decide a case in the preliminary ruling proceedings, but upon a reference from a national court, it rules on the point of either interpretation or validity of EU law relevant for the dispute.[112] As the proceedings are not initiated by any EU institutions but by national courts, and the CJEU is not empowered to invalidate a national law, enforcement of democratic values through preliminary rulings to confront threats to domestic democracy may appear feeble. However, recall also that the Court's preliminary rulings, which represent an authoritative interpretation of EU law, are generally binding, *i.e.*, have *erga omnes* effects.[113] Consequently, preliminary rulings appear to be the most efficient EU law enforcement measure against the Member States[114] and crucial for maintaining European integrations, as the application of direct effect and supremacy doctrines, developed within the proceedings, clearly indicates. In reality, the CJEU used the first opportunity to send a strong message against populist court-packing in Poland through its preliminary ruling. Consider its novel approach in the A.K. and Others case.[115]

To increase its impact on the justice system, after targeting the Constitutional Court and the Supreme Court, Poland's ruling populists extended a packing plan to the National Council of the Judiciary (the body responsible for judicial appointments, the NCJ) and the Disciplinary Chamber of the Supreme Court.[116] Under the 2017 reform law, the NCJ was staffed entirely by members either elected or appointed by the ruling party (out of 25 members, 23 were chosen by politicians).[117] Thus, the ruling populists created yet another 'executive' body. The NCJ soon participated in the packing of the Disciplinary Chamber of the Supreme Court, mostly with the regime supporters.[118]

The disputes that gave rise to the CJEU preliminary ruling involved the NCJ's rejection of granting term extensions to three judges (two Supreme Court judges and a judge of the Supreme Administrative Court). Their retirement age was lowered under the 2017 Supreme Court Act, which earlier, in the 2018

112 For more, see Craig and de Búrca, *supra* note 27, pp.464–507.

113 M. Broberg, 'Preliminary References as a Means for Enforcing EU Law', in Jakab and Kochenov (eds.), *supra* note 15, p.107.

114 *Ibid.*, p.111.

115 *A.K. and Others v. Sąd Najwyższy (Supreme Court)* (Independence of the Disciplinary Chamber), *supra* note 85.

116 For a broad discussion, see, *e.g.*, K.G. Roszczynialska and K. Krystian Markiewicz, 'Disciplinary Proceedings as an Instrument for Breaking the Rule of Law in Poland', *Hague Journal on the Rule of Law*, 2020, available at https://doi.org/10.1007/s40803-020-00146-y.

117 *A.K. and Others*, para.143.

118 *Ibid.*, para.469.

infringement case mentioned above, was found to violate EU law.[119] The Polish government did amend the Act in response to the CJEU interim measure, but it was never repealed *ex tunc*.[120] Anyhow, under its provisions, before granting consent for term extension in each particular case, the President of the Republic should have obtained an opinion of the NCJ.[121] The said law also created the Disciplinary Chamber of the Supreme Court and envisaged its exclusive jurisdiction in case of disputes.[122] In the cases concerned, the judges brought separate actions before the Labour and Social Insurance Chamber of the Polish Supreme Court, because the Disciplinary Chamber was not yet formed, asserting that the opinions of the NCJ, unfavourable to them, *inter alia*, violated judicial independence guarantees under Article 19 (1) TEU, Article 47 of the Charter, and Article 9 (1) of 2000/78 Directive prohibiting age discrimination.[123]

Concerned by the 'independence' of the Disciplinary Chamber, to which the cases should have been referred, the Labour and Social Insurance Chamber of the Polish Supreme Court submitted three requests for a preliminary ruling, asking the CJEU to interpret the guarantees of judicial independence and a general framework for equal treatment in employment and occupation. The CJEU joined the requests, and in A.K. and Others set out standards of judicial independence in the Union and took a revolutionary approach to implement EU law in the Member States.

The CJEU built a preliminary ruling on its previous ruling in the infringement case, confirming that the Member States were required to comply with the obligations deriving from EU law, even though the organisation of justice in the Member States falls within their competences.[124] It then recalled that Article 47 of the Charter safeguards the fundamental right to an effective remedy that encompasses everyone's right to a fair hearing by an independent and impartial tribunal.[125] The CJEU interpreted the requirements of independence and impartiality relying heavily on the related European Court of Human Rights jurisprudence,[126] but did not miss the opportunity to underline that the independence and impartiality are essential components of the rule of law, protected as the EU identity value in Article 2 TEU and shared by the Member States.[127] Having said that, it warned that the separation of the powers principle and justice *in a democratic society* imply two major requests: (a) that the body involved in the procedure for the appointment of judges must be independent from the legislature and the executive; and (b) that the courts in exercising their jurisdictions

119 *Ibid.*, paras.37–39.
120 *Ibid.*, paras.87–89. For a discussion, see E. Zelazna, 'The Rule of Law Crisis Deepens in Poland after *A.K. v. Krajowa Rada Sadownictwa and CP, DO v. Sąd Najwyższy*', *European Papers*, Vol.4, No.3, 2019, p.908.
121 *A.K. and Others*, para.17.
122 *Ibid.*, paras.21–26.
123 *Ibid.*, paras.37–39.
124 *Ibid.*, paras.82–84.
125 *Ibid.*, para.119.
126 *Ibid.*, paras.126–130.
127 *Ibid.*, para.120.

must be protected from any direct or indirect influence liable to have an effect on their decisions.[128]

In what followed, the CJEU left it to the referring Polish court to determine whether the Disciplinary Chamber met the criteria of an independent and impartial tribunal. Nonetheless, it hinted that the Disciplinary Chamber's composition, circumstances of its creation and the scope of its jurisdiction, when taken together, could confirm concerns regarding its independence and impartiality.[129] As Bogdanowicz rightly notes, this is not what the CJEU usually do in the preliminary ruling procedure, as it leaves a final decision to be made by the referring court.[130] This time, it determined the outcome of the proceedings before the referring national court by taking the position regarding criteria it should use to examine whether the NCJ was an independent and impartial tribunal and whether such qualifications possessed a judicial body whose judges were appointed with the participation of the NCJ.[131]

There is another CJEU intervention in the case that sheds light on its potential to turn the Union militant. For the first time, the Court used the principle of the primacy of EU law as a militant tool to confront the erosion of domestic democracy. Starting from the premise that the principle requires all Member State bodies to give the full effect of the EU law, it ruled that Article 47 of the Charter and Article 9 (1) of Directive 2000/78/EC must be interpreted as 'precluding cases concerning the application of EU law from falling within the exclusive jurisdiction of a court which is not an independent and impartial tribunal'.[132] Consequently, any provision of a domestic law that grants jurisdiction to a court not meeting the requirements of independence and impartiality must be disregarded, and jurisdiction given to the court, which qualifies as an independent and impartial tribunal.[133] As this was a preliminary ruling and not the infringement case, it was, in the end, the Polish Supreme Court that found that the Disciplinary Chamber was not an independent and impartial tribunal and, therefore, could not be regarded as a court within the meaning of EU law.[134]

The further developments indicate that the CJEU's preliminary ruling pushed the EU to use the Court in its full capacity to preclude illiberal threats to domestic democracy. The ultimate effects of the CJEU's preliminary ruling in *A.K. and Others* implied obedience of any court in Poland, as each of them might come into a situation to implement EU law. The populists reacted and, in December 2019, adopted new legislation, known as the 'Muzzle Law', prohibiting courts to

128 *Ibid.*, paras.121–125.
129 *Ibid.*, paras.146–152.
130 P. Bogdanowicz, *Legal Opinion about the Consequences of Judgment of the Court of Justice of the European Union on the National Council of the Judiciary and the Disciplinary Chamber in the Light of European Union Law*, Warsaw, The Batory Foundation, 2020, p.8.
131 *Ibid.*, p.9.
132 *A.K. and Others*, para.171.
133 *Ibid.*
134 For more, see Kochenov, Scheppele and Grabowska-Moroz, *supra* note 3, p.70.

question judicial appointments and penalising judges who find, applying the *A.K. and Others* test, a domestic court not independent.[135] Poland's open opposition to EU law made the Commission request interim measures in the infringement case referred to the Court in October 2019, in which the CJEU was asked to suspend the functioning of the Disciplinary Chamber of the Supreme Court.[136] The CJEU granted interim measures pending its final judgment, concluding that the functioning of the Disciplinary Chamber 'is likely to cause serious and irreparable harm to the EU legal order'. The Commission also initiated a new infringement proceeding against Poland that is still pending, on the grounds that the 'Muzzle Law' undermines the judicial independence of Polish judges, is incompatible with the primacy of EU law, prevents Polish courts from directly applying EU law, and from requesting preliminary rulings on the questions regarding judicial independence.[137]

Undoubtedly, a strong declaration on judicial independence and the CJEU's more or less direct intervention in A.K. and Others stand as a powerful rejoinder to those who considered the preliminary ruling procedure only a mechanism to obtain from the CJEU advice on how to interpret EU law in a concrete case. A.K. and Others illustrates that the advising time has passed, at least in cases when threats to domestic democracy may seriously undermine the EU legal order.

5 Conclusion

This chapter concerns strategic techniques to confront democratic backsliding in the EU Member States. The increasing rise of populism in Hungary and Poland testifies that a politically structured EU militant democracy response is not necessarily thriving. On the contrary, as the Union significantly delayed activation of the sanction mechanism envisaged in the Treaties, the ruling populists in Hungary and Poland have progressed in transforming their political system into illiberal democracy. Moreover, instead of returning to the core democratic values, they started accusing the Union of being a threat to domestic democracy and Europe itself.[138] When the EU finally went militant and activated the sanction mechanism against Poland and Hungary, it became evident that difficulties in using the Article 7 disciplinary arm made EU democracy more vulnerable than it had been previously thought. The problem here to stay is its efficacy – obtaining the political will for Article 7 implementation – as imposing sanctions requires a rather dialogical approach and can be vetoed by any Member State.

135 *Ibid.* For a detailed discussion on 'Muzzle Law', see Roszczynialska and Markiewicz, *supra* note 116.

136 Kochenov, Scheppele and Grabowska-Moroz, *supra* note 3, p.70.

137 European Commission, Press Release, 29 April 2020, available at https://ec.europa.eu/commission/presscorner/detail/en/ip_20_772.

138 For example, Viktor Orbán, the Hungarian leader, accused the EU of 'abuse of power'. See at https://www.dw.com/en/hungarys-viktor-orban-accuses-eu-of-abuse-of-power/a-45442385

As some comparative examples show, judges might compensate for political failures in defending democracy. For example, the US lower courts that blocked US President Donald Trump's travel ban,[139] the UK Supreme Court, which made UK politicians go back to parliament to implement the Brexit vote,[140] and the Israeli Supreme Court, which rescued the legislature's review over an annual budget[141] managed to resist the populism and defend the separation of powers on which constitutional democracies rest.[142]

As shown in this chapter, the CJEU's militant approach to court-packing in Poland sheds light on how judicial avenues, like the infringement proceedings and a preliminary ruling, if rightly and timely articulated, and accompanied by interim measures and the EU integration saving doctrines, may help defend EU democracy. But the court-packing cases are just a good start. A proposed militant approach, *i.e.*, novel use of the existing judicial toolkit, may prove effective in confronting other democratic backsliding modalities, including 'unconstitutional constitutional amendments' or weakening of the fundamental rights. This is not to say that the CJEU alone can save the EU democracy, but to suggest that judicial intervention is also consistent with its militant defence. However, the bottom line here is the problem of mindset: without the democrats, there is no democracy.

139 Several US lower courts blocked Trump's travel ban policy. See, *e.g.*, *State v. Trump*, 265 F. Supp. 3d 1140 (2017); *International Refugee Assistance Project v. Donald Trump*, No. 17–1351 (2017); *Aziz et al. v. Trump et al.*, No. 1:2017cv00116 – Document 111 (E.D. Va. 2017).

140 *R (Miller) v. Secretary of State for Exiting the European Union*, UKSC 5 (2017).

141 *Ramat Gan Academic Center of Law and Business v. Knesset*, HCJ 8260/16 (2017).

142 For a discussion, see, *e.g.*, S. Issacharoff, 'Judicial Review in Troubled Times: Stabilizing Democracy in a Second-Best World', *North Carolina Law Review*, Vol.98, No.1, 2019, pp.1–58.

Part III

Judicial activism and illiberal constitutionalism

5 An illiberal turn or a counter-constitutional revolution?

About the Polish Constitutional Tribunal before and after 2015

Aleksandra Kustra-Rogatka

1 Introduction

In Poland, significant changes have occurred since 2015, consisting of the gradual dismantling of the existing system of checks and balances and the subordination of judiciary power to executive power.[1] Due to the fact that the current parliamentary majority has ignored the text of the constitution and the previous jurisprudence of the Constitutional Tribunal, this is referred to as *constitutional breakdown*,[2] *constitutional crisis*,[3] *rule of law crisis*,[4] *democratic backsliding*,[5] *populist backsliding*[6] as well as *statutory anticonstitutionalism*.[7] These academic and journalistic terms aim to conceptualise Poland's gradual departure from the paradigm of liberal constitutionalism.[8] While critics of this phenomenon point out that the

1 Cf. W. Sadurski, Poland's Constitutional Breakdown, Oxford University Press, Ewa Łętowska & Aneta Wiewiórowska-Domagalska, A 'good' change in the Polish Constitutional Tribunal?, 1 OSTEUROPA RECHT 79 (2016); Ewa Łętowska, The current dismantling of the rule of law in Poland (5 June 2018), https://ruleoflaw.pl/the-currentdismantling- of-the-rule-of-law-in-poland/.

2 W. Sadurski, Poland's Constitutional Breakdown, Oxford University Press 2019.

3 Among many: M. Matczak, The Clash of Powers in Poland's Rule of Law Crisis: Tools of Attack and Self-Defense, Hague Journal on the Rule of Law 2020, M. Matczak, Poland: From Paradigm to Pariah? Polish Constitutional Crisis – Facts and Interpretations, https://ruleoflaw.pl/poland-from-paradigm-pariah-polish-constitutional-crisis-facts-and-interpretations/; Aleksandra Kustra, Poland's Constitutional Crisis. From Court-packing Agenda to Denial of Constitutional Court's Judgments, Toruńskie Studia Polsko-Włoskie/Studi Polacco-Italiani di Torun, vol. XII 2016, pp. 343–366.

4 Among many: A. Kustra-Rogatka, Country Report. Poland Rule of Law Overview, https://democracy-reporting.org/ua/dri_publications/country-report-the-rule-of-law-in-poland/.

5 Among many: W. Przybylski, Explaining Eastern Europe: Can Poland's Backsliding Be Stopped? Journal of Democracy 2018, vol. 29, issue 3, pp. 52–64.

6 W. Sadurski, How Democracy Dies (in Poland): A Case Study of Anti-Constitutional Populist Backsliding, Sydney Law School Legal Studies Research Paper no. 18/01 (2018).

7 M. Bernatt, M. Ziółkowski, Statutory Anti-Constitutionalism, Washington International Law Journal 2019, vol. 28, pp. 485–525.

8 For more on this phenomenon cf. Tom Ginsburg, Aziz Z. Huq, Mila Versteeg, The Coming Demise of Liberal Constitutionalism? The University of Chicago Law Review, 2018, vol. 85, no. 2, pp. 239–255.

DOI: 10.4324/9781003200666-9

use of the salami-slice strategy leads to a gradual transformation of the political system towards authoritarianism,[9] supporters of the changes consider them a necessary systemic correction, finding legitimisation in the will of a sovereign nation.[10]

The purpose of this chapter is to assess the systemic changes that have affected the first target of the Law and Justice [Pol: PiS] government – the Constitutional Tribunal. A comparative analysis of the government's actions aimed at dismantling the existing tripartite division of power proves that the primary target are counter-majoritarian institutions that mainly include constitutional courts. Typically, two strategies are used: court-packing or curbing, sometimes used simultaneously. In the case of the Polish Constitutional Tribunal, the first step involved undermining the social authority of the Constitutional Tribunal. Then, a court-packing strategy was applied, and after a period when the judicial activity of the Constitutional Tribunal was effectively frozen until the President of the Constitutional Tribunal position was filled with someone favourable to the government, the Polish constitutional court once again began to issue rulings on politically controversial cases, legitimising the unconstitutional actions of the parliamentary majority.[11] An analysis of the political role and jurisprudence of the Constitutional Tribunal after 2015 will be made from a specific theoretical perspective that aims to answer the question posed in the title: are we witnessing an illiberal turn or a (counter-) constitutional revolution?

2 Theoretical background

The definition of 'illiberal' refers to the notions of illiberal democracy[12] and illiberal constitutionalism[13] used in public and academic discussions on recent reforms (with or without quotation marks, depending on the side of the dispute). The term illiberal democracy was initially used purely descriptively, to capture the nature of the political system of states undergoing systemic transition, where, however, the model of Western liberal democracy had not been adopted (defined as a political system marked not only by free and fair elections, but also by the rule of law, a separation of powers, and the protection of basic liberties of free speech, assembly, religion and property).[14] Currently, however, this concept has taken on

9 B. Bugaric, Central Europe's descent into autocracy: A constitutional analysis of authoritarian populism.
10 A. Czarnota, Populistyczny konstytucjonalizm czy nowy konstytucjonalizm?, Krytyka Prawa 2019, vol. 11, no. 1, pp. 9–10.
11 Cf. W. Sadurski, Polish Constitutional Tribunal Under Law and Justice: From an Activist Court, to a Paralysed Tribunal, to a Governmental Enabler, Hague Journal on the Rule of Law.
12 A. Antoszewski, Demokracja nieliberalna jako projekt polityczny, Przegląd Europejski 2018, no. 2, pp. 11–31.
13 T. Drinoczi, A. Bień-Kacała, Illiberal Constitutionalism: The Case of Hungary and Poland, German Law Journal, 2019, vol. 20, s. 1140–1166.
14 F. Zakaria, The Rise of Illiberal Democracy, Foreign Affairs 1997, vol. 76, no. 6, pp. 22–23.

a normative character and is used to describe a political project that postulates the necessity to reinterpret the main principles of democracy, such as national sovereignty, representation or separation of power, and to reject the liberal-democratic consensus that prevailed after World War II in Western Europe.[15] One of Hungarian Prime Minister Viktor Orban's speeches, in which illiberal democracy is presented as a political project that constitutes the optimal solution for Hungarian society, is considered to have been the beginning of this approach.[16] It involves a thorough modification aimed in two directions simultaneously: restoring closer ties between the ruled and the ruling and increasing the effectiveness of the latter in solving pressing social problems.[17] Although the term illiberal democracy does not function in practice in the political language of Polish politicians, the arguments used in the rhetoric of Law and Justice supporters for returning to a 'simple democracy' – based on representation of the nation in society[18] and the legitimacy of all actions of the parliamentary majority and the government through selected parliamentary elections – refer to the political project of illiberal democracy.

In turn, illiberal constitutionalism is defined as 'capturing the constitution and constitutionalism with legal means such as formal and informal constitutional change and packing and paralyzing the constitutional court'.[19] Illiberal constitutionalism thus conceived is supported by the misunderstood concept of political constitutionalism, relying heavily on the emotional components of national identity and is conceived as a particular phase in the process of democratic decay or the backsliding from liberal constitutionalism towards an authoritarian regime.[20] However, as some academics highlight, by adding the illiberal epithet to the words democracy and constitutionalism, the neologisms 'illiberal democracy' and 'illiberal constitutionalism' are in fact oxymorons, as liberalism is not merely a limit on the public power of the majority, but also a constitutive precondition for democracy, which provides for the rule of law, checks and balances, and guaranteed fundamental rights.[21]

15 A. Antoszewski, Demokracja nieliberalna jako projekt polityczny, Przegląd Europejski 2018, no. 2, p. 11; R. Wodak, Entering the 'post-shame era': The rise of illiberal democracy, populism and neo-authoritarianism in Europe, Global Discourse 2019, vol. 9, no. 1, p. 195.

16 Full Text of Victor Orban's Speech at Bájle Tuşnad of 26 July 2014, quoted further as Orban (2014), dostępny online, www.budapest-beacon.com.

17 A. Antoszewski, Demokracja nieliberalna jako projekt polityczny, Przegląd Europejski 2018, number 2, s. 12.

18 Przemówienie Jarosława Kaczyńskiego na konwencji Law and Justice z 7.09.2019, quote after: https://oko.press/kaczynski-jeden-narod-jeden-kosciol-demokracja-skonstruowana-prosto-kazdy-dobry-polak-musi/.

19 T. Drinoczi, A. Bień-Kacała, Illiberal Constitutionalism: The Case of Hungary and Poland, German Law Journal 2019, vol. 20, s. 1141.

20 T. Drinoczi, A. Bień-Kacała, Illiberal Constitutionalism. The Case of Hungary and Poland, German Law Journal 2019, vol. 20, s. 1141.

21 G. Halmai, The Making of 'Illiberal Constitutionalism' with or without a New Constitution. The Case of Hungary and Poland, s. 1–2, G. Halmai, Illiberalism in East-Central Europe, EUI Working Paper LAW 2019/05.

The term constitutional revolution is currently used in many different ways.[22] One of the most basic ones is Hans Kelsen's understanding of 'constitutional revolution' as a change to, or a replacement of, the (formal, written) constitution in a way that is incompatible with the constitutional amendment process.[23] However, this definition of constitutional revolution is not helpful while examining significant systemic changes that take place without interfering with the text of the constitution. In this case, it would seem to be more appropriate to refer to the notion of 'constitutional moment' as defined by Bruce Ackerman.[24] The 'constitutional moment' is a phenomenon whereby – under the conditions indicated by Ackerman – the constitution is modified in violation of the procedural requirements of constitutional amendment or outside the constitutional amendment procedure.[25] Therefore, the concept of 'constitutional moment' allows constitutional revolutions that enjoy strong public support to be legitimised. Ackerman bases his views on the assumptions of the dualist theory of democracy (distinguishing between higher lawmaking and normal politic) and reinterpreted popular constitutionalism. The traditional approach to popular constitutionalism recognises judicial review (or at least a version of it involving judicial supremacy) as an anti-democratic element of the political system.[26] On the other hand, Bruce Ackerman accepts that the sovereign (the People) at certain historical moments of political mobilisation may also bring about a significant systemic change (a kind of constitutional revolution) precisely through interpretation of the constitution in the process of constitutional review.[27] The jurisprudence of the US Supreme Court thus becomes an expression of popular lawmaking. The consequence of such a take on the role of the Supreme Court is a modified understanding of the basic ideas of the philosophy of law and political philosophy, such as representation or democracy. The concept of the people is separated from the relationship with a specific empirical community. It is worth adding that this process of conceptually transforming elite organs into representatives of the sovereign will go beyond the American context, as exemplified by the concepts of Pierre

22 For more on the subject of constitutional revolution and revolutional constitutionalism cf. G.J. Jacobson, Theorizing the Constitutional Revolution, Journal of Law and Courts 2016, vol. 2, no. 1, pp. 1–32; G. J. Jacobson, Y. Roznai, Constitutional Revolution, Yale University Press 2020; B. Ackerman, Revolutionary Constitutions. Charismatic Leadership and the Rule of Law, Harvard University Press 2019; R. Albert, Revolutionary Constitutionalism. Law, Legitimacy, Power, Hart Publishing 2020; S. Gardbaum, Revolutionary Constitutionalism, International Journal of Constitutional Law 2017, vol. 15, no. 1, pp. 173–200.

23 H. Kelsen, General Theory of Law and State 1967, p. 209.

24 B. Ackerman, We, the People, Volume 1: Foundations, Harvard University Press, 1991.

25 B. Ackerman, We, the People, Volume 1: Foundations, Harvard University Press, 1991.

26 J. Waldron, Law and Disagreement, Oxford University Press, Oxford 1999; M. Tushnet, Taking the Constitution Away from the Courts, Princeton University Press, Princeton 1999; L. Kramer, The People Themselves: Popular Constitutionalism and Judicial Review, Oxford University Press, Oxford 2004; L. Kramer, Popular Constitutionalism, California Law Review 2004, vol. 92, pp. 959–1012.

27 B. Ackerman, We the people, Foundations, Harvard University Press 1993, str. 23–25.

Rosanvallon and Dominique Rousseau.[28] In Bruce Ackerman's theory, for the people to take over the constitutive power thereby enabling constitutional amendment, four phases must occur: signalling, proposal, general deliberation and codification. Ackerman presents these stages against the background of a model view, where the political movement has received sufficient support to guarantee its participation in the process of higher legislation.[29]

Bruce Ackerman's theory of constitutional moment was originally formulated in relation to the US political system and takes into account its specificity.[30] Nevertheless, numerous academic attempts to apply Ackerman's theory to systemic changes occurring in other countries[31] may justify asking whether Poland is now facing a constitutional moment, and if the activity of the Constitutional Tribunal after 2015 can be conceptualised as a manifestation of popular lawmaking. It should be noted, however, that Bruce Ackerman's theory of constitutional moment fits within the paradigm of liberal revolution.[32] Although revolution means the reorganisation of collective life according to new principles, according to Ackerman, in modern liberal democracies it is impossible to amend all these principles and that a revolution may be described as 'total'. That is why liberal revolutionists insist on limiting the scope of the transformations as much as possible. Thus, a revolution in the liberal approach means that, despite significant systemic changes, it does not break with a certain continuity.[33]

In the case of the systemic changes taking place in Poland since 2015, there is no doubt that there will be some systemic continuity, yet their nature and the accompanying political rhetoric prove that they are illiberal in nature and are described by most constitutionalists as a symptom of the crisis of the rule of law as well as democratic backsliding. So, one must consider whether, despite their illiberal nature, they fit within the model formulated by Bruce Ackerman. If not, then it is possible to conceptualise them as an (illiberal) counter-constitutional revolution, i.e. a revolution which, despite maintaining nominal systemic continuity, due to its illiberal nature, constitutes a breach of the essence of the current (liberal)

28 P. Rosanvallon, La Légitimité démocratique. Impartialité, réflexivité, proximité, Paryż 2008, D. Rousseau, Constitutionnalisme et démocratie, https://laviedesidees.fr/IMG/pdf/20080919_drousseau.pdf.

29 B. Ackerman, We the people, Foundations, Harvard University Press 1993, str. 266.

30 S. Choudhry, Ackerman's Higher Lawmaking in Comparative Constitutional Perspective: Constitutional Moments as Constitutional Failures?, International Journal of Constitutional Law 2008, vol. 6, issue 2, p. 196.

31 B. Ackerman, The Future of Liberal Revolution, Yale University Press 1992; S. Choudhry, Ackerman's Higher Lawmaking in Comparative Constitutional Perspective: Constitutional Moments as Constitutional Failures?, International Journal of Constitutional Law 2008, vol. 6, issue 2, pp. 193–230; R. Dixon, G. Baldwin, Globalizing Constitutional Moments? A Reflection on the Japanese Article 9 Debate, The American Journal of Comparative Law, 2019, vol. 67, issue 1, pp. 145–176; C. Powell, Libya: A Multilateral Constitutional Moment?, American Journal of International Law 2012, vol. 106, issue 2, pp. 298–316.

32 B. Ackerman, The Future of the Liberal Revolution, Yale University Press 1992.

33 B. Ackerman, The Future of the Liberal Revolution, Yale University Press, pp. 9–11.

constitution. Such a hypothesis requires consideration of the role of the Constitutional Tribunal in the ongoing process of change. Can the activity of the Constitutional Tribunal after 2015 be described as an element of the counter-constitutional revolution?

The question posed in the title (illiberal turn or counter-constitutional revolution) does not present a completely mutually exclusive alternative. Recognising the activity of the Constitutional Tribunal after 2015 as an illiberal turn (referring to the notions of illiberal democracy and illiberal constitutionalism) does not preclude its simultaneous classification as an element of the counter-constitutional revolution in the sense given above. However, such a conceptualisation means that the activities of the Constitutional Tribunal, as well as other systemic changes taking place in Poland since 2015, do not fit within the model of Bruce Ackerman's constitutional moment and the constitutional revolution (carried out within the liberal paradigm).

The answer to the title question requires an analysis of the activities of the Constitutional Tribunal in a broader historical context.

3 The Polish Constitutional Tribunal before 2015

The history of judicial review in Poland is relatively short (compared to the United States or some countries in Western Europe) and is just over 30 years old. The decision to introduce a centralised model of constitutional review and to establish the Constitutional Tribunal was made in 1982, still during the period of martial law.[34] The Constitutional Tribunal was established by the Act of 26 March 1982, amending the Constitution of the Polish People's Republic. Thus, Poland was the only country from the socialist bloc (apart from Yugoslavia[35]), where judicial constitutional review was introduced to the political system before the system transformation.[36] From the very beginning, the Constitutional Tribunal was treated as an 'unwanted child' of the socialist regime.[37] The introduction of a judicial review of constitutionality (similarly to the establishment of the State Tribunal in the same act of constitutional amendment as well as the appointment of the Ombudsman in 1987) was a response to growing social discontent caused by the

34 Martial law was introduced on 13 December 1981 throughout the Polish People's Republic. Martial law was introduced by a resolution of the State Council of 12 December 1981, at the request of the Military Council for National Salvation – a temporary, unconstitutional authority, de facto superior to the constitutional state authorities. Martial law was not lifted until 22 July 1983 (it was suspended from 31 December 1982). During its duration, a total of 10,131 activists associated with 'Solidarity' (a nationwide trade union established in 1980, which turned into the main centre of opposition to the government of the Polish People's Republic) were interned, and about 40 people lost their lives.

35 Yugoslavia established a constitutional court in 1963.

36 Ján Mazák, The European model of constitutional review of legislation, https://www.venice.coe.int/SACJF/2006_02_Venice_Strasbourg/report_mazak.htm.

37 M. Brzezinski, in Constitutional 'Refolution' in the Ex-Communist World: The Rule of Law, American University International Law Review 1997, vol. 12, pp. 90–91.

economic crisis. The authorities were afraid of the new institution; hence it took three years to work on the law that would enable the functioning of the Constitutional Tribunal, during which time a total of 15 projects of the legal act were drafted.[38] The Act of 29 April 1985, which was finally passed, was a compromise between supporters of judicial constitutional review coming mainly from legal circles and the political majority still rooted psychologically in a system based on the supremacy of the parliament (and in fact of the socialist party). The position and powers of the Tribunal were limited. Decisions on the unconstitutionality of laws were not final and could be rejected by a resolution of the Sejm adopted by a two-thirds majority. (It should be added, however, that the same majority was needed to amend the Constitution of the Polish People's Republic.)

The Constitutional Tribunal officially began adjudicating on 1 January 1986. Its members consisted of 12 judges elected for an eight-year term. The first three years of the Constitutional Tribunal was a period of quite conservative jurisprudence. Until the end of 1988, the Constitutional Tribunal focused on the control of sub-statutory acts. Only three of the 33 cases adjudicated by the Constitutional Tribunal in 1986–1989 concerned legal acts, and only one was found to be unconstitutional.[39]

After 1989, the Constitutional Tribunal's activism grew significantly. This was influenced (apart from the dynamically changing political situation in the country) by a significant shift in the composition of the Constitutional Tribunal; half of the judges ended their terms of office and in November 1989 they were replaced by six new ones, supported by Solidarity.[40] With this 'refreshed line-up', the Constitutional Tribunal played a key role in the most important phase of the political transformation. The basic tool in this process turned out to be the activist interpretation, introduced in December 1989 to Art. 1 of the Constitution of the Polish People's Republic of 1952, of the rule of law (literally: a democratic state ruled by law).[41] In its jurisprudence, the Constitutional Tribunal assumed that as a consequence of the principle of a democratic state ruled by law introduced to Art. 1 of the Constitution of the Polish People's Republic, then a number of other important constitutional principles and fundamental rights would come into force (not explicitly included in the then-binding text of the constitution), such as the tripartition of power,[42] the prohibition of legal retroactivity,[43] the principle of

38 Robert Alberski: Trybunał Konstytucyjny w polskich systemach politycznych. Wrocław: Wydawnictwo Uniwersytetu Wrocławskiego, 2010, s. 112.

39 Aleksandra Kustra-Rogatka, The Polish Constitutional Court and the Political 'Refolution' after 1989: Between the Continuity and Discontinuity of the Constitutional Narrative, Wroclaw Review of Law, Administration and Economics 2016, vol. 6, pp. 66–67.

40 Aleksandra Kustra-Rogatka, The Polish Constitutional Court and the Political 'Refolution' after 1989: Between the Continuity and Discontinuity of the Constitutional Narrative, Wroclaw Review of Law, Administration and Economics 2016, vol. 6, pp. 67–68.

41 Dz. U. z 1989 r. No. 75, Item 444.

42 The Constitutional Tribunal ruling of 19 August 1992, U 6/92.

43 The Constitutional Tribunal ruling of 22 August 1990, K 7/90.

citizens' trust in the state and the law it creates[44] (meaning, *inter alia*, the duty to take into account the legal and social effects of a new law when creating inter-temporal provisions), the principle of equality,[45] the right to a fair trial[46] and the right to privacy.[47] On the one hand, this activism of the Constitutional Tribunal allowed for a rapid transition of the legal system, but on the other hand, it was also criticised by some legal philosophers.[48]

Art. 2 of the 1997 Constitution of the Republic of Poland, currently in force, repeats the wording of Art. 1 of the Constitution of 1952 (in the version after the amendment of 1989), and the Constitutional Tribunal, after the Constitution of 1997 entered into force, concluded that the jurisprudence developed so far regarding the principles of the rule of law remains valid,[49] although some of the previous constitutional principles and fundamental rights, previously derived from the rule of law, were clearly entered into the text of the Constitution of 1997 (including the principle of the tripartition of power,[50] *nullum crimen sine lege*,[51] the right to a fair trial[52] and the right to privacy[53]).

The Constitution of 1997 strengthened the current political position of the Constitutional Tribunal, mainly by introducing the finality of judgments given by the Constitutional Tribunal.[54] Moreover, it modified the existing regulations regarding the composition and jurisdictions of the Constitutional Tribunal. The number of judges increased from 12 to 15, which was justified by the extension of the jurisdictions of the Constitutional Tribunal, mainly to adjudicating on constitutional complaints. The judges' term of office was extended from eight to nine years.[55] The only, but significant, loss of the existing jurisdictions concerned the establishment (in the form of abstract resolutions) of the so-called generally applicable interpretation of law.[56] These changes at the constitutional level needed

44 The Constitutional Tribunal ruling of 22 August 1990, K 7/90.
45 The Constitutional Tribunal ruling of 8 May 1990, K 1/90.
46 The Constitutional Tribunal ruling of 7 January 1990, K 8/91.
47 The Constitutional Tribunal ruling of 24 June 1997, K 21/96.
48 L. Morawski, Spór o pojęcie państwa prawnego, 'Państwo i Prawo' 4/1994, pp. 3–12.
49 Judgment of the Constitutional Tribunal of 25 November 1997, K 26/97.
50 Art. 10 of the 1997 Constitution.
51 Art. 42(1) of the 1997 Constitution.
52 Art. 45 of the 1997 Constitution.
53 Art. 47 of the 1997 Constitution.
54 The Sejm, under a transitional provision (Art. 239 (1) of the 1997 Constitution), could for two more years (until 17 October 1999) reject by a majority of two-thirds votes in the presence of at least half of the statutory number of deputies the decisions of the Constitutional Tribunal on the unconstitutionality of legal acts, but only those enacted before the entry into force of the new constitution. The same did not apply to judgments issued as a result of legal questions referred to the Tribunal by courts (these were final).
55 Leszek Garlicki (ed.), Konstytucja Rzeczypospolitej Polskiej. Komentarz,vol. IV. Warszawa: Wydawnictwo Sejmowe 2005, p. 4 (Chapter VIII. art. 194), pp. 4–8.
56 Piotr Winczorek, Komentarz do Konstytucji Rzeczypospolitej Polskiej z dnia 2 kwietnia 1997 roku. Warszawa: Wydawnictwo Liber 2008, p. 371.

to be reflected and detailed at the statutory level, which led to the adoption of the new Constitutional Tribunal Act (the Act of 1 August 1997).[57]

Pursuant to the binding Constitution, the scope of the Constitutional Tribunal's jurisdiction includes what may be broadly understood as constitutional review (both *ex ante* and *ex post*, including legal questions from courts and constitutional complaints), adjudication on the unconstitutionality of objectives and activities of political parties, resolving jurisdiction disputes (between central, constitutional organs of state) and adjudicating on the temporary replacement of the President of the Republic of Poland by the Marshal of the Sejm (when the President himself cannot delegate his duties to the Marshal).[58]

After 1997, the Constitutional Tribunal built up its constitutional and social authority fairly consistently. After a relatively short space of time, citizens became convinced of the need for constitutional complaint, introduced in 1997, which in Poland means the typical constitutional control of a legal provision (rather than a court ruling or an administrative decision *per se*). The number of legal questions from courts also increased. Of course, as is the case with any constitutional court, some judgments of the Polish Constitutional Tribunal have been severely criticised, but until 2015 the Constitutional Tribunal had been an organ of state that had enjoyed considerable social authority, and until 2015 had never been the object of a direct political attack.[59]

4 The political background of the rule of law crisis in Poland

The formal start of the crisis surrounding the Constitutional Tribunal was the adoption in June 2015 of a new act on the Constitutional Tribunal (the Act of 25 June 2015), which was to replace the 1997 act in force. Although the assumptions of the draft act were developed by a team that included, among others, retired Constitutional Tribunal judges,[60] and the draft itself was primarily aimed at streamlining the proceedings by the Constitutional Tribunal, while the draft bill was being processed by the Sejm, one MP from the then ruling coalition (Civic Platform–Polish People's Party) submitted a draft of an unconstitutional transitional provision establishing a 30-day deadline for submitting candidates for Constitutional Tribunal judges. This provision was to apply to candidates chosen to replace five judges of the Tribunal whose terms of office expired in November and December 2015. The official justification for its introduction was the desire to avoid a situation in which the work of the Constitutional Tribunal would be blocked due to a failure to promptly fill the 5 judicial vacancies in relation to the

57 Journal of Laws of 1997, no. 102, item 643, as amended.

58 Cf. Art. 188, Art. 189, Art. 79, Art. 122, Art. 193 and Art. 131(1) of the 1997 Constitution.

59 Aleksandra Kustra, Poland's Constitutional Crisis. From Court-packing Agenda to Denial of Constitutional Court's Judgments, Toruńskie Studia Polsko-Włoskie/Studi Polacco-Italiani di Torun 2016, vol. XII, p. 344.

60 M. Szuleka, M. Wolny, M. Szwed, Kryzys konstytucyjny w Polsce 2015–2016, Helsińska Fundacja Praw Człowieka, 2016, p. 10.

upcoming parliamentary elections and the possibility that a situation may arise whereby the new Sejm would not fill the vacancies in time. However, this was in fact a question of the then ruling coalition filling the five judges' posts, since they were afraid of defeat in the upcoming parliamentary elections.

The controversial provision, despite numerous critical voices, was included in the final version of the adopted act of law, which entered into force on 30 August 2015. According to the adopted transitional provision, 5 new Constitutional Tribunal judges were chosen by the previous Sejm during its final session, i.e. 8–9 October 2015 (the so-called October judges). In response, a group of MPs from the then opposition (including, in particular, Law and Justice MPs) submitted a request to the constitutional court to review the constitutionality of the provisions of the Act of 25 June 2015. At the same time, President Andrzej Duda (who had held the office of the head of state since August 2015, and previously a European parliamentarian elected from the Law and Justice list) did not take the oath from the so-called October judges.[61] It is worth adding that until 2015 the President had never delayed taking the oath from the Constitutional Tribunal judges appointed by Sejm. Nevertheless, the President of Poland, Andrzej Duda, uplifted a mere formality to a codetermination mechanism without any constitutional basis therefore and refused to take the oath of office from all the five 'October judges'. As a consequence, three seats in the Constitutional Tribunal remained vacant. The newly selected judges became trapped in a procedural deadlock, and the pending replacement process was frozen.[62]

In the parliamentary elections on 25 October 2015, Law and Justice (previously in opposition) won 37.5 per cent of the votes and obtained 235 seats in the Sejm. This result made it possible to form a government on its own – for the first time since the 1989 elections.[63] However, Law and Justice's victory meant that the earlier motion to the Constitutional Tribunal to examine the constitutionality of the controversial transitional provision of the new act on the Constitutional Tribunal was withdrawn (which meant that the proceedings in this case were discontinued).[64] It is worth adding that after Law and Justice withdrew the motion, the opposition submitted a motion to the Constitutional Tribunal that duplicated Law and Justice's previous allegations, including the unconstitutionality of the controversial transitional provision of the act.[65] Obviously, this move was of a

61 A. Rytel-Warzocha, A. Szmyt, Kilka uwag na temat aktualnych przemian konstytucyjnych w Polsce, in Dookoła Wojtek... : księga pamiątkowa poświęcona Doktorowi Arturowi Wojciechowi Preisnerowi, eds. R. Balicki, M. Jabłoński, K. Wójtowicz, 2018, p. 190.

62 A. Kustra, The Polish Constitutional Crisis ... Studia Polsko-Włoskie, s. 346–347. See also A. Śledzińska-Simon, A. Śledzińska-Simon, available at: Midnight Judges: Poland's Constitutional Tribunal Caught Between Political Fronts, VerfBlog, 2015/11/23, http://verfassungsblog.de/midnight-judges-polands-constitutional-tribunal-caught-between-political-fronts/.

63 A. Szmyt, Spór o tryb wyboru i kadencję Prezesa Trybunału Konstytucyjnego., Przegląd Sejmowy 2016, no. 2 (133), p. 10.

64 M. Szuleka, M. Wolny, M. Szwed, *Kryzys konstytucyjny* ..., pp. 12–15.

65 Motion of 17 November 2015, case K 34/15.

pragmatic nature – to give the Constitutional Tribunal a chance to resolve the constitutional problem which had been, in a constitutionally questionable manner, resolved by the Sejm at the statutory level. The fact that Law and Justice withdrew its motion to the Constitutional Tribunal after winning the parliamentary elections sheds a slightly different light on the causes of the crisis surrounding the Constitutional Tribunal in Poland. This proves the ill will of Law and Justice. The controversial transitional provision introduced into the Act of 2015 was only a convenient pretext to start the implementation of the long-planned deep system changes, carried out via acts that ignored the Constitution of 1997.

In order to fully explain the genesis of the rule of law crisis in Poland that began in 2015, a slightly broader political and social context should be outlined. Law and Justice had already been a member of a ruling coalition in 2005–2007. The parliamentary crisis in 2007, however, led to an early parliamentary election in 2007, won by Civic Platform [Pol: Platforma Obywatelska] – the second largest party on the Polish political scene. For two terms of the Sejm, Civic Platform formed a ruling coalition with the Polish People's Party [Pol: Polskie Stronnictwo Ludowe] until their defeat in the parliamentary elections. Back in 2005–2007, Law and Justice had already used the political slogan that they would build a 'Fourth Republic', postulating the need to make fundamental changes in the Polish political system and criticising the constitutional foundations of the Third Republic (this is how the Polish state was defined in the Constitution of 1997).[66] The postulates of Law and Justice assumed, among others, a moral revival in public life, based on national and democratic traditions, the necessity to re-create many laws and institutions, social solidarity (in opposition to economic neoliberalism) and the primacy of Polish constitutional law over international law. One of the main elements of the political programme of the Law and Justice Party was the reforming of the judiciary, justified not only by the prolonged duration of court proceedings, but also by the communist past of some Polish judges.

After winning the parliamentary elections in 2015, Law and Justice resumed the implementation of its political postulates. Nevertheless, in accordance with the rule of law, a political plan to build a state based on such a thoroughly modified constitutional axiology and based on a significantly modified political system requires a formal constitutional amendment. Law and Justice, although it won the parliamentary elections in 2015 and 2019, did not obtain the majority necessary in Poland to amend the constitution (two-thirds in the Sejm and an absolute majority in the Senate).[67] All system reforms were introduced through statute law.

A broader time perspective (taking into account the years 2015–2020) enables one to form the thesis that the introduction of a controversial transitional provision to the final version of the Constitutional Tribunal Act of 2015 was the formal beginning of the constitutional crisis surrounding the Constitutional Tribunal, but the deeper causes of the ongoing crisis of the rule of law in Poland lie elsewhere

66 The official name of the Polish state is the 'Republic of Poland'.

67 The procedure for amending the Polish Basic Law is governed by Art. 235 of the Constitution.

and are related to Law and Justice's efforts to implement – at all costs – its own political vision of the state, even in violation of the constitutional norms. The transitional provision in the 2015 Constitutional Tribunal Act, which allowed the Sejm to elect five judges of the Constitutional Tribunal with *pro futuro* effect, was an obvious and cardinal error of the then ruling coalition, and its real goal was to stop (in a manner violating the Constitution) the forthcoming political tsunami.[68]

5 The fight over the Constitutional Tribunal: 2015–2016

After victory in the 2015 parliamentary elections, the Sejm immediately began working on the amendment to the 2015 Constitutional Tribunal Act on the Constitutional Tribunal. According to the official rhetoric of the new parliamentary majority, it was supposed to remedy the constitutional flaws in this law. The amendment to the act was rushed through on 19 November 2015 (hereinafter, the amendment of 19 November 2015), and a day later it was signed by Law and Justice-aligned President Duda. The amendment came into force after 14 days of *vacatio legis*. In addition to the repeal (with retroactive effect) of the controversial transitional provision, the amendment provided for, *inter alia*:

1 the introduction of a new transitional provision, under which candidates for Constitutional Tribunal judges replacing those whose term of office expires in 2015 had to be submitted within seven days of the entry into force of the amendment,
2 expiry of the term of office of the current President and Vice-President of the Constitutional Tribunal within three months from the date of entry into force of the act and the election of a new President of the Constitutional Tribunal under new rules.[69]

On 25 November, just a few days after the adoption of the amendment of 19 November 2015, the parliament declared 'no legal force' regarding five previous Sejm resolutions (resolutions from 8 October) regulating the election of new judges for the Constitutional Tribunal.[70] Again, despite numerous objections, including from the Constitutional Tribunal itself,[71] the resolutions were adopted

68 The Venice Commission issued an opinion during March 2016 that 'the conflict over the Constitutional Tribunal originated from the activities of the previous Sejm' and that 'both the previous and the present parliamentary majority took unconstitutional actions'.
69 M. Szuleka, M. Wolny, M. Szwed, Kryzys konstytucyjny …, p. 17.
70 A. Rytel-Warzocha, A. Szmyt, Kilka uwag…, p. 190.
71 As a reaction to the Sejm's resolutions of 25 November, on 30 November the Constitutional Tribunal held in a full court sitting and issued an injunction ordering all public authorities to abstain from any actions which might undermine the effectiveness of the pending review of constitutionality of the law. The injunction was preventive in nature, had the effect of final judgment and was binding to those to whom it was addressed. Its aim was to make sure that any future decision given in the case on merits by the Constitutional Tribunal would be enforceable and devoid of purpose.

and published, regardless of the lack of legal basis for doing so.[72] At the same session, the Sejm also amended the Sejm Regulations, allowing the Marshal of the Sejm to set a date for presenting candidates for judges of the Constitutional Tribunal.[73] The deadline was set for 1 December 2015. A day later, on 2 December, the Sejm elected five new judges (the so-called December judges), thus ignoring the Constitutional Tribunal's recommendations to refrain from performing any activities until the Tribunal had issued a ruling in this case.[74]

In the judgment of 3 December 2015 (K 34/15), the Tribunal ruled on the opposition's motion, which repeated accusations from the previously withdrawn Law and Justice motion. The Constitutional Tribunal found that most of the provisions of the law that had previously criticised Law and Justice were consistent with the constitution. At the same time, the Constitutional Tribunal ruled that the controversial transitional provision of the 2015 Constitutional Tribunal Act was partially inconsistent with the constitution – in so far as it concerned two judges whose terms of office ended after the first session of the newly elected Sejm. The Constitutional Tribunal found that the election of three judges of the Tribunal in place of those judges whose term of office ended in November was consistent with the constitution. In justification of the Constitutional Tribunal's judgment, it was stressed that the constitution infers the obligation of the Sejm to elect a judge of the Tribunal during the term of office during which the position of a judge of the Tribunal was vacated. The expression 'the Constitutional Tribunal is composed of 15 judges individually elected by the Sejm' indicates that it is not about any Sejm, but one whose temporal scope coincides with the date of expiry or expiry of the term of office of a judge of the Tribunal. Of course, it is possible that a situation may arise whereby the Sejm may not be able to fill the position of a judge of the Tribunal due to various extenuating circumstances, such as, for example, the lack of support for a candidate or short deadlines for the election procedure due to imminent parliamentary elections. In such a case, the obligation to elect a judge of the Tribunal naturally passes to the next Sejm. A temporary vacancy in the composition of the Tribunal is also constitutionally acceptable, provided that it is the result of a combination of justified extenuating circumstances, and not a strategy or measure chosen by a state authority.[75] The Constitutional Tribunal also emphasised that accepting the oath from a newly elected judge is the responsibility of the President and should be made immediately,[76] and 'upon the entry into force of this judgment, no state authority has any legal grounds to question – as

Cf. A. Kustra, Poland's Constitutional Crisis, T.T. Koncewicz, T. T. Koncewicz, Bruised but not dead (yet): The Polish Constitutional Court has spoken, available at: http://verfassungsblog.de/bruised-but-not-dead-yet-the-polish-constitutional-courthas-spoken-2/.

72 M. Szuleka, M. Wolny, M. Szwed, Kryzys konstytucyjny ..., p. 18

73 Resolution of the Sejm of the Republic of Poland of 26 November 2015 on amendments to the Regulations of the Sejm of the Republic of Poland, M.P. 2015 item 1136.

74 M. Szuleka, M. Wolny, M. Szwed, Kryzys konstytucyjny ..., p. 19.

75 Cf. part III point 6.17 of the justification of the judgment K 34/15.

76 M. Szuleka, M. Wolny, M. Szwed, Kryzys konstytucyjny ..., pp. 20–21.

unconstitutional – these provisions regulating the element of the procedure for electing a judge of the Tribunal'.[77]

The constitutional crisis could have been resolved after judgment 34/15 of the Constitutional Tribunal. Law and Justice, however, aimed not so much at reforming the unconstitutional legal status, but at a genuine 'hostile takeover' of the Constitutional Tribunal. This thesis is confirmed by the proceedings of Prime Minister B. Kempa, who did not allow the judgment of the Constitutional Tribunal to be published (as is necessary for it to impart legal effects).[78] Ultimately, the judgment was published in the *Journal of Laws*, almost two weeks after its announcement. However, a new ace was yet to be played – a new amending act put forward by Law and Justice on 15 December 2015.[79]

After its entry into force, the amendment of 19 November 2015 was brought to the Constitutional Tribunal for appeal (joint motions of the Ombudsman, the National Council of the Judiciary, the First President of the Supreme Court and a group of opposition MPs). The applicants questioned both the content of the provisions of the amendment of 19 November 2015 and the procedure for adopting the act. The Tribunal resolved this case in a judgment issued on 9 December 2015 (ref. K 35/15). The Constitutional Tribunal found unconstitutional, *inter alia*, provisions on the re-election of judges, as well as on the dismissal of the function of the then President and Vice-President of the Constitutional Tribunal.[80] At the same time, although it strongly criticised the legislative procedure regarding work on the act, it found that it did not infringe the provisions of the Constitution, but 'only' the provisions of the Sejm's regulations.

In response to the judgments of the Constitutional Tribunal in cases K 34/15 and K 35/15, Law and Justice began work on another amendment to the 2015 Act on the Constitutional Tribunal. In a controversial manner, the act was passed on 22 December 2015 (hereinafter the amendment of 22 December 2015). It entered into force on 28 December 2015 on the day of its announcement, without *vacatio legis*.[81] The act introduced new regulations concerning proceedings before the Constitutional Tribunal, which de facto resulted in freezing the judicial activity of this body. *Inter alia*, the act imposed the obligation to adjudicate in almost all cases with a full court and in the order in which cases were submitted (rather than their weight), increased the number of full judges from nine to 13, and introduced the requirement of a two-thirds majority to issue a final judgment in place of the simple majority.

An appeal was brought to the Constitutional Tribunal against the amendment of 22 December 2015 by a group of opposition MPs, the First President of the Supreme Court, the Ombudsman and the National Council of the Judiciary. On 9 March 2016, the Tribunal of 12 judges issued a judgment in this case (K 47/15)

77 Judgment of the Constitutional Tribunal of 3 December 2015, file ref. no. K 34/15
78 In the opinion of the Prime Minister, the judgment was passed without a proper panel of judges and is therefore invalid. Cf. A. Kustra,
79 A. Kustra, Poland's Constitutional Crisis…, p. 350.
80 Judgment of the Constitutional Tribunal of 9 December 2015, file ref. No. K 35/15.
81 Journal of Laws of 2015, item 2217.

and ruled that the amendment of 22 December 2015 was entirely inconsistent with the constitution (both the legislative procedure and the content of the act were deemed unconstitutional). After the ruling, Prime Minister Beata Szydło announced that it would not be published because, in her opinion, adjudicating without the provisions of the new law was a violation of the procedure. She referred to the judgment in case K 47/15 as 'the position of some judges of the Constitutional Tribunal'. The judgment was not published in the official journal until 5 June 2018.

In response to the judgment of the Constitutional Tribunal in case K 47/15, Law and Justice began work on a completely new act on the Constitutional Tribunal in June 2016 (which was to replace the 2015 Act, which is still in force). Once again, the draft act evoked numerous reservations as to its compliance with the Constitution. It made provision for the introduction of numerous solutions subordinating the Constitutional Tribunal to the executive authority. Finally, the act was passed on 22 July 2016. In its judgment of 11 August 2016, the Tribunal found a number of key innovations in this act unconstitutional. The judgment of 11 August 2016 was also published in the official journal on 5 June 2018.[82]

The actions taken by the ruling majority in 2015–2016 can be summarised as a phase of progressive judicial paralysis for the Constitutional Tribunal.[83] Law and Justice was aware that the plan to take over the constitutional court would take time. As long as the majority of the composition were old judges, and the then President of the Constitutional Tribunal, Andrzej Rzepliński, did not allow stand-in judges to adjudicate, Law and Justice was unable to take full control of the Constitutional Tribunal. Therefore, at the end of 2016, with the term of office of the incumbent President of the Constitutional Tribunal drawing to a close, the choice of a new President became the key issue.

6 The final stage of the Constitutional Tribunal takeover: 2017–2018

Andrzej Rzepliński's term of office ended on 19 December 2016. Until the appointment of a new President, his duties should have been shouldered by Stanisław Biernat, the then Vice-President of the Constitutional Tribunal. Such a procedure would have guaranteed the lawfulness of the procedure for selecting a new President. Pursuant to the Constitution, he or she is appointed by the President of the Republic of Poland from among the candidates presented by the General Assembly of the Judges of the Tribunal. The General Assembly is chaired by the President (and in his or her place by the Vice-President). Unfortunately, the day after the end of Andrzej Rzepliński's term of office, President Andrzej

82 Judgment of the Constitutional Tribunal from 11 August 2016, file ref. no. K 39/16, Journal of Laws 2018, item 1078.

83 Cf. Sadurski, Polish Constitutional Tribunal Under Law and Justice: From an Activist Court, to a Paralyzes Tribunal, to a Governmental Enabler, Hague Journal on the Rule of Law 2018, vol. 11, issue 2, p. 65.

Duda decided to appoint Julia Przyłębska (one of the December judges) as 'the acting President of the Constitutional Tribunal'. One of Przyłębska's first decisions after taking over the actual leadership of the Constitutional Tribunal was to allow 'stand-in judges' to adjudicate and perform other judicial activities.

The meeting of the General Assembly, the subject of which was the selection of candidates for the President of the Tribunal, was held on 20 December 2016. Six judges took part in the vote on the selection of candidates for the President. Eight refused to participate in the vote, indicating the procedural flaws of the convened General Assembly. One of the judges could not participate in the Assembly due to being on leave, but Przyłębska decided not to postpone the appointment of candidates for the President of the Constitutional Tribunal (despite protests from some judges). In the end, J. Przyłębska was supported by five of the 15 judges of the Constitutional Tribunal (three of these 15 were 'stand-in judges'). On 21 December 2016, President Andrzej Duda appointed the President of the Constitutional Tribunal (Mariusz Muszyński – one of the 'stand-in judges' – became the Vice-President).

The legally flawed appointment of Julia Przyłębska as the President of the Constitutional Tribunal marks the beginning of the last phase of the 'takeover of the Constitutional Tribunal' by Law and Justice. It led to a significant decrease in judicial activity, the destabilisation of this body, a reduction in the number of cases (especially constitutional complaints and legal questions from courts), as well as a significant extension of the average longest deliberation period.[84] This proves the ineffectiveness of the 'reforms' of the Constitutional Tribunal introduced by subsequent amendments, which in fact had a negative impact on the functioning of the Polish constitutional court. The act on the organization and proceedings before the Constitutional Tribunal passed on 30 November 2016 (hereinafter the Act of 30 November 2016) prepared the legislative ground for the final stage of the Constitutional Tribunal takeover. Apart from the reorganisation of the current administrative structure of the Constitutional Tribunal (liquidation of the existing Constitutional Tribunal Office as of 31 December 2018), one significant consequence of this act was the provision amending the existing rules for excluding a judge from the adjudication panel. In practice, the new statutory regulations allowed Julia Przyłębska to manipulate the panel of judges in numerous ways.[85]

Currently, the Constitutional Tribunal (composed of 15 judges) consists of 14 judges elected by the Sejm of the current term of office, and thus supported by Law and Justice. One of the so-called 'old judges' Leon Kieres will end his nine-year term on 23 July 2021. Of the 14 judges elected by Law and Justice votes, three are still 'stand-in judges', i.e. those who take the place of three judges legally elected in October 2015 (two of the 'stand-in judges' appointed in December 2015 have died, and the present parliamentary majority chose new ones to replace

84 B. Szepietowska, Działalność orzecznicza ..., s. 9–10

85 M. Ziółkowski, Zmiana składu orzekającego Trybunału Konstytucyjnego. In: Funkcjonowanie Trybunału Konstytucyjnego w latach 2014–2017, The Stefan Batory Foundation 2018 pp. 135–137

them). The two candidacies (regarding non-stand-in judges) that caused the most controversy in the public debate were former parliamentarians associated with the current government: Krystyna Pawłowicz and Stanisław Piotrowicz.

7 The counter-constitutional case law of the Constitutional Tribunal in 2019–2020

After a fairly long period of effective paralysis of this body's operations, when, with the end of the so-called old judges' term of office, the majority of judges chosen by the current Sejm began to form, the Constitutional Tribunal began to adjudicate again, including in cases with a strong political context. The three most important decisions that are significant from the perspective of evaluating the judicature of the Constitutional Tribunal after Law and Justice took over this body are the judgment of 25 March 2019 regarding the constitutionality of the National Council of the Judiciary reformed by Law and Justice (K 12/18) and two judgments directly relating to internal problems related to the implementation of the Court of Justice of the European Union judgment of 19 November 2019 on the legality of the Disciplinary Chamber of the Supreme Court and (indirectly) the National Council of the Judiciary: the judgment of 20 April 2020 (U 2/20) and the decision of 21 April 2020 (Kpt 1/20). Significantly, in the last two resolutions, the role of judge-rapporteur was played by the aforementioned former parliamentarians, who actively participated in pushing through the reform of the judicial authorities and were known for their radically negative opinions about Polish courts.

Analysis of the Constitutional Tribunal's new jurisprudence in cases with a strong political accent should facilitate an answer to the question of whether we are dealing with an illiberal turn of the Constitutional Tribunal itself and if this new jurisprudence can be conceptualised as the last stage of Bruce Ackerman's constitutional moment.

All of the aforementioned resolutions aroused controversy in public opinion. Each of them is also a breach in the previous line of Constitutional Tribunal jurisprudence.

Judgment K 12/18 concerned new provisions introduced by Law and Justice regulating the composition of the National Council of the Judiciary – a body which, according to the constitution, is designed to safeguard the independence of judges. Law and Justice changed the method of appointing those members of the National Council of the Judiciary who are to represent judges (15 out of a total of 25 members). Currently, these judges are elected by the Sejm (and not by the judges themselves as previously).[86] The terms of office of the existing judges-members of the National Council of the Judiciary have been terminated.[87] This change was heavily criticised by the majority of constitutionalists and opposition politicians as being unconstitutional. Nevertheless, the Constitutional Tribunal, in its judgment of 25 March 2019, found the challenged provisions of the Act on the National Council of the Judiciary to be consistent with the constitution. At the

86 Art. 9a and 11a of the Act.
87 Art. 6 of the Act.

same time, it found the provision allowing the Supreme Administrative Court to appeal against the resolutions of the National Council of the Judiciary containing motions for the appointment of judges of the Supreme Court to be unconstitutional.

Evaluation of judgment K 12/18 requires taking into account the broader context of the systemic changes introduced in Poland since 2015. After the takeover of the Constitutional Tribunal, the next target of Law and Justice were the remaining judicial authorities, including the National Council of the Judiciary, which plays an important role in the process of appointing judges in Poland (judges are appointed by the President, but at the request of the National Court Register, which reviews the candidates). Thus, taking control of the National Council of the Judiciary was a key element in the strategy of appointing judges (including Supreme Court judges) favourable to Law and Justice.

The 1997 Constitution states in Art. 187 (1) that 'the National Council of the Judiciary shall be composed as follows: (…) 15 judges chosen from amongst the judges of the Supreme Court, common courts, administrative courts and military courts'. A literal reading of the Constitution does not, therefore, prohibit the election of members of the National Council of the Judiciary representing judges by the Sejm. Moreover, a comparative analysis of the composition of similar bodies operating in other countries leads to the conclusion that there is no single standard in this regard, and the solutions adopted in individual countries differ significantly from each other. Sometimes judges are a minority in the composition of bodies performing a role similar to that of the National Council of the Judiciary.[88] Nevertheless, in the case of the Polish National Council of the Judiciary, a key element in assessing the new procedure for appointing a significant part of the composition of the National Council of the Judiciary (members who are judges) is the introduction of a provision interrupting the term of office of the current composition of the National Council of the Judiciary. The previous jurisprudence of the Constitutional Tribunal – first of all, the judgment of 23 March 2006 (K 4/06) in full court concerning similar changes in the National Broadcasting Council – clearly indicates that such moves by the legislator are inconsistent with the Constitution.[89] Judgment K 12/18 concerning the National Council of the Judiciary (issued not in full court but in a panel of five) therefore represents a radical shift in the position of the Constitutional Tribunal in this respect.

The temporal and political context of the enactment of the amendment to the Act on the National Council of the Judiciary indicates that its real purpose was to take control of a constitutional body by ensuring its influence over the majority of the composition of the National Council of the Judiciary. Such a political practice is well known and is sometimes used in other countries, but is always treated as a violation of the institutional balance and the rule of law. By accepting it at the

88 Cf. P. Albers, W. Voermans, Councils for the Judiciary in EU Countries, https://www.researchgate.net/publication/228153259_Councils_for_the_Judiciary_in_EU_Countries; D. Kosař, Beyond Judicial Councils: Forms, Rationales and Impact of Judicial Self-Governance in Europe, German Law Journal 2018, vol. 19, issue 7, pp. 1567–1612.

89 Part IV point 3 of judgment K 4/06.

constitutional level, the Constitutional Tribunal has played the role of a body which *post factum* legitimises the violation of the constitution by the parliament.

Two more of the aforementioned judgments also concern what is broadly understood as the 'reform' of the judiciary carried out by Law and Justice, but they refer to another body whose composition has changed as a result of the amendments introduced, i.e. the Supreme Court. Moreover, both of these decisions are directly related to the EU law context.

In the judgment of 20 April 2020 (U 2/20), the Constitutional Tribunal found the resolution of the joint chambers of the Supreme Court of 23 January 2020 to be unconstitutional. At a national level, this resolution implemented the judgment of the Court of Justice of the European Union of 19 November 2019, which concerned the 'reform' of the Supreme Court introduced by Law and Justice.

In addition to lowering the retirement age of judges (which the Court of Justice of the European Union found inconsistent with EU law in the case of the European Commission v. Poland C-619/18[90]), one of the elements of this 'reform' was the introduction of two new chambers to the Supreme Court: the Extraordinary Control and Public Affairs Chamber (which is responsible, *inter alia*, for adjudicating on the validity of elections) and the Disciplinary Chamber (which adjudicates in cases of the disciplinary liability of judges). The Court of Justice of the European Union judgment of 19 November 2019 concerned the compliance of the second of the above-mentioned new chambers of the Supreme Court, as well as the National Council of the Judiciary indirectly, with the EU. The Court of Justice of the European Union did not decide (as the Attorney General did) to state openly that the Disciplinary Chamber of the Supreme Court does not meet the EU standard of an independent and impartial tribunal within the meaning of Article 47 of the Charter of Fundamental Rights, yet considered that the objective circumstances in which the Chamber was formed, its characteristics and the means by which its members have been appointed were capable of giving rise to legitimate doubts, in the minds of subjects of the law, as to the imperviousness of that court to external factors, in particular, as to the direct or indirect influence of the legislature and the executive and its neutrality with respect to the interests before it.[91]

The Court of Justice of the European Union gave the floor to the referring Supreme Court and pointed out that it is for the national court to determine, in the light of all the relevant factors, whether the Disciplinary Chamber meets the standard of an independent and impartial court. Moreover, the Court of Justice of the European Union stated loud and clear that if that is not the case, the principle of the primacy of EU law thus requires the national court to revert the relevant provisions of the Polish law.[92]

90 Judgment of the Court of Justice of the European Union of 24 June 2019.

91 A. Kustra-Rogatka, Country Report: The Rule of Law in Poland, available at: https://democracy-reporting.org/my/dri_publications/country-report-the-rule-of-law-in-poland/.

92 The resolution of the formation of the combined Civil Chamber, Criminal Chamber and Labour and Social Security Chamber of 23 January 2020, case BSA I-4110–1/20; English translation available at: http://www.sn.pl/aktualnosci/SiteAssets/Lists/Wydarzenia/AllItems/BSA%20I-4110-1_20_English.pdf.

On 23 January 2020, the Supreme Court sitting in the three chambers bench issued a binding resolution that indeed such a bench composition in the case of newly appointed Supreme Court justices is contrary to the law and their rulings may be challenged. In the case of common courts, however, it must be verified if the defect of the appointment procedure leads, in specific circumstances, to a breach of the standard of independence and impartiality. The Supreme Court held that the resolution applies to decisions issued with the involvement of judges of the Disciplinary Chamber regardless of the date on which these judgments are issued, whereas in case of other judicial bench the resolution does not act retroactively.[93]

The judgment of the Constitutional Tribunal of 20 April 2020 is another proof of its new role. It is transforming into a body used in fierce political games, not only at the national level, but also related to Poland's membership of the EU. The resolution aimed at blocking the effects of the Court of Justice of the European Union judgment of 19 November 2019 is also a transgression of the constitutional powers of the Constitutional Tribunal – indeed this concerns the constitutionality of the judicial decision (resolution of the Supreme Court), rather than a normative act. In its previous jurisprudence, the Constitutional Tribunal repeatedly indicated that in the event of doubts arising as to whether a given act falls within the sphere of applying a law or legislation, the decisive factor is not the form but the content of the act.[94] Nevertheless, in this case, there is no 'normative novelty' in the resolution of the Supreme Court of 23 January 2020, which only implements the judgment of the Court of Justice of the European Union at the national level. The political idea behind U 2/20 was to open the way for the controversial Disciplinary Chamber of the Supreme Court to resume judicial activity. Moreover, the judgment of the Constitutional Tribunal was issued shortly after the Court of Justice of the European Union decided to issue interim measures and suspend the activities of the Supreme Court Disciplinary Chamber.[95]

The decision of 21 April 2020 complements the Eurosceptic turn in the narrative of the Constitutional Tribunal and the questioning of the legality of the resolution of the Supreme Court of 23 January 2020. This decision formally resolves two 'jurisdiction disputes': one between the Sejm and the Supreme Court, and the other between the President and the Supreme Court. The first was thought to concern whether the Supreme Court had the power to issue the resolution of 23 January 2020. The second involved whether the Supreme Court could assess the legality of the act of appointing a judge (which is executed by the President). The basic problem related to the decision of the Constitutional Tribunal of 21 April 2020 is that neither one nor the other doubts of the applicants should be qualified as a dispute over jurisdiction. According to the previous jurisprudence of the Constitutional Tribunal, a dispute over jurisdiction is a situation where two or more bodies are deemed

93 A. Kustra-Rogatka, Country Report: The Rule of Law in Poland, available at: https://democracy-reporting.org/my/dri_publications/country-report-the-rule-of-law-in-poland/.

94 Cf. M. Zubik, 'Akt normatywny' jako przedmiot kontroli Trybunału Konstytucyjnego, Gdańskie Studia Prawnicze 2014, vol. XXXI, pp. 731–744.

95 Decision of the Court of Justice of the European Union of 8 April 2020, case C-791/19.

competent to resolve a given case (positive dispute), or two or more bodies consider that they do not have jurisdiction to resolve a given case (negative dispute).[96] The jurisdiction of the Supreme Court to issue the resolution of 23 January 2020 does not directly interfere with the sphere of jurisdiction of the Sejm or the President. It indirectly assesses the legality of these bodies' actions, but does not interfere with the jurisdictions of the legislative or executive power. The Constitutional Tribunal's resolution of 21 April 2020 is a breach in the existing – and rather self-restrained – jurisprudence of the Constitutional Tribunal concerning disputes over jurisdiction. Although the alleged constitutional problem is embedded in the sphere of domestic law, the decision of 21 April (as well as the judgment of 20 April) is a decision of fundamental importance for relations between Poland and the EU. The previous jurisprudence of the Constitutional Tribunal concerning the constitutional aspects of EU membership (including the status of EU law within the Polish legal order) has followed the 'course' set by the constitutional courts of the Member States. The Polish Constitutional Tribunal was certainly not as Europhile as the Belgian constitutional court or the Austrian Federal Constitutional Tribunal[97], but its jurisprudence in EU-related matters cannot be called Eurosceptic. The Constitutional Tribunal has repeatedly highlighted the primacy of the Polish constitution,[98] but in practice it has always adjudicated in such a way as to ensure the effective application of EU law within the Polish legal order.[99] Therefore, the judgment of 20 April 2020 and the decision of 21 April 2020 are not only a breakthrough in the existing jurisprudence on purely domestic issues, but also an evident shift towards the Eurosceptic trait of illiberalism.

8 Conclusions

An analysis of the changes that have taken place in the Constitutional Tribunal since Law and Justice took power in 2015 leads to the conclusion that this typically counter-majoritarian institution has radically changed its role. From a fairly

96 Cf. S. Wronkowska-Jaśkiewicz, Kilka uwag o sporze kompetencyjnym między Sejmem RP i Sądem Najwyższym oraz Prezydentem RP i Sądem Najwyższym, 'Palestra' 2020/5, pp. 46–59.

97 Such an evaluation of the jurisprudence of the Belgian SK and Austrian SK is primarily due to the fact that these courts are the leaders in the number of questions referred for a preliminary ruling to the CJEU. Nevertheless, in recent years, certain decisions concerning the membership of said courts in the EU have raised a great deal of controversy. Cf. P. Gérard, W. Verrijdt, Belgian Constitutional Court Adopts National Identity Discourse Belgian Constitutional Court no. 62/2016, 28 April 2016, European Constitutional Law Review 2017, vol. 13, pp. 182–205; A. Orator, The Decision of the Austrian *Verfassungsgerichtshof* on the EU Charter of Fundamental Rights: An Instrument of Leverage or Rearguard Action?, German Law Journal 2016, vol. 16, issue 6, pp. 1429–1448.

98 K 18/04, P 1/05, SK 45/09, K 32/09.

99 For example, P 1/05, in which the Constitutional Tribunal obliged the parliament to amend the constitution so as to ensure its compliance with the European Arrest Warrant and obliged the courts to apply the Framework Decision on the EAW until the amendment to the constitution entered into force.

activist court, one of the main actors of the political transition of the 1990s, it became a body which post-factum legitimises the systemic changes violating the Constitution of 1997. The court-packing strategy and the paralysis of the Constitutional Tribunal, which continued until Julia Przyłębska was appointed President of the Constitutional Tribunal, were elements of a broader political project to take over all organs of the judiciary. The rhetoric of Law and Justice criticising the Constitutional Tribunal was one of the tools used to undermine the social authority of this institution. Actions aimed at taking over the constitutional court fit into the concept of illiberal democracy, understood both on the descriptive (Faraki's definition) and normative levels (a political programme referring to the idea of majority democracy and political constitutionalism with the aim of destroying the existing separation of powers (check and balance) and creating a state that would correspond to the vision of the current parliamentary majority).

In formal terms, the shifts that have occurred in the Constitutional Tribunal since 2015 are a manifestation of 'illiberal constitutionalism', one of whose key elements is 'packing and paralysing the constitutional court'.[100] The rulings of the Constitutional Tribunal from 2019–2020 presented in this chapter prove that there has already been an 'illiberal turn' in the Constitutional Tribunal itself. This body has resumed adjudication on cases with a strong political context. Apart from the issues related to the formal shortcomings of these decisions (with the participation of so-called 'stand-in judges'), the content of the analysed judgments proves that an illiberal turn has indeed occurred. They formally legitimise actions of the parliament that violate the constitution. The last two of the discussed decisions of the Constitutional Tribunal, due to their significant impact on Poland's membership of the EU, also prove that illiberalism vehemently challenges the European project, rejects all dialogue, agreed norms and established conventions.[101]

The conceptualisation of the shift that took place in the Constitutional Tribunal after 2015 as an 'illiberal turn' concerns both the formal level (the shortcomings in the procedure for appointing Constitutional Tribunal judges, the participation of 'stand-in judges' in adjudication panels, the flawed procedure of appointing the President of the Constitutional Tribunal, the manipulation of Constitutional Tribunal adjudication boards) and the legitimisation of violations of the constitution by the parliamentary majority.

Nevertheless, the definition of changes in the Constitutional Tribunal after 2015 as an 'illiberal' turn does not exclude the question of the legitimacy of the 'new' jurisprudence of the Constitutional Tribunal as an element of the constitutional revolution (in a broader sense, going beyond the paradigm of the strictly legal constitutionalism). It is in this context that one must consider whether Poland currently faces a constitutional moment and the new jurisprudence of the Constitutional Tribunal may be considered judicial higher-law making. The

100 T. Drinoczi, A. Bień-Kacała, Illiberal Constitutionalism: The Case of Hungary and Poland, German Law Journal 2019, vol. 20, p. 1141.

101 R. Wodak, Entering the 'post-shame era'; The rise of illiberal democracy, populism and neo-authoritarianism in Europe, Global Discourse 2019, vol. 9, no. 1, pp. 195–213.

legitimacy of these questions – particularly in the context of Poland – is confirmed by one of the academic interpretations of Bruce Ackerman's constitutional theory formulated by Sujit Choudhry. He claims that:

> some of Ackerman's constitutional moments are, in reality, moments of constitutive constitutional politics, the very character of which leads to constitutional failure and breakdown. As a consequence, Ackerman should be read not as a theorist of constitutional change proceeding through mass democratic mobilisation. Rather, Ackerman should be read as a theorist of constitutional crisis.[102]

As noted by M. Ziółkowski, the emphasis on the sovereignty of the parliament and its privileged position among the organs of the public authorities, which is characteristic of Law and Justice rhetoric, is in contradiction with the concept of dualistic democracy, and only through a dualistic concept of democracy can we speak of a constitutional moment.[103] It is also worth adding that Law and Justice, referring to the fundamental assumptions of political constitutionalism, distorts them. The identification of the essence of constitutionalism with the idea of dynamic self-determination of the political community, characteristic of political constitutionalism, should not, however, be confused with the permissibility of making so-called systemic adjustments beyond the current constitutional framework. Political constitutionalism presupposes a consensual vision of politics, and sees the constitution as a set of rules and institutions that enable emerging conflicts to be managed.[104]

Moreover, the concept of the constitutional moment assumes that a constitutional change does not break the continuity of the system, and thus represent a complete revolution. That is also why, in order to apply the concept of the constitutional moment to Polish historical and political conditions, one must accept the legacy of constitutionalism from the period of transformation.[105] However, the Law and Justice rhetoric is based on criticism of the Polish political transition and the postulate for refabricating the political foundations of the state. Finally, in

102 Sujit Choudhry, Ackerman's Higher Lawmaking in Comparative Constitutional Perspective: Constitutional Moments as Constitutional Failures?

103 M. Ziółkowski, 2018: dlaczego nie ma momentu konstytucyjnego w Polsce? Analiza momentu konstytucyjnego prof. Bruce'a Ackermana w kontekście prawnych i politycznych dyskusji w Polsce, Archiwum Osiatyńskiego 2018, https://archiwumosiatynskiego.pl/wpis-w-debacie/2018-dlaczego-nie-ma-momentu-konstytucyjnego-w-polsce/.

104 Cf. P. Minkkinen, Political constitutionalism versus political constitutional theory: Law, power, and politics, International Journal of Constitutional Law 2013, vol. 11, no. 3, p. 585.

105 M. Ziółkowski, 2018: dlaczego nie ma momentu konstytucyjnego w Polsce? Analiza momentu konstytucyjnego prof. Bruce'a Ackermana w kontekście prawnych i politycznych dyskusji w Polsce, Archiwum Osiatyńskiego 2018, https://archiwumosiatynskiego.pl/wpis-w-debacie/2018-dlaczego-nie-ma-momentu-konstytucyjnego-w-polsce/.

reference to Ackerman's concept, one should not omit the crucial point that a constitutional judiciary must exist independent of the supreme authority. The independence and impartiality of the constitutional judiciary is an inherent part of the debate on amending the constitution. The role of the constitutional court is crucial in the final stage of the higher lawmaking process, as it reinterprets the provisions of the constitution and verifies the conformity of constitutional reform made outside the formal procedure with the constitution (which is tantamount to legitimising high lawmaking). Therefore, in Poland's case, it is difficult to speak of a constitutional moment. A flawed parliamentary procedure, which resulted in the appointment of 'stand-in judges', the manner whereby the President of the Constitutional Tribunal was appointed in breach of the constitution, defective adjudication panels as well as the manipulation of adjudication panels all preclude the application of Bruce Ackerman's concept to Polish legal reality.[106] These features of the systemic changes taking place in Poland, in particular those that affected the Constitutional Tribunal, also make it pointless to consider in detail whether there were three stages in Poland preceding the final phase of the constitutional moment, which is the stage of legal codification.[107]

The changes that have occurred in Poland since 2015 should really be conceptualised as an illiberal, counter-constitutional revolution. Its aim, despite maintaining the nominal continuity of the system, is to destroy the essence of the current constitution. The role of the Constitutional Tribunal in this ongoing process is complex. Initially, it was the object of criticism and direct political attack, which led to the undermining of its social authority. Subsequently, a parliamentary majority led to the takeover of this institution. The Constitutional Tribunal thus captured became an actor in a gloomy political spectacle. As an active entity participating in the counter-constitutional revolution, the Constitutional Tribunal *post factum* legitimises violations of the Constitution perpetrated by the parliamentary majority and acts as a governmental enabler.

106 M. Ziółkowski, 2018: dlaczego nie ma momentu konstytucyjnego w Polsce? Analiza momentu konstytucyjnego prof. Bruce'a Ackermana w kontekście prawnych i politycznych dyskusji w Polsce, Archiwum Osiatyńskiego 2018, https://archiwumosiatynskiego.pl/wpis-w-debacie/2018-dlaczego-nie-ma-momentu-konstytucyjnego-w-polsce/.

107 B. Ackerman, We the people, Foundations, Harvard University Press 1993, pp. 272–290.

Romania is an interesting case study of activism in this respect, with peculiarities related to the 'politicisation' of the Constitutional Court, because in the recent decade the Court has been used as a powerful weapon by some political actors against their opponents.

2 Constitutional courts and judicial activism

The debate on judicial activism of courts in general and of constitutional courts is a recurring one in constitutional law scholarship. Judicial activism has been understood in different ways, depending on the type of judicial system and on the 'model' of constitutional review applied in various countries. The concept is related to the idea of the constitution as a 'living document',[7] which has to evolve permanently, in line with societal changes and needs. This adaptation of the relatively stable normative text to a changing society can be achieved through various means, among which is judicial activism. Constitutional adjudication can thus become a vector of change through judicial activism. But how can judicial activism be defined? In a more general wording, expressed in American scholarship, it is 'a practice of the federal courts of imposing their moral, social, political and economic views on the country'.[8] The explanation for the need of such imposition may be, in the same author's view, that 'the kind of Government envisaged by the Constitution is incapable of coping with contemporary conditions'.[9] Although the courts may not always be very well prepared to fill that void, as 'they are trained in the law, not in mental health, penology, race relations, school and business administration', the recourse to judicial activism is inevitable, because even the political powers demand such action.

In a more nuanced opinion, there is a difference between 'active courts' versus 'passive courts', and 'activist courts' versus 'restrained courts'. Thus, 'an ***active*** court can be defined as one that is more likely to strike down or otherwise modify the actions taken by other branches of government. A *passive* court is one which routinely defers to legislative and executive judgment.'[10] However, in the author's view, an active court is not always an activist court. A court becomes activist only when it, 'without constitutional authorization, imposes its own views'.[11] Therefore, the activist nature of the court's activity depends on the nature and extent of the powers that it exercises: if they are authorised and/or required by the constitution, then the court cannot be deemed as 'activist', as all it does is remain within the limits created by the fundamental law.

7 Thurgood Marshall, *The Constitution: A Living Document* (1987). Text available at http://thurgoodmarshall.com/the-bicentennial-speech/.

8 Iredell Jenkins, *Judicial Activism and Constitutional Government*, in (1984) 29 (1) American Journal of Jurisprudence, p. 173.

9 Ibidem, p. 185.

10 Jorge M.Farinacci-Fernos, *Constitutionally Required Judicial Activism. Re-examining the Role of Courts in Modern Constitutional Adjudication*, in (2018) 28 Kansas Journal of Law and Public Policy, p. 38.

11 Ibidem, p. 70.

A broader definition of judicial activism is proposed by Brian Galligan: 'control or influence by the judiciary over political or administrative institutions, processes and outcomes'.[12] I partially agree with Farinacci-Fernos that this definition is more accurate when it applies to control or influence exercised by courts (including constitutional courts) outside the scope of their constitutionally limited powers. The fact that a constitutional court strikes down legislation by exercising its constitutional powers of review is not the same as interfering with the state powers while exceeding its constitutional powers of review of legislation or control of the authorities. This distinction is especially true when constitutional courts become involved in politics. Judicial activism was also seen as 'the frequency with which courts rule that policies passed by government institutions are unconstitutional'.[13]

What are the contexts in which a contemporary constitutional court can become activist and what are the benefits, if any, of this activism? Are there more types of judicial activism or does it just depend on the context? For space reasons, I will not develop the answers to all these questions, but it is worth mentioning that, if improperly used, judicial activism of constitutional courts can become a 'double-edged sword'.

One legitimate context of judicial activism would be a vague constitutional text which needs either an update or a more precise interpretation from the constitutional court. In this case, the court acts as an interpreter but the thin line between a negative and a positive legislator can easily be broken.

Another context of judicial activism is the willingness of the RCC to protect its own powers or even to exceed these powers, in order to fulfil a certain goal. Usually, this goal is a political one and sometimes it is determined by the political influence of the governmental majority within the court. This type of activism could be used under the guise of protection of constitutional values, in order to interfere with the normal functioning of state powers – such as the executive or even the judiciary. 'Judicial populism',[14] understood as a 'case-law that would enhance popular sovereignty, prioritise constitutional identity, restrict pluralism, diminish checks and balances, relativize fundamental rights or simply seek to give effect to public perceptions or endorse populist views of the government', is a derivative of this type of judicial activism. S. Tănăsescu further explains this relationship:

> in some instances judicial activism of constitutional courts may prove instrumental for popular constitutionalism. If judicial activism is not merely a certain propensity of constitutional judges to invalidate decisions taken by other legitimate actors in order to enforce their own vision of the Constitution, but it also encompasses an overlap of that vision with the vision on the

12 Brian Galligan, *Judicial Activism in Australia*, in Kenneth M. Holland (ed.), *Judicial Activism in Comparative Perspective*, St. Martin's Press, New York, 1991, p. 71.

13 Kirill M. Bumin, *Judicial Institutionalization and Judicial Activism of the Post-Communist Constitutional Courts*, in (2017) 10 (2) Journal of Politics and Law, p. 56.

14 Simina Tănăsescu, *Can Constitutional Courts Become Populist?* in Martin Belov (ed.), *The Role of Courts in Contemporary Legal Orders*, Eleven International Publishing, 2019, pp. 308–309.

> Constitution held by the majority of the population, the distance between judicial activism and judicial populism becomes very thin, particularly when the balance is tilted in the direction of majoritarian views.[15]

The latter case makes judicial activism closer to 'political servility' of the constitutional court, which can become very dangerous for the rule of law.

In non-consolidated democracies, where the political power can easily become instrumentalised in order to serve personal or group interests of certain politicians or political parties, judicial activism can become a 'constitutional tsunami', when the constitutional court exceeds its powers and becomes a positive legislator and/or interferes with the judicial power or, more generally, with the structure and functioning of the very constitutional system. In other cases, post-communist constitutional courts are less activist in relation to the political powers and more activist as players in interpreting the constitution in respect of EU membership.[16] Other courts channel their activism towards human rights protection.[17]

Many of these abovementioned cases or contexts of judicial activism can be detected in the case law of the RCC in recent years. Some of them will be illustrated in the following sections with relevant decisions.

3 Is the Romanian Constitutional Court an 'activist' court?

In the following sections, I argue that the Romanian Constitutional Court, after a long period of restraint (1992–2012), became more and more activist, but not always consistent with its own case law. The most relevant example is the caselaw regarding the powers of the President of Romania. I also argue that, by exceeding its prescribed constitutional powers, the Court made this activism turn the wrong way and may become a potential threat to the rule of law, which the Court is called to defend.

3.1 The Romanian Constitutional Court's design – brief overview

Following the demise of the communist regime in 1989, Romania, like all the other countries of Central and Eastern Europe (CEE), proceeded, with more hesitant steps than other countries in the region, on the path of democracy. After an enthusiastic revolutionary start, shadowed by the turmoil of the years 1990–1991, when democratic values were put at risk by political uncertainty and by the miners' riots against anti-communist protesters, the situation settled with the adoption, in December 1991, of the new Constitution, which established, among others, the Constitutional Court. Romania was thus part of the 'third wave' of constitutional

15 Ibidem, p. 313.

16 Martin Belov, *Constitutional Courts as Ultimate Players in Multilevel Constituent Power Game*, in Martin Belov (ed.), *Courts, Politics and Constitutional Law. Judicialization of Politics and Politicization of the Judiciary*, Routledge, 2020, p. 158.

17 Bumin, op. cit., supra, note 13, p. 62.

review enshrined in transition democracies.[18] Among the reasons for adopting the Kelsenian model of constitutional review, to the detriment of the American model (which had existed in Romania between 1912 and 1940) were the distrust in the judiciary, too often identified as faithful to the former communist power,[19] but also the will to break with the communist past and to join the European organisations (Council of Europe and European Union). A constitutional court was seen, as in the other countries in the region, as a part of the 'passport' necessary for the 'return to Europe'.

The RCC was established by the 1991 Constitution in a separate title (Title V), as an independent institution, outside the judicial system. The Court actually started to function in 1992, after the adoption of the organic law on its organisation and functioning. Its competencies and procedures were amended over the years, both at the constitutional and at the legislative level. The first constitutional amendment, from 2003, gave the Court new powers and endowed the organic legislator with the ability to introduce even more powers of the Court in the future. This happened by subsequent changes of the Court's organic law and increased the political role of the Court.

At first, during the transition period, the RCC was seen as a 'negative legislator', as it had mainly the power to review legislation – both by means of abstract and concrete review, with a mission to correct and adapt the legislation to the new political context. The Constitution also gave the Court limited power of electoral and political parties' review, as well as an advisory power in relation to the political liability of the head of state. In 2003, by constitutional amendment, it was added to the Court's power to solve 'legal conflicts of a constitutional nature'[20] and to review international treaties and agreements. In 2004 and 2010, two additional

18 Andrew Harding, Peter Leyland, Tania Groppi, *Constitutional Courts: Forms, Functions and Practice in Comparative Perspective*, in Andrew Harding, Peter Leyland (eds.), *Constitutional Courts. A Comparative Study*, Wildy, Simmonds & Hill Publishing, 2009, p. 12.

19 However, as Lach and Sadurski very correctly put it, 'it would be neither just to describe ordinary judges as obedient servants of the communist authorities, nor would it be correct to portray the constitutional courts as exclusively consisting of individuals untainted by associations with the former regime' (Lach and Sadurski, op. cit., note 3, p. 59).

20 The Venice Commission, in its *Opinion on the Draft Law Amending the Constitution of Romania* (2003), expressed its concerns about the new power to solve legal conflicts of constitutional nature: 'It should be made clear that the reference is to conflicts of a legal nature and not to those of a political nature. A constitutional court must remain what it is: i.e. a court with jurisdiction only to "declare what the law is". To that extent, such a dispute between institutions is a progress of the State governed by law. On the other hand, a Constitutional Court is not a body for mediation between the powers of the State, responsible for appeasing disputes between them and for finding a "political" solution for their differences. [...] However, the proposed text goes further. It appears to embrace all conflicts between the public authorities concerning the interpretation and application of the Constitution in a specific situation. The concept of "conflict" remains to be defined.' (CDL-AD (2003) 4, available at https://www.venice.coe.int/webforms/documents/?pdf=CDL-AD(2003)004-e, last visited on 17 July 2020).

powers were introduced by the organic law: the power to review the laws on constitutional amendments *after* the final adoption by the Parliament and the power to review the constitutionality of parliamentary resolutions, other than the chambers' Standing Orders (which were already under the Court's jurisdiction).

3.2 Politicisation of the Constitutional Court: Crisis and beyond

The RCC was, at the beginning, a revolutionary court, both literally and figuratively: literally, as it was established by a post-revolutionary Constitution and it was a departure from the concept of constitutional review that existed in Romania before the totalitarian era; figuratively, the Court started to be revolutionary in some of its early decisions, but not as activist as the Hungarian or Polish courts of the same period (1992–1999).[21]

In 2000, the RCC revolutionised the Romanian ordinary courts' approach towards human rights and the Strasbourg case law, by taking ECtHR judgments more into account.[22]

This approach did not, however, increase the activism of the Court in respect of human rights, but it managed to increase the awareness of the ordinary courts regarding the European Convention on Human Rights. Nevertheless, the Court's case law in this respect cannot be considered truly 'activist', because it was its duty to interpret the Constitution in the light of human rights treaties, according to Article 20 of the Constitution.

As mentioned above, in 2003, the Court received, by way of constitutional amendment, a power that passed unnoticed at the time, but became a 'revolutionary' power over the years: the power to solve legal conflicts of a constitutional nature between public authorities. This power allowed the Court, especially in the last five years (2017–2021), to become more and more involved in politics, showing an 'activism' that took a different turn than one should expect from its declared role as 'guardian of the Constitution' and guardian of the rule of law.

In this context, it must be mentioned that independence of the judiciary from political and other interests has been a recurring issue in the debate about Romania's EU adhesion and, after 2007, EU membership. In 2006, the European Commission established a monitoring mechanism, the 'Cooperation and Verification Mechanism' (hereinafter CVM), which is focused on two main issues: strengthening the independence of justice and increasing the fight against corruption. In the Commission's reports issued within this mechanism, the RCC is deemed to be one of the paragons of independence and the rule of law. For example, whereas in the European Commission's reports of 2010, 2011 and 2012, the RCC was scarcely mentioned, in the reports of 2013, 2014 and 2017, it suddenly became a central figure:

21 Bianca Selejan-Guţan, *The Constitution of Romania. A Contextual Analysis*, Hart Publishing/Bloomsbury, 2016, pp. 166–167.

22 See, for details, Iulia Motoc, Crina Kaufman, *Romania and the European Convention on Human Rights: A Dialogue of Judges*, in Iulia Motoc, Ineta Ziemele (eds.), *The Impact of the ECHR on Democratic Change in Central and Eastern Europe*, Cambridge University Press, 2016, pp. 330–349.

> While the Constitution and the Constitutional Court's role and decisions have been respected, commitments regarding the independence of the judiciary and regarding the response to integrity rulings have not been adequately implemented. [...] What is important is that the process of constitutional reform progresses in full respect of fundamental values such as respect for the rule of law and the separation of powers. This includes continued respect for the Constitutional Court as the guarantor of the supremacy of the Constitution.
>
> (CVM Report on Romania, January 2013)

> The Constitution and the Constitutional Court are at the heart of the rule of law. [...] The [Constitutional] Court will continue to have a key role in defending key principles like the separation of powers, including any future discussion on Constitutional change.
>
> (CVM Report on Romania, January 2014)

> Throughout 2016, the judiciary (represented by the High Court of Cassation and Justice and the Superior Council of the Magistracy) and the Constitutional Court continued to support judicial independence as institutional actors contributing to the balance of power.
>
> (CVM Report on Romania, January 2017)

A change of heart occurred in the recent years, especially starting with 2017, when the government changed after the general elections of 2016 and the new political power started an offensive against the independence of the judiciary and the anti-corruption measures. Thus, in the more recent report of 2018, the actions of the RCC were seen as affecting the irreversibility of the fight against corruption:

> At the same time as the legal amendments [*on the laws of the judiciary*, n.n.], specific decisions have underlined the consequences of the concentration of power in the hands of the Minister of Justice. This was the case first with the dismissal of the Chief Prosecutor of the National Anti-Corruption Directorate (DNA) at the request of the Minister of Justice. In a first stage, the President of Romania rejected the proposed dismissal, in line with the negative opinion of the Superior Council of the Magistracy. However, a Constitutional Court Decision in May on the dismissal procedure reinforced the trend of increased power for the Minister [...]. These developments also have consequences for the irreversibility of the fight against corruption.
>
> (CVM Report on Romania, November 2018)[23]

23 The Commission also stated, in an explanatory note to its comments on the Constitutional Court, that 'The Venice Commission also pointed to inconsistencies in the case law of the Constitutional Court where previous decisions did not raise issues of constitutionality in relation to the President's role in the appointment procedure of top prosecutors and had even stated that the role of the President in that procedure could not be purely formal' (CVM Progress Report 2018, p. 4, note 18).

Finally, in 2019, the Commission explicitly said that:

> The Constitutional Court rulings directly impact ongoing high-level corruption cases, entailing delays and restarts of trials, and have allowed the re-opening of several final cases, under certain conditions. The full consequences are yet to unfold. This clear knock-on on the process of justice also raised broader doubts about the sustainability of the progress made so far by Romania in the fight against corruption.
>
> (CVM Progress Report on Romania, October 2019)

How did the RCC become, from an institution placed on a rule-of-law pedestal, one whose certain actions endanger the very values that it was defending a few years ago?

The constitutional crisis that took place in the summer of 2012 'raised the Constitutional Court to a position of influence and public visibility that it had never before enjoyed'.[24] Nevertheless, even then, the RCC has not acted in a completely politically free and objective manner. Therefore, the powers by which the Court exercised a certain judicial control of the political power has frequently had a 'boomerang' effect, generating the struggle of the political forces to subdue the independence of the Court by using different means of pressure.

Formally, there are some constitutional and legal guarantees of the independence of RCC judges towards political authorities which appointed them: irremovability, impossibility of term renewal, disciplinary autonomy, certain incompatibilities established by the Constitution and by the organic law. However, even if there would be a suspicion of lack of impartiality, according to the organic law, constitutional judges cannot be recused and may not abstain from judging a case.

The political influence starts, as in many other countries, with the appointment process. The appointing authorities are, like in most Kelsenian constitutional review systems, the chambers of parliament and the head of state. However, as the constitutional requirements are rather loose and there is little transparency in the choice of candidates, conflicts frequently took place in respect of the election of judges. In the Parliament's chambers, no supermajority is required for electing constitutional judges: the chambers elect the judges with absolute simple majority (half plus one of the total number of members). Therefore, the ruling majority usually manages to impose its candidates, regardless the result of the 'quality' hearings in the legal committee. In some cases, the appointment procedure of the constitutional judges was transformed into an open battle between the majority and the opposition.[25]

24 Bogdan Iancu, *Separation of Powers and the Rule of Law in Romania: The Crisis in Concepts and Contexts*, in Armin von Bogdandy, Pal Sonnevend (eds.), *Constitutional Crisis in the European Constitutional Area*, Hart Publishing, 2015, p. 155.

25 In 2010, the election of a constitutional judge in the Chamber of Deputies was annulled and repeated for procedural reasons because allegedly the 'wrong' candidate had won, whereas at the Senate, there was an open 'surveillance' of the 'secret' voting process by the representatives of the majority.

The recurring political fights for the appointment of constitutional judges created around the Court a suspicion of partiality (that, despite the obligation of independence and impartiality, there are 'teams' within the Court, serving the interests of the political majorities who appointed them). Unfortunately, the Court did not always act so as to refute this suspicion and sometimes it became an instrumentalised organ.[26]

This tendency manifested especially when the Court exercised its ancillary powers, because they bring the Court in closer contact with the political institutions. From the perspective of the whole Romanian constitutional judicial culture, 'in spite of its post-2003 gain in influence, prerogative and Westernization, the RCC does not appear to have acquired the essential features of a credible judicial culture'.[27]

Controlling the other state powers gave the Court the incentive to become a distinct branch of power itself, interfering with its role of neutral arbiter. Even when reviewing legislation, the Court frequently exceeded its competence and openly interfered with the legislative power, thus trespassing its own limits of an independent 'negative' legislator.

In the following sections, I will briefly examine how the RCC recently manifested its 'activism'[28] in decisions that distorted the balance of state powers, informally amended some constitutional provisions and even interfered directly with the exercise of certain state powers, such as the judiciary.

3.3 Activism in the constitutional review of legislation and of constitutional amendments

Abstract review of legislation is considered the most 'politicised' type of constitutional review within the Kelsenian model.[29] Within its abstract review powers, the RCC can be addressed with an 'objection of unconstitutionality' of a law before promulgation, by authorities from all branches of power: the President of Romania, one of the presidents of the Chambers of Parliament, the High Court of Cassation and Justice (hereinafter HCCJ), at least 50 deputies or 25 senators, and by the Ombudsman. However, in the last few years, decisions issued in the concrete review of legislation, i.e. by means of the referral of unconstitutionality,[30] had an impact on the judicial activity and became an example of RCC activism taking the wrong turn.

26 Ibidem, p. 166 and *passim*.

27 Bogdan Iancu, *Constitutional-Judicial Culture in Romania – Ambivalence and Possibility*, in Manuel Guțan, Bianca Selejan-Guțan (eds.), *Europeanization and Judicial Culture in Contemporary Democracies*, Hamangiu, 2014, p. 147.

28 On the Romanian Constitutional Court's 'activism' before 2014, see Elena-Simina Tănăsescu, *The Romanian Constitutional Judge: Lost in Transition*, in Miodrag Jovanovic (ed.), *Constitutional Review and Democracy*, Eleven International Publishing, 2015, pp. 223–252.

29 Ginsburg and Garoupa, op. cit., supra, note 1, p. 548.

30 Selejan-Guțan (2016), op. cit., supra, note 21, pp. 173–175.

After the already famous decisions from the 2012 constitutional crisis, especially the ones regarding the referendum law,[31] the RCC adopted a more moderate approach in exercising its constitutional review powers (2013–2017). The context of the recent changes was the coming to power of a new political majority and the intensification of the attempts to weaken the judiciary and especially the fight anti-corruption. The main legislative initiatives of the new political majority in this direction were important changes to the Criminal Code (especially related to the 'neutralisation' of corruption offences),[32] to the Code of Criminal Procedure and, most importantly, to the laws on the organisation of the judiciary. For space reasons, I will only quote a few relevant examples of the approach of the RCC to these legislative changes. One of the techniques used by the Court in its most recent case law, 'in order to achieve specific targets',[33] is the modulation of the effects of its own decisions, 'in a manner that obliges the legislator to adopt specific laws, practically as drafted by the Court'.[34] For example, in *Decision 466/2019*, the Court stated that the challenged legal provisions had already been declared unconstitutional by the Court, and therefore 'the margin of appreciation of the Parliament [to adopt a new law] is limited, because the legislator is compelled to re-analyse the normative substance of the law exclusively to bring it in line with the decision of the Court'. Therefore, the only choice of the legislator is to draft the new law as instructed by the RCC and thus transform the Court into a positive legislator. The decision concerned, *inter alia*, the articles from the Criminal Code on the abuse of office, a frequent corruption offence in Romania.

In a similar 'activist' manner, through *Decisions 874/2018, 220/2019* and *55/2020*, the RCC interfered with the judicial power. In the first two cases, regarding the Code of Civil Procedure and the Code of Criminal Procedure respectively, the Court expanded the effects of its previous decisions with a retroactive effect, thus interfering with the outcome of pending cases before ordinary courts. In *Decision 874/2018*, the Court even 'declared unconstitutional' an interpretative decision of the HCCJ, an act which is not under its jurisdiction, while in *Decision 26/2019*, the Court decided that pending criminal cases on corruption offences must be

31 Bogdan Iancu, *Romania under EU Influence: Note on the Constitutive Limits of External Constitutional Interventions*, in (2012) 12 (2) *Romanian Journal of Political Science*, pp. 61–70; Bianca Selejan-Guţan, *The Illusion of the Romanian Constitution?*, I-CONnect, the blog of the International Journal of Constitutional Law, 2012, at http://www.iconnectblog.com/2012/12/the-illusion-of-the-romanian-constitution/.

32 See, for details, Bianca Selejan-Guţan, *'We Don't Need No Constitution' – On a Sad EU Membership Anniversary in Romania*, Verfassungsblog, 1 February 2017, https://verfassungsblog.de/we-dont-need-no-constitution-on-a-sad-eu-membership-anniversary-in-romania/; Bianca Selejan-Guţan, *Failing to Struggle or Struggling to Fail? On the New Judiciary Legislation Changes in Romania*, Verfassungsblog, 31 January 2018, https://verfassungsblog.de/failing-to-struggle-or-struggling-to-fail-on-the-new-judiciary-legislation-changes-in-romania.

33 Bianca Selejan-Guţan, Elena-Simina Tănăsescu, *Romania*, in Richard Albert, David Landau, Pietro Faraguna, Simon Drugda (eds.), *2019 Global Review of Constitutional Law*, I-Connect/Clough Center Boston College Law School, forthcoming 2020.

34 Ibidem.

reviewed if the evidence had been gathered by targeted surveillance, because such means of surveillance cannot be used in ordinary criminal procedures, but only in matters pertaining to national security.

In the same vein, in *Decision 55/2020*, by declaring unconstitutional an article from the Law on National Security, the Court practically removed from hundreds of criminal files the evidence collected with the help of the technical surveillance of the intelligence service, even though such surveillance had been ordered by a judge. At the same time, the Court stated that similar recordings, if taken by means of private individuals, are allowed as evidence, 'because the Code of Criminal Procedure (CCP) does not prohibit them' [N.B. the CCP did not prohibit the abovementioned ones either]. Two judges, L.-D. Stanciu and E.-S. Tănăsescu, wrote a very well-documented separate opinion, in which they said, firstly, that 'it is out of our understanding why the text that provides the use as evidence of recordings made by the authorities that perform duties regarding intelligence collection is unconstitutional [...] whereas the text that provides the use as evidence of recordings made by private parties or any other persons is constitutional'. Moreover, the dissenting judges rightly emphasized that the decision exceeds the jurisdiction of the Court and interferes with the jurisdiction of the ordinary courts, as well with the competence of the legislator.[35]

3.4 Activism in solving conflicts between authorities

As neither the Constitution nor the organic law defines them in any way, the RCC established that its power of solving conflicts between authorities is circumscribed to the following requirements: the 'conflict' should be of a legal nature; the conflict should have a constitutional basis. As regards the contents of the conflict, the Court defined it as the existence of: 'acts or actions by which one or more authorities arrogate powers, attributions or competencies which, according to the Constitution, belong to other public authorities, or the omission from the part of some authorities, by means of declining their competence or of refusing to carry out certain acts within their competence' (*Decision 144/2005*), or 'any legal conflict situations born directly from the constitutional text' (*Decision 901/2009*).

These types of decisions not only brought the Court into the centre of political fights, but also enable us to detect the main directions in which the Court's activism was headed in the last five years: dismantling the powers of the President of Romania and interfering with the activity of the judiciary. Also, in this context, as stated by E.S. Tănăsescu, 'the RCC has gradually embraced a populist agenda in the area of criminal repression of corruption'.[36]

One of the first controversial cases was the conflict between the Prime Minister and the President from June 2012, over the participation at the reunion of the European Council. In a highly controversial decision, the Court decided in favour of the President, arguing, *inter alia*, that 'taking into account that these

35 RCC, Decision 55/2020, Separate Opinion, §2, §13.
36 Tănăsescu (2019), op. cit, supra, note 14, p. 315.

[meetings] entail conclusion of treaties on behalf of Romania, the participation of the head of state, which has the power to conclude treaties in this field, is needed'. However, as it was pointed out in the scholarship:

> Are acts adopted by the European Council 'international treaties'? And also, even supposing that on the occasion of a European Council meeting a treaty is signed by the States' representatives, [...] that act is not an act of the European Council (and even not of the Union itself). Significant examples are international agreements concluded by eurozone members. On the other hand, acts adopted by the European Council under simplified revision procedures (Article 48 TEU) are by no means (classic) international acts.[37]

This decision is a part of the series of RCC decisions that enhanced presidential powers between 2009 and 2012.[38] Arguably assuming Maurice Duverger's definition of semi-presidentialism (which is not widely accepted in today's constitutional scholarship, being considered outdated[39]), the Court has interpreted constitutional text so as to increase presidential powers:[40] in the silence of the text, the Court ruled that the president has the right to refuse only once, by reasoned decision, the proposal of the Prime Minister to appoint a minister on a vacated ministerial post and also that the president may refuse only once the appointment of a magistrate proposed by the Superior Council of Magistracy (whereas usually the head of state power to appoint judges is only formal).

This favourable attitude towards the presidential powers dramatically shifted in 2017, due to a completely different political context and under a completely different political majority (including within the Court itself). The Court started to gradually diminish the presidential powers, in a series of decisions ruling upon 'legal conflicts of constitutional nature', by discovering such conflicts where they did not exist or by reinventing existing interpretations of the Constitution.[41]

Thus, in 2019, the Court found that there was a 'legal conflict of constitutional nature' as a result of the refusal of the President of Romania to revoke a few ministers and to appoint ad interim ministers at the proposal of the Prime Minister, in the circumstances of a governmental reshuffle. During the reshuffle, a change of the political composition of the Government occurred, due to the withdrawal from the Government of one of the parties from the majority coalition.

37 Constantin Mihai Banu, *Comments on the representation of Romania in the European Council and on its consequences for democratic accountability*, in (2014) 14 (1) *International and Comparative Law Review/Mezinárodní a srovnávací právní revue*, p. 13.

38 Tănăsescu (2015), op. cit., note 28.

39 Robert Elgie, *Duverger, Semi-presidentialism and the Supposed French Archetype*, in (2009) 32 (2) *West European Politics*, pp. 248–267.

40 Bogdan Dima, *Shaping the Role of the President: The Influence of the Romanian Constitutional Court's Jurisprudence*, in Guțan and Selejan-Guțan, op. cit., supra, note 27, pp.112–116.

41 See also Karoly Benke, *Shaping and Dismantling Semi-presidentialism Through Constitutional Adjudication. An Ongoing Romanian Experience,* in (2019) 2 Romanian Journal of Comparative Law, p. 301

As the Constitution requires that, in such a case, the Prime Minister should seek the approval of the Parliament, the President did not appoint the suggested ad interim ministers. Although the Court stated that there was no legal conflict of a constitutional nature, it still required the President to 'immediately give a written and motivated answer' regarding the refusal to appoint ad interim ministers. In the same decision, the Court ruled that there was such a conflict due to the refusal of the President to revoke the reshuffled ministers and that the President is obliged to issue the decrees of revocation. This, too, was a case of political conflict and not a legal one, as stated by the dissenting judges, E.S. Tănăsescu and L.D. Stanciu.[42]

Perhaps the most famous and controversial decision on constitutional conflicts from the last five years was *Decision 358/2018*, by which the Court ordered the President of Romania to issue a decree on a particular matter involving the judiciary – i.e. a decree dismissing the chief prosecutor of the anti-corruption office. The procedure was initiated by the Minister of Justice, who, according to the law on judicial organisation, had to request the advisory opinion of the Superior Council of Magistracy (SCM) before submitting the proposal to the President of Romania. The SCM gave a negative opinion and the President, upon receiving the proposal, refused to dismiss the chief prosecutor. The Prime Minister then addressed the RCC with a request to solve a constitutional conflict between the Minister of Justice and the President, as a result of the President's refusal. Although the appointment and dismissal of chief prosecutors is not a power of the President established by the Constitution, but by an organic law, and thus the case did not fit in its own definition, the RCC decided that it was still a 'constitutional conflict'. In doing that, the Court argued that the administrative litigation courts do not have jurisdiction in this case, although the refusal of the President had an administrative nature. In doing this, the Court practically 'established that a minister enjoys greater discretionary powers than a directly elected President of the republic'[43] and, as a result, drastically diminished the powers of the President by ordering him to issue the dismissal decree (which he did in July 2018). This decision was considered 'a turning point in the functioning of the political regime in Romania: while the guardian of the Constitution has, apparently, trespassed its boundaries, the President of Romania remained compliant with the principles of the rule of law'.[44] The decision is also part of the 'rollercoaster' case law regarding the powers of the President of Romania: from the increasing of these powers via the decisions from 2009–2012 to a dramatic decreasing via the case law of 2018–2019.

Decision 358/2018 had another – unexpected – outcome, this time at the European Court of Human Rights. The dismissed chief prosecutor, Laura-Codruța Kövesi, complained to the Strasbourg Court for the violation of her rights to a fair

42 See also RCC, Decision 875/2018.

43 Bianca Selejan-Guțan, Elena-Simina Tănăsescu, *Romania*, in Richard Albert, David Landau, Pietro Faraguna, Simon Drugda (eds.), 2018 Global Review of Constitutional Law, I-Connect/Clough Center Boston College Law School, 2019, http://www.iconnectblog.com/2019/10/now-available-the-2018-global-review-of-constitutional-law/.

44 Ibidem.

trial and of freedom of expression, because she had no possibility to intervene and defend herself in the dismissal procedure (as the RCC ruled that the administrative courts were not competent in the case) and because the decision of her dismissal was taken on grounds of her opinions and not for professional faults. The European Court found in favour of the applicant on both complaints and, in the part concerning the alleged violation of Article 6 of the Convention, it held that:

> in the absence of domestic case law examples of similar cases and in view of the binding and specific nature of the decision adopted by the Constitutional Court in the current case, the Court is not convinced that the applicant had an available domestic remedy for effectively attacking in court [...] the reasons of her removal from the position of chief-prosecutor of the DNA by the presidential decree of 9 July 2018 in accordance with the judgment of the Constitutional Court of 30 May 2018.[45]

The Strasbourg Court also said that 'the respondent State impaired the very essence of the applicant's right of access to a court *owing to* [my emphasis, B.S.-G.] the specific boundaries for a review of her case set down in the ruling of the Constitutional Court'[46] and, accordingly, found a violation of Ms. Kövesi's right of access to a court.

Another highly controversial result of the Constitutional Court's 'activism' in solving constitutional conflicts was the interference with the judicial power. *Decision 685/2018*, which regarded the changes brought to the laws on the judiciary in the same year, is a relevant example. One of these changes required that all members of the five-judges panels (the last-instance panels) of the High Court of Cassation and Justice (the supreme court of the land) should be drawn at the beginning of the calendar year. The current practice was the draw of four members, whereas the fifth was appointed *ex officio*, according to a decision of the HCCJ ruling board. The RCC did not rule on this matter within one of its constitutional review powers, but was addressed by the Prime Minister with a request to solve a 'conflict of constitutional nature' between the Parliament and the HCCJ on the grounds that the Supreme Court refused to apply the new law immediately. Thus, in the first place, by addressing the Constitutional Court, the Government (which was not a part of the alleged conflict) interfered in a matter that could have been solved within the judiciary itself. Secondly, the Constitutional Court, by declaring that there was a conflict and by 'solving' it in its own way, interfered with the judiciary, more specifically infringed the principle of *res iudicata*, as many cases were prone to reopening as a result of the Court's decision. In its decision, the CC admitted to interfere in the judicial process, by stating that 'by solving this conflict [the CC] substituted the ordinary citizens, who would be otherwise compelled to seek justice in courts'.[47]

45 ECtHR, *Kövesi v. Romania* (2020), §154.
46 Ibidem, §157.
47 Selejan-Guțan and Tănăsescu, op. cit., supra, note 43.

Another case in which the RCC interfered with the principle of *res iudicata* was *Decision 417/2019*, where, in the same manner (by solving a 'legal conflict of constitutional nature' between the Parliament and the HCCJ, at the request of the President of the Chamber of Deputies this time), the RCC stated that the five-judges panels ruling on corruption cases should be formed by judges 'specialised in ruling upon corruption', according to a law from 2000. The HCCJ and the judiciary in general interpreted this law, over the years, in an extensive way and said that all judges that rule upon criminal cases at the level of the HCCJ were specialised *ope legis* in corruption cases. The RCC did not agree and said that all panels which, between 2003 and 2018, were not constituted by 'specialised' judges[48] were in breach of the law and therefore null and void. The cases decided by these panels should be reopened. The decision was adopted with a very thin majority – five to four – and all four minority constitutional judges wrote separate opinions. However, the decision was adopted and severely encroached the principle of *res iudicata*.[49]

3.5 The Court as 'activist judge' of its own powers

In the period that coincided with the gradual increase of its 'activism' with a political dimension, the RCC also started to protect and expand its own powers and interests, by 'seizing every opportunity to increase its powers [at] the expense of its partners or competitors, legislator and judiciary alike, while also showing a propensity to invalidate decisions taken by them in order to enforce its own vision upon the Constitution and, sometimes, its own political vision'.[50]

The power of the Court to review parliamentary resolutions enhanced its activism. The power was introduced by *Law no. 177/2010* amending the organic law of the Court and includes the review the constitutionality of all resolutions adopted by the chambers of parliament (other than the Standing Orders of the chambers, which already were included in the Court's competence via the Constitution). From the outset, this disposition was criticised by the majority of the doctrine, because of its obvious political purpose: submitting the Parliament to the Court's review which, at the time of the changes, was the object of a real 'battle' between the political parties for the nomination of new judges, with the obvious purpose to create a 'new majority' within the Court. Such a power is very rare in other democratic constitutional review systems (one of these rare examples being Latvia).[51] And this, because the traditional role of a Constitutional Court,

48 In Romania, there is no formal specialisation of judges, except for general criminal law, civil law and administrative law. There are no judges who specialise in homicide cases, in theft cases or in rape cases. Judges follow initial and continuous trainings in various areas, and, because of the European Commission's monitoring mechanism, a special regard was given to trainings related to corruption offences.

49 Selejan-Guțan and Tănăsescu, op. cit., supra, note 33.

50 Tănăsescu (2015), op. cit., supra, note 28, p. 246.

51 Arne Mavcic, *Powers of Constitutional Courts and Equivalent Bodies*. European Commission for Democracy Through Law, CDL-JU(98)10, p. 3.

despite being granted other ancillary powers, must remain the constitutionality review of legislation, and only in subsidiary a 'microconstitutionality review' (of judicial or administrative acts). This traditional role should prevent a constitutional court from having the power to become involved in the political game, by checking acts with a political stake, such as, in the Romanian case, parliamentary resolutions (for example, the US Supreme Court imposing the condition that the cases brought before it should lack a political character, as well as the 'cases and controversy' requirement).

The first failed attempt to change the law back was made in June 2012. The amending law was challenged before its promulgation and the Court had to decide on its constitutionality. By *Decision 727/2012*, the Court proved a manifest tendency to transform into an omnipotent and intangible organ, situated above the Parliament and any other authority, using as a single argument 'the respect of the rule of law'. No instance, said the Court, may give an opinion on the Court's activity: 'to appreciate and decide on the activity of the Constitutional Court [...] means its incorrect reception and, moreover, to ignore the substance of its fundamental role'.

In this Decision, the Court exceeded its constitutional limits for many reasons: a) it acted against its 'negative legislator' role, thus 'replacing' the legislator, even the constituent legislator, by giving a 'constitutional rank' to organic law provisions: 'although the power of reviewing parliamentary resolutions was given by the Court's organic law, it obtained a constitutional value by virtue of Article 146 (l) of the Constitution'.; b) it expressly limited the competence of the Parliament, by stating that, if there was 'the possibility to limit, eliminate or reduce these powers [of the Court, introduced by the same legislator] [...] this would mean to distort the goal of perfecting the constitutional democracy'. However, in an earlier decision from 2011, examining a constitutional amendment initiative, the Court had admitted that the powers introduced by virtue of Article 146 (l) of the Constitution had a 'legal rank' and not a 'constitutional rank' and proposed the elimination of this constitutional provision altogether (*Decision 799/2011*); c) in its reasoning, the Court uses no solid legal or constitutional argument: it only repeats that such a review is 'important for the functioning of the rule of law and for the respect of the balance of powers'. Indirectly, the Court proclaims itself the sole guardian of democracy by means of checking any act of parliament, becoming thus a 'universal reviewer', claiming to be 'above the political conflicts which are inherent to the relationships between the majority and the opposition'. By doing this, the Court ignored precisely the fact that, this kind of review makes it a referee of the parliamentary activity and thus a potential instrument used by one of the parties in such type of political conflicts.

In sum, the very practice of the Court shows that, in exercising this power, it examined resolutions with purely political stakes: appointments and dismissals from office, the vote of confidence procedure, resolutions on lifting the parliamentary immunity, etc.

In 2014, in a decision regarding a draft law of constitutional amendment (which has never been adopted), the Court reiterated this view and held that, if the constitutional legislator wishes to remove from the Constitution the possibility of the ordinary legislator to add new powers of the RCC (namely Article 146 letter l), it should first 'constitutionalise' the two powers already added by means of this Article, because otherwise the removal would 'breach the right to access to constitutional justice for the defence of constitutional values, principles and rules, i.e. the suppression of a guarantee of these values, rules and principles, which include the sphere of fundamental rights and freedoms'.[52] If this assertion might be true for the review of laws amending the Constitution (although, in this case, it would situate itself above the parliamentary two-thirds supermajority which can adopt such a law), the Court did not explain how the review of parliamentary resolutions would encompass a guarantee of fundamental rights and freedoms.

This case of judicial activism proves right what T. Ginsburg and Z. Elkins had said:

> [T]he involvement of courts in ancillary tasks has the potential to undermine their ability to conduct effective constitutional review, precisely because it pulls them into political conflicts. [...] The prestige of constitutional courts in general, their reputation for neutrality [...] creates an incentive to give them complex political problems to resolve. There is, however, a risk that constitutional courts will be drawn into inherently unwinnable zero-sum conflicts, which require deft maneuvering and skillful action. In new democracies, at least, it is not obvious that the courts themselves will always be up to the task.[53]

Another striking case in which the RCC acted as a defender not only of its general jurisdiction but of its own majority power was that of the separate opinions formulated to the Court's decisions. Thus, in 2017, following a series of critical, separate opinions formulated by certain judges, the plenum of the Court adopted, with a majority vote, *Internal Ruling no. 1/2017*, where it said that the right of judges to write a dissenting or concurring opinion is limited by a 'duty of self-restraint' and that there must be a 'reverence' manifested by 'any legal subject' as regards the fundamental institution of the Constitutional Court, 'a duty that belongs especially to Constitutional Court judges'. Based on these premises, the Ruling prohibited the publication of any opinions that comprise 'sententious, ostentatious, provocative or political remarks, as well as those which may lead to such an outcome'. Following an administrative case brought by a young lawyer before the Court of Appeals of Bucharest (the complaint held that the separate opinions are highly relevant to the legal profession and should be published at the same time with the Court's decisions), the Internal Ruling was annulled by the Court of Appeal. The RCC adopted, in July 2018, another Internal Ruling that changed some parts of the first one, but not in an essential manner. *Inter alia*, the new ruling says that 'the separate opinion cannot transgress beyond the opinion of the judge in order to become a precise criticism of the Constitutional Court's decision and it cannot be a direct attack against the latter'.[54]

52 RCC, Decision 80/2014 on the legislative proposal to revise the Constitution.
53 Tom Ginsburg, Zachary Elkins, *Ancillary Powers of Constitutional Courts*, in (2009) 87 Texas Law Review, p. 1431.
54 RCC, Internal Ruling no. 1/2018.

4 Conclusion

In the debate on judicial activism of constitutional courts, within their competences to control political power, a legitimate question arises: who controls the reviewer, in our case, the constitutional court? Should the constitutional court become more influential, through its activism, in respect of political authorities? The answer to this question depends largely on the degree of democratic development of a particular constitutional system, on the constitutional culture of the given country and, not in the least, on the degree of professionalisation of the constitutional court itself. As B. Iancu rightly put it:

> In the abstract and on the presupposition of a healthy constitutional culture and generally accepted normative standards, a strong constitutional court is a guarantee of the supremacy of the constitution and consequently of the rule of law. In a context such as the one described above [the post-communist Romanian context] an increase of the power of the constitutional tribunal is not necessarily conducive to the legal integration and normalisation of the political order. Judicial power without accountability may just as easily lead to perverse forms of politicisation under the guise of constitutional principles.[55]

In the case of the Romanian Constitutional Court, the particular cases of activism that were analysed are hard to explain, especially when one takes into account the moderate attitude of the Court in the first years of its existence. This initial self-restraint is partly due to the fact that the Court started its activity when the Constitution had just been enacted and it needed to be consolidated as a reference standard and not in the absence or in the process of drafting a new constitution, like in other countries in the region. A possible explanation for the Court's activism in the last decade could be the fact that the political fights in the period 2007–2009 (a period of co-habitation between the President and the Government, which entailed a suspension from office of the former) generated a 'competition' between constitutional judges and supreme court judges in imposing their views on the main controversial issues.[56] Another possible explanation for the Court's activism could be the actual failure of the democratic transition. In fact, Romania remains a 'non-consolidated' democracy, where the political actors are still not mature enough to solve their conflicts by applying the mechanisms of the balance of powers, and they refer them instead to the RCC, transforming it into the most powerful political actor, and by bringing it into the heart of politics. At this point, the Constitutional Court has a choice: to remain in the limits set by the original spirit of the Constitution (a 'negative legislator' designated to remove the unconstitutional errors from the legislation) or to be caught in political games that question its very role in the constitutional architecture.

55 Iancu, op. cit., supra, note 24, p. 162.
56 Tănăsescu (2015), op. cit., supra, note 28, p. 249.

In this context, two possibilities of reform are thus envisaged: first, to curtail, via constitutional amendments, those of the Court's powers that come into close contact with the political game, thus avoiding the risk that the Court is being used as a political instrument. Nevertheless, due to the Court's expressed reluctance to give up the ancillary powers by denying the autonomy of the legislator in this respect and by creating thus a new limit to the constitutional amendment, this will be very difficult to achieve.

A second possibility would be to increase the degree of professionalisation and of ethical accountability of the constitutional judges, by changing the criteria (more career judges, not affected by political affiliation and used to the independence requirements, more academics and specialists in constitutional law, which would bring added quality to the Court's interpretations) and procedures of appointment (more transparency, the increase of the majority required to appoint constitutional judges by the chambers of Parliament, so that they will be appointed by consensus and not unilaterally by the ruling majority).

In addition, the whole paradigm of the Court constantly invoking its own power and authority against others should be reconsidered, because, as E.S. Tănăsescu points out, 'it is a sad and worrying situation for a judge who feels obliged to resort to arguments of authority instead of laying its authority on legal arguments'.[57] In the absence of such an internal reform, the Court's public image and the public trust in its objective and professional decisions would be significantly shattered and would fuel the discourse which questions the utility of its very existence. In any case, and subject to thorough reforms, a form of judicial control of political power should be maintained, through the force of constitutional interpretation of norms, as a powerful tool in consolidating the rule of law.

57 Ibidem, p. 248.

7 The revolutionary role of constitutional courts in Morocco and Jordan as a contemporary example from the MENA region

Hadeel S. Abu Hussein

1 Introduction

Establishing the constitutional court (hereafter the CC) is a critical function of the state and is understood as a key element of demonstrating a state's democratic identity. Furthermore, CCs are essential monitoring bodies in democratic countries. The establishment of the CC is a catalyst in a society in transition or reforming towards democracy, as the court plays many significant roles in the application and understanding of constitutions, as well as in the protection of human rights and the rule of law. This is not a new mechanism; various countries such as France, Germany and Egypt use CCs to enforce and promote the rule of law, establish legitimacy, impose the separation and balance of powers, and protect the fundamental rights of citizens. The court protects individuals' rights by offering a forum for resolving disputes and holding distinctive political participants accountable to their constitutional obligations. Additionally, such courts can offer political protection for the opposition.[1]

Major political concerns following the Arab Spring uprising in the Middle East and North Africa (hereafter MENA) region lead to compromises between political powers. Judicial independence is viewed as a cornerstone of the rule of law, and as such a crucial component of democratic transitions. But in the context of democratic monarchies and their democratisation, the definition of judicial independence may require modification to take into account the unique challenges of moving to a system of rule by the people. Particularly, an independent judiciary and judicial review may slow down legislative and constitutional reform by engaging in a form of constitutional review designed to shield the preferences of the

1 After authoritarian rule, establishing a constitutional court can be a symbol of the end of the authoritarian period and the start of a new democratic era on one hand; on the other, constitutional justice is often a delicate position in states that are 'legally' emerging between reserve and weakness, 'so as not to unnecessarily aggravate spaces under democratic construction', or in the extreme, between development and consolidation or legitimisation of a process that is quite authoritarian. Rainer Grote and Tilmann J. Röder, Constitutionalism, Human Rights, and Islam after the Arab Spring, Oxford University Press (2016), Part 6 Constitutional Courts: New Guardians of the Constitutions? 6.2. Morocco's Constitutional Court after the 2011 Reforms, Oxford Constitutional Law. Nadia Bernoussi.

DOI: 10.4324/9781003200666-11

elite from democratic reversal. This chapter examines this problem through a detailed exploration of the CC's role and cases in Morocco and Jordan to illustrate the future risk of a narrow definition of judicial review and judicial independence. Also, it explores the appropriate balance between autonomy and accountability in the CCs during periods of transition from monarchy to democracy or of democratic strengthening and suggests how there is a space for future developments of a judicial activism approach instead of one of self-restraint.

The wave of Arab Spring protests in the MENA region led to a wide range of results, and each country in the region, and subsequently their judicial systems, was affected to varying extents, causing a number of constitutional transitions and reforms. The exceptional circumstances of the upsurge-built momentum within those countries initiated improvements to their legal systems, such as constitutional judicial review. Countries have done this by adopting or considering amendments to reflect the governments' commitments to the rule of law.

The Kingdom of Morocco took the lead by rapidly drafting and adopting a new constitution on 29 July 2011.[2] The new constitution of the Kingdom of Morocco replaces the previous one and offers a careful framework for transitional arrangements.[3] The Hashemite Kingdom of Jordan also reformed its existing constitution in September 2011. Palestinian authorities followed in April 2016 and established a new Supreme CC of Palestine. The Court was created by presidential decree, based on Articles 103 and 104 of the Basic Law of Palestine 2003 (amended 2005)[4] and the Supreme Constitutional Court 2006 (amended 2012).[5] The Supreme Constitutional Court of Palestine holds supremacy over all lower courts. The purpose of establishing the Supreme Constitutional Court of Palestine was to maintain clarity and legitimacy, ensure appropriate separation of powers and independence of judges, and to embed the democratic system and the Court into Palestinian national norms.[6,7]

Consequently, many countries saw the emergence of the CC as essential to strengthening the role of the courts in protecting and implementing the constitution. Others, such as Tunisia, improved their existing constitutional system by amending the appointment process or expanding the CCs' functions to guarantee the rule of law. Some other countries, such as Lebanon, did not undertake any constitutional reforms.

To summarise, this chapter presents an assessment of the revolutionary role of CCs in the MENA region and a detailed examination of the establishment of CCs in Morocco and Jordan, which are engaged in constitutional reforms to varying degrees. We will study the CCs' activities and judgments related to constitutional

2 Moroccan Official Gazette (19 July 2011). https://www.constituteproject.org/constitution/Morocco_2011.pdf.

3 Art. 176–180, ibid.

4 Basic Law of the Palestinian National Authority (2003) (amended 2005), 18 March 2003.

5 Law on the Supreme Constitutional Court No. (3) of 2006. Official Gazette, number 62, 25 March 2006, at 93.

6 Ibid.

7 The guiding principles of the Law on the Supreme Constitutional Court 2006.

reform in the two monarchies and the extent to which the CCs established and carried out decisions autonomously or were more subject to political decisions in the reform process. Did it really challenge the notion of the supreme authoritarian regime? While the monarchies could impose legislative change, the CCs were, at best, partially able to enforce these laws or to impose legislative change, limiting the impact of the CCs in reality.

2 Methodology

The methodology I have adopted in this chapter is mainly a case law method, consulting primary and secondary sources such as statuary acts, court decisions, parliamentary discussion, reports and other studies; I will apply a legal research methodology given the fact that the study is doctrinal. The principal tools applied are historical and descriptive methods to trace the details of the CC evaluation in Morocco and Jordan; the historical perspectives of the monarchy, democracy and the judicial system in Jordan and Morocco; and the statutory and constitutional schemes relating to those issues.

3 Constitutional amendments in parliamentary monarchies

In legal form, constitutional amendments are not neutral acts or technical matters; they are reactions to major political interests and are used by political powers that opposed one another. The recent constitutional amendments in Jordan and Morocco are no exceptions to this rule. The constitutional amendments followed a long process of evolution in the democratic demands of the people, were shaped by the requirements of regionalisation and of reforming the structure of the state, and were meant to strengthen the democratic nature of the state. Therefore, the constitutional amendments originated within the democratic transition debate, the rule of law and attempts to ensure good governance;[8] however, each of the Arab monarchies experienced different challenges associated with their authoritarian rule in the context of the Arab Spring.[9] While some authoritarian regimes have been ousted,[10] the Arab

8 Rainer Grote and Tilmann J. Röder, Constitutionalism, Human Rights, and Islam after the Arab spring, Oxford University Press (2016), Part 6 Constitutional Courts: New Guardians of the Constitutions? 6.2. Morocco's Constitutional Court after the 2011 Reforms, Oxford Constitutional Law. Nadia Bernoussi.

9 For example, the monarchy in Bahrain represented by Sunni Khalifa has been under massive pressure from the Shiite majority yet survived the crises in February and March 2011 using a mixture of repression tools. Jordan, Kuwait and Morocco received unprecedented criticism of the ruling monarchs; Oman and Saudi Arabia experienced a new form of activism; smaller Gulf monarchies such as the United Arab Emirates and Qatar have remained largely calm. André Bank, Thomas Richter and Anna Sunik, 'Durable, yet Different: Monarchies in the Arab Spring', 4(2) Journal of Arabian Studies (December 2014), 136–179.

10 For example, Tunisia, Egypt, Yemen and Libya; André Bank, Thomas Richter and Anna Sunik, 'Durable, yet Different: Monarchies in the Arab Spring', 4(2) Journal of Arabian Studies (December 2014), 136–179.

monarchies remain relatively stable. Generally, the monarchies have been unaffected by the Arab Spring upheaval and have remained relatively durable.

The main focus of this section is to draw attention to the diverse strategies that were used by the monarchies to endure the challenges created by the Arab Spring, in particular non-Gulf monarchies including Morocco and Jordan,[11] and to highlight the constitutional reforms proposed by those two monarchies as a strategy for countering the protests in the first months of 2011.[12] Morocco defined itself as following 'moderate Islamic religion, national unity with multiple tributaries, the connotational monarch and democratic choice'.[13] Meanwhile, the Hashemite Kingdom of Jordan describes its system of government as being parliamentary, monarchical and hereditary to support the contention that the parliamentary aspects preceded the monarchical aspects of government, as stated in article 1: 'The Hashemite Kingdom of Jordan is an independent sovereign Arab State. It is indivisible and no part of it may be ceded. The Jordanian people is a part of the Arab Nation, and its ruling regime is parliamentary with a hereditary monarchy.'[14] Those parliamentary monarchies emerged relatively unhurt from the region's uprisings. During the Arab Spring protests, a popular movement emerged in Jordan and Morocco; among other demands, the protests called for constitutional monarchies to limit the kings' powers, elected governments, security reform and the formation of CCs to appease popular sentiment. Both kings accepted, and they proposed constitutional amendments as a first step in the right direction. Hence, the Moroccan and Jordanian constitutional reforms led to the establishment of the CCs.

These contemporary examples are useful for exploring the extent to which the establishment of CCs can be revolutionary and provide a dominant nature to the public debate over political reform. The Arab Spring generated a spirit of cooperation between revolutionary groups, with calls to implement democratic reforms, demands for democratisation, and attempts to promote human rights and judicial independence. First, we examine and present an overview of the law, amendments and articles that established and defined the role of the CCs, in Jordan and then in Morocco.

11 In the Arab world, there are eight authoritarian monarchies in the region. There is typically a distinction between two monarchies in the MENA region, a first group consisting of the six monarchies in Gulf States monarchies (Saudi Arabia, Qatar, Bahrain, United Arab Emirates, Kuwait and the Sultanate of Oman), and a second group comprised of the non-Gulf monarchies of Jordan and Morocco. The monarchies have experienced quite different challenges to their authoritarian rule in the context of the Arab Spring. Michael Herb, All in the Family: Absolutism, Revolution, and Democracy in the Middle Eastern Monarchies, State University of New York Press (1999); Russell E. Lucas, 'Monarchical Authoritarianism: Survival and Political Liberalization in a Middle Eastern Regime Type', 36(1) International Journal of Middle East Studies (2004), 103–119; G. Luciani, 'Allocation v. Production State', in The Rentier State, eds. H. Beblawi and G. Luciani (1987), 63–84; Zoltan Barany, 'Unrest and State Response in Arab Monarchies', 24(2) Mediterranean Quarterly (2013), 5–38.

12 André Bank, 'Jordan and Morocco: Pacification through Constitutional Reform?' in Protest, Revolt and Regime Change in the Arab World: Actors, Challenges, Implications and Policy Options, ed. Muriel Asseburg (2012), 31–33.

13 Article 1, Moroccan Official Gazette (19 July 2011).

14 Jordan Constitution, Jordanian Official Gazette no. 5117 (1 October 2011).

3.1 Jordan

Jordan was influenced by developments in the Arab Spring, and King Abdullah II formed a Royal Commission to review the need to amend the constitution.[15] After passing through parliament and government approval, the amendments were published and issued in the Official Gazette of Jordan and set to come into effect on 1 October 2011. The major amendments to the constitution included the creation of the CC, with 'oversight on the constitutionality of the applicable laws and regulations'. Articles 58 and 59 of the Constitution of Jordan[16] articulate the formation of the CC as crucial for the future as a guarantor of the separation of powers, a regulator of respect for the sovereignty of law, and a protector of citizens' fundamental rights in accordance with the constitution.[17]

Law No. 15 of 2012, which was passed with an absolute majority of the parliament, established the Constitution Court Law, which declared the financial and administrative independence of the CC. Additionally, the law describes the role of the CC in monitoring the constitutionality of laws and regulations in force. Therefore, the CC's role is mainly overseeing the constitutionality of regulations and interpreting legal texts.[18] Furthermore, the CC interprets provisions of the constitution, when requested by either a decision of the Council of Minsters or by resolution taken by the Senate or the Chamber of Deputies, and issues its judgments in the name of the king.[19] Therefore, the CC is a reliable gauge of the judiciary system's autonomy, and the CC's independence preserves citizens' rights and freedoms, as guaranteed by the Jordanian Constitution. Nonetheless, some laws and regulations might violate the constitution.

15 In May 2011, the king formed a Royal Commission of ten dignitaries in order to introduce any needed constitutional amendments. A closer examination of the Royal Commission discloses several factors to indicate the problematic formation of the commission that lack professionalism due to lack of experts' appointment engagement. The Royal Commission submitted its recommendation to the king following more than three months of secret meetings. The proposed recommendations suggested amending 68 paragraphs grouped in 37 articles of the constitution. In turn, on the recommendations and the advice of his inner circle, the king directed the government and the two houses of parliament to finalise the amendments within 30 days. The Council of Ministries, composed of 30 Ministers then, followed by the House of Representatives, composed of 120 members, needed 27 days to finalise the constitutional amendments, which left the Senate only three days to make any observations. Three days were not enough time for the 60 members of the Senate to review the amendments, so the Senate decided to approve the amendments without a single change or observation. Jordanian Official Gazette no. 5117 (1 October 2011).

16 Ibid.

17 Article 5 of the Constitutional Court Law of 2012; King Abdullah II issued a royal decree on 6 October 2012, appointing a president and eight members of the newly established Constitution Court.

18 Article 4, ibid.

19 El Jarida al Rasmiyya 07/06/2012, no. 5161, pp. 2519–2528.

The Jordanian CC is one of the most recently created CCs in the Arab world;[20] it was founded in 2012.[21] It was introduced to promote the role of law and legal transparency.[22] Across history, legal reform has been an ongoing process in every nation.[23] However, the Jordanian CC faces many challenges that have resulted in calls for its reform. It is important to highlight that the people's demands following the Arab Spring were not the first attempt by the people of Jordan to demand their individual rights and freedoms. A similar endeavour was attempted in April 1989, when the Jordanian people raised their voices against the corruption and the monopoly of the elite, and a powerful government that had revoked individuals' rights and freedoms. During that time, Jordan changed into a state controlled by powerful men rather than a state of law.[24] This uprising pressed for reform and asked for changes from the authorities. The late King Hussein responded with drastic measures, such as changing the government, holding elections for a new House of Representatives, and forming a commission to propose a National Charter.[25]

In October 1991, the National Charter was declared.[26] However, the charter was never implemented; it had merely been a way to appease the people and make it appear as if Jordan had moved towards democracy, while in fact nothing had been reformed. The rule of men overshadowed the rule of law.[27] If we connect the dots, we understand why the Arab Spring was a golden opportunity to rise again and call for genuine reform.

A closer examination of Jordanian CC provisions[28] is necessary and even challenging,[29] and can be considered a slippery slope instead of a way to fulfil the people's

20 Constitution of the Hashemite Kingdom of Jordan, 1 January 1952, amended in 2011, art. 59/1; Law No. 15 of 2012 (Constitutional Court Law), 6 June 2013, art. 15/A (Jordan).

21 Issam Saliba, 'Jordan: Constitutional Law Court Newly Established in Jordan', Global Legal Monitor, Library of Congress (3 December 2012).

22 Alt'adaliat Al Dusturia alidafat almuhima fi a'maliat alislah alsiyasya wata'ziz aldimuqrtia, Petra (7 July 2017) [Arabic] (Significant Constitutional amendments to strengthen democracy).

23 Anne Daily, 'Federalism and families', 143 U. PA. L. Rev., 1787, 1828 (1994–1995); Scott Grinsell, 'Caste and Problem of Social Reform in Indian Equality Law', 35 Yale J. Intl L., 199, 218 (2010).

24 Rainer Grote and Tilmann J. Röder, Constitutionalism, Human Rights, and Islam after the Arab Spring, Oxford University Press (2016), Part 6 Constitutional Courts: New Guardians of the Constitutions? 6.4. Constitutional Reform and the Rise of Constitutional Adjudication in Jordan: Background, Issues, and Controversies, Mahamad Hammouri.

25 Drastic measures were taken, such as abolishing martial law [according to the martial law, the cognisance of deciding the accusation against a citizen was given to the State Security Court (Martial Court) subject to the approval of the Martial Governor, whose decisions are not subject to any court appeal.], which was in application until 1991.

26 Text of the charter: http://www.kinghussein.gov.jo/charter-national.htlm.

27 Rainer Grote and Tilmann J. Röder, Constitutionalism, Human Rights, and Islam after the Arab Spring, Oxford University Press (2016), Part 6 Constitutional Courts: New Guardians of the Constitutions? (p. 724).

28 Articles 58–61 of the Constitution of Jordan, Jordanian Official Gazette no. 5117 (1 October 2011).

29 Since the 1990s Jordanians have been requesting the establishment of the JCC.

demands. It worked de facto to suit the government. Examples of such provisions include the questionable appointment system. The nine judges of the Jordanian CC are appointed by government decision that must be approved by the King. By law, only the government, the House of Representatives and the Senate are empowered to bring direct action to the Jordanian CC to decide on the constitutionality of laws. Therefore, neither individuals nor political parties can bring direct action before the Jordanian CC. Furthermore, according to Article 60 of the Jordanian Constitution, the Higher Court will judge whether or not a petition of unconstitutionality should be referred to the Jordanian CC. Thus, it is a long process for cases to reach the Jordanian CC, creating a burden for the parties that might undermine justice due to the lengthy process.[30]

3.2 *Morocco*

Almost at the same time, constitutional reforms took place in Morocco, where the king, on the advice of his advisor, formed a Royal Commission.[31] After studying the matter, the Commission formulated a draft amendment to discuss reforms in the meetings with civil society members which followed. Ultimately, the conclusion of those meetings was turned into provisions in the Constitution of Morocco.[32]

Like Jordan, Morocco is another example of a country establishing a new CC with expanded functions to represent a changing Kingdom of Morocco.[33] King Mohammed VI installed the new CC, following the 2011 Moroccan Constitution,[34] and the Constitutional Council is to be replaced by the Constitutional Court[35] following the 2011 Moroccan Constitution.[36] The judiciary's independence will be enhanced, according to Article 130 of the Moroccan Constitution. The Moroccan CC is comprised of 12 judges: six of them elected in secret, of which three are elected by the House of Representatives, and three by the Senate. The secretary general of the High Scientific Council proposes one judge's name to the king (one of the remaining six judges). Furthermore, the five other judges are appointed by the king. Therefore, the executive authority can only influence the appointment of the minority of the judges.[37] It inherits all of its prerogatives and adjudges new ones, with expanded powers as might be brought before a court of law.

30 Article 60 of the Jordanian Constitution, Jordanian Official Gazette no. 5117 (1 October 2011).

31 The Royal Commission comprises 19 notable law professors, who also discussed the suggestions and amendments with skilled experts; cf. Madie Schutte, 'Post-Election Reflection: Morocco's 2011 Constitutional Referendum' (16 August 2011).

32 Moroccan Official Gazette (19 July 2011).

33 Articles 113–116 of the new constitution provide a better basis for the independence of the judiciary from the executive power by giving more authority to the Higher Judicial Council. Article 6 states, 'the law is the supreme expression of the will of the nation' and provides new guarantees for the primacy of law over individuals and public institutions.

34 Moroccan Official Gazette (19 July 2011).

35 Article 129, ibid.

36 Ibid.

37 Article 130, ibid.

The 2011 Moroccan Constitution[38] introduced the Moroccan CC in the name of protecting the rights and freedoms of citizens and ensuring the organic laws, ordinary laws and regulations of both houses of parliament conform to the Constitution. Additionally, the Moroccan CC has essential powers to check the constitutionality of international conventions and rule on disputes within the context of the new regionalisation of the country.[39] Moreover, according to Article 133 of the Moroccan Constitution, any entitled individual can plead the unconstitutionality of a law before any judge in Morocco who in turn has the jurisdiction to refer the case to the Moroccan CC based on merit to support the petition.[40]

Therefore, the constitutional amendments are a de facto method that the monarchy uses to restore the confidence of the people and re-establish social connection to reform common ground with the people. Drawing attention to the law being equal, the amendments promote social justice to found a true democracy. It is worth noting that the 2011 constitutional amendments were not unprecedented but followed Morocco adopting a gradual and systematic approach, where in 1992 constitutional amendments anticipated substantial human rights amendments, restructuring of the powers of the monarchy, increased powers for the constituted bodies and new institutions, such as the Constitutional Council.[41] Soon after, in 1996, additional constitutional amendments that proposed dualism had a positive influence on the legislative process and the organisation of the state authorities. As mentioned, the new constitution of 29 July 2011[42] proposed transitional arrangements.[43] As explained earlier, this was the second time that the constituted authority acted drastically to wipe out the former legal system.[44] Cultivated by the conclusions of the Equity and Reconciliation Authority[45] and by reports on the fiftieth anniversary of the Moroccan parliament, the new constitution promised regionalisation of the universal democratic standards. The process of drafting the constitutional amendment was progressive in comparison with the previous reforms, and the legitimacy was reflected in several behaviours, such as professionalism by appointing the Advisory Committee for the Revision of the Constitution.[46] It was followed by a political follow-up and consultation mechanism.[47]

38 Ibid.
39 Articles 132 and 133, ibid.
40 Article 133, ibid.
41 Abdelatif Menouni. 'Lectures dans le Project de Constitution révisée', in Driss Basri, Michel Rousset and George Vedel (eds.), Révision de la Constitution Marocaine, Imprimerie Royale (1992), 55–82.
42 Moroccan Official Gazette (19 July 2011).
43 Articles 176–180, ibid.
44 Article 103 of the constitution stipulated that 'the Constitution promulgated by Zahīr No. 1–70–177 of the 27 journada I 1390 (July 1970) shall be revoked'.
45 Instance Equité et Réconciliation (IER).
46 The Advisory Committee for the Revision of the Constitution chaired by Abedltif Menoumi.
47 Mohamed Moatassim chairs the political mechanism for the follow-up, consultation and exchange of views on the draft revision of the constitution.

3.3 Judicial review v. monarchy

A primary question to explore the reform would be to ask if there is a legal philosophy behind the reform. We are dealing with two parliamentary-monarchical regimes in Jordan and Morocco. For instance, one of the steps that King Abdullah II of Jordan took while attempting to establish constitutional monarchy[48] was establishing the Jordanian CC, as mentioned earlier.[49] It is similar to the Moroccan CC,[50] but has the right to strike down any unconstitutional law or regulations provided to the Jordanian CC.

The Moroccan CC imposes challenges first to the legitimacy question and second to checks and balances.[51] Legitimacy in a monarchical regime is not an easy question to tackle. Courts in most democratic monarchical systems are able to announce certain laws as unconstitutional, but the courts are not authorised to strike down these laws. For instance, in the United Kingdom, courts can issue a non-binding declaration of unconstitutionality.[52] Hence, despite the unconstitutionality of a law, the law is still valid.[53] Under republican systems, the constitutional courts provide various venues, meaning that in non-monarchic republican regimes the right to render unconstitutional law as invalid is acceptable.[54] Therefore, compared to other monarchical regimes, the Jordanian CC and Moroccan CC competencies are unconventional and delicate.

One additional challenge that cannot be ignored is the checks and balances between the king, the CC and the parliament. One straightforward example is that in the Jordanian CC the king appoints judges.[55] According to the constitutional amendments of 2011, the right to abolish any unconstitutional amendments is given to the Jordanian CCs' judges,[56] but the constitutional amendments did not give any weight to the parliament.[57] Consequently, all the privilege was given to the king.[58] In Morocco, before the constitutional amendments of 2011, Article 93 handed the parliament members, whom the public elected,[59] the ability to

48 Layth Kamal Nsrawin, Athar al-ta'edilat al-dustorya li-"am 2011, ealaa al-sulutat al-'amat fi al'urdun, http://www.parliament.gov.sy/SD08/MSF/1435494620_.PDF.
49 Constitutional Overview, Hashemite Kingdom of Jordan, Constitution – Al Court (2017), http://www.cco.gov.jo/en-us/About-the-Court/Constitutional-Overview.
50 Moroccan Official Gazette (19 July 2011).
51 Article 130, ibid.
52 David Jenkins, Common Law Declarations of Unconstitutionality, 7 Int. J. Const. L. 183, 200 (2009).
53 Ibid.
54 For instance, Marbury v. Madison, 5 U.S. 137, 138 (1803).
55 Article 15/A; Tom Ginsburg and Nuno Garoupa, Building Reputation in Constitutional Courts, Political and Judicial Audiences, 28 Ariz. J. Int. and Comp. L. (2011), 539, 547.
56 Article 15/B, ibid.
57 Article 5/A, ibid.
58 Article 15/A, ibid.; in theory, the sole source of the JCC's legitimacy is the king, and if he opposes any law, he can strike down the law through the Jordanian Constitutional Court. Hypothetically, this might be a tool used against the public will.
59 Article 93, Constitution of Kingdom of Morocco.

challenge the king's decision in the event of his rejection or confirmation of new laws. In the constitutional amendments, the state paradigm based on the rule of law and the constitutional justice theme is a critical element in the contemporary state.[60]

3.4 Groundwork comparison between the Jordanian Constitutional Court and Moroccan Constitutional Court

The following analysis briefly explores a comparison between the functions of the CC of Morocco and the CC of Jordan.

First, the 2011 Moroccan Constitution[61] introduced the CC in the name of protecting the rights and freedoms of citizens and ensured that the organic laws, ordinary laws and regulations of both houses of parliament conform to the constitution. Moreover, a CC has essential powers to check the constitutionality of international conventions and rule on disputes within the context of the new regionalisation of the country.[62] Analogously, Jordan was influenced by this development as mentioned above. The significant amendments to the constitution included the creation of the CC[63] to articulate the formation of a CC as crucial for the future as a guarantor of separation of powers, a regulator of respect for the sovereignty of law, and protector of citizens' fundamental rights under the constitution.[64] Besides, the law describes the role of the CC in monitoring the constitutionality of laws and regulations in force. Therefore, the constitutional CC's role is primarily overseeing the constitutionality and regulations as well as interpreting legal texts.[65] The CC will interpret provisions of the constitution when requested, either by a decision of the Council of Ministers or by a resolution taken by the Senate or the Chamber of Deputies, and issue its judgments in the name of the king.[66] Therefore, the CC is a dependable measurement of the judicial system's independence, and the CC's objectivity preserves citizens' rights and freedoms, as guaranteed by the Jordanian Constitution. Nonetheless, some laws and regulations might violate the constitution.

Second, in Morocco the new amendment to Article 133 of the Moroccan Constitution[67] deals with an objection of unconstitutionality. It is important to mention that this is a useful tool, introduced in the name of protecting the rights and freedoms of citizens. Hence, the Moroccan CC guarantees that organic laws,

60 It is important to acknowledge that since the 1980s Morocco has witnessed the emergence and universality phenomenon.

61 Moroccan Official Gazette (19 July 2011).

62 Articles 132 and 133 of the 2011 Constitution detail the competencies of the Constitutional Court.

63 Ibid.

64 Article 5 of the Constitutional Court Law of 2012. King Abdullah II issued a royal decree on 6 October 2012, appointing a president and eight members of a newly established Constitutional Court.

65 Article 4, ibid.

66 El Jarida al Rasmiyya 07/06/2012, no. 5161, pp. 2519 –2528 [Arabic] (Official Newspaper, 07/06/2012, no. 5161, pp. 2519–2528).

67 Moroccan Official Gazette (19 July 2011).

ordinary laws and regulations conform to the constitution. This mechanism would offer the right for any political party involved in legal proceedings before the CC to challenge a statuary provision if constitutional rights were violated.[68] This opening of the option of questioning the constitutionality of a law that is already in force leads to the mechanism of ex post constitutional review. The 2011 Constitution offers a degree of ex-post review of legislation, as well as ex-ante review. The most critical issue in the Jordanian court is linked with the mechanism provided by Article 11 of the 2012 law. It provides that a judge, when deemed justified, cannot refer the question directly to the CC when the parties raise a challenge to constitutionality during a judicial proceeding. Rather, she or he must refer the case to the Court of Cassation, which is the only judicial body entrusted with the exclusive power to raise the question of constitutionality. The Jordanian law adopted a rigid and centralised system of control over the lower courts, which does not favour access to the CC, while in the Moroccan system the power of referring questions of constitutionality is widespread among all courts.

Third, the 2011 Constitution is the first Moroccan Constitution to allow private litigants to challenge the constitutionality of laws concerning the determination of the conditions and modalities of raising the issue of unconstitutionality of a law.[69] Under Law No. 15.86, private litigants are allowed to raise the issue of constitutionality before any courts, including for the first time the Court of Appeals and the Court of Cassation.[70] In other words, even if a litigant did not raise the issue of constitutionality before the lower court, he or she can still bring it up before the higher courts, including the Court of Cassation.[71]

Nevertheless, the Jordanian system[72] keeps the exclusivity of governmental bodies in submitting complaints, which causes a restrictive prohibition on individuals to use the path of the CC and limits their right to access the court.[73] Furthermore, in Jordan, there is a requirement that complaints need to pass a double filter, either through the institutional path – by going through governmental bodies – or through a referral from the Court of Cassation. Hence, the Court of Cassation conducts primary reviews of cases before referring them to the CC.[74] For instance, in Germany, Spain and Turkey, the direct complaint by individual or groups is sent to the CC for the protection of fundamental rights. The arguments put forward in favour of the direct individual complaint point out the possibility of offering citizens a 'residual' remedy before a body like the CC. When all the ordinary remedies have been

68 Prior to this reform, litigants could not challenge constitutionality of any statute, similar to Article 61–1 of the French Constitution.

69 On 6 February 2018, Morocco's Parliament approved, in accordance with Article 133 of the 2011 Moroccan Constitution, Law No. 15.86: website of the Ministry in Charge of Relations with the Parliament (in Arabic) http://www.mcrp.gov.ma/pdf/Lois/Projets/86.15/Representants/SP_LEC_2.pdf.

70 Article 3 of Law No. 15.86.

71 Article 5 of Law No. 15.86.

72 The Italian system also has not introduced the direct complaint by individuals.

73 Article 6(1) of European Convention on Human Rights.

74 However, individuals who are part of a lawsuit in court can also contest the unconstitutionality of laws and regulations.

exhausted, or when a case cannot be brought before an ordinary judge, the recourse to the direct individual complaint could favour the public's knowledge of the role of the CC and enhance in the future a broader access to the CC by the lower courts and individual judges.[75]

Fourth, in Morocco, the CC may also now rule on the conformity of international conventions with the constitution. While the Jordanian court does not include this directly, as part of Morocco's international legal obligations recognised in international law, it is included as reflected in the jurisprudence of international human rights bodies, while in Jordan, it was not mentioned as a direct obligation by the CC law.

Finally, in both Morocco[76] and Jordan, CC decisions are binding, not subject to appeal, and must be enforced by public authorities. Furthermore, they both have an executive branch that contains vast power concerning appointments for the CC judges. In addition, both CCs indicate that the courts' proceedings are confidential.[77]

To conclude, it is important to highlight that developments and intentions have shown a growing commitment to carrying out an efficient constitutional review and accordingly a move towards judicial independence. Both CCs are trying to push their way toward a useful judicial review of legislation. The judicial and political traditions and the current needs of every country play an essential role in the framework and the functioning of the system of constitutional review. Accordingly, the functions of the CCs have critical importance regarding ensuring the court's competence, independence and impartiality, as well as its effectiveness in upholding the rule of law and protecting and enforcing human rights.

4 The revolutionary role of the Constitutional Court as protector of freedom, individual rights and human rights

The CC's role in any country is associated with the concept of how the people approach their government. How do legal systems protect their interests?[78] That might vary due to the judicial review that was established in each country.[79]

75 Ekince, Saglaw, 'Individual application to the Turkish Constitutional Court', Publications of the Constitutional Court of Turkey Ankara (2015).

76 Article 134; on 6 February 2018, Morocco's Parliament approved, in accordance with Article 133 of the 2011 Moroccan Constitution, Law No. 15.86: website of the Ministry in Charge of Relations with the Parliament (in Arabic).

77 Article 18 of the amendment of the Constitution of Jordan.

78 H.S. Toubat, E. Mahafzeh and H.A. Balas, 'Oversight on the Constitutionality of Laws: A Case Study of the Jordanian Constitutional Court', J. Pol'y & Globalization (2019), 82, 17.

79 L.K. Nasrawin, 'Protecting Human Rights through Constitutional Adjudication – Jordan as a Case Study', 25(2) Digest of Middle East Studies (2016), 264–284; In the Unites States, for example, change occurred in the people's attitude towards their own government due to the judicial review that was established that imposed on the Constitutional Court to adapt to the people's attitudes regardless of the circumstances linked with freedoms and rights limitations.

In the MENA region, the understanding of freedoms and citizen protection is a debated matter and one of the main causes of the Arab Spring protests. This section will examine the CC's role in freedom protection and individuals' rights and basic freedoms. The CC forms the legal framework for more democratic societies in Morocco and Jordan, by balancing the judiciary and democracy.[80] The challenges that the CCs face are to find the right balance between the court's duties towards the people on one hand and the duties towards the state on the other hand.[81] The determination is based on the legislation in each state. Accordingly, in some cases, this could produce a political position; in other cases, a resolution could be accessible without facing any conflicts. Some might claim that the role and regulation of the CC in public life is the ruling party's responsibility in ordinary and extraordinary circumstances. Thus, a CC has to deal with challenges based on the legislation and the resolution.[82] Therefore, a CC should support and protect human rights and freedoms to play an active role in the MENA region, keeping in mind some principal elements, such as the responsibility of judges and lawyers and the awareness of the public. The hope is that CCs will have an actual judicial role in protecting human rights and freedoms, enhancing justice and advancing the rule of law in the MENA region.[83] At a theoretical level, the public demand in the region played a crucial role in establishing the CCs to provide a judicial review to invalidate the regulations and laws opposed to constitutions and in violation of human rights and freedom. However, the review procedures proposed by the new amendment provisions are particularly ambiguous. Therefore, the cynics argue that the review procedure is unnecessary and not helpful. To build a human rights-oriented and progressive jurisprudence, it is essential for a CC to maintain the independence of the judiciary and judges while deciding a constitutional issue. This will remain a problematic aspect under examination, due, for instance, to the direct intervention of the king in Jordan in judges' appointments.[84] It increases trust among the public if the judicial system in general and the CC in particular are reliable and key elements in human rights and freedom. A CC does not have exclusive powers over protection of the human rights and freedoms of citizens, as indeed the king remains the protector in a monarchical regime. Likewise, in Morocco, the king, for example, remains a protector 'of the rights and freedoms of citizens, male and female, and of groups'.[85] Parallel with the previous constitution, in

80 M. Abu-Karaki, R.S. Faqir and M.A.K. Marashadah, 'Democracy & Judicial Controlling in Jordan: A Constitutional Study', 4 J. Pol. & L. (2011), 180.

81 L.K. Nasrawin, 'Protecting Human Rights through Constitutional Adjudication – Jordan as a Case Study', 25(2) Digest of Middle East Studies (2016), 264–284.

82 T. Ginsburg, 'Building Reputation in Constitutional Courts: Political and Judicial audiences', 28 Arizona Journal of International and Comparative Law (2011), 539–568.

83 In Jordan, as one example. L.K. Nasrawin, 'Protecting Human Rights through Constitutional Adjudication – Jordan as a Case Study', 25(2) Digest of Middle East Studies (2016), 264–284.

84 Article 5 A. For instance, the judges' appointment process rests solely with the king of Jordan.

85 Article 42, Moroccan Official Gazette (19 July 2011).

monarchies the question of the degree of involvement of the king in the constitution and the laws is still open, despite the efforts to empower judges. Under the new constitution, the judges remain 'in charge of protection of rights and freedom'.[86]

5 Legitimacy and hegemony: Drawing the balance for the future

This section describes the anticipated narrative supported by the general opinion to explain that the decision to establish constitutional courts in Morocco and Jordan[87] emerged as a result of the Arab Spring protests, rather than the regimes' defence mechanisms and sense of security to provide creative solutions as a way of handling crises, particularly in monarchical regimes, to provide democratic reforms and introduce changes. To do so, the current exploration details the history and background of the idea of the CC.

5.1 Theoretical insight

We will discuss here to what extent the Arab Spring conforms to the historical experience of constructing a CC. In democratic states, constitutional courts are vital columns of the civil state and essential monitoring bodies. CCs oversee the immunity of the parliamentary and democratic systems and play many significant roles in applying and understanding constitutions. This is not a new mechanism; various countries use CCs to enforce and promote the rule of law and legitimacy, impose separation and balance of powers, protect fundamental rights of citizens and individuals, offer a forum for resolving disputes, and hold distinctive political participants accountable to their constitutional obligations. Additionally, such courts can provide political protection for the opposition.[88] In contrast with the first opinion, others claim that once a CC is established, it often enables the sovereign apparatus to reserve its hegemony and supremacy, advance its political goals and deflect threats.[89] In Egypt, for instance, the regime established and designed the Supreme CC[90] to support its economic

86 Article 117, ibid.; for example, Article 66 of the French Constitution states that the judicial authority is the guardian of individual freedom.

87 In Tunisia, the decision on the importance of the creation of a constitutional court was made, yet the fulfilment has not yet started.

88 After authoritarian rule, establishing a constitutional court can be a symbol of the end of the authoritarian period and the start of a new democratic era.

89 T. Ginsburg and T. Moustafa, 'Introduction', in Rule by Law (2008), 11–12, 15–19; R. Hirschl, Towards juristocracy: The origins and consequences of the new constitutionalism. Harvard University Press (2009), 8; H. Shambayati, 'Courts in Semi-Democratic/Authoritarian Regimes', in Rule by Law (2008), 285–287; T. Ginsburg, 'Constitutional Review', in Oxford Handbook of Law and Politics (2008), 92; A. Trochev, 'Less democracy, more courts: A puzzle of judicial review in Russia', 38(3) Law & Society Review (2004), 513–548.

90 Supreme Constitutional Court established in 1979.

need.[91] However, the regime in Egypt[92] granted the Supreme CC the freedom and autonomy to protect property rights and facilitate economic development. Yet, the Supreme CC ultimately was able to exercise unanticipated amounts of political autonomy.[93]

5.2 A glimpse into the continuity and rupture of the Arab Spring

It is important to highlight that because little has been written on the CCs, we cannot obscure the political implications of their establishment, particularly in monarchies such as Jordan and Morocco.

The 2011 protests in the MENA region brought political change that was as vital and powerful as it was rapid. In the following years, as a consequence, academic analyses emphasised the movement's regional aspects, focused on the outcome of the Arab Spring movement and explored how monarchies[94] survived while other countries – the republics – were overthrown.[95] It is noteworthy that the subsequent scholarship, unlike the initial historiography, moved away from such analyses and concentrated more on reflecting on how the Arab Spring transformed existing political trends in a given country.[96] The outbreak of the Arab Spring renewed the regimes' need to demonstrate that they were engaged in democratic reforms to satisfy both domestic protesters and the international community. The context of the Arab Spring also led Jordan and Morocco to become conceptually bound to the idea of the democratic reforms with the foundation of the CCs. Arab monarchies and regimes

91 T. Moustafa, The struggle for constitutional power: Law, politics, and economic development in Egypt. Cambridge University Press (2007), 69–89; N.J. Brown, Constitutions in a nonconstitutional world: Arab basic laws and the prospects for accountable government. Suny Press (2012), 61–65.

92 The regime during the rule of Anwar Sadat 1970–1981.

93 T. Moustafa, The struggle for constitutional power: law, politics, and economic development in Egypt. Cambridge University Press (2007), 69–89; N.J. Brown, Constitutions in a nonconstitutional world: Arab basic laws and the prospects for accountable government. Suny Press (2012), 61–65.

94 Monarchies such as Jordan, Morocco and the Gulf monarchies.

95 B. Ryan (ed.), Identity politics in the women's movement. NYU Press (2001), 564; F. G. Gause III, 'Why Middle East studies missed the Arab Spring: The myth of authoritarian stability', Foreign affairs (2011), 81–90; S.L. Yom and F.G. Gause III, 'Resilient royals: How Arab monarchies hang on', 23(4) Journal of Democracy (2012), 74–88; A. Bank, T. Richter and A. Sunik, 'Durable, yet different: Monarchies in the Arab Spring', 4(2) Journal of Arabian Studies (2014), 163–179; N. Köprülü, 'Consolidated monarchies in the post-"Arab Spring" era: The case of Jordan', 20(3) Israel Affairs (2014), 318–332; M. Beck and S. Hüser, 'Jordan and the "Arab spring": No challenge, no change?', 24(1) Middle East Critique (2015), 83–97; H. Ghanem, The Arab Spring Five Years Later Volume One: Toward Greater Inclusiveness. Brookings Institution Press (2016), 7–8.

96 R. Brynen, P.W. Moore, B.F Salloukh and M.J. Zahar, Beyond the Arab spring: Authoritarianism & democratization in the Arab world (vol. 4). Boulder, CO: Lynne Rienner Publishers (2012); S.L. Yom 'The new landscape of Jordanian politics: Social opposition, fiscal crisis, and the Arab spring', 42(3) British Journal of Middle Eastern Studies (2015), 284–300.

sought to appease domestic protesters and address external concerns by establishing new CCs as evidence of improvements in the field of judicial review.[97]

The Arab Spring manifested, among other things, the people's simple request for transformation within their own regimes in pursuit of freedom, including freedom of expression. In other words, they aimed to acquire basic human rights protections to achieve democratic reforms within their domestic regimes, as well as basic human rights, economic concerns,[98] equality and political rights. Hence, the 2011 protests initiated a continuity of transformation requests concerning existing political trends, including economic change, which drove the civil resistance that started after the protests. Thus, the accumulation of economic criticism created a powerful supporting call for political change. In due course, these economic grievances morphed into political debates that were largely divorced from the broader regional dynamics.[99] Economic concerns were the direct cause of the protests in the MENA region, and they prompted a political debate that was energised and emboldened by those regional developments. As a result, the monarchy initiated rapid political change by reshuffling the cabinet and government and offering a package of constitutional amendments, thus introducing political reforms and amendments through the proposed establishment of the CC.

An in-depth examination of the efforts of legislators in drafting the CC law reveals the deliberate complexity that led to the legislative amendments required to establish the court by tracing the relevant political processes.

In addition, one of the first major steps the regimes took to appease the protesters[100] to avoid the Arab Spring in their countries was to propose amendments to the system. The proposed changes included the foundation of the CC, but it can be argued that this was not the only motive behind the court's establishment. As one crucial argument states, the regimes and monarchies established the CC to improve their image with the international community. In addition, the desire to improve their international standing would make such regimes appear to favour reforms. Thus, improving the regime's image and international standing was of primary importance.

The CC can be a tool for promoting human rights and democracy, even though powerful regimes consistently resist this idea, as well as the idea that the CC's functionality derives from the powerful threat it poses in the form of judicial review and democratic protections. The main question on which this section focuses is whether the CC's initiatives were a de facto commitment to democracy on the part of those regimes. An examination of their decisions reveals that the substantial reforms that were so enthusiastically anticipated did not de facto occur in Jordan and Morocco. The CC only preserved and reaffirmed the existing legislative strategy as a new but regular court that followed powerful mainstream

97 N. Sultany Law and revolution: Legitimacy and constitutionalism after the Arab Spring. Oxford University Press (2017), 265–269.

98 For example, requesting more government services and improving living standards.

99 J.A Clark, 'Municipalities go to market: Economic reform and political contestation in Jordan', 17(3) Mediterranean Politics (2012), 358–375.

100 S.L. Yom, 'Jordan: The ruse of reform', 24(3) Journal of Democracy (2013), 127–139.

governmental and monarchical institutions. Because the CC compromises the existing power structure and its judicial review is the opposite of a revolution, the purpose of its establishment was far from sincere. The ineffectiveness of the CC in terms of its understanding of democratic governance matched what could be contemplated as the Western models ules of democracy. Ideally, argument would arise as a result of critiquing the imported Western institution while ignoring its local legal foundations. That can be expressed in terms of the tension that emerged between the lawmakers' political visions and implementation in reality. The CC establishment law was intended to strengthen the court's authority and introduce it as a relevant player in Jordan and Morocco's political-judicial processes, while ensuring the CC's decisions remained independent. In the case of Jordan, for instance, the CC would be more independent if its judicial review powers included the question of the constitutionality of draft laws before their promulgation, not simply afterwards. Also, for instance the CC judges should not sit in hearing of their dissent rulings. Furthermore, judges and lawyers could appeal directly to the CC. Solutions might include the power of constitutional interpretation itself. Debunking the CC's decisions and limiting its functionality in terms of judicial review shifts the CC towards an analytical focus and from the people to the regime, causing its motivations to differ from popular demands for revolutionary reform. Hence, the CC can be considered a political institution.

Almost a decade after the inception of the CCs in Morocco and Jordan, the question of their role within the government's political system remains. Does the CC fulfil its role? It was advertised as facilitating the separation of powers and thus promoting democracy in the region. Therefore, the involvement of politicians and legislators in the CC was deemed paramount to preserving regimes' existing political order in which the monarchy has the final word. This tension creates a kind of CC that is diametrically opposed to people's expectations. Choices made by the king, such as the appointment of a judge, are examples that reveal the regime's raison d'être vis-a-vis its post-Arab Spring reform efforts. Consequently, the CC is a wing to maintain the regime's control over the popular political discourse and, thus, preserve its hegemony.

6 Surviving the constitutionalism paradox; judicial self-restraint approach rather than judicial activism

As discussed earlier, the purpose of establishing the CCs in Morocco and Jordan was to present them as newly established institutes that would elevate the independent judiciary, and that judges would engage in judicial activist activities by promoting human rights through an independent judiciary's professional implementation. As King Abdullah of Jordan declared, the CC would be one of the 'new democratic institutions concerned with bolstering the rule of law and ensuring that justice [was] served to all'; also for the regime, 'the rule of law is the umbrella that protects the march towards democracy and reform in Jordan'.[101]

101 King Abdullah website, 'The Rule of Law and Citizenship'.

Therefore, the assumption was that the Jordanian CC would be the guardian of democratic reform and protector of the rule of law.[102] Furthermore, it would defend the people's liberties and rights through offering constitutional interpretation and supervision.[103] The magnitudes of the CC as activist courts should logically raise the bar while dealing with time-sensitive cases in order to echo the people's demands. Nonetheless, up to this point, the CCs in Morocco and Jordan, based on their decisions, were inclined to favour adopting a judicial self-restraint approach rather than judicial activism. It has become clear that for economic, political, security and cultural reasons, most of the CCs' establishment, including judges, value order stability above almost all else. More broadly, it has the impression that the CCs are willing to endure an alarming degree of human rights violations and dismiss the demands of the public if deemed necessary for national security and to restore order on the streets. Hence, the self-restraint approach adopted might be reflected in the concrete case enrolled in the Jordanian CC – 'gas deal' judgment[104] (we will discuss this in more detail bellow) – which could be an illustration of the resemblance of the CC judges with other judges in the system. They are unified in guarding the authority's interests, while viewing judiciary accountability as an enforcement arm of the state rather than engaging with the activism judiciary role of promoting the public good and supporting the public demand.

Understanding the self-restraint in the CC might be an indication on the proposed constitutional reforms that included the establishment of the CC by the monarchy in Morocco and Jordan by arguing that it is a proposal for 'surviving constitutionalism';[105] instead of those reforms democratising the country, they propose to guarantee the regimes, and that might explain the judicial self-restraint that CC judges embrace. The challenge of the young CCs in Morocco and Jordan is to develop a revolutionary judicial review that aims to limit arbitrary power and human rights violations. Hence the CC in Morocco and Jordan should propose active judicial review to reflect demand and appease discontent. On the contrary, the approach of judicial self-restraint (that so far dominates) includes upholding regime stability and continuity. It is essential to understand the power of the sovereign in these monarchies despite the proposed reforms, which could explain the self-restraint approaches of the CC. For instance (as mentioned earlier), in Morocco the appointment of half of the CC judges is made by the sovereign.[106] The situation is more critical in Jordan, as all the judges are appointed by the king.[107] That might create a

102 King Abdullah website, 'The Rule of Law and Citizenship'.

103 Definition of the Court, Website of the CC.

104 Constitutional Court 2019-2 case 2 (2019).

105 J.O. Frosini and F. Biagi, 'Transition from Authoritarian Rule following the Arab Uprising: A Matter of Variables', in J.O. Frosinin and F. Biagi (eds.), Political and Constitutional Transition in North Africa: Actors and Factors (2014). Francesco Biagi, 'Will Surviving Constitutionalism in Morocco and Jordan Work in the Long Run? A Comparison with Three Past Authoritarian Regimes', 3(4) Cambridge International Law (2014), 1240–1259.

106 Article 130, Moroccan Constitution.

107 Article 58 of the Jordanian Constitution grants the king the sole power to appoint the judges of the CC.

slippery slope, a risk of creating a CC with regime-friendly judges, And, therefore, they might tend to adopt the self-restraint approach, as the king continues to hold the essential powers and continues to be 'the master of the political game'.[108] Furthermore, it preserves regime control and hegemony of those reluctant to sacrifice any real power that would allow the CC to play an activist role. In turn, the CC would be used as an instrument to increase the legitimacy of the regime without decreasing the executive monarchy power over each kingdom.

Accordingly, in the 'gas deal' case,[109] for example – in a nutshell, the deliberation background of the decision associated with a contract between a Jordanian energy company and an Israeli company – the Jordanian CC interpretation dealt with the following central questions: firstly, dealing with the deal's lack of parliamentary approval; and secondly, if the 'gas deal' is a substantial matter of Jordanian public interest.[110] The Jordanian CC decided that the contract does not require parliament approval, as a contract was signed between two private companies.[111] Hence, the Jordanian CC deliberately avoided the debate and decided to favour the validity of the 'gas deal'. Furthermore, The Jordanian CC decided that as the 'gas deal' was conducted between companies, not states, it was no longer a matter of public purview. The Jordanian CC adopted a self-restraint approach and wavered to clarify the blurred line between law and politics, and review the case nature as merely political rather than legal, and confirmed the Jordanian CC part of the apparatus. It is essential to emphasise that the Jordanian CC adopted a self-restraint approach, despite the ongoing public protest held in Jordan against the 'gas deal'. Instead of taking a progressive judicial activism step against corruption, the Jordanian CC decision dealt mostly on legal technicalities that generate little public interest; and therefore the country avoided intervening in two of the most public and politically delicate issues in a Jordanian context – Israel[112] and the economy. Furthermore, the Jordanian CC decision had immediate political consequences: the Jordanian CC role ensured that the politics of the executives – king and government – are respected, and it built the

108 A. Tourabi, 'Constitutional Reform Morocco: Reform in Times of Revolution' (2011).

109 Constitutional Court Decision 2019-2 case 2 (2019). According to Article 19, the CC Law and the Jordanian CC deliberation are confidential; hence there is no public hearing. The CC publishes its decisions with dissenting opinions in the official gazette as well as on its website (unlike the Moroccan CC). Article 33-2 of the Jordanian Constitution states that: 'Treaties and agreements which entail any expenditure to treasury of the State or affect the public or private rights of the Jordanians shall not be valid unless approved by Parliament'.

110 Constitutional Court 2019-2 case 2 (2019). Article 33-2 of the Jordanian Constitution states that: 'Treaties and agreements which entail any expenditure to treasury of the State or affect the public or private rights of the Jordanians shall not be valid unless approved by Parliament'.

111 Constitutional Court 2019-2 case 2 (2019), 7–9.

112 Despite the 1994 peace treaty between the Israeli government and Jordan, public opinion disapproves of the normalisation of the relationship, and anti-normalisation campaigns against that are active. Israel as a political issue unites Jordanians, in particular the opposition.

impression that the CC publicly fulfilled the role as a self-restraint court. Consequently, the decision signalled that the Jordanian CC would participate in the government's decision to run its course. Therefore, this case perhaps indicates how the Jordanian CC deals with its power; instead of entrenching a reformed activist role to appeal to the ideas of democracy and develop an independent institutional personality by this decision, it preserved the existing structure of power. Examining the background of the case and its final decision reveals how the Jordanian CC remained relatively quiet in the Jordanian public discourse, implementing self-restraint methodology without purported significant judicial revolutionary decisions.[113]

6.1 Prospective towards more judicial activism

Despite the above-mentioned, and the conservative, narrow interpretation of the CC, there is a glimmer of hope that the CC still can play revolutionary role to contribute in revolutionising the system. Here are several recommendations. First, Article 133 of the Moroccan CC Law[114] proposes ex-ante review that permits a concrete constitutional review; the article stipulated 'the CC shall have the competence to look into an exception of unconstitutionality raised in the course of the trial when one of the parties argues that the law on which the outcome of a trial depends undermines the rights and freedoms guaranteed by the Constitution'.[115] The addition of ex-post review is significant as it authorised the Moroccan CC to strengthen its status as a counter-majoritarian body. Therefore, the Moroccan CC may contribute effectively to the democratisation progression in the future in comparison with previous reforms. Second, the supremacy of the international convention over domestic law that the new Moroccan constitution proposes is an accessible tool for proposing judicial activism and revolutionising the system by opposing any law that contradicts the international protocols in cases of anti-domestic laws conflicting with international law. In other words, the Moroccan constitution respects the supremacy of international conventions; accordingly, national legislation must be brought into line with international standards of protection of human rights, and civil and economic rights. If put in use by the Moroccan CC judges (adopting a broad interpretation approach), the supremacy of international conventions could be an inspirational resource for developing the activism.[116]

Third, there is a proposal for the significant revolutionarily influence of the CC, which is possible by opting for systematic interpretations of the constitution rather than a literal interpretation.[117] Suppose the CC reviews the illegitimacy of laws that restrict the freedoms or political competition and reviews critical legislative

113 Right to date, as of the writing of this chapter.
114 Article 133, Moroccan Constitution.
115 Article 133, Moroccan Constitution.
116 It is also important to highlight that the constitution states the supremacy of international convention, yet 'within the framework of the provision of the Constitution, the laws of the Kingdom, and respect for the immutable national identity'.
117 Inspiring example of the Tribunal Constitution of Chile, where the Tribunal Constitution, since its first judgments, shows that it is the voice of the people by

acts carefully wherever it considers being in contract with the rights of freedoms provided in the constitution. In that case, that can indicate that the CC might fill the role of guardian of the constitution and play judicial revolution by providing equal protection under the law, freedom of association and political rights. The CC can play a crucial role in ensuring that the reform is meaningful and reflects the people's demands, and it can be a human rights protector and safeguard economic and political rights. Suppose the CC wants to fill the gap by granting the people political, civil and economic rights, and is willing to confront the executive directly when the latter opposes the political liberation. The fourth recommendation is to start relying on international human rights conventions and offer to guarantee adequate protection of fundamental rights and freedoms, such as freedom of expression, freedom of the press, freedom of association and more. However, careful observation of the 'gas deal'[118] judgment as an example might indicate that the high expectations from the CC are not in the right place, and the CC is envisaged as a supporter of the executive instead of constraining its power.

Finally, the undeclared purpose of establishing the CC in Morocco and Jordan and their constitutional reforms proposed was to calm the streets in the short run and strengthen and increase the monarchy's legitimacy and preserve it in the long run. Hopefully the CC will end up producing revolutionarily judicial decisions. It remains to be seen how CC judges will interpret the provisions and new constitution, and intervene in promoting human rights and democratisation and echo the people's demands in the future; their path is full of challenges. Nonetheless, the initial purpose behind establishing the CC in Morocco and Jordan was to contribute to the regimes' solidity and continuity, to address the public frustration and avoid revolution in the short term. In the long term, the CC judges can still demonstrate judicial activism that strives for policy-making and engages in judicial politics. It may boomerang and produce a democratic outcome by reinforcing judicial independence through leading concrete constitutional review in the CC decisions.[119] Thus, the CC might one day turn into an effective revolutionarily tool and restrain the powers of the monarchy and executives, and contribute to the establishment of a more democratic form of government. The CC should be revolutionary, useful, reliable and reformist in order to promote progressive politics while balancing court intervention without violating the separation of powers and finding the balance between the high expectation of judicial activism and the disillusionment of narrow self-restraint typified by a non-interfering approach.

7 Epilogue: On the future of constitutional courts

This chapter looked at the CC reforms undertaken in Morocco and Jordan and examined their revolutionary aspects. A close examination of the cases shows that the

challenging the undemocratic illiberal military government, and not becoming a regime's ally. Sentencia Rol. No. 33, D.O., 3 October 1985.

118 Constitutional Court 2019-2 case 2 (2019).

119 For example, in Moroccan case subsequently declaring the supremacy of international conventions over domestic legislation, pledge a greater protection of fundamental rights.

motivation behind the establishment of the CC was strengthening the representation of freedoms and human dignity in a democratic parliamentary monarchy in which people lived under a totalitarian regime with a parliamentary façade. The CC failed to undertake an activist judiciary approach in order to represent the popular will and make decisions that served the people's interests.[120] Even more critically, the CC turned into an additional arm of the executive authority, similar to the other courts in the judiciary system, which constrained its agenda by embracing self-restraint rather than judicial activism. This included, for instance, the empowerment of the security agencies at the expense of civil institutions. Thus, instead of expanding freedoms and protecting human rights, it restricted them. Human rights continue to be violated, and civil society organisations continue to deteriorate. Such practices strengthen the regime while weakening the people. Nonetheless, the establishment of the CC was expected to lead to judicial activism, realistic reform and a revolutionary role in promoting human rights and freedoms. The process is still new and includes reviewing the CCs upcoming judgments. The establishment of the CC has therefore been more a result of urgent reform due to tense conditions linked partially to the Arab Spring protests and other local protest than a natural evolution towards democracy and independent judicial review. However, some positive aspects of the CC include improvement to judicial review and strengthening the rule of law throughout interpretation of the CC and review of laws and regulations. The results of these improvements, as well as the establishment of the CC, remain incomplete, and they have never fully eliminated the dominance of the executive authority over other authorities, particularly the legislative authority, potentially raising questions concerning independence. However, they do add a democratic aspect to those regimes. Thus, in principle and in aspiration, their adoption has contributed to a civil, democratic and pluralistic regime based on the people's desire for political reforms and substantial amendments due to the Arab Spring uprising. The CC is one example that the regime could use to increase its legitimacy and ensure its effectiveness by presenting itself as a model for promoting human rights in the region. This must be evaluated gradually by following the CC's judgments and influence.

Despite the establishment of the CC in those countries, however, the appointments of the judges limited the efficacy of the court as a judicial institution. For instance, appointments made by the king of Jordan lacked intrinsic judicial independence because of the judges' reputations and close relationships with the regime. They perpetuate links with the regime, political structure or monarchy and remain temporary constellations of powerful individuals. Thus, instead of fulfilling revolutionary steps towards real reform sought by protesters in the streets, the CC can be described as the de facto embodiment of a conservative establishment. Hence, the conservative decisions of the CC are far from its enthusiastic revolutionary ideals.

120 In 2019 the Jordanian Constitutional Court discussed the Jordanian energy company and Israeli gas company case: Constitutional Court Decision 2019-2; in that decision the Constitutional Court embraced the role that was carved out for it by political forces – it signalled the Constitutional Court's active participation in enabling the government's decision to run its course. The Constitutional Court decided in favour of the government political interest.

Finally, it is beyond the scope of this chapter to determine the exact degree of the CC's success, as it is still in the early stages of its development, and the extent to which politics are involved in its judgments and decisions remains unclear. It is essential to note that the CC is still young, and its terminology and mechanisms will develop with more experience and cases. However, the overall spirit of its establishment suggests that the CC and its judges intended to promote human rights, judiciary review and activism, and constitutional changes. The CC promotes the separation of powers, ensures individual rights and thereby facilitates the rule of law. Against this backdrop, some might imply that the foundation of the CC is a concrete political change by the regime in response to the protesters' requests, but it appears to be something different. A comparison of the instrumentalist view on the political utility of the CC vis-à-vis the Arab Spring uprising shows the protests created an urgent demand that forced the regime to propose unprecedented amendments. This is the framework of which the CC is considered a part. Thus, the establishment of the CC became a significant symbol of the regime's supposedly good-faith efforts to reform. In light of this, the question is whether the establishment of the CC was merely a symbolic act or a reflection of the regime's intent to capture the positive momentum of the Arab Spring while considering the CC as a political symbol. After the fact, establishing a new institution and touting it as a milestone of democratic reform helped to increase the regime's credibility in the eyes of the protesters and the international community, as the CC represented a main pillar of democratic governance.[121]

In conclusion, the difference between the practice and rule of law can frequently be ambiguous.[122] Future CC judgments and observations will clarify whether the CCs of Morocco and Jordan will take steps to intervene with a revolutionarily steady voice. This will depend on the depth of the law interpretation of the CC judges and whether they are keen on taking concrete, steady steps and playing a fundamental role in transitional justice towards a democratic state that promotes human rights and freedoms. The examples of the role of older CCs in the MENA region is a source of worry because the CC is where the political establishment fights democratic change instead of promoting it.[123] However, I will argue that the CC, in the long run, may become a significant restraint on the regime and propose a revolutionary role that involves more judicial independence and strength in the future. Therefore, the CC in Morocco and Jordan may

121 L.K. Nasrawin, 'Protecting Human Rights through Constitutional Adjudication – Jordan as a Case Study', 25(2) Digest of Middle East Studies (2016), 276; M. Abu-Karaki, R.S. Faqir and M.A.K. Marashdah, 'Democracy & Judicial Controlling in Jordan: A Constitutional Study', 4 J. Pol. & L. (2011), 180.

122 'The problem is how to secure the enforcement of … rights – how to turn the commitment on paper into a reality in practice' Cherie Booth, Arab Judicial Forum 2003, Judicial Systems in the 21st Century, September 15–17, 2003, Manama.

123 Rainer Grote and Tilmann J. Röder, Constitutionalism, Human Rights, and Islam after the Arab Spring, Oxford University Press (2016), Part 1 Power and Legitimacy, 1.6 The Arab Spring and Constitutional Reforms in Jordan: A Historical and Legal Appraisal, Awn Shawkat Al-Khasawneh, Oxford Constitution of the World, 138.

rebound in the long run and could become effective in restraining the authorities' power in the future, and the CC judgments will contain some essential democratic innovations and broaden judicial activism in order to satisfy the public and fulfil their demands.

Part IV

Judicial activism and emergency constitutionalism

8 Mastering emergency situations

The activist role of the Bulgarian Constitutional Court in redefining the constitutional design of war, state of siege and state of emergency

Martin Belov

1 Introduction

This chapter explores the role of the Constitutional Court in emergency situations. It provides a case study that is focused on Bulgaria and the activity of the Bulgarian Constitutional Court. There are several reasons for this choice of research. The constitutional foundations of the emergency situations in Bulgaria are rather austere.[1] The 1991 Bulgarian Constitution provides for war, state of siege or state of emergency, thus offering an exhaustive official scheme of the valid alternatives to the constitutional normalcy. However, the constitutional approach is rather formal-procedural, thus leaving space for interpretation and for further development of the constitutional text by the ordinary legislator or by the Constitutional Court.

Moreover, the Bulgarian Constitutional Court is rather activist. Indeed, it refrains from explicit engagement with judicial dialogue with international and supranational courts.[2] Thus, it is accomplishing judicial self-restraint in matters related to supranational constitutionalism, global constitutionalism and global governance.[3] In contrast, the Bulgarian Constitutional Court's standing towards domestic matters and in the domestic arena is activist. This is very much visible especially in respect of the Court's engagement in redrawing the scheme of institutional competences and separation of powers at the national level. Thus, the Bulgarian Constitutional Court is a key player in shaping and further developing the constitutional model of separation of powers. This practice contravenes the principles of popular sovereignty, democracy and separation of powers.

The focus of this chapter will be precisely on the activist engagement of the Bulgarian Constitutional Court in reshaping the constitutional competences of key state institutions via activist interpretation of constitutional provisions related to

1 See Belov, M., A. Tsekov Covid-19 Pandemic and Its Impact on Parliamentarism in Bulgaria. A self-restricting of the control power, available at: https://www.robert-schuman.eu/en/doc/ouvrages/FRS_Parliament_Bulgaria.pdf.

2 Belov, M. Judicial Dialogue, The Hague, Eleven, 2019.

3 Belov, M. Courts, Politics and Constitutional Law. Judicialization of Politics and Politicization of the Judiciary, Abingdon, Routledge, 2020.

DOI: 10.4324/9781003200666-13

emergency situations (war, state of siege, state of emergency) and to the institutional design of the national defence. Elsewhere I have demonstrated the role of this court as an ultimate player in multilevel constitutional games on the border between national and supranational constitutionalism.[4] Here I will focus on the role of the Court as quasi-constituent power reshaping the demarcation lines between the legislative and the executive power and redrawing the lines of competence between the Parliament and government.

The activism of the Court is visible especially in defining and redrafting the lines of competence of the central state institutions – the Parliament, government, etc. – with regard to the model of their engagement in emergency situations. The most recent example is its Decision No. 10 of 2020 related to the introduction of the 'extraordinary epidemic situation' in the Bulgarian legal order. Thus, a topical event, namely the response of the Bulgarian legal order to the Covid-19 pandemic, has triggered a new wave of concerns regarding the impact of the Bulgarian Constitutional Court on the institutional design for mastering of emergency situations in Bulgaria.

The chapter will start with an outline of the constitutional model for crisis management provided by the 1991 Bulgarian Constitution. It will offer structured information regarding the regimes for crisis management enshrined in the Bulgarian Constitution as instruments for mastering of emergency situations. Moreover, it will discuss the stance of the Bulgarian constitutional legislator on the conceptualisation of the emergency, the permissible deviations from constitutional normalcy it provides, the tools for its mastering, and their implied philosophy and institutional logic. In other words, the chapter will offer a brief but informative critical account of the constitutional model for emergency situations management in Bulgaria. The analysis will shed light on the reason why there are no other emergency regimes provided by the 1991 Constitution. This will be of crucial importance for convincingly raising the claim of unconstitutionality of other emergency regimes created by virtue of the ordinary legislation and subsequently legitimated by activist jurisprudence of the Constitutional Court.

In that regard, the support of the Constitutional Court's practice for the adoption of unconstitutional legislation providing for additional regimes of emergency situations will be defined in terms of judicial activism. To sum up: the first part of the chapter will engage with emergency constitutional politics and emergency constitutional regimes serving as a playground for judicial activism and, vice versa, being themselves framed and shaped by activist case law of the Bulgarian Constitutional Court.

The constitutional regime of crisis management, reflecting the original constitutional position on it, will be contrasted with the provision of different emergency regimes in the ordinary legislation in Bulgaria. It will be shown that the

4 See Belov, M. Constitutional Courts as Ultimate Players in Multilevel Constituent Power Games: The Bulgarian Case. In: Belov, M. (ed.) Courts, Politics and Constitutional Law. Judicialization of Politics and Politicization of the Judiciary, Abingdon, Routledge, 2019, pp. 152–173.

Parliament develops the constitutional framework for crisis management too extensively, especially with a view to the 'extraordinary epidemic situation' introduced with the amendment of the Health Act on the occasion of the outbreak of the Covid-19 pandemic.

Furthermore, the chapter focuses on the judicial activism of the Bulgarian Constitutional Court. The most important cases of judicial activism of the Bulgarian Constitutional Court, which powerfully develops further the constitution using its open texture,[5] will be briefly outlined. Thus, the immense power of the Court will be demonstrated on the basis of this short but informative overview of its jurisprudence, showing both its key role as strategic player mastering constitutional design and safeguarding institutional adjustment and power balancing and as key danger for the maintenance of the constitutionally enshrined model of separation of powers.

Special attention is devoted to the judicial activism of the Bulgarian Constitutional Court related to mastering of emergency situations. The activist stance of the Court regarding issues of war, state of siege, state of emergency and other – in fact unconstitutional – regimes of emergency measures, such as the 'extraordinary epidemic situation' and the 'state of disaster', is researched in a complex way. First, the case law of the Bulgarian Constitutional Court related to military emergency situations and to the constitutional scheme for management of national defence issues is critically assessed. Second, the chapter devotes special attention to Decision No. 10 of 2020 which concerns the health-related emergency ('extraordinary epidemic situation') introduced through ordinary legislation via amendment of an act of Parliament. Third, the Court's policy towards both national defence-related emergency situations and an extraordinary epidemic situation is compared. This comparison sheds additional light on the judicial activism of the Bulgarian Constitutional Court in the sphere of constitutional emergency politics and leads to important conclusions.

In brief, this chapter has been provoked by a concrete topical issue. This is the introduction of the unconstitutional 'extraordinary epidemic situation' by virtue of amendments to the Health Act in 2020 in Bulgaria, which has been declared constitutional by the Bulgarian Constitutional Court. However, this is a good occasion for broader assessment of the role of the Bulgarian Constitutional Court as activist constitutional jurisdiction which visibly and deliberately redraws the separation of powers – more precisely the demarcation line between constituent and constituted powers and between legislative and executive powers.

2 The legal shapes of war, state of siege and state of emergency in the Bulgarian Constitution and legislation

2.1 War, state of siege and state of emergency in the Bulgarian Constitution

The Bulgarian Constitution provides for special constitutional regimes of emergency situations. It outlines three such regimes, namely war, state of siege and

5 For the open texture of law, see Hart, H.L.A. The Concept of Law, Oxford, Oxford University Press, 1997, pp. 124–136.

state of emergency. These regimes exhaust the constitutionally permitted exceptions from constitutional normalcy. No other exceptional situations, allowing for redistribution of power between the state institutions or for limitations of constitutional rights, can be created either by the Parliament or by the Constitutional Court. Other forms of exceptional situations may be established by the ordinary legislator only if they do not concern the constitutional scheme for separation of powers and do not limit constitutional rights in a formal sense as rights provided by the constitution.

This constitutional framework for emergency policy-making is binding on all state institutions, including the Parliament and the Constitutional Court. In that regard, the Constitutional Court is allowed to explain the concept of war, state of siege or state of emergency, to clarify implied meaning and to control the constitutionality of acts of Parliament or acts of the President which may contravene the constitutional model for mastering of emergency situations in case such proceedings are initiated in front of it by institutions which have the competence to approach the Court. According to the Bulgarian Constitution institutions which may approach the Court with demand for issuing of abstract interpretative decisions or decisions for control of constitutionality of sub-constitutional acts are one-fifth of the MPs, the President of the Republic, the Council of Ministers, the Supreme Court of Cassation, the Supreme Administrative Court and the State Prosecutor General. When acts of Parliament are supposed to infringe constitutional rights the procedure for declaration of their unconstitutionality may be initiated in front of the Constitutional Court also by the national ombudsman and the Supreme Bar Council.

The open texture of the concepts of war, state of siege and state of emergency, the lack of mature discussion on these issues in the Bulgarian scientific and public discourse, and the already established traditions of judicial activism of the Bulgarian Constitutional Court allow for their rather discretionary and wide interpretation by the Court. In fact, until the outbreak of the Covid-19 pandemic, no discussion on the problems of emergency situations, their constitutional and legislative framework and the constitutional delimitation between extraordinary situations and normalcy took place. The Covid-19 pandemic has triggered such intense public discourse in a rather chaotic way with no sound scientific background. In fact, the expert opinions given to the Constitutional Court's case No. 10 of 2020 are the exception since they focus on the question of whether a new form of emergency situation – the 'extraordinary epidemic situation' – is constitutionally permitted.

The activist practice of the Court must be critically assessed with regard to the overall initial intention of the Bulgarian constitutional legislator for defining the constitutional foundations of the emergency situations. The reconstruction of the constitutional legislator's standing on the problems of emergency situations can be assessed in a threefold manner. First, the history of emergency constitutional policy and the constitutional foundations of the emergency situations in Bulgarian constitutionalism must be briefly summarised. Second, the philosophy of the scheme of emergency constitutionalism in the contemporary Bulgarian constitutional model must be explained. Third, the concrete normative parameters of the three forms of constitutionally provided emergency situations – war, state of siege and state of emergency – must be outlined. This will be done with regard to the constitutional shapes of war, state of siege and state of emergency and with a view to the provision of their outlook in the acts of Parliament which are supposed to further develop the constitution.

Emergency constitutionalism is deeply discredited in Bulgarian constitutional history. This is due to the misuse of emergency situations during the period of constitutional monarchy (1879–1947). In fact, the application of the first Bulgarian constitution – the 1879 Tarnovo Constitution – was deeply marked by emergency situations when the constitutional provisions for emergency were largely misused and misinterpreted in order to promote authoritarianism with a central role of the monarch or the Prime Minister in its establishment. This may be one of the reasons why until 2020 there had been no case of emergency situation (shaped as either state of siege or as state of emergency) in the last phase of the development of Bulgarian constitutional history after the fall of the Berlin Wall. In that regard, the declaration of a state of emergency from 13 March 2020 until 13 May 2020 subsequently replaced by 'extraordinary epidemic situation' is a great exception. It should be considered a huge deviation from the constitutional normalcy and as an expression of the will of the emerging 'health leviathan', imposing non-transparent, inefficient, disproportional and imbalanced human rights restrictions justified in the context of 'health Ernstfall'.[6]

The first Bulgarian Constitution – the 1879 Tarnovo Constitution – in article 47 gave the regime provision for emergency situations. According to this provision, in case of external or internal threat to the state, if the Parliament cannot be summoned, the monarch on proposal and under the joint responsibility of the Council of Ministers can govern by decrees. These decrees must be approved on the first possible session of the Parliament. The government by decrees cannot concern tax issues since taxes must always be adopted by the Parliament.

Article 47 of the Tarnovo Constitution has been largely misused by the Bulgarian monarchs for declaring emergency situations to promote the establishment of their authoritarian regimes. Thus, the constitutional provision of emergency situations has been frequently used as a loophole and main entrance for authoritarianism turning the emergency situations into normalcy.[7]

6 For the concept of 'Ernstfall', see Schmitt, C. Political Theology: Four Chapters on the Concept of Sovereignty, Chicago, University of Chicago Press, 2006, pp. 5–16. For the health emergency and the 'health Ernstfall' produced by pandemics as well as for the 'health leviathan', see Belov, M. The Role of Fear Politics in Global Constitutional 'Ernstfall'. Images of Fear under Covid-19 Health Paternalism, in Belov, M. (ed.) Populist Constitutionalism and Illiberal Democracies Between Constitutional Imagination, Normative Entrenchment and Political Reality, Cambridge, Intersentia, 2021, pp. 187–221.

7 See Belov, M. Establishment of the Modern Constitutional Principles in Bulgaria. The Tarnovo Constitution of 1879. In: Stolleis, M. (ed.) Konflikt und Koexistenz. Die Rechtsordnungen Südosteuropas im 19. und 20. Jahrhundert. Band 1: Rumänien, Bulgarien, Griechenland. Frankfurt am Main, Vittorio Klostermann Verlag, 2015, pp. 859–897; Belov, M. Executive Power Metamorphoses in the History of the Balkan Constitutionalism: Between the Imperatives of the Constitutional Teleology and the Potentialities of the Political Reality. Romanian Journal of Comparative Law, vol. 5, issue 2, 2014, pp. 299–360.

The logic behind the regimes of the emergency situations established by the 1947 and 1971 Constitutions is actually also generally adopted and broadly followed by the current 1991 Bulgarian Constitution. All three constitutions try to concentrate the ultimate decisions for making recourse to emergency power in the Parliament. They grant the competence to propose the declaration of emergency to the executive power institutions (more precisely to the government) or to institutions performing the function of the head of state (the Presidium (the 1947 Constitution), the State Council (the 1971 Constitution), or the President of the Republic (the 1991 Constitution)). All three constitutions allow just-mentioned institutions performing the function of head of state to intervene with a declaration of emergency regimes only in case the Parliament cannot be summoned. They safeguard the right of the National Assembly to subsequently confirm or renounce such declaration. Moreover, while the 1947 Constitution operates with two main concepts – war and 'other extraordinary situation' – the 1971 Constitution is the forerunner of the three main forms of emergency situations provided by the 1991 Constitution: the war, the state of siege and the state of emergency. All three constitutions also contain provisions related to the military power offering models for constitutional distribution of the competences related to the defence and maintenance of public order and the regimes of mobilisation.

There are several important differences between the three constitutions under consideration with regard to the way they organise the emergency situations. More precisely, one of these differences consists of the fact that the 1991 Constitution and the 1947 and 1971 Constitutions ascribe some competences in emergency situations to a single head of state (the President) or to collective institutions (Presidium of the National Assembly or State Council) with competences related to the emergency situations. Moreover, the 1991 Constitution establishes constitutional liberal democracy, while the previous two Constitutions of 1947 and 1971 provide for a Soviet type of governmental system.

Several conclusions can be made on the basis of this short overview of the constitutional models of emergency situations in the history of Bulgarian constitutionalism. All Bulgarian constitutions provide for regimes of state of exception. These regimes proliferate in number. The emergency situation has been just one type in the 1879 Tarnovo Constitution, two types in the 1947 Constitution and three types in the 1971 and the 1991 Constitutions. The emergency situations also get more concrete in shape in the last two constitutions. Nevertheless, none of the Bulgarian constitutions contain very detailed constitutional provisions of the state of exception systematically united in a single chapter or consequent list of constitutional provisions. The state of exception has a bad history in Bulgarian constitutionalism. Thus, the recourse to a state of exception in one of its constitutionally provided forms – the state of emergency – in 2020 recalls negative memories and is rather exceptional. The introduction of an 'extraordinary epidemic situation' as an intermediate regime between state of exception (state of emergency) and constitutional normalcy that has been approved as constitutional by the Constitutional Court is a further step in the establishment of misuse with exceptional powers legitimated by the constitutional jurisdiction, as will be shown later in this chapter.

Due to space constraints I will not explore in further detail the history of emergency situations, emergency power and emergency policy-making in Bulgaria. I will focus on the constitutional model for emergency situations in the contemporary Bulgarian constitutional model in order to specifically outline the role of the Constitutional Court and its impact on constitutional emergency.

There are three possible main conceptual and comparative models for regulating the emergency situations. The first one provides for relatively extensive constitutional provisions of the emergency situations. The constitutional provisions of emergency situations may even be concentrated systematically in a separate chapter or otherwise united under the concept of 'emergency constitution'.[8] The logic behind this model is that the constitution must provide not only for the principles and the overall framework of the exceptional and emergency situations. It must also regulate in detail the different regimes of constitutional emergency with its concrete issues related to human rights and institutional design.

The second model for a constitutional attitude towards the emergency situations is the one proposed by Walter Benjamin and Giorgio Agamben.[9] Briefly summarised, it claims that there is no need for a state of emergency. Moreover, the state of emergency regulated in the constitution is dangerous. The idea is that even in crisis situations the state must safeguard all constitutional rights and the constitutionally enshrined balance of power between the state institutions must be preserved. The fear is that if the constitution allows for emergency situations, this may offer insights and legitimation for the political players to misuse them, thus triggering temptations for the establishment of authoritarian regimes and for promoting the emergency as 'the new normal'.

The third model is a variant of the first one. It rests upon the need for constitutional provision of emergency situations. However, it provides only for the main aspects of these situations, allowing the ordinary legislator to further develop and concretise the emergency situations broadly regulated on constitutional level.

The 1991 Constitution belongs to the third model. It enumerates all possible forms of constitutional emergency (war, state of siege and state of emergency) and broadly outlines their main aspects. However, this constitution allows for the further development of these forms of constitutional emergency by the Parliament. Implicitly, it also makes possible their further development via constitutional interpretation delivered by the Constitutional Court. It will be demonstrated, however, that the Constitutional Court interprets rather broadly the constitutional provisions related not only to these three constitutional regimes of emergency, but also the provisions of the constitutional framework of the military defence of the public order. Moreover, the Constitutional Court justifies the introduction of new forms of emergency via ordinary legislation (acts of Parliament) which is

8 For the concept of emergency constitution, see Ackerman, B. The Emergency Constitution. The Yale Law Journal, vol. 113, no. 5, March 2004, p. 1029 and the following.

9 See Agamben, G. Homo Sacer II, Kritika i humanisam, Sofi a 2019 (in Bulgarian), p. 13 and the following; and Benjamin, W. On the Concept of History, CreateSpace Independent Publishing Platform, 2009.

unconstitutional. These forms of judicial activism of the Court will be discussed in detail after the presentation of the constitutional foundations of the war, state of siege and state of emergency and their implementation on legislative level in the acts of Parliament.

The 1991 Constitution contains three groups of provisions that aim at mastering emergency situations. Altogether they form the constitutional policy towards emergency situations, shape the constitutional framework of emergency constitutionalism and serve as a constitutional basis for their further development by virtue of acts of Parliament. The first group includes the regimes of constitutional emergency defining the overall parameters of emergency constitutionalism. The second group comprises the human rights safeguards in times of war, state of siege or state of emergency. The third group encompasses the institutional design for crisis management and for protection of national security and public order.

It has been mentioned that war, state of siege and state of emergency are the three regimes provided by the 1991 Constitution for mastering of emergency situations. War, state of siege and state of emergency can be declared by the National Assembly. If the Parliament is not in session and cannot be summoned immediately, then war, state of siege and state of emergency can also be declared by the President of the Republic in case of immediate attack against the state or a need for immediate fulfilment of duties for collective defence stemming from an international treaty. In such case the National Assembly must be immediately summoned.

War, state of siege and state of emergency can be declared by the Parliament on proposal of the President of the Republic or the Council of Ministers. The state of siege and state of emergency can be national (covering the whole territory of the state) or local (focused on a specific part of it). Last but not least, in the event of war, state of siege or state of emergency which has occurred during the term of the National Assembly or after the expiry thereof, the period of the credentials thereof shall be extended until the lapse of these circumstances.[10]

The second group of constitutional provisions concerns the safeguards of human rights in case of war, state of siege or state of emergency. Article 57, paragraph 1 of the Constitution declares the fundamental rights to be irrevocable. However, most of them can be limited during war, state of siege or state of emergency. Here it should be stressed that the human rights can be limited only during these three permissible forms of emergency, but not in the context of other emergency regimes invented by the ordinary legislator and provided by (in fact) unconstitutional acts of Parliament.

According to Article 57, paragraph 3 of the Constitution, upon declaration of war, state of siege or state of emergency, the exercise of particular citizens' rights may be temporarily restricted by statute, with the exception of the rights provided for in Article 28, Article 29, paragraphs 1, 2 and 3, Article 32, paragraph 1, and

10 See Tanchev, E., M. Belov The Governmental System of the Republic of Bulgaria. In: Chronovski, N., J. Petretei, T. Drinoczi (eds.) Governmental Systems of Central and Eastern European States, Warsaw, Kluwer Polska, 2011, p. 95; Belov, M. Constitutional Law in Bulgaria, Kluwer, 2019, p. 248.

Article 37 of the Constitution. This means that the following constitutional rights cannot be restricted during these emergency regimes: the right to life, the prohibition of torture, cruel, inhuman and degrading treatment, or forcible assimilation, the prohibition of compulsory medical, scientific or other experimentation without their voluntary written consent, the right to privacy and the freedom of conscience, thought and religion.

The third group of constitutional provisions includes the institutional design for distribution of competences in the military, defence and maintenance of national security. It has been mentioned that the National Assembly is the key factor for declaring of war, state of siege or state of emergency, while the President of the Republic acts as a reserve when the Parliament is not in session. Furthermore, the Council of Ministers and the President of the Republic are key proactive veto players[11] that can propose declaration of one of the three constitutionally provided regimes of state of exception.

Nevertheless, there are also other important competences related to defence and national security. According to Article 9, paragraph 2 of the Constitution the activity of the armed forces has to be regulated by an act of Parliament. However, this empowerment of the Parliament must not be understood as a blank cheque. It must be in compliance with the constitutional model for distribution of competences in the sphere of national defence. More precisely, the acts of Parliament cannot establish emergency situations different from the war, state of siege and state of emergency as provided in the Constitution which have as a consequence the redistribution of the constitutionally enshrined model of separation of powers or allow for the limitation of constitutional rights. Such emergency situations may be established only if they do not produce such results and lead only to a shift of competences provided by the ordinary legislation or to limitation of rights which do not have constitutional standing. Any legislative provisions, establishing regimes that aim at the achievement of the results of one of the three constitutionally provided emergency situations without explicitly framing them as war, state of siege or state of emergency, must be deemed unconstitutional. Their potential approval by the Constitutional Court should be considered unconstitutional as well while also raising the problem of who should control the unconstitutional jurisprudence of this supreme guardian of the constitution.[12]

Furthermore, there are also constitutional provisions establishing the institutional design of the state power in the sphere of war, national security and public defence. They will be discussed later in this chapter in conjunction with their activist interpretation by the Constitutional Court.

11 See Belov, M. The Separation of Powers and the Veto Players in the Contemporary Constitutionalism. Essay on the Actual Dimensions of the Institutionalization of the Power Dynamics. In Kirov, Pl. (ed.) National and European Dimensions of the Contemporary Constitutionalism, vol. I, Sofia, St. Kliment Ochridski University Press, 2010 (in Bulgarian).

12 Vinx, L. (ed.) The Guardian of the Constitution: Hans Kelsen and Carl Schmitt on the Limits of Constitutional Law (Cambridge Studies in Constitutional Law), Cambridge, Cambridge University Press, 2015

2.2 War, state of siege and state of emergency in Bulgarian legislation: Other emergency situations created by an act of Parliament

There are four acts of Parliament which contain detailed legislative provisions for emergency situations. These are the Defence and Military Troops Act, the Counter-Terrorism Act, the Protection against Disasters Act and the Health Act. The Defence and Military Troops Act develops further the first two types of emergency situations provided by the Constitution – war and state of siege. Hence, it does not introduce any new forms of emergency situations differing from the constitutionally provided ones. The Defence and Military Troops Act just sets more concrete parameters of the legal foundations of war and state of siege in the Bulgarian legal order. It only further develops the constitutional model for crisis management related to the gravest emergency situations –war and state of siege. It allows for human rights limitations with due respect to the constitutional provisions related to that issue.

The same is true for the Counter-Terrorism Act. It provides for a specific case of state of emergency. This is the state of emergency in case of terrorist attack. The Counter-Terrorism Act regulates the institutional response to terrorism and the related human rights restrictions in compliance with the Constitution. It operates with one of the three constitutionally permitted forms of emergency situations – the state of emergency – and does not invent new forms of exceptional situations allowing for deviation from the established constitutional order.

The Counter-Terrorism Act and the Defence and Military Troops Act dispose only with the tool-kit provided by the Constitution. They provide only for constitutionally permissible forms for mastering of emergency situations, thus preserving the overall constitutional model for dealing with the state of exception. They are a necessary continuation of this model. They are a logical result of the rather austere provision of states of exception in the Bulgarian Constitution due to which it belongs to the third model for coping with an emergency situation, as has been explained above.

In contrast to the Counter-Terrorism Act and the Defence and Military Troops Act, the Protection against Disasters Act and the Health Act provide for unconstitutional regimes of exception. These are the emergency epidemic situations introduced by the Health Act in 2020 following the unconstitutional example of the Protection against Disasters Act that has introduced the unconstitutional 'state of disaster' as early as 2006.

The state of disaster is in fact a variant of the state of emergency. It must be regulated as such with the formal, procedural and substantial consequences of this subsuming. However, the state of disaster introduced by the Protection against Disasters Act deviates from the constitutional framework of the state of emergency in many aspects. It infringes the key role of the National Assembly in emergency situations by providing for an alternative – and unconstitutional – procedure for declaration of states of disaster. In contrast to the state of emergency which is declared by the National Assembly on proposal of the President of the Republic or the Council of Ministers, the state of disaster is declared by the Council of Ministers on proposal of the Minister of Interior. Thus, the Parliament is deprived of its role as ultimate safeguard for democracy, rule of law and human rights.

The Protection against Disasters Act concentrates emergency powers in the executive power institutions – the government and the Minister of Interior – in an unconstitutional way. Nevertheless, the Protection against Disasters Act tries to at least formally comply with the requirements of proportionality in substantial and temporal aspects. It sets maximal terms for the duration of the state of disaster, thus defining loose temporal limits at the discretion of the institutions of executive power. It also explicitly requires the state institutions to perform proportionality checks for the introduced measures.

However, this fact does not make the provisions of the Protection against Disasters Act introducing the state of disaster constitutional. They are unconstitutional not only due to the above-mentioned infringement of the constitutional model of distribution of competences for declaration and mastering of emergency situations. The state of disaster is unconstitutional also because the Protection against Disasters Act allows for limitation of constitutional rights (e.g. the freedom of movement, the freedom of professional activity, personal integrity, etc.) which can be eventually restrained only during war, state of siege or state of emergency, but not in the context of 'state of disaster'. Thus, the state of disaster remains a legislative invention which is largely unconstitutional.

These dangerous provisions of the Protection against Disasters Act remained largely unknown until the unconstitutional state of disaster was used as a row model for the introduction of the 'extraordinary epidemic situation' in 2020 by virtue of an amendment in the Health Act. The analogous creation of an unconstitutional form of state of exception in 2020 is not even the worst problem. What is especially problematic is that the Health Act did not even provide for either concrete time limitations of the 'extraordinary epidemic situation' or for more specific safeguards for the proportionality of the introduced emergency measures. On top of this, the constitutionality of the 'extraordinary epidemic situation' has been confirmed by the Constitutional Court in its Decision No. 10 of 2020 which grounded its argumentation partially in the unconstitutional provisions of the state of disaster in the Protection against Disasters Act. This clear case of judicial activism which is also an instance of overt violation of the Constitution by the Constitutional Court will be a central topic of the subsequent analysis in the remaining part of this chapter.

Let's briefly summarise the legal framework of the 'extraordinary epidemic situation' as it is provided by the recent amendments of the Health Act introduced in 2020 in the course of the adopted governmental anti-pandemic measures. The Health Act introduces an 'extraordinary epidemic situation'. In contrast to the emergency situations introduced by the Counter-Terrorism Act and the Defence and Military Troops Act, and similarly by the Protection against Disasters Act, it is not legislative further development of the constitutionally provided state of emergency but a brand-new form of emergency regime which expands its realm in an unconstitutional manner. This is due to the following reasons.

The 'extraordinary epidemic situation' is not provided by the Constitution. It is created by the Parliament with the idea only to allow the government to concentrate power and to restrict human rights in a rather discretionary manner under the pretext of the fight against the pandemic. The only constitutionally permissible way for the government to combat pandemic situations is by declaring a state of emergency.[13] The government did so for two months during the period 13 March 2020 to 13 May 2020. However, under the pressure of public opinion it wanted to move to a regime that resembled normality but at the same time still be able to restrict human rights, bypass official democratic channels of government and provide for a mixed semi-authoritarian and semi-technocratic regime masquerading as democracy. That is why the pro-governmental parliamentary majority has adopted the amendments to the Health Act allowing the establishment of an 'extraordinary epidemic situation' as a fig leaf for a regime which is a de facto state of emergency but must look like something that is close to normalcy.

The 'extraordinary epidemic situation' is provided in a way which contains no sufficient indicators that will allow for its justification on the basis of the principles of proportionality and balancing of constitutional rights. It deviates from the constitutional model for distribution of powers related to emergency situations, bypassing the National Assembly and placing largely uncontrollable power in the hands of the government, the Minister of Health and the Chief Health Inspector. The introduction of an 'extraordinary epidemic situation' is dependent on vague and abstract alternatively formulated concepts such as 'the existence of [a] pathogen with high epidemic potential' (this can be even the regular flu), the existence of a pathogen which is 'unusual for the region, the season or the population' (this can be a flu during the summer), which causes disease and which has unusual symptoms, or there are 'registered cases of the disease among the medical personnel' (meaning that the infection of nurses and doctors may also be a legitimate ground for emergency). To sum up, an 'extraordinary epidemic situation' with the above-mentioned detrimental effects on the rule of law, democracy, human rights and separation of powers may be declared by the government on the recommendation of the Minister of Health acting on a proposal of the Chief Health Inspector, for example in case there are infected medical specialists or if there is a disease which is unusual for Bulgaria. This obviously contradicts the principle of proportionality and balancing of human rights and is overtly unconstitutional.

3 Role of the Constitutional Court in shaping and mastering an emergency situation

4.1 The judicial activism of the Bulgarian Constitutional Court

The Bulgarian Constitutional Court does not have a very long history. It was established in 1991 by the last Bulgarian Constitution and started its functioning one year later. However, it has a rather long and well-established tradition of judicial activism.[14] Indeed, there are many cases which have been decided with

13 For a similar conclusion and proposal, see Djordje Gardasevic's chapter in this edited volume.

14 See, e.g., Decision No. 3 of 2003, Decision No. 3 of 2004 and Decision No. 8 of 2005, which massively redraft the demarcation line between the two institutions of the

judicial self-restraint. There are even cases in which the Court could or even should have demonstrated its clout, but did not do so. However, there are plenty of examples of overt and unrestrained judicial activism which has redrawn the demarcation lines between the competences of constitutional institutions and has produced extensive implications of new meaning in the open texture of the constitutional provisions.

I have to make an admission here and say that I am not explicitly against judicial activism. In fact, I believe that judicial activism can be possible, justifiable and in many cases even necessary. The role of courts has changed throughout the history of modern statehood.[15] They should not necessarily be a power which is *en quelque facon nulle*, as suggested a long time ago by Montesquieu. Judicial activism may be necessary in order to promote change, adjust the constitutional and legal order to the demands of the socio-political context and establish a feasible system of human rights and rule of law. This does not preclude the fact, however, that judicial activism in general and the development of constitutional standards by the constitutional courts via extensive interpretation of the constitution allowed by its 'open texture' is in sharp contradiction with established principles of constitutional law such as popular sovereignty, separation of powers and democracy. I am just briefly marking this conceptual problem and will not discuss it in detail due to space constraints. This is really one of the topical issues of contemporary constitutionalism which cannot be solved in few lines. Nevertheless, judicial activism might be rather problematic when it concerns the constitutional model of emergency situations and the emergency policy of the state. The combination of judicial activism, power-hungry executive and technocratic expansion in the sphere of separation of powers and constitutional rights might have dangerous results related to democracy, rule of law and human rights protections.

Again, the judicial activism of the Bulgarian Constitutional Court is also not a negative phenomenon per se. In fact, the Court in quite a number of cases did an excellent job adjusting the Constitution to the demands of the socio-political reality and giving informative interpretation, elucidating many obscure or unclear elements of the constitutional texture, and thus of the constitutional order. Therefore, the Court has been not only a defender of the rule of law, democracy and human rights, but also a promoter of constitutional change leading to the adaptation of the constitutional text to the constitutional context.

constituent power – the National Assembly and the Grand National Assembly. Thus, the Court has actually defined the spheres of competences of the constituent power while it is supposed to be constituted power. For more about these issues, see Belov, M. Constitutional Courts as Ultimate Players in Multilevel Constituent Power Games: The Bulgarian Case. In: Belov, M. (ed.) Courts, Politics and Constitutional Law. Judicialization of Politics and Politicization of the Judiciary, Abingdon, Routledge, 2019, pp. 160–166.

15 See Belov, M. Global Rule of Law instead of Global Democracy? Legitimacy of Global Judicial Empire on the Edge between Westphalian and post-Westphalian Constitutionalism. In: Belov, M. (ed.) The Role of Courts in Contemporary Legal Orders, The Hague, Eleven, 2019.

Nevertheless, the perils of judicial activism both in general and in the Bulgarian case should not be underestimated. That is why I will outline here the Bulgarian Constitutional Court's case law on the constitutional provisions devoted to mastering of emergency situations. I will first expose the activist role of the Constitutional Court in shaping and mastering military emergency situations. Then, I will explore the activist role of the Constitutional Court in shaping and mastering health-related emergency situations. I will focus on the recent case No. 10 of 2020, which wrongly declared constitutional the 'extraordinary epidemic situation' established by the amendments of the Health Act related to the Covid-19 pandemic.

4.2 The activist role of the Constitutional Court in shaping and mastering military emergency situations

The constitutional foundations of the national defence can be briefly summarised in the following way. The National Assembly has monopoly over the decision of the most important issues – the declaration of war, state of siege or state of emergency, the ratification of the most important treaties related to national defence and security. The Parliament allows the sending and use of Bulgarian military troops abroad as well as the transition or deployment of foreign military troops on Bulgarian territory. The international treaties with political or military character must be ratified by the National Assembly by virtue of an act of Parliament. The Parliament adopts the legislative framework of the national defence. The National Assembly also asserts control over the Council of Ministers, the Minister of Defence and the Minister of Interior and may engage their political liability.

The Council of Ministers determine the foreign, national defence and national security politics. It determines its strategic lines and shapes and its tactical key points. The government further develops the legislative framework of national security and defence through normative, general and individual administrative acts. The Council of Ministers is competent to propose to the Parliament the declaration of war, state of siege or state of emergency. The Minister of Defence is responsible for the defence policy following the overall governmental policy and acting in accordance with the EU law, the Constitution, the acts of Parliament and the acts of the Council of Ministers. He of she must also cooperate with the President of the Republic in defence matters.

The President of the Republic is the commander in chief of the armed forces both in times of peace and war. He also presides over the Advisory Council for National Defence. The President of the Republic appoints and dismisses the high military ranks and assigns military decorations on proposal of the Council of Ministers. The President of the Republic declares general or partial mobilisation on the proposal of the Council of Ministers. The President of the Republic declares war in case of military invasion against the country or when the immediate fulfilment of international obligations for collective defence is necessary, as well as a state of siege or state of emergency when the National Assembly is not in session. In this case the National Assembly must be summoned immediately in order to pronounce on this declaration.

This is the relatively simple but clear structure of the 'military constitution' in the contemporary Bulgarian constitutional order. The Constitution provides for an intelligible framework not only for the emergency situations (war, state of siege and state of emergency) but for the whole constitutional model of the national defence. However, the Constitutional Court has adopted two interpretative decisions in this domain. Decision No. 5 of 1999 and Decision No. 1 of 2003 of the Constitutional Court give abstract and binding interpretation on some of the most important issues related to the sphere of national security and defence. They are clear examples of judicial activism and demonstrate the central role of the Constitutional Court in shaping and mastering military emergency situations. The overall reason for these two decisions is that they interpret rather extensively the constitutional text, imply new meaning in it, and thus enable the political institutions and more precisely the government to accomplish its military and defence policy in rather a discretionary way through diminishing its constitutional restraints. Thus, the Constitutional Court promotes specific constitutional politics in the sphere of national defence and emergency situations in the sphere of military and defence policy-making, developing the Constitution in a questionable manner. Here is a brief summary of these two Constitutional Court decisions which illustrate this conclusion.

Decision No. 5 of 1999 was adopted on the initiative of the Council of Ministers, who had approached the Constitutional Court with the following two interpretative questions:

1 In case of international treaty that has already been ratified with an act of Parliament by the National Assembly and has entered into force which regulates issues related to the transition of foreign military troops through the Bulgarian territory or their deployment on it, namely: the type of the military troops, the aims of their transition or deployment and the term of the validity of the treaty, should the government ask for permission the National Assembly in each concrete case of transition or deployment. The Council of Ministers believes that such permission is not necessary because it is granted via parliamentary decision, while the international treaty has already been ratified via an act of Parliament which has superior legal force.
2 Should military troops that transit or are deployed on Bulgarian territory be considered as military troops of a foreign state or international organisation if they are accomplishing these manoeuvres in accordance with an international treaty which has been ratified with an act of Parliament and has entered into force for Bulgaria. For example, if the Republic of Bulgaria is attacked by a foreign state and in accordance with an international treaty, it has to receive military help from foreign states or international organisations; it is necessary that the National Assembly must give permission in each concrete case.

It has been mentioned above that the Constitution has clear and explicit provision that in all of the above-mentioned cases there must be an explicit and formal decision of the National Assembly. Indeed, such constitutional provision makes the accomplishment of the transition and deployment of military troops a bit more complicated in terms of procedure and may create some delay. However, this is the explicit will of the constitutional legislator. If it is considered to be inadequate or to produce unreasonable impediments for a wartime use of military troops, then the text should have been explicitly amended by the institutions of the constituent power and not through an interpretative decision of the Constitutional Court.

However, exactly the opposite has been done due to contextual reasons related to political opportunity and expedience. The Constitutional Court has decided that if the international military treaty has been ratified with an act of Parliament by the National Assembly, if is published and entered into force and if it contains clauses for the transition or deployment of foreign military troops through or on Bulgarian territory, then there is no need for a special decision of the Parliament which allows each concrete transition or deployment. Thus, the Constitutional Court has in fact amended the Constitution and has allowed the government to acquire competences in the sphere of national defence which were initially vested in the Parliament by an explicit constitutional provision.

Moreover, the Constitutional Court stipulates in Decision No. 5 of 1999 that in case of international obligations for mutual military support that are a result of an international treaty, ratified with an act of Parliament by the National Assembly, published and entered into force the deployment or transition of military troops of such alliance on Bulgarian territory, can be accomplished with a decision of the government and a special decision of the Parliament is not necessary.

This line of reasoning has been continued by the Constitutional Court in its Decision No. 1 of 2003. According to it the military troops of a political or military union, or the member states of such union or those of allied states that are parties to an international treaty which is ratified via an act of Parliament by the National Assembly, published and entered into force for the Republic of Bulgaria, are not foreign troops according to the meaning of Article 84, point 11 of the Constitution if their transition or deployment through or in the territory of Bulgaria is related to the accomplishment of alliance obligations.

The decision of the National Assembly in accordance with Article 84, point 11 of the Constitution is not necessary in case of sending and use of Bulgarian military forces outside of the territory of the state as well as in case of transition or deployment of foreign military troops through it when this is done in the course of implementation of alliance obligations stemming from an international treaty which is ratified via an act of Parliament by the National Assembly, published and entered into force for the Republic of Bulgaria in accordance with Article 85, paragraph 1, point 11 of the Constitution.

A decision of the National Assembly for each concrete case related to the hypotheses provided by Article 84, point 11 of the Constitution is not necessary if a separate act of Parliament enlists exhaustively the aims, procedure and conditions for fulfilment of the Bulgarian obligations stemming from an international treaty which is ratified via an act of Parliament by the National Assembly, published and entered into force for the Republic of Bulgaria that foresees the sending of

Bulgarian military troops outside of the country or the transition or deployment of allied military forces through or on Bulgarian territory.

The joint effect of these two Constitutional Court decisions is the redrawing of the scheme of competences in the sphere of national defence between the key players in it – the National Assembly and the Council of Ministers – in favour of the latter. Thus, the Constitutional Court has rewritten the Bulgarian Constitution, strengthening the role of the government in national defence for reasons of expediency, efficiency and political and military appropriateness. Just one clear example for this extensive and obvious judicial activism: according to Decision No. 1 of 2003 the military troops of NATO countries are not foreign troops if they are on Bulgarian soil for the fulfilment of their alliance obligations. There is no single provision or even word in the text of the Bulgarian Constitution which allows for such a conclusion of the Court.

It will be shown that such an activist stance of the Bulgarian Constitutional Court is not an exception. On the contrary, Decision No. 10 of 2020 adopted in the context of the Covid-19 pandemic is a clear continuation of the same line of reasoning and of the same trend for strengthening the role of the government in case of emergency situations to the detriment of the National Assembly and parliamentarism in general.

4.3 The activist role of the Constitutional Court in shaping and mastering health-related emergency situations

The 'extraordinary epidemic situation' that was introduced in 2020 by virtue of amendments in the Health Act has been described above. It is just one of the many unconstitutional activities undertaken by the Bulgarian authorities during the Covid-19 pandemic, disrespecting and infringing the rule of law and democracy. Most of the measures adopted have been disproportional and did not take into account the balancing between the protection of life and health and the other constitutionally provided rights such as freedom of movement, privacy rights, the right to education, the freedom of speech, etc.

The state of emergency was declared by the National Assembly on proposal of the Council of Ministers for the period of two months (13 March 2020 to 13 May 2020). However, it has been considered largely disproportional, especially with a view to the relationship between the lockdown and the rather low number of cases of Covid-19 in the country during the above-mentioned period. Thus, the government and its parliamentary majority have been forced by public opinion to renounce the continuation of the state of emergency after 13 May 2020. The state of emergency had detrimental effects on the economy as well, so the government itself wanted to go beyond it while keeping the possibility of restricting rights and shifting power towards the executive and its technocratic advisers. Hence, the government wanted to have an intermediate regime at its disposal – a hybrid regime which is not exactly a state of emergency but allows for the adoption of emergency measures. More precisely, the idea was to preserve the shift of power from the Parliament to the government, the Minister of Health and the expert advisory institutions – the National Operative Headquarters and the Chief Health Inspector.

This is the reason why the government and its parliamentary majority came up with this idea – to introduce an 'extraordinary epidemic situation', formally different from the state of emergency, following the example of the state of disaster introduced in 2006 by the Protection against Disasters Act. The hope of the government was that this 'extraordinary epidemic situation' would allow for a restriction of human rights and for the imposition of harsh measures with detrimental impacts on society, education, culture and normal life in general while removing the claim that governance by emergency measures needs to comply with the requirements of legal certainty, proportionality, transparency and has to have some clear temporal limits. Moreover, the government needed a legal excuse for the shift of power from the Parliament to the government, and the technocratic advisory bodies the latter deprived of any constitutional status and legitimacy.

In this context, the President of the Republic has approached the Constitutional Court with the claim that the amendments in the Health Act that enabled the introduction of an 'extraordinary epidemic situation' on 14 May 2020, which is still in force, are unconstitutional. The constitutional proceedings had been initiated on the same day as the 'extraordinary epidemic situation' had entered into force – on 14 May 2020. More precisely, the President of the Republic suggested that Article 63, paragraphs 2–7 of the Health Act contravene Article 57, paragraph 3 (inviolability of constitutional rights in times of war, state of siege or state of emergency), Article 61 (the duty of the citizens to cooperate with the state and help the society in case of disasters and other emergency situations), Article 4 (rule of law) and Article 8 (separation of powers) of the Constitution.

The Constitutional Court has rejected the claims of the President of the Republic. Thus, it has confirmed the constitutionality of the above-mentioned provisions of the Health Act and consequently provided that the introduction of the 'extraordinary epidemic situation' is compliant with the Constitution.

This decision of the Constitutional Court is unconstitutional. It shows the risk of unconstitutional Constitutional Court decisions. Unconstitutional constitutional amendments is one of the hottest topics in contemporary constitutional theory.[16] The scientific debate is focused mainly on the challenges which formal constitutional amendments that are unconstitutional on formal, procedural or substantial grounds create for constitutional theory or political practice. The overall claim produced as a result of this debate is that the constitutional legislator may also act unconstitutionally if the constitutional amendments are introduced in an unconstitutional manner or infringe the main constitutional principles, the core of the constitution or constitutional identity. Of course, the opinions which are the legitimate grounds for unconstitutionality of constitutional amendments are rather divergent. In Bulgaria there is even a decision of the Constitutional Court

16 See Roznai, Y. Unconstitutional Constitutional Amendments – The Migration and Success of a Constitutional Idea. The American Journal of Comparative Law, vol. 61, no. 3 (summer 2013), pp. 657–719; Roznai, Y. Unconstitutional Constitutional Amendments. The Limits of Amendment Powers, Oxford, OUP, 2019, pp. 1–368; Yap, P. The Conundrum of Unconstitutional Constitutional Amendments. Global Constitutionalism, vol. 4, issue 1, 2015, pp. 114–136.

which has declared a formal constitutional amendment adopted by the National Assembly instead of a special covenant – the Grand National Assembly – to be unconstitutional. This is Decision No. 7 of 2006.

However, in parallel to the risk of constitutional infringement inflicted by the institutions of the constituent power via formal constitutional amendment, there is also the threat of unconstitutional constitutional amendment accomplished by the Constitutional Court through their interpretative decisions or via any other decision that accomplishes 'virtual amendment of the Constitution'.[17] I believe that this is the case with Decision No. 10 of 2020 adopted by the Bulgarian Constitutional Court. Here are the reasons for my claim.

Indeed, the very construction of the concept of unconstitutional constitutional amendment produced by the Constitutional Court's decision is rather questionable since the Courts are not supposed to be able to amend the Constitution. This is true if we stick to the traditional theory of clear separation between constituent and constituted powers. In such case the Constitutional Court must be an institution that belongs to the constituted powers having the competence to only clarify meaning enshrined by the constitutional legislator while sticking to judicial self-restraint.

However, constitutional courts nowadays typically perform judicial activism, as their explicit or implicit constitutional policy uses the 'open texture' of the constitutional provisions[18] in order to further develop the constitution. This is the case also with the Court of Justice of the EU and the European Court of Human Rights. This phenomenon is usually defined as a 'virtual amendment of the Constitution'[19] via judicial activism. Many contemporary Constitutional Courts perform such activist jurisprudential development of the Constitution. Thus, we must not reject the possibility of 'unconstitutional constitutional amendment' via constitutional interpretation and the case law of the courts. On the contrary, constitutional theory must expose such cases, critically assess them and suggest strategies for their prevention.

In the motives to Decision No. 10 of 2020 the Constitutional Court wrongly assumes that the emergency situations inevitably lead to constitutional dictatorship. In fact, the Court structures an important part of its argument around the concept of 'constitutional dictatorship', which is not a valid concept of Bulgarian constitutional law, as correctly noted by Judge Georgi Angelov in his dissenting opinion[20]. Indeed, the emergency situations are 'emergency regimes' as the Court points out, but this does not lead to any legitimation of dictatorship – constitutional or unconstitutional. Hence, the Court speculatively builds its argument around a purely theoretical concept which is of marginal importance even for the theory and derives arguments addressing the issue of the constitutionality of the

17 See Tanchev E., M. Belov Constitutional Gradualism: Adapting to EU Membership and Improving the Judiciary in the Bulgarian Constitution. European Public Law, vol. 14, issue 1, March 2008.

18 See Hart, H.L.A. op. cit.

19 See Tanchev E., M. Belov supra.

20 See http://www.constcourt.bg/bg/Acts/GetHtmlContent/cbb2555e-31e8-411b-b65e-4894857937cf

'extraordinary epidemic situation'. This is a clear example of judicial activism by the Court by virtue of which it creates justification for unconstitutional legislative inventions such as the 'extraordinary epidemic situation'. Unfortunately, the argumentation strategy of the court, structured on the basis of recourse to 'constitutional dictatorship', has repercussions also for the overall conceptualisation of the constitutionally provided emergency situations (war, state of siege or state of emergency).

The Court correctly provides a brief historical analysis of the emergency situation in Bulgarian constitutional history. It also rightly points out the international agreements of which the Republic of Bulgaria is part which define the concept of emergency situation. The Court's decision (as well as the dissenting opinions) engage also with linguistic analysis and comparison of the terms 'extraordinary epidemic situation' and 'state of emergency', which are denominated by different words in the Bulgarian language ('ёбстанёвка' and 'пёлёжение'). The linguistic analysis in fact contributes to the blurring of the conceptual clarity with the deliberate aim to justify the constitutionality of the 'extraordinary epidemic situation'.

Nevertheless, the Court comes to the wrong conclusion that the Parliament has not violated the constitutional provisions for emergency by creating an emergency situation which deviates from its requirements. The long line of historic and comparative argumentation and the definition of the concept of emergency do not really prove the thesis of the Court that the 'extraordinary epidemic situation' is compliant with the Bulgarian Constitution. The Court has not been able to solidly prove its main thesis that underlines the decision. The discretionary imposition of 'extraordinary epidemic situation' coinciding with the concept of state of emergency, but regulated as a different concept, initiated on the discretionary decision of the Minister of Health on suggestion of experts without any parliamentary involvement, its temporal non-restrictedness, the rather vague and wide criteria for its imposition and the substantial shift in competences from the legislative to the executive power are in contrast to the key idea enshrined in the Constitution regarding regulation of emergency. This is the idea to have only three types of emergency – war, state of siege and state of emergency – declared exclusively by the Parliament when it is possible to be summoned. Hence, the 'extraordinary epidemic situation' contravenes the principle of separation of powers since no 'constitutional dictatorship' is permissible even in a state of emergency and the Constitution clearly requires the involvement of the National Assembly in mastering emergency situations.

Another great danger of the introduction of the 'extraordinary epidemic situation' is that it allows for a disproportionate restriction of constitutional rights. These restrictions are introduced by the ordinary legislator without taking into account basic elements of the constitutional principle of rule of law. These are the predictability and transparency in the introduction of human rights limitations, legal certainty, the proportionality in human rights limitations, the balancing of rights and the need for involvement of the Parliament in the imposition of such restrictions. The Bulgarian Constitution provides for proportional human rights limitations which are related to the three possible emergency situations – war, state of siege and state of emergency. They are not applicable to an 'extraordinary epidemic situation' which is constitutionally null and void and does not grant legitimacy for the restriction of any constitutional right. This constitutional logic is in conflict with the legislative provisions of the Health Act by virtue of which the 'extraordinary epidemic situation' has been introduced. Thus, the 'extraordinary epidemic situation' contradicts the principle of rule of law and is unconstitutional also on that ground.

It must be noted that Decision No. 10 of 2020 was adopted with only nine votes because there were three dissenting judges who wrote two dissenting opinions that contain their reasons and arguments for disagreement with the majority in the Court which had been behind the decision. The one dissenting opinion is jointly written by the Constitutional Court judges Tanya Raikovska and Atanas Semov. The other dissenting opinion is written by the Constitutional Court judge Georgi Angelov.

Some of the arguments for unconstitutionality of the 'extraordinary epidemic situation' discussed here are shared also by leading experts in law or medicine in their advisory opinions to this case.[21] I cannot discuss them here due to space constraints. However, I will briefly focus on the two dissenting opinions of the above-mentioned three Constitutional Court judges. Similarly to the expert advisory opinions, the dissenting opinions do not possess either validity or normativity. Nevertheless, they demonstrate alternative judicial logic and serve as an important source of information for the eventual weaknesses in the argumentation and the conclusions of the Constitutional Court enshrined in its decision.

In their dissenting opinion, judges Tanya Raikovska and Atanas Semov stipulate that

'the principle of safeguarding of the legitimate legal expectations and the principles of proportionality are of fundamental importance for the rule of law. The continuous introduction of disproportional anti-pandemic measures which do not take into account the balance of constitutional rights as well as their subsequent chaotic and frequently partial abolition are severe infringement of the rule of law'.[22]

In their dissenting opinion, Tanya Raikovska and Atanas Semov raise important claims. They believe that the 'extraordinary epidemic situation' is a variant of the state of emergency and must be defined as such. They think that the procedure for declaration of this 'extraordinary epidemic situation' is clear – it is the procedure for a declaration of a state of emergency – and it has not been taken into account. The judges believe also that the 'extraordinary epidemic situation' contradicts the rule of law and the separation of powers, with a view to both an unconstitutional shift of competences from the Parliament to the Minister of Health and expert institutions and the infringement of the constitutional safeguards for restriction of constitutionally provided human rights.

21 See the expert advisory opinions given by the Bulgarian Attorneys for Human Rights, Prof. Vasil Mrachkov, Prof. Tsvetan Sivkov, Prof. Radka Argirova and attorney Maria Sharkova. These opinions contain many arguments related to my criticism of Decision No. 10 of 2020 expressed in this chapter.

22 See http://www.constcourt.bg/bg/Acts/GetHtmlContent/0c77871a-a6c3-461e-9e2a-a3d1ced420b0

Linguistic comparison is accomplished also by Judge Georgi Angelov in his dissenting opinion. On its basis, he comes to the conclusion that the constitutional concept of 'state of emergency' and the 'extraordinary epidemic situation' as a concept provided by an act of Parliament are mutually related as type to subtype, and the former includes the latter. Thus, the 'extraordinary epidemic situation' is a variant of the state of emergency and must be declared only by the National Assembly and not by the government. Hence, the introduction of an 'extraordinary epidemic situation' is unconstitutional since it shifts power and competences in an unconstitutional way. Judge Angelov believes that the legislative provisions that introduced the 'extraordinary epidemic situation' are unconstitutional also because the concretisation of the reasons for declaration of a state of emergency in the Health Act limit the constitutional competence. He also challenges the rather questionable recourse to the concept of constitutional dictatorship and the reasoning of the Court's majority in the motives of Decision No. 10 of 2020 that the extraordinary situation is a legitimate constitutional dictatorship in which deviations from the constitutional model of separation of powers provided for times of normality are permissible. Judge Angelov correctly concludes that 'transformation of the constitutional order' in times of emergency is constitutionally non-permissible.

Last but not least, Decision No. 10 of 2020 of the Constitutional Court is a dangerous precedent also because it indirectly legitimises the other form of unconstitutional deviation from the constitutional model of state of emergency. This is the 'state of disaster' discussed above. Thus, the Court paves the way for the future introduction of further unconstitutional forms of emergency situations on the discretion of the parliamentary majority pressured by its government.

4 Conclusion

The Constitutional Court must be a key safeguard for the rule of law and democracy, for the supremacy of the Constitution, respect for international treaties and EU law, and the separation of powers between state institutions. Its activity is crucial for the existence of a feasible system of rule of law, separation of powers and democracy. The Constitutional Court must be a predictable protagonist of human rights. When performing in an activist or counter-majoritarian way, this should be done with due respect for the principles of transparency, proportionality and balancing of human rights.

The Bulgarian Constitutional Court has been rather activist in the sphere of emergency situations. It has extensively and further developed the constitutional model for distribution of competences in the sphere of national defence and emergency situations. Thus, the Constitutional Court has largely intervened in and engaged with constitutional emergency politics and has contributed to the shaping of emergency constitutionalism and the 'military constitution' in Bulgaria.

The case law of the Bulgarian Constitutional Court has favoured the executive branch of power. It has shifted core competences in the sphere of emergency and military constitution towards the government and to the detriment of the

Parliament. In some of the cases this has been justified with pragmatic reasons related to improving the efficiency of policy-making in national defence. In other cases, the case law of the Court has led to paradoxical results which overtly contradict the explicit will of the constitutional legislator.

The recent Decision No. 10 of 2020 of the Constitutional Court is especially problematic. It has legitimised an unconstitutional new form of emergency – the 'extraordinary epidemic situation' – introduced by the Parliament in a 'rush and hush' manner during the 2020 Covid-19 pandemic. This decision allows for an unconstitutional shift of power from the National Assembly to the executive power institutions and even to unaccountable and non-elected experts, which contravenes the model of separation of powers. Especially problematic is the fact that such a shift concerns the already sensitive sphere of extraordinary situations. Moreover, Decision No. 10 of 2020 of the Constitutional Court justifies the legislative invention of the 'extraordinary epidemic situation', which contains no safeguards for proportionality, balancing and predictability in the restriction of constitutionally enshrined rights, thus violating not only the principles of democracy and separation of powers but also the rule of law. In that regard, Decision No. 10 of 2020 of the Constitutional Court is a clear example of the danger of judicial activism.

9 Activism of the Croatian Constitutional Court and Covid-19

A Bridge Too Far

Djordje Gardasevic

1 Introduction

Even though the circumstances surrounding the spread of Covid-19 are not a typical emergency such as war or imminent threat to the survival of the state, their consequences have strongly impacted global living conditions in a way that only a grave crisis can do. It also seems that the present pandemic definitely tends to be put in the category of unprecedented cases.[1] So once again, for constitutional lawyers the central question is this: how do we appropriately balance between powers that governments strive for in their attempts to respond effectively to the threat and liberty that under extraordinary circumstances inevitably comes under attack?

My chapter is focused on the specific Croatian experiences with the Covid-19 crisis. In the second part of the chapter I first present the legal framework under which the national authorities have so far dealt with the pandemic. In principle, Croatia decided not to invoke the constitutional provisions on the situation of a 'severe natural disaster' and thus opted for applying special legislation. Furthermore, I add a presentation of all the decisions of the Croatian Constitutional Court by virtue of which in September 2020 it reviewed constitutionality both the laws and special regulations enacted for combating the pandemic. In the third part of the chapter I first give some general remarks on the position of the rule of law principle in contexts of emergencies and on the possible role of courts thereof. In the following part, I focus on the evaluation of the case law of the Croatian Constitutional Court. My general conclusion is that the Court in the 'corona cases', with only a few exceptions, was largely deferential to the undertakings of the Government. My personal opinion, however, is that the Court should have taken a different path and that it should have been more active in examining the totality of Covid-19 anti-epidemic measures in Croatia. In the remaining section of this chapter I will try to explain the reasons for that conclusion.

1 See: UN News: Covid-19 pandemic, an 'unprecedented wake-up call' for all inhabitants of Mother Earth, at: https://news.un.org/en/story/2020/04/1062322, 21 October 2020.

DOI: 10.4324/9781003200666-14

2 Covid-19 pandemic in Croatia

The forms of state of emergency in the Croatian Constitution are regulated in two central provisions. Article 17 deals with criteria on restrictions of fundamental rights and freedoms and may be applied in a state of war, immediate threat to the independence and unity of the State, or in the event of severe natural disasters. In such cases, it is the exclusive power of the Parliament to decide on restrictions of rights, with a two-thirds majority of all of its members, provided it is able to convene. If the Parliament is unable to meet, decision rests with the President of the Republic, who acts only at the proposal of the Government and upon the counter-signature of the Prime Minister. Apart from that, Article 17 explicitly imposes application of the proportionality principle and prohibition of discrimination. Finally, it excludes that constitutional guarantees on some core right may be subject to restriction, even in the case of an immediate threat to the existence of the State.[2] On the other hand, Article 101 regulates emergency decrees enacted by the President of the Republic, in a state of war, an immediate threat to the independence, unity and existence of the State, or in situations where the governmental bodies are prevented from performing their constitutional duties regularly. Except for the state of war, the Prime Minister must countersign emergency decrees. At the same time, those decrees must always be presented to the Parliament, as soon as it convenes. The Parliament must approve enacted decrees or they lose legal force. The Constitutional Court retains its jurisdiction to rule on constitutionality of emergency measures. However, there is no rule similar to Article 16 of the French Constitution, for example, that would set up specific time limits as to when the Court could or should be called to express itself on the existence of conditions mandating application of a state of emergency. There is no time limit as to when the Court should deliver its decision on constitutionality of a particular emergency decree either.

Faced with the Covid-19 threat, Croatia proclaimed an epidemic on 11 March 2020. Despite the growing and global spread of the virus, Croatian authorities decided to act on the basis of powers conferred by the special legislative acts and did not invoke Article 17 of the Constitution. In order to better understand the situation, I am here presenting explications related to two special laws that, up to this date, have served as the legal ground for dealing with the pandemic.

The first step made for the purpose of strengthening the special powers intended to be used was an amendment made to the Law on the Civil Protection System. A newly added Article 22.a thereof provided that the body called 'the National Civil Protection Headquarters'[3] has the power to 'render decisions and guidelines to be implemented by the civil protection authorities of the local and regional governments' in case of 'specific circumstances involving an unpredictable

2 For the English translation of the Croatian Constitution, see: https://www.constituteproject.org/constitution/Croatia_2013?lang=en, 13 October 2020.

3 Further: 'the Headquarters'.

or uncontrollable event or state endangering the lives and health of citizens'. According to Article 22.a, those 'decisions' and 'guidelines' are enacted 'for the purpose of protecting the lives and health of citizens'.[4] It is to be noted that the amendment to the Law on the Civil Protection System was enacted after only one day of parliamentary deliberations with 108 votes for the amendment. This made an overwhelming majority, extending beyond two-thirds of all parliamentary representatives.[5] Immediately after this amendment, the Headquarters started to enact anti-epidemic measures, the first one being the temporary restriction of crossing the state borders.[6]

On the other hand, even before the pandemic, the Croatian parliament enacted the Infectious Diseases Protection Law which provides for a range of anti-epidemic measures, but in its version in force in March it also prescribed that application of those measures could be imposed only on the basis of a decision of the Minister of Health and not the Headquarters. After roughly a month, this law was also amended in order to provide that the Headquarters receive the same power as the Minister. The amendment also prescribed that the Headquarters issues its decisions under direct control of the Government (Article 47 of the Infectious Diseases Protection Law).[7] This came as a legal necessity because in the period before the amendment it was exclusively the Headquarters that was deciding on special measures, solely on Article 22.a. This in turn opened the issue of the retroactivity of the amendment, which I will come back to later.

The Croatian Constitutional Court expressed its position regarding special anti-epidemic measures in a series of decisions delivered on 14 September 2020. I should immediately stress that the most important outcome thereof was the Court's validation of all the Headquarters' decisions with just one exception. Moreover, the Court ruled that it had no constitutional power to review the decision of the Parliament to act within the rules provided for normal situations (Article 16 of the Constitution), thus excluding itself from pronouncing whether a state of severe natural disaster (Article 17 of the Constitution) should have been proclaimed regardless.

Among those several decisions of the Court, the prominent place belongs to the one in which it dealt with constitutionality of amendments to the Law on the Civil

4 For a wider description of the Croatian legislative response to the Covid-19 threat, see also: Bačić Selanec, N., Croatia's Response to COVID-19: On Legal Form and Constitutional Safeguards in Times of Pandemic, at: https://verfassungsblog.de/croatias-response-to-covid-19-on-legal-form-and-constitutional-safeguards-in-times-of-pandemic/, 25 October 2020.

5 The amendment to the Law on the Civil Protection System was enacted already on 18 March 2020. It entered into force the following day.

6 The Headquarters enacted this particular decision already on 19 March 2020. All the decisions of the Headquarters are available (in Croatian) at: https://civilna-zastita.gov.hr/odluke-stozera-civilne-zastite-rh-za-sprecavanje-sirenja-zaraze-koronavirusom/2304, 28 October 2020.

7 The amendment to the Infectious Diseases Protection Law was enacted already on 17 April 2020. It entered into force on 18 April.

Protection System and the Infectious Diseases Protection Law.[8] I will now present those two combined cases.[9]

The arguments submitted by the applicants who sought the constitutional review of the two laws may be summarised in a few points. First, they claimed that the Parliament erred in deciding to amend the laws through an ordinary procedure, without first proclaiming the state of a severe natural disaster, as foreseen in Article 17 of the Constitution. Moreover, that meant that the amendments to two laws, affecting constitutionally protected rights and freedoms, should have been enacted with the two-thirds majority of all parliamentary representatives. In addition, it was argued that the contested amendments actually transferred special powers to the Headquarters even though such powers inherently belonged to the Parliament, which under the Constitution was the sole organ to decide on rights and freedoms in scenarios such as the present pandemic. Some of the applicants argued that the Parliament did have a constitutional power to retroactively validate decision of the headquarters but that this should have been done only within the Article 17 scheme, whereas others contested the possibility of retroactivity in general. Finally, the applicants pointed to the lack of a legitimate aim, that it was impossible to review the necessity and proportionality of enacted measures, that the measures actually were not subject to either judicial or parliamentary control and that they had an indeterminate time validity.

As to the crucial issue in the whole case – the one related to the necessity of applying Article 17 of the Constitution – the Court stressed that the Parliament had two options to regulate restrictions on fundamental rights and freedoms. The first was to enact new laws through an ordinary procedure foreseen for ordinary times, with the majority of all representatives,[10] while the second was to use Article 17 and a two-thirds majority. The Court, however, expressly said that the decision as to which of those two models should be applied in the present case belonged exclusively to the Parliament and not to the Court. The Court retained only its power to review constitutionality of particular decisions restricting rights and freedoms, even if they would be enacted within the realm of Article 17, should that have been the case.[11]

8 Decision of the Croatian Constitutional Court: U-I-1372/2020, 14 September 2020.

9 Apart from this particular decision, the Constitutional Court on the same day delivered its opinion in two additional cases, dealing with constitutionality of amendments to the Law on Local Elections and the Law on Catering Activities, also enacted in the context of the present pandemic. I will not go into details describing those two decisions separately because the Court itself there also referred to its main argumentation revealed in the decision dealing with the Law on the Civil Protection System and the Infectious Diseases Protection Law.

10 Article 16 of the Constitution prescribes the rule for restrictions of rights and freedoms in the following way: 'Freedoms and rights may only be restricted by law in order to protect freedoms and rights of others, public order, public morality and health. Every restriction of freedoms or rights shall be proportional to the nature of the necessity for restriction in each individual case.' On the other hand, Article 83 of the Constitution commands that laws regulating rights and freedoms the Parliament must enact by a majority of all of its representatives.

11 The Constitutional Court took the same approach, thus rejecting the use of Article 17 of the Constitution sought by the applicant, in a related case delivered the same day, and upholding the amendments to the Law on Local Elections. By those

As to the issue of legality of the Headquarters, the Court concluded that said body was properly empowered to act in new circumstances through both Article 22.a and Article 47. Moreover, the Court added that the pandemic/epidemic of Covid-19 did constitute 'specific circumstances' that endangered the health of the population in terms of Article 22.a and that, therefore, by enacting those amendments the Parliament actually constructed a legal framework in which both the Minister of Health and the Headquarters had powers to act.[12] Additionally, the Court stated that the specific measures enacted as a result of specific circumstances could last only for the duration of the pandemic.

In relation to the issue of control, the Court said that the Headquarters was undoubtedly an executive body and that it was under direct supervision of the Government, which, in turn, was itself under control of the Parliament and the Constitutional Court. This also meant that, according to the Court, there was always a possibility that the Parliament could ask for a report from the Government on the application of concrete measures and on the overall work of the Headquarters. Concrete measures of the Headquarters were also firmly defined as acts falling under both judicial and constitutional review.

The issue of a legitimate aim in this particular case was solved easily by relying on the interest of protection of health, but the Court clarified that it could not here go into reviewing the elements of proportionality and necessity, thus saving this for cases in which it would deal precisely with concrete anti-epidemic measures.

In the most striking section of this part of the Decision – the one related to the issue of retroactivity – the Court concluded that this problem actually did not exist because the Headquarters from the beginning had legal grounds for acting, not on basis of Article 47, but rather through Article 22.a. According to the Court, Article 47 thus did not have a retroactive effect, but rather it only clarified powers already conferred to the Headquarters by Article 22.a.

The three dissenters in this case offered a range of counter-arguments to the majority opinion.[13]

amendments, the Government was empowered to postpone local elections, which it actually did, in two municipalities. Although those specific elections were later held, the three dissenting judges pointed both to the necessity of applying Article 17 of the Constitution and to the fact that the contested Law, as abstractly written, actually allowed for an indeterminate postponement of local elections in cases of 'specific circumstances'. Here also, the formulation of those circumstances in said law was almost identical to the one I already described in reference to Article 22.a of the Law on the Civil Protection System. See: Decision of the Croatian Constitutional Court: U-I-1925/2020, 14 September 2020.

12 In its submission to the Court, the Government firmly claimed that the circumstances did not constitute a 'natural disaster' but rather an unpredicted state of special circumstances that in their totality were endangering the lives and health of citizens in the entire territory of the State. To this it added that the state for the first time was faced with a new legal situation, unpredicted in the existing law and explicitly denied relevance of Article 17 of the Constitution. See: Decision of the Croatian Constitutional Court: U-I-1372/2020, 14 September 2020.

13 The three dissenting judges were Andrej Abramović, Lovorka Kušan and Goran Selanec. As to the merits, judges Branko Brkić and Rajko Mlinarić, in their concurring

Firstly, they posited that there was no possibility to claim that one specific situation may be solved by choosing between two (competing) constitutional norms (Article 16 or Article 17 of the Constitution). In other words, each case should be dealt with by exclusively applying the relevant norm. Here the dissenters also warned that the optional approach actually contained a major advantage for the Government because it was obvious that no parliamentary majority, under such a scheme, would ever agree to binding itself to the two-thirds requirement if it could operate under a simple (absolute) majority. Additionally, they stressed that, for the sake of legal certainty, the state of a severe natural disaster should have been proclaimed. This meant that emergency as such finds its basis in the facts of the case itself, and not in the legal act of proclamation,[14] the proof of which was also that the 'special circumstances', as defined by the Law on the Civil Protection System, indeed were used to legally validate the actions of the Headquarters. The dissenters also insisted that the very existence of a state of emergency was a fact arising from the global situation surrounding Covid-19. To further strengthen the same line of reasoning, they focused on the specific definition contained in Article 22.a of the Law on the Civil Protection System and concluded that it perfectly fits the constitutional notion of a state of 'severe natural disaster' itself.

On the sub-issue of the consequences arising from the states of emergency, the dissenters stressed that there existed a crucial legal difference between laws reserved for ordinary times and those meant to regulate crises (different parliamentary majorities required for their adoption). Consequently, from the strict legal point of view, that meant that an ordinary majority of representatives could not decide that the two-thirds of votes was actually not necessary. Moreover, for the dissenters, it was exactly the Court's duty to verify if the proper procedure of enactment of laws was followed.

opinions stated that activation of Article 17 of the Constitution would not benefit the interest of expediency and efficiency of indispensable safety measures. Judge Brkić even stated that Article 17 could not be activated here because the case did not involve 'state of emergency' ('severe natural disaster' are the exact words in the Constitution) but rather 'obviously a state that will last, become regular, the one with which the whole global population, including the Republic of Croatia, is faced and in which it will live in the future'. See: Decision of the Croatian Constitutional Court: U-I-1372/2020, 14 September 2020 (concurring opinions of Judges R. Mlinarić and B. Brkić).

14 The Constitutional Court forwarded the same argument, regarding the act of proclamation of an emergency, already in its 1992 decision. See: Decision of the Croatian Constitutional Court: U-I-179/1991, 24 June 1992. The dissenters made another parallel here, the one with the 1990s war, which itself was never declared. The US Supreme Court offered the same argument in the Prize cases: 'This greatest of civil wars was not gradually developed by popular commotion, tumultuous assemblies, or local unorganised insurrections. However long may have been its previous conception, it nevertheless sprung forth suddenly from the parent brain, a Minerva in the full panoply of war. The President was bound to meet it in the shape it presented itself, without waiting for Congress to baptize it with a name; and no name given to it by him or them could change the fact.' See: Prize Cases, 67 U.S. 668, 669 (1862).

The dissenters also criticised arguments, pursued in public debates surrounding the situation, that a proper and full parliamentary control over special measure was not possible, pointing to practices in other states that proved otherwise. To this they added two additional reasons for the claim that proclamation of an emergency was actually beneficial for society: first, because both the European Convention on Human Rights and the International Covenant on Civil and Political Rights asked for temporary application of emergency measures; and, second, because the proportionality principle contained in Article 17 of the Croatian Constitution actually imposed a lower burden of proof for necessity than its counterpart in Article 16.[15] For all those reasons they concluded that restrictions of rights and freedoms should have been decided by the two-thirds majority in the Parliament, thus according to the prescription of Article 17 of the Constitution.

What then follows in the dissenting opinion is a rather heavy criticism on two special points: legal status of the Headquarters and retroactivity of the amendment to the Infectious Diseases Protection Law. As to the first point, the dissenters concluded that, due to its composition, its powers and the way it is controlled, the Headquarters truly represents a 'Clone of the Government'. In fact, they stressed, the Headquarters was made of members elected by the Government according to political criteria, was led by the Minister of Interior and included most of the ministers of the Government, with only a few exceptions. This way, it was actually a political body, a fact that totally undermined its independence from the Government and overturned the desired purpose of its functioning. In other words, instead of having in it experts who would advise relevant ministers on how to deal with the crisis, it was the ministries who delegated their representatives in the Headquarters so that it could more easily do the job. Moreover, judicial oversight of the Headquarters was here also put in question, not only because the Constitutional Court was in heavy delay in delivering its review, but also because ordinary courts were, during the pandemic and according to instructions of the Headquarters itself, mainly out of action.[16] As to the powers of the Headquarters, the dissenters criticised the overall and temporally indeterminate 'delegation' of powers made to it through Article 22.a of the Law on the Civil Protection System, specifically the prerogative to render

15 Article 16 of the Croatian Constitution regulates restrictions of rights in ordinary times and prescribes that 'every restriction of freedoms or rights shall be proportional to the nature of the necessity for restriction in each individual case'. On the other hand, Article 17 imposes a lower standard in emergencies and commands that 'the extent of such restrictions shall be adequate to the nature of the danger'.

16 For the same objection in the Bulgarian case, see: Vassileva, R., Bulgaria: COVID-19 as an Excuse to Solidify Autocracy?, at: https://verfassungsblog.de/bulgaria-covid-19-as-an-excuse-to-solidify-autocracy/, 25 October 2020. For similar staying of ordinary courts, as well as for the silence of the Constitutional Court regarding the emergency measures in the Serbian case, see: Marinković, T., Fight Against Covid-19 in Serbia: Saving the Nation or Securing the Re-Election?, at: https://verfassungsblog.de/fight-against-covid-19-in-serbia-saving-the-nation-or-securing-the-re-election/, 25 October 2020.

'decisions and guidelines'.[17] In their view, this resulted in the Headquarters becoming a 'parallel legislator headed by the Minister of Interior'. Finally, they found inadmissible a solution according to which the Headquarters was 'allegedly' empowered to act through Article 22.a along with the Minister of Health, who could act on the basis of Article 47 of the Infectious Diseases Protection Law. For those reasons, the dissenters concluded that Article 22.a was unconstitutional. And on the second point, the dissenters rejected that there was no issue of retroactivity of Article 47 in this case: for them, retroactivity clearly did exist and should have been justified. Since it was not justified, the dissenters pointed to unconstitutionality in this respect as well.[18]

Apart from the decisions made in abstract constitutional review of the laws I already described, the Constitutional Court also reviewed several decisions of the Headquarters imposing concrete anti-epidemic measures. Those may be summarised in three separate categories.

In three cases, the Court rejected going into merits because the applicants, according to the Court, did not further relevant reasons justifying their claims and because the contested decisions of the Headquarters ceased to apply before the Court delivered its opinions in mid-September.[19] In the first case, the Court

17 In a related case delivered the same day, the majority in the Constitutional Court also concluded that through the contested law the Headquarters acquired general power to enact special measures during 'unforeseen special circumstances that could not have been counteracted, and which were endangering the lives and health of the people'. In this case, the Court dealt with the power of the Headquarters to regulate working hours in catering businesses during the pandemic. See: Decision of the Croatian Constitutional Court: U-I-2162/2020, 14 September 2020. The same dissenters objected to this point in this case as well.

18 Decision of the Croatian Constitutional Court: U-I-1372/2020, 14 September 2020 (A. Abramović, L. Kušan and G. Selanec, dissenting). In a separate dissent, the same judges objected that the Court should have taken the whole case into docket on its own motion, that it should have done it months before and that separate motions for review of constitutionality should have been distributed equally among several judges, instead of having been given to only one rapporteur. Their objections become even more serious with their statement that they received the first draft of the opinion from the judge rapporteur only on 3 September, thus 11 days before the Court published its decisions. Additionally, they complained that a public hearing, which they advocated for, was not held. See: Decision of the Croatian Constitutional Court: U-I-1372/2020, 14 September 2020 (L. Kušan, A. Abramović and G. Selanec, dissenting). In yet the third joined dissent, they heavily criticised the whole legal model upon which the Headquarters was based, especially the fact that by it the Headquarters, unlike the Minister of Health, was not directly accountable to the Parliament. They also objected on several other grounds, including that it remained unclear whether the Headquarters had a timely limited mandate to act and by which exact procedure it was acting. See: Decision of the Croatian Constitutional Court: U-I-1372/2020, 14 September 2020 (G. Selanec, L. Kušan and A. Abramović, dissenting).

19 This, however, provoked the three dissenting judges to object to the majority reasoning on three grounds: first, that it was not true that the applicants in those cases had not submitted relevant reasons in support of their claims on constitutionality of contested measures; second, that it was not the fault of the applicants that the Constitutional Court waited several months to deliver its opinions; and third, that the

concluded that the ban on crossing the state borders was both appropriate and necessary since most of the European countries, from the beginning of March until the beginning of May, applied similar measures with the objective of preventing the uncontrolled spread of the virus. The Court also added that concrete damages that might have been inflicted upon the applicants should be solved in individual judicial proceedings, including the constitutional complaint, and not in an abstract review before the Constitutional Court.[20] In the second case, the Court concluded the same, this time in reference to the Headquarters' decision that prohibited leaving the place of residence.[21] In the third case within this category, the Court rejected the applicants' motion for constitutional review in reference to several decisions restricting public assemblies, work of shops and markets, provision of some other services, sport and cultural activities, as well as cemetery ceremonies.[22]

On the other hand, the Court did undertake a substantial review of the Headquarters' decision on the duty to wear face protection masks, from the point of Article 35 of the Constitution, guaranteeing personal and family life, dignity, reputation and honour. In the Court's view, the article implied positive obligations on the state in its efforts to protect health and the conclusion was that the measure in the existing circumstances was both rational and necessary. This way, the Court accepted justifications of the Government thereof which claimed that it acted on the basis of both the recommendations of various expert groups, including the World Health Organization, and on the basis of several scientific researches.[23]

Court should have applied its own power to review the decisions notwithstanding the fact that those decisions meanwhile ceased to apply. See: Decisions of the Croatian Constitutional Court: U-II-1312/2020, U-II-2027/2020, U-II-1373/2020, 14 September 2020 (A. Abramović, L. Kušan and G. Selanec, dissenting).

20 Decisions of the Croatian Constitutional Court: U-II-2027/2020, 14 September 2020. The applicant in this case stressed that the exclusions to the decision did not allow travelling for specific purposes, such as in case of seeking a job in another country or for medical interventions or for performing parental duties.

21 Decisions of the Croatian Constitutional Court: U-II-1312/2020, 14 September 2020. In this case the applicants argued that the decision of the Headquarters infringed upon the freedom of movement, that it discriminated against people in small municipalities who had to travel in order to purchase food and medicine, that it did not precisely foresee the time period of its application and that it should have been enacted by the Parliament, according to Article 17 of the Constitution.

22 Decisions of the Croatian Constitutional Court: U-II-1373/2020, 14 September 2020. The Court thus rejected as ill-founded the applicants' arguments that the imposed measures infringed the constitutional principle of equality, entrepreneurial freedoms, freedom of movement, right to work and freedom of assembly.

23 Decision of the Croatian Constitutional Court: U-II-3170/2020, 14 September 2020. The three dissenting judges, however, pointed out that there undoubtedly existed an intrusion into the personal freedom, which should have been properly justified by the Government. Taking into account the fact that the duty to wear masks was imposed only in June 2020, thus months after the actual outbreak of the pandemic, the dissenters objected on the ground of both the rational basis for the measure and its necessity. See: Decisions of the Croatian Constitutional Court: U-II-

Finally, the Court struck down the decision of the Headquarters, which prohibited work of shops, markets and similar businesses on Sundays exclusively. The contested measure was part of the 'relaxation' strategy of the Government and was enacted after a wide March 'lockdown' already ended. Taking into consideration that shops did work on Sundays even during the lockdown and that the Government in its submission firmly claimed that for shops the most frequent day of the week was actually Friday, the Court concluded that the measure breached the principle of proportionality.[24]

I conclude this overview of the Court's case law with an additional case in which it unanimously struck down the standing orders of the Parliament that regulated its operation in circumstances of epidemic. In short, the challenged section reduced the number of representatives allowed to be present in the parliamentary hall during debates, time of their expositions and number of their replies. At the same time, it allowed for voting of all representatives by electronic means or from different rooms apart from the main hall. Parliamentary committees were also allowed to use audio or video conference means of communication. The Court concluded that there obviously existed appropriate alternative means for organising sessions of the Parliament, which would not infringe rights and duties of representatives based on their free mandate.[25]

In one specific aspect, however, the Court remained completely silent. It did not pronounce itself on the fact that the challenged section of the standing orders prescribed that the decision to put the whole Parliament into the reduced mode of operation rested with the presidency of the Parliament alone. Moreover, the presidency could 'determine' this special mode of work only on the basis of a decision already issued by the body declaring the epidemic, i.e. the Government. Having in mind that by this scheme the presidency, counting only six persons and, of course, reflecting a significantly reduced parliamentary majority, had the exclusive power of deciding how long this mode of operation for the rest of 151 parliamentarians

3170/2020, 14 September 2020 (A. Abramović, L. Kušan and G. Selanec, dissenting).

24 Decision of the Croatian Constitutional Court: U-II-2379/2020, 14 September 2020. In one dissent, Judge D. Mlakar argued that the Court should have rejected the case as it did for the first category of cases. In another, Judge M. Šumanović claimed that the Court's decision to take the case into consideration represented an ungrounded judicial activism, taking into account that no specific motion for review was sent to it. On the merits, Šumanović advocated a relaxed standard of review in reference to proportionality. In their dissents, however, both judges, although not willing to invoke application of Article 17 of the Constitution, expressly stated that the Covid-19 situation amounted to 'health risk without a precedent' (M. Šumanović) and 'emergency situation' (D. Mlakar). On the other hand, three judges (G. Selanec, L. Kušan and A. Abramović) concurred, stressing that the Court should have applied Article 17 of the Constitution in the first place, and since it did not, it gravely erred in interpreting the elements of appropriateness of the measure and its necessity. See: Decision of the Croatian Constitutional Court: U-II-2379/2020, 14 September 2020 (G. Selanec, L. Kušan and A. Abramović, concurring).

25 Decision of the Croatian Constitutional Court: U-I-4208/2020, 20 October 2020.

would last, I strongly believe that this also represented an obvious example of the breach of the separation of powers principle.

3 Rule of law and its 'emergency exceptions'

Conviction that real emergencies are, by definition, actually unpredictable or having *sui generis* origin is deeply embedded in the Western history of political theory and constitutional law. And if causes of emergencies cannot be predicted, then, logically, the same goes for their consequences. In practice, it means that with every new genuine emergency we urgently require new tools to fight the threat. Consider in this context, for instance, the American debates on the War on Terror as falling under neither the 'crime' nor the 'war' paradigm and the consequent claims that this requires new categories, such as 'enemy combatants', or new procedures, such as those before military commission in Guantanamo.[26] The comparative experiences, including the Croatian example, make no exception here.[27]

Notable adages such as *Inter arma silent leges, Salus rei publicae suprema lex esto* or *Necessitas legem non habet* were known centuries before J. Locke reopened the issue in his discourses on the 'prerogative', which has the right to act 'according to discretion, for the public good, without the prescription of the law, and sometimes even against it'.[28] But Locke deserves much more attention here because his argument, in terms of causes and consequences, was completely formulated. It is already with him that we find not only the practical problem of law-making power which 'is not always in being, and is usually too numerous, and so too slow for the

26 See generally: Ackerman, B., Before the Next Attack – Preserving Civil Liberties in an Age of Terrorism, Yale University Press, New Haven and London (2006); Ackerman, B., The Emergency Constitution, 113 Yale Law Journal 1029 (2004); Posner, E.A. and Vermeule, A., Terror in the Balance – Security, Liberty and the Courts, Oxford University Press, New York (2007); Posner, R.A., Not a Suicide Pact – The Constitution in a Time of National Emergency, Oxford University Press, New York (2006); Yoo, J., The Powers of War and Peace – The Constitution and Foreign Affairs after 9/11, The University of Chicago Press, Chicago and London (2006); Gross, O. and Ní Aoláin, F., Law in Times of Crisis – Emergency Powers in Theory and Practice, Cambridge University Press, New York (2006). See also: Gardasevic, Djordje, American Lessons Learned – European Future Rethought?, 66 Collected Papers of Zagreb Law Faculty 1 (February 2016), pp. 61–86 (at: http://hrcak.srce.hr/index.php?show=clanak&id_clanak_jezik=232266&lang=en, 25 October 2020).

27 In this context, see also the French example: Platon, S., From One State of Emergency to Another – Emergency Powers in France, at: https://verfassungsblog.de/from-one-state-of-emergency-to-another-emergency-powers-in-france/, 25 October 2020. It is also worth noting here the historical practices of governments seeking new powers when confronted with new threats. Consider, for example, the enactment of the English 1914 Defence of the Realm Act and the French enabling acts from the same year, which, respectively, ended both the martial law and the state of siege philosophy. Similar almost all-encompassing delegation may be found in the 2001 Authorization for Use of Military Force in the United States.

28 Locke, J., *The Works of John Locke in Nine Volumes*, 12th ed., Rivington, London, 1824, vol. 4.

dispatch requisite to execution'. He also warns of 'legislators not being able to foresee, and provide by laws, for all that may be useful to the community'. What Locke envisions is that 'the executor of the laws having the power in his hands, has by the common law of nature a right to make use of it for the good of the society, in many cases, where the municipal law has given no direction, till the legislative can conveniently be assembled to provide for it'.[29] It is, however, worth noting that Locke was not an advocate of a completely unrestrained executive, such as we find with C. Schmitt, because from a normative point of view the prerogative must always be used 'for the good of the people, and not manifestly against it'.

These postulates found their intellectual echo in, to remain with the classics, both the French and the Americans. Thus, J.J. Rousseau warned that 'The inflexibility natural to laws, which hinders their bending to events, may in certain cases be pernicious, and, in a crisis, even occasion the ruin of the State', and then stressed that 'as there are at thousand occurrences for which the legislator has not provided, it is a very necessary part of foresight to perceive that everything cannot be foreseen'.[30] Similarly, A. Hamilton pointed out that powers needed for the common defence 'ought to exist without limitation, because it is impossible to foresee or define the extent and variety of national exigencies, or the correspondent extent and variety of the means which may be necessary to satisfy them'.[31]

All this had already been said long before C. Schmitt proposed his theory of an actually unfettered sovereign and his interpretation of the 'exception'.[32] But Schmitt's completely reductionist belief that 'the most guidance the constitution can provide is to indicate who can act in such a case' (i.e. of extreme peril) was soon rejected by C.L. Rossiter and C.J. Friedrich and their concepts of 'Constitutional Dictatorship'.[33] Besides his famous 11 criteria of constitutional dictatorship, Rossiter posited three 'fundamental facts' of his theory. The first was that 'the complex system of government of the democratic, constitutional state is essentially designed to function under normal, peaceful conditions, and is often unequal to the exigencies of a great national crisis'. The second was that 'in time of crisis a democratic, constitutional government must be temporarily altered to whatever degree is necessary to overcome the peril and restore normal conditions', with an unavoidable consequence that 'the government will have more power and

29 For a comparison, see here the crisis measures undertaken by the Hungarian government in the March 'interim period'. See: Kovács, K., Hungary's Orbánistan: A Complete Arsenal of Emergency Powers, at: https://verfassungsblog.de/hungarys-orbanistan-a-complete-arsenal-of-emergency-powers/, 25 October 2020.

30 Rousseau, J.J., Du Contrat Social, Les éditions du cheval ailé, Genève (1947).

31 Federalist No. 23.

32 Schmitt, C., Political Theology: Four Chapters on the Concept of Sovereignty, University of Chicago Press (2005).

33 Rossiter, C. L., *Constitutional Dictatorship – Crisis Government in the Modern Democracies*, Princeton University Press, Princeton, 1948.; Friedrich, C. J., *Constitutional Government and Democracy – Theory and Practice in Europe and America*, Fourth Edition, Blaisdell Publishing Company (A Division of Ginn and Company), Waltham, Massachusetts – Toronto – London, 1968.

the people fewer rights'. And the third of Rossiter's warnings was that 'this strong government, which in some instances might become an outright dictatorship, can have no other purposes than the preservation of the independence of the state, the maintenance of the existing constitutional order, and the defense of the political and social liberties of the people'.[34]

Those were, in fact, lessons learned after World War II. After bitter experiences from the 'Schmittean' era, they strongly advocated for bringing the rule of law back into action. What they actually meant is that emergencies are not a legal 'black hole' and that, despite an unavoidable need for certain accommodations, there have to be some restrictions on governments acting in crisis.

Once the rule of law in emergencies is back in action, the problem I would like to further address here is what exact role is thus given to the 'judicial-review mechanism'.[35] Due to their insight into long-standing national experiences, including debates surrounding the 'War on Terror', I believe that American authors are especially inspiring here. Nevertheless, their views on the position of courts in emergencies vary greatly,[36] along the usual lines.[37]

34 Rossiter, C.L., Constitutional Dictatorship – Crisis Government in the Modern Democracies, pp. 5–7.

35 Tushnet, M., Controlling Executive Power in the War on Terrorism, 118 Harv. L. Rev. 2673 (2005), pp. 2673–2682.

36 One of the notable aspects of the American debate on the past is that there exist rather different interpretations of it. Thus, for example, E.A. Posner and A. Vermeule explain two differing views on history in the security vs. liberty context (history either as a 'political and constitutional failure' or as a 'political and constitutional success'). This, in their view, consequently leads to adoption of either 'civil libertarianism' or 'deferential' view. See: Posner, E.A. and Vermeule, A., Terror in the Balance – Security, Liberty and the Courts, op. cit. While those two authors affirm the deferential view, explaining that historically it was successful, others criticise emergency 'overreactions' and claim that they later led to regret. For this, see: Stone, G.R., War Fever, 69 Missouri Law Review (2004), pp. 1131–1132; Stone, G.R., Perilous Times – Free Speech in Wartime (From the Sedition Act of 1798 to the War on Terrorism), W.W. Norton, New York (2004), pp. 12–14; Cole, D., No Reason to Believe: Radical Skepticism, Emergency Power, and Constitutional Constraint, 75 U. Chi. L. Rev. 1329 (2008), p. 1329. See also: Cole, D., The New McCarthyism: Repeating History in the War on Terrorism, 38 Harv. C.R.-C.L. L. Rev. 1 (2003), pp. 1–30. For an excellent overview of relevant precedents in American history, as used by various opposing approaches that favour either an active or deferential judicial role in emergencies (the 'Milligan thesis' and the 'Crisis thesis'), see: Epstein, L., Ho, D.E., King, G., Segal, J. A., The Supreme Court during Crisis: How War Affects Only Non-War Cases, 80 New York University Law Review 1 (2005), pp. 1–116. The most quoted American cases in that context, according to those authors, are: United States v. Curtiss-Wright Export Corp., Youngstown Sheet & Tube Co. v. Sawyer, Ex parte Milligan and Korematsu v. United States, 323 U.S. 214 (1944).

37 On this, see also: Gardasevic, Djordje, American Lessons Learned – European Future Rethought?, op. cit. The following short reference to the American doctrine here is inevitably reduced and my primary attention is to emphasise its overall importance for European debates as well, in terms of general issues raised and possible interpretations offered.

Thus, for instance, 'civil libertarians'[38] argue for a strong role of courts and for that they offer various reasons, for instance, that courts have the advantage of not being politically accountable and are not under pressure to act quickly and decisively, as it is expected from political branches; moreover, that courts are advantaged compared to other branches because they 'assess the legality of measures long after they have been adopted, which means that courts may bring more perspective to the question than those acting in the midst of the emergency'; or, that 'the fact that legal decisions must offer a statement of reasons that then binds future cases contributes to the judiciary's ability to exert control over the next emergency'; further, that judicial case law 'in the long run [...] establish[es] principles that are critical to checking future government abuse', and that 'the formalities of the judicial process mandate the creation of an official record that may facilitate reaching a just result' and 'may make subsequent assessments, beyond the heat of the moment, more reliable'.[39] On the other hand, the 'executive unilateralists' often rely on particular advantages of the executive,[40] argue for 'flexible' interpretations of the Constitution in favour of inherent executive and against unspecified judicial powers[41] or stress that, basically, judges are not experts for national security matters.[42]

38 Here I draw from the inspiring division of American authors on 'executive unilateralists', 'civil libertarians' and those that further some type of the third way, such as the 'process-based institutional approach'. See: Issacharoff, S. and Pildes, R.H., Emergency Contexts Without Emergency Powers: The United States' Constitutional Approach to Rights during Wartime, International Journal of Constitutional Law, Vol. 2 (2004), pp. 296–333; Rosenfeld, M., Judicial Balancing in Times of Stress: Comparing the American, British, and Israeli approaches to the War on Terror, 27 Cardozo Law Review 2079 (2006), pp. 2079–2151. For a related division on 'National Security Maximalism' and 'Liberty Maximalism', see: Sunstein, C.R., Minimalism at War, John M. Olin Law & Economics Working Paper No. 231 (2nd series), Public Law and Legal Theory Working Paper No. 80, University of Chicago (2004). See also: Sunstein, C.R., National Security, Liberty, and the D.C. Circuit, 73 Geo. Wash. L. Rev. 693 (2004–2005), pp. 693–708.

39 In addition, see also the arguments that the long-standing practice of American judges to defer to other governmental branches in security issues, characteristic until 1950s, was later reversed through 'rejection' of the 'logical' presumption of deference either by the newly construed case law or through various forms of political excuse for past mistakes or overreactions. On this, see: Stone, G.R., National Security v. Civil Liberties, 95 Cal. L. Rev. 2203 (2007), pp. 2203–2212; Cole, D., Judging the Next Emergency: Judicial Review and Individual Rights in Times of Crisis, 101 Mich. L. Rev. 2565 (2002–2003), pp. 2565–2595.

40 See the arguments furthered by A. Hamilton in: Federalist No. 70 (A. Hamilton), The Executive Department Further Considered, 18 March 1788; Federalist No. 74 (A. Hamilton), The Command of the Military and Naval Forces, and the Pardoning Power of the Executive, 25 March 1788.

41 See: Yoo, J., The Powers of War and Peace – the Constitution and Foreign Affairs after 9/11, op. cit., pp. 11 and 18.

42 See: Posner, R.A., Not a Suicide Pact – the Constitution in a Time of National Emergency, op. cit., pp. 9 and 35; Posner, E.A. and Vermeule, A., Terror in the Balance – Security, Liberty and the Courts, op. cit., p. 49. However, one must also note that recent American experiences in the 'War on Terror' showed that the Supreme Court to some extent did act to restrict the executive discretion. Moreover, the Court also undertook

From the historical perspective, the actual outcome of the Court's Covid-19 decisions probably could have been expected. In fact, the Court's precedents for that purpose include only one decision dating back to the 1990s war.[43] In reviewing presidential emergency decrees thereof in 1992, the Court, in a totally deferential approach, rejected all arguments submitted by the applicants. Most strikingly, the Court completely ignored the strict constitutional command that the President could decide on restrictions of constitutionally protected rights and freedoms only if the Parliament was not able to convene, which factually was not the case.[44] In a manner that executive unilateralists would largely greet, the Court simply stated that the President had an independent, or 'inherent', power to act. Admittedly, to this the Court valued also that the contested decrees were in the meantime approved by the legislative body as well. But even so, one may easily conclude that the Court followed a well-known scheme of a clear unilateral executive exception, followed by subsequent parliamentary ratification and resulting in a hugely deferential ('process-based'[45]) judicial validation.[46]

When viewing the Court's case law in the corona cases, one may easily notice that, save for the decision in the 'Sunday' and the 'Standing Orders of the Parliament' cases, it allowed for all safety measures to be applied.[47] But before

some judicial activism, such as is visible, for instance, in its application of the Matthews v. Eldridge test in the Hamdi v. Rumsfeld case. Other relevant cases here include opinions in Rasul v. Bush, Hamdan v. Rumsfeld and Boumediene v. Bush.

43 Decision of the Croatian Constitutional Court: U-I-179/1991, 24 June 1992. For an additional description of this decision, see also: Gardasevic, Djordje, Croatian Constitutional Adjudication in Times of Stress, in: New Challenges to Constitutional Adjudication in Europe – A Comparative Perspective, Zoltán Szente and Fruszina Gárdos-Orosz (eds.), Routledge (2018), pp. 27–44.; Gardasevic, Djordje, American Lessons Learned – European Future Rethought?, op. cit.

44 Two additional issues that the Court analysed in this case were the presidential power to unilaterally proclaim an emergency and his power to enact measures with retroactive effect.

45 For this approach, see: Issacharoff, S. and Pildes, R.H., Emergency Contexts Without Emergency Powers: The United States' Constitutional Approach to Rights during Wartime, op. cit. See also: Issacharoff, S. and Pildes, R.H., Between Civil Libertarianism and Executive Unilateralism: An Institutional Process Approach to Rights During Wartime, in: The Constitution in Wartime – Beyond Alarmism and Complacency, Tushnet, M. (ed.), Duke University Press, Duke and London, 2005., pp. 161–197.

46 This scheme is well known in comparative practice. See, for instance: the Prize cases, 2 Black (67 U.S.) 635 (1863). Additionally, I believe that such a 'liberal model' of 'emergency powers' might be typical for constitutional systems in their rudimentary form in which, despite formal proclamations, there exists neither a true concept of 'fundamental rights' nor an effective system of judicial review. For the 'liberal model', see: Lobel, J., Emergency Power and the Decline of Liberalism, 98 Yale. L. J. 1385 (1988–1989).

47 One additional exception to this is found in the Court's statement issued prior to the July 2020 parliamentary elections in which it warned the State Electoral Committee that it was unacceptable to deny the right to vote to persons having a virus and thus being in isolation. This, however, was not a decision of the Court in formal proceedings, but rather its general statement. See: Statement and Warning of the Constitutional Court, U-VII-2980/2020, 3 July 2020.

concluding that the Court was hugely deferential to political branches, and not activist, it is necessary to see what it could or should have done instead.

The crucial point to be made is, of course, that the Court avoided answering the question whether the emergency Article 17 of the Constitution should nevertheless have been used. In that context, comparative practice might suggest that courts usually defer to other branches in emergency issues, and even more so when they are dealing specifically with proclamation of an emergency than when deciding on specific measures.[48] Despite that, it is also true that there do exist models in which even proclamation of emergency is at some point made subject of a special review, at least theoretically,[49] whereas the dissenting judges in the Croatian case also strongly advocated for application of Article 17. From that point of view, I also think that the Court should have thoroughly examined that particular argument, if for nothing else than the fact that, while avoiding interpreting the Constitution, it did interpret Article 22.a of the Law on the Civil Protection System. In fact, having in mind that Article 17 and Article 22.a contain substantively the same provisions, it is, as a matter of legal interpretation, completely unclear why the Court allowed for introduction of the legal definition of 'special circumstances' at the expense of the constitutional term of 'a severe natural disaster'.[50]

This brings me to the next point, the fact that in the corona cases the Court accepted the proposition of a *sui generis* origin of the 'threat'. More precisely, it is quite clear that the *sui generis* qualification of the epidemic in the Croatian case stems from three crucial points: the rejection of the application of Article 17 of the Constitution, the amendments to the Law on the Civil Protection System and the Infectious Diseases Protection Law and, finally, from the explicit conclusions of the Croatian Constitutional Court. Moreover, in terms of theoretical connection

48 On that point, O. Gross and F. Ní Aoláin generally observe the following: 'practice shows that domestic courts tend to support the government's position either by invoking such judicial mechanisms as the political questions doctrine and standing to prevent themselves from having to decide the matter brought before them on the merits, or, when deciding a case on its merits, accepting the government's position. That tendency of the courts becomes even more pronounced when they deal with cases *durante bello* as opposed to deciding them when the crisis is over'. See: Gross, O, i Ní Aoláin, F., Law in Times of Crisis – Emergency Powers in Theory and Practice, op. cit., p. 63.

49 See Article 16 of the French Constitution.

50 Of course, one may take here the following observation made by the dissenting judges in the case dealing with constitutionality of two main 'corona statutes': 'Let us analyze a bit that peculiar and erroneous conclusion that the Parliament may 'choose' between constitutional norms: should that be true, that would mean that a simple majority could decide all that for what the Constitution requires a qualified two-thirds majority. But, which government would then put a stone of opposition around its neck, when it can enact the same regulations itself, by a simple majority? Constitution is not a cake-shop in which everyone chooses what his or her appetite at a certain moment wishes. If two norms collide, then one of them certainly must, and another must not be applied.' See: Decision of the Croatian Constitutional Court: U-I-1372/2020, 14 September 2020 (A. Abramović, L. Kušan and G. Selanec, dissenting).

between causes and consequences of emergencies, the Court went even further than the Government when it established that during the first month of the pandemic there was no gap in the legal framework regulating the work of the Headquarters.[51] This, of course, largely resembles Locke's, Hamilton's and Rousseau's conceptions I had previously mentioned. At the same time, in my own opinion, this fact represents the most troubling aspect of the Court's standing. This is so because the reference to 'special circumstances' and the Headquarters' extensive power to enact 'decisions' and 'guidelines' is thus not restrained by a requirement that such decisions and guidelines ought to be grounded in other laws, with more specific and enumerated powers of said body.[52]

On the other hand, the existing legal framework under which the Headquarters has acted so far contains neither some strict sunset clauses nor an additional model of, at least periodical, parliamentary control of anti-corona measures, outside of ordinary means of supervision over the Government.[53] This surely would be the case had the Court accepted the emergency model. For that purpose, Article 17 of the Constitution prescribes that in cases of severe natural disasters restrictions of rights must be decided by a two-thirds majority in the Parliament. Admittedly, in the words of Article 17, there exists no further specification as to whether the two-thirds parliamentary approval is necessary for all decisions restricting constitutional rights or just for those that require adoption of new laws. An activist court could go so far as to claim that even in cases of all restrictions of rights there needs to be the two-thirds parliamentary approval, possibly within a short period of time following the enactment of special measures. I personally believe, however, that the latter solution would appropriately balance between the need to act quickly, on the basis of powers already within the laws adopted before the emergency, and possible need to acquire new legal anti-epidemic tools of reaction.[54] Had the Court been activist, it could have clarified that problem as well. But it did not.

51 In relation to the April amendments to the Infectious Diseases Protection Law, even the Government stated that those were needed to retroactively validate the decisions of the Headquarters enacted in the meantime. This was due to the fact that within this interim period it was the Minister of Health who was the only one upon which the law conferred the power to activate safety measures.

52 Admittedly, however, the Law on the Civil Protection System contains a provision according to which the decisions and guidelines must be enacted for the purpose of 'protecting the lives and health of citizens'.

53 The dissenting judges also heavily criticised the lack of appropriate control by ordinary courts, in a separate section of their opinion, concerning the application of the self-isolation safety measure. They pointed out that the Infectious Diseases Protection Law allows for such a judicial control only if a self-isolated person is found in breach of the measure and not when the measure itself is imposed. See: Decision of the Croatian Constitutional Court: U-I-1372/2020, 14 September 2020 (G. Selanec, L. Kušan and A. Abramović, dissenting).

54 This is also the position taken by the dissenting judges. See: Decision of the Croatian Constitutional Court: U-I-1372/2020, 14 September 2020 (G. Selanec, L. Kušan and A. Abramović, dissenting). In fact, at the very beginning of the pandemic in spring 2020, the Government proposed a bill allowing tracking of mobile phones for the purpose of controlling the spread of the virus. This bill was never enacted into a

As to the applied level of judicial scrutiny, the Court seems to have opted for some type of review between the executive unilateralism and the 'process-based institutional approach'.[55] This is even more curious when one has in mind that the whole time the Court acted under the pretext of normal conditions, in which the regular proportionality review is required.

Finally, in the Croatian constitutional settings, the Court does have the power to start a constitutional review of its own will. Nevertheless, and despite the initiative of the dissenting judges,[56] it took it more than five months to finally deliver its opinions in mid-September.

All in all, I think that expecting the Croatian Constitutional Court to take an activist role in reviewing the measures of the Government in a delicate safety context might still be a bridge too far.

4 Conclusion

Emergencies inevitably require application of unusual measures. This especially goes for global threats, such as is the spread of the Covid-19 virus. In my opinion, the present pandemic in the Croatian context undoubtedly represents the case of a 'severe natural disaster', foreseen in Article 17 of the Croatian Constitution.

At the same time, the emergency model made on the basis of Article 17 is not to be read as the 'state of exception' that leads to unrestrained discretion of the executive, but rather as an expression of the concept of constitutional 'checks and balances', that is of the rule of law. I personally believe that it should have been activated.

law, but the case represents a clear example of a new measure which, under Article 17 of the Constitution, would need to be approved by a two-thirds majority in the Parliament. On the other hand, that the two-thirds majority is not an unachievable goal even in emergencies is clear from the fact that the Parliament enacted the amendments to the Law on the Civil Protection System with 108 representatives voting for it (the two-thirds in the Croatian case is 101 votes).

55 S. Issacharoff and R.H. Pildes describe well that approach in the American context, in my opinion also applicable here: 'American courts have gravitated toward intermediate institutional options that reject the more extreme claims of either executive unilateralists or civil libertarian idealists. Contrary to the modern civil libertarian stance, the American courts have only rarely addressed these issues through the framework of individual constitutional rights. Yet contrary to the executive unilateralist position, courts have also been reluctant to find that the executive has unfettered discretion to make liberty/security trade-offs. Instead, the courts have developed a process-based, institutionally oriented (as opposed to rights-oriented) framework for examining the legality of governmental action in extreme security contexts. Through this process-based approach, American courts have sought to shift the responsibility for these difficult decisions away from themselves and toward the joint action of the most democratic branches of the government.' See: Issacharoff, S. and Pildes, R.H., Emergency Contexts Without Emergency Powers: The United States' Constitutional Approach to Rights during Wartime, op. cit., p. 297.

56 See: Decision of the Croatian Constitutional Court: U-I-1372/2020, 14 September 2020 (L. Kušan, A. Abramović and G. Selanec, dissenting).

In that scenario, Article 17 would have placed upon the undertakings of the Croatian authorities dealing with the threat more appropriate means of democratic parliamentary control. On the other hand, judicial review mechanism would still be in place for protecting both the constitutionally guaranteed rights and freedoms and for checking upon the crisis measures of the Government.

Ironically for the Constitutional Court, the application of Article 17 would have also given it more fuel for being deferent to political branches because the proportionality principle included in Article 17 allows for far more flexibility than its counterpart in Article 16. This way, the Court approved some sort of 'Business as Usual' model to the whole situation,[57] even though in practice it largely moved out of the way of the Government.

Such an approach, of course, comes with significant costs. Judicial validation of governmental crisis actions as being under the framework of an ordinary situation not only blurs the distinction between a regular and an emergency constitution. It also establishes a 'principle' that 'then lies about like a loaded weapon ready for the hand of any authority that can bring forward a plausible claim of an urgent need'.[58]

57 For the application of the 'Business as Usual Model' in the Slovenian case, see: Zagorc, S. and Bardutzky, S., Business as Usual, but to the Unusual Extremes: Slovenia and Covid-19, at: https://verfassungsblog.de/business-as-usual-but-to-the-unusual-extremes-slovenia-and-covid-19/, 25 October 2020.

58 Korematsu v. United States, 323 U.S. 246 (1944) (Justice Jackson, dissenting).

Conclusion

We are witnessing the deep transformation of our constitutional civilisation. The pillars of constitutional democracy that we have inherited from the nineteenth and twentieth centuries have been profoundly shaken. Fractures are visible with regard to all elements of representative democracy. The concepts of representation, democracy, party democracy and liberal democracy are largely contested. They are altogether exposed to both traditional and novel challenges.

Traditionally constitutional democracy is prone to conflict. It is a system that is open for challenges related to social disorder, protest, disagreement and contestation.[1] Hence, implosion and explosion of constitutional democracy can be expected as a result of the conflictual nature of constitutional democracy. In this context, the courts are supposed to be guardians of legality, neutral arbiters in constitutional battles for power, and ultimate guardians of human rights. Disadvantaged in terms of democratic legitimacy courts are possessing other valuable constitutional resources – neutrality, expertise and political and populist detachment. At least, this is the idea that underlines the courts' institutional design during Western legal modernity.

There is also a range of novel challenges to which the courts are exposed. The expansion of 'constitutionalism beyond statehood'[2] in recent decades, quite visible since the beginning of the 1990s, confronted constitutional theory and practice with the problem of 'ordering of constitutional orders'.[3] Regardless of whether multilevel constitutionalism or constitutional pluralism has been used as an explanatory or ordering scheme for the emergence and development of international and administrative orders with elements of constitutionalism, supranational constitutionalism was on the rise. Additionally, it was paralleled by more demanding

1 See Belov, M. Peace, Discontent and Constitutional Law. Challenges to Constitutional Order and Democracy, Routledge, 2021.

2 See Dobner, Petra and Martin Loughlin (eds.) Twilight of Constitutionalism? Oxford, Oxford University Press, 2010; and Walker, N. 'Taking Constitutionalism beyond the State', Political Studies, vol. 56, no. 3, 2008, pp. 519–543.

3 For the concept of 'ordering of constitutional orders', see Tanchev, E. 'The Contemporary Supranational Constitutional Pluralism or the Ordering of Constitutional Orders' in P. Kirov (ed.) Constitutional Studies 2012–2013 (Sofia, 'St. Kliment Ohridski' University Press, 2014), pp. 171–198 (in Bulgarian).

DOI: 10.4324/9781003200666-15

and far-reaching concepts and phenomena such as global constitutionalism and global governance.

Thus, the courts were confronted with plurality of legal orders, some of which even had constitutional features. The ordinary courts were overburdened with the application of international and supranational legal standards drifting away from jurisprudential routine practices of the twentieth century. This overburdening has been simultaneously conceptual, epistemic and cultural. However, the constitutional and the supreme courts especially acquired novel roles and functions within composite, pluralist, multi-layered constitutional (dis)order. They gained the status of gatekeepers of the domestic constitutional and legal order functioning at the same time as transmitters of international and supranational law. Thus, the constitutional and supreme courts gradually became a sort of membrane on the edge between national, international, supranational and global legal orders. Naturally, this novel and extremely contested position allowed them to expand in the political realm, to engage in constitutional politics, to shape constitutional axiology, to promote constitutional teleology and to become important factors in constitutional ontology.

Hence, globalisation, internationalisation of constitutional law and constitutionalisation of international law massively promoted judicial activism. They served as natural and quasi-objective justifications of judicial activism legitimising both the new political engagement of courts and the combination of revolutionary and imperial standing of supreme, constitutional, international and supranational courts.

The combination of challenges stemming from globalisation is paralleled and exacerbated by a range of to an extent interrelated political developments that are changing profoundly the socio-political context in which the courts exist and function. The expansion of neo-liberal globalisation and its ongoing crisis, the rise of illiberalism, illiberal constitutionalism, authoritarian constitutionalism and constitutional populism, the clash between extreme versions of liberalism and conservatism, globalism and nationalism jointly produce poisonous constitutional climate and shape a dangerous power network.

The courts are currently embedded in this power field of intense friction between political extremities. They are stretched between powerful political factors pursuing divergent and frequently controversial and antagonistic political agendas. Supreme and constitutional, international and supranational courts are in possession of important tools by virtue of which they can engage in policy-making going beyond their role of neutral arbiters and safeguards of legality and increasingly performing as political players and even as law-makers.[4] Moreover, they also have the incentive and even the justification to go beyond legalism and self-restraint and to engage in constitutional politics via judicial activism.

This book offers more questions than answers. Its aims has been to raise the awareness of the impact of judicialisation of politics, politicisation of the judiciary, judicial activism and even imperial judicial politics of constitutionalism,

4 See Florczak-Wątor, M. Judicial Law-Making in European Constitutional Courts, Routledge, 2020.

constitutional theory and constitutional law. The focus of the book is on the role of courts in the context of globalisation, emergency constitutionalism and rising illiberalism and technocracy. The provocative chapters have been framed by the overall issue of judicial activism, blurring the lines between law and politics and offering the courts the chance to have a revolutionary impact on a national, international, supranational and global level of public power and legal ordering. A revolutionary impact has rather detrimental effects on legal certainty, proportionality and balancing as key elements of rule of law.

Several conclusions can be made on the basis of the intellectual and scientific discourse offered by the contributors to this edited volume in their respective chapters. The conclusions are made on the basis of solid theoretical arguments launched by the authors and are further developed and exemplified through comparative research and illustrative case studies. Hence, judicial activism is viewed through the prism of legal and socio-legal methodology in a theoretical and comparative perspective. The analysis and the conclusions that stem from it are grounded predominantly in European experience mostly within the EU legal and constitutional context.

First, courts, especially constitutional and supreme courts, play a central role for both constitutional orders and political systems. The apex courts (supreme and constitutional courts) are simultaneously legal and political players, being bridges between law and politics. Thus, they are strategic assets for the social and the political system with constitutional standing and role in a double sense. More precisely, they are instruments for the adjustment of the legal order to the social, economic and political context and technocratic engines for promotion of legal, political and constitutional reform. In this regard, courts' performance and especially their case law have both legal and socio-legal implications. Thus, the apex courts trigger legal, political and constitutional reform directly by virtue of activist judicial interpretation of the constitutional texture or indirectly by outlining and framing its key areas or topics. Such institutional behaviour deeply impacts both legal and political orders and is rather contested as well.

Second, judicial activism is both strategy and tactics. It is used for strategic reallocation of the courts within the overall scheme of power distribution and accomplishment, undermining the role of the demos and the democratically elected institutions. Thus, judicial activism is a challenge to separation of powers and democracy. Paradoxically, in the long term, judicial activism may both hamper and promote democracy. It will redefine our concepts of democracy and separation of powers. Judicial activism is at the same time also a tactical tool for shaping and forming different, important judicial policies. It is a tactical tool embedded in and dependent on the rule of law.

Third, courts are entrenched on the conceptual, normative and empirical borderline between law and politics in a twofold way. They are influencing politics and are engaging in policy-making. They are not only correctives of illegal policies, safeguards of rights and arbiters of constitutionally provided competences. Apex courts are also policy-initiators going well beyond traditional theories of democracy and separation of powers. At the same time, courts – especially supreme and constitutional courts – are also influenced by political factors and considerations. They are being politically influenced in a range of ways. Thus, the issue of judicial independence and judicial impartiality should be reassessed in the light of illiberalism, authoritarianism and populism. Several contributions to this book show different ways of improper and unconstitutional politicisation of constitutional courts.

Fourth, courts are gatekeepers of national constitutionalism. They are membranes between national, international and supranational legal orders. They are engaged in multilevel constitutional and political games, being the ultimate players in the context of constitutional pluralism to the extent of gradually evolving to the standing of global judicial empire. Hence, the book assesses the impact of globalisation on judicial activism and revolutionary or evolutionary judicial policy-making also through the prism of the interaction between a multitude of legal and constitutional orders. It demonstrates how globalisation, supranationalisation and vertical proliferation of power fosters and creates justifications for judicial activism.

Fifth, apex courts – the supreme, constitutional, international and supranational courts – are revolutionising the constitutional law and modern constitutionalism in multiple ways. They are putting pressure on ideas, concepts and paradigms with fundamental importance for contemporary constitutionalism and constitutional law. They are blurring the line between law and politics. Courts are challenging key principles of constitutional law, most visibly rule of law, democracy and separation of powers. They are producing important effects and side-effects in both authoritarian and democratic constitutional orders, being one of the main promoters of technocracy in the form of juristocracy.[5] Thus, courts are increasingly functioning as triggers of constitutional revolution, which rather paradoxically is sometimes achieved in an evolutionary manner. Thus, judicial activism goes hand in hand with (re)evolutionary courts.

Sixth, judicial activism is especially visible, important and problematic under extreme conditions. Emergency situations foster judicial activism. They allow supreme and constitutional courts to actively engage in protecting human rights, declaring unconstitutionality or illegality of acts or competence infringements and explain constitutional and international law provisions related to democracy and rule of law standards. Thus, courts may be promoters of justice and rule of law in emergency situations. Nevertheless, they may also be contributing to human rights and competence infringements in emergency situations being accomplices of the political institutions belonging to the legislative and executive power and even to technocratic expert bodies with little or no constitutional standing and legitimacy. Hence, judicial activism in emergency situations might be very detrimental to certainty, proportionality, balancing of rights and institutional competences, thus presenting itself as an impediment to rule of law and democracy. This finding, exemplified by several contributions to this volume, brings again to the front the advantages, but also the huge risks, that judicial activism imposes on key principles of constitutionalism. Hence, the book should be considered also as an invitation for critical thinking.

5 See Hirschl, R. Towards Juristocracy: The Origins and Consequences of the New Constitutionalism, Harvard University Press, 2007.

Index

9/11 terror attacks 16

A and B v. Norway 73
Abbasov v. Azerbaijan 68
Abdullah II 149, 153, 161
Absinth 47n20
abuse of office 135
accountability 143, 146, 162; ethical 144; governmental 74, 78; principle of 80
ACHR *see* American Convention on Human Rights
Ackerman, Bruce 104–106, 117, 123–124
acquis 89
activist courts 6–7, 11, 127, 162
administrative courts 1, 118, 138
administrative sanctions 72–73
Advisory Committee for the Revision of the Constitution 152
Agamben, Giorgio 177
age discrimination 92, 95
A.K. and Others v. Sąd Najwyższy (Supreme Court) 94–97
Albuquerque, Pinto de 73
American Convention on Human Rights (ACHR) 65
Amsterdam Treaty 84
ancillary powers 125, 134, 141, 144
Angelov, Georgi 189, 191, 192
anti-constitutionalism 5, 12, 16
apex courts, 9, 16, 43–60, 215, 216; in Germany 54–56; role of 44–45; in Switzerland 45–54; *see also* constitutional courts; supreme courts
Arab Spring 13–14, 145–150, 157–160, 166–167
Austria 45–46, 56–58, 85, 125
Austrian Constitutional Court 9, 56, 58
Austrian Federal Constitution Tribunal 121
authoritarian constitutionalism 5, 6, 7, 8, 14, 16, 214, 216
authoritarianism 17, 88, 102, 103, 145n1, 147, 148n11, 175, 177

Basic Law of Palestine 146
Belgian Constitutional Court 121
Benjamin, Walter 177
Besselink, L. 87
Biernat, Stanisław 115
bilateral treaties 46, 48, 58
Bogdanowicz, P. 96
Brexit 98
Brown v. Board of Education of Topeka 33, 34
Budget Treaties 80
Bulgaria 14, 125; constitutional courts 15–15, 171–93; constitutions 14, 172–182, 185–189; *see also* Bulgarian Constitutional Court
Bulgarian Constitutional Court 14–15, 171–193
Búrca, G. de 78

CEE *see* Central and Eastern Europe
Central and Eastern Europe (CEE) 129
Chernobyl case *see Parliament v. Council*
Choudhry, Sujit 123
Civic Platform 111
Civic Platform–Polish People's Party 109
civil law 63
'civil libertarianism' 206n36, 207, 211n55
Civil Rights Act 1964 33
CJEU *see* Court of Justice of the European Union
Code of Civil Procedure 135
Code of Criminal Procedure (Italy) 66, 70
Code of Criminal Procedure (Romania) 135, 136

Commission v. Ireland 93
Commission v. Poland 90–93, 119
common law 63
Community Law 82
conscience, freedom of 179
constitutional amendments 47–48, 58, 104–106, 111, 130–131, 134–136, 141–142, 144, 166, 188–189; in parliamentary monarchies 147–156
constitutional breakdown 101
Constitutional Council 151, 152
constitutional courts 1, 2, 6, 8–9, 12–14, 145, 213, 214–216; 'active' 127; 'activist' 127; and ancillary powers 125, 134; in ; Bulgaria 14–15, 171–93; characteristics of 23–24, 32, 34; and democracy 25–26; functional perspective 29; and health-related emergency situations 187–192; institutional perspective 27–28; as interpreters of the law 30–31; in Jordan 145–168; and judicial activism 127–129, 143; and military emergency situations 184–187; in Morocco 145–168; outcomes of decisions 39–40; 'passive' 127; and politics 25–42, 126–127, 131–134, 141; post-communist 129; role of 26–27, 29, 124, 140–141, 149–150, 182–192; stand-alone 56; structural perspective 28; *see also* Austrian Constitutional Court; Belgian Constitutional Court; Bulgarian Constitutional Court; Croatian Constitutional Court; German Constitutional Court; Italian Constitutional Court; Polish Constitutional Court; Romanian Constitutional Court
constitutional crisis 101
constitutional democracy 1, 3, 7, 10, 15, 83, 141, 213
'constitutional dictatorship' 15, 189, 190, 205
constitutionalism: authoritarian 5, 6, 7, 8, 14, 16, 214, 216; 'beyond statehood' 7, 213; emergency 4, 5, 8, 14, 16, 178, 215; illiberal 4, 8, 11, 12, 14, 16, 102, 103; key principles of 3, 59–60; national 2, 216; pandemic 5, 14; paternalistic 5; political 103; popular 104, 128; populist 4, 7, 11, 12, 214; as socio-legal phenomenon 7; sub-national 2; supranational 2
constitutional justice 13–14, 142, 145n1
constitutional law: and international treaties 44–45, 49–53, 56–59; national 44
constitutional moment 12, 104–106, 117, 122–124
constitutional norms 44, 45, 48, 49, 51, 53, 112, 199, 209n50
constitutional orders 1–2, 3, 6, 7, 9, 15, 215, 216
constitutional politics 2, 4, 6, 8, 11, 15, 23, 123, 185, 214; emergency 14, 172
constitutional review 24, 25, 26, 32, 45–46, 127; American model 130; in Austria 56, 57; in Croatia 197–198, 201, 202, 211; in Germany 54; in Jordan 155, 156, 164–165; Kelsenian model 130, 133, 134; in Morocco 155, 156, 164–165; in Poland 106–107, 109; in Romania 13, 126, 129, 131, 133–136, 139, 140, 142; in Switzerland 53–54; in the United States 104
'constitutional revolution' 104, 216
Constitution Court Law 149
constitutions: in Austria 56–58; in Bulgaria 14, 172–182, 185–189; flexibility 43, 45, 55; in Germany 54–56; and international law 43–60; in Italy 67–68; in Jordan 146, 149, 151, 154–155; as 'living documents' 127; malleability 47, 53, 59; in Morocco 146, 151–152, 154–155, 164; in Poland 106–108, 111; as political product 26–27; as political symbol 30; in Romania 129–132, 136, 138, 141; in Switzerland 46–47, 57–58
construction abuse 73
Cooperation and Verification Mechanism (CVM) 131–133
corruption 76, 131–133, 135–136, 140, 150
'counter-constitutional revolution' 12
Counter-Terrorism Act 180
Court of Appeals of Bucharest 142
Court of Justice of the European Union (CJEU) 9, 11, 77, 80–82, 86, 89–98, 117, 119–120
Court of Luxembourg 73
court-packing 89–90, 92–94, 102, 122
courts: activist 6–7, 11, 127, 162; administrative 1, 118, 138; 'beyond statehood' 9; and impartiality 1, 68, 95–96, 120, 133; international 2, 9–10; and liberal-democratic constitutionalism 1, 3; mitigating power of 48; and policy-making 2, 4; revolutionary 4–6; role of 2–3, 8, 44–45, 215; supranational 2, 3, 6, 9–10, 14, 171, 214, 216; supreme 2,

9, 214–216; *see also* apex courts; constitutional courts
Covid-19 pandemic 1, 16, 173, 174, 187; and Croatian Constitutional Court 194–212; *see also* pandemic constitutionalism
Criminal Code 135
criminal justice 10, 63–73
criminal offence 51, 71
criminal proceedings 63, 65–67, 135–136; qualifying as 71–72; reopening of 68–70
Croatia 125; constitutional review in 197–198, 201, 202, 211; *see also* Croatian Constitutional Court
Croatian Constitutional Court 14, 194–212
cruel, inhumane and degrading treatment 179
CVM *see* Cooperation and Verification Mechanism
Czech Republic 125

death penalty 49
'December judges' 113
Defence and Military Troops Act 180
democracy 2; and conflict 126, 213; constitutional 1, 3, 7, 10, 15, 83, 141, 213; and constitutional courts 25–26; 'constructive deconstruction' of 3; contemporary understanding of 78; dualistic concept of 104, 123; erosion of 86, 88, 96; and European Union 11, 74–98; illiberal 7–8, 10, 12, 93, 97, 102–103, 106, 122; liberal 83, 102, 105; 'minimum substantive core' of 74, 78; non-consolidated 13, 129, 143; paradox of 83; participatory 79, 81; and power 78, 80; principles of 59–60, 80; representative 1, 5, 11, 79, 80, 81, 213; and rule of law 89; 'simple' 103; *see also* militant democracy
democracy-endangering actions 83
democratic backsliding 5, 8, 12, 16, 77, 85–86, 88–90, 92–93, 97, 101; *see also* democratic decay
democratic decay 103; *see also* democratic backsliding
'democratic minimum core' 11, 74
democratic monarchies 145–146; *see also* parliamentary monarchies
'democratic striving approach' 78
dependant variable 46
de-segregation 34
detention 63, 66–67
direct effect doctrine 82
disputes 95
Dixon, Rosalyn 74, 78
DNA *see* National Anti-Corruption Directorate
domestic law 43; and EU law 57; and European Convention on Human Rights (ECHR) 50, 52; and international law 44–45, 49–52, 55–57, 164
double jeopardy *see ne bis in idem*
double punishment 72–73
Drozd and Januseck v. France and Spain 66
dualism 46n16, 54, 104, 123, 152
Duda, Andrzej 110, 112, 116
Duverger, Maurice 137
Dworkin, Ronald 33
Dyzenhaus, D. 84

ECtHR *see* European Court of Human Rights
Egypt 158–159
elections 74, 78
Elkins, Z. 142
emergency constitutionalism 4, 5, 8, 14, 16, 178, 215
emergency powers clause 83
emergency situations 14–15, 172–193; as 'emergency regimes' 189; health-related 187–192; military 184–187; role of constitutional courts 182–192; and rule of law 204–211; *see also* state of emergency; state of exception; state of siege; war
'empire of courts' 3
'enemy combatants' 204
Engel's criteria 71
environmental policies 73
equal treatment 34, 95
Equity and Reconciliation Authority 152
ethnicity 33
European Commission (EC) 76, 79, 85, 131; Directive 2000/78/EC 92, 96
European Convention on Human Rights (ECHR) 49–50, 52–53, 58, 64–73, 131, 200
European Council 85–86, 137
European Court of Human Rights (ECtHR) 9–10, 53, 58, 66–70, 131, 138–139; and militant democracy 83–84; and *res judicata* 63–73; subsidiarity of 64
European Parliament 81, 82, 85
European Union (EU): and Austria 56–58; and democracy 11, 74–98; and Germany

54; key principles 75n7; primacy of law 57, 96–97, 119; and rule of law 75–76; sanction mechanisms 76–77, 85–86, 91; and Switzerland 46, 48, 50–52; values 75–76, 78–79, 85, 87–88, 93–97
Euroscepticism 120–121
executive power institutions 1, 176, 181, 193
'executive unilaterism' 207, 208, 211
expression, freedom of 160
'expulsion of criminal foreigners' initiative 49, 51, 55
'extraordinary epidemic situation' 181–182, 187–188, 190–193

face protection masks 202
fair trial, right to 70, 92, 108
family life, right to 49
Farinacci-Fernos, Jorge M. 128
fascist movement 83
Federal Supreme Court of Switzerland 9, 46, 49–51, 53, 58, 59
financial austerity 16
financial crisis 1, 16
fines 93
forcible assimilation 179
Foucault, Michel 41
France 125
Frankenberg, G. 89
freedom of assembly 83
freedom of conscience 179
freedom of expression 160
freedom of religion 179
freedom of speech 83
freedom of thought 179
Freedom Party 85
freedoms: and constitutional courts 156–158; fundamental 142, 165, 195, 197; restriction of 83–84, 197
free movement 47n 21, 49, 50–51
free speech 83
'friction surface' 44
Friedrich, C.J. 205
function-effects 36–37, 40
fundamental legal principles 39
fundamental rights 55, 64, 68–71, 78–80, 82, 83, 95, 98, 103, 107–108, 119, 142, 149, 154, 155, 165; and populism 74–76

Galligan, Brian 128
'gas deal' case 163–164
Gençel v. Turkey 68
German Federal Constitutional Court 9, 54–56, 58
Germany 45–46, 54–56, 125, 155; apex courts 54–56; constitutional review in 54; and European Union (EU) 54; *see also* German Federal Constitutional Court
Ginsburg, T. 142
giudice dell'esecuzione 67, 70
Glantz v. Finland 71
globalisation 214–216
globalism 4
Global North 1, 16
gouvernement des juges 7
governmental accountability 74, 78
'government of judges' 23
Grande Stevens and others v. Italy 71–73
Grundgesetz 54, 55, 58
Guantanamo 204

Haider, Jörg 85
Hamilton, A. 205, 210
hate speech 83
HCCJ *see* High Court of Cassation and Justice
Health Act 2020 173, 180–182, 187–188, 191, 192
'health Earnstfall' 175
'health Leviathan' 5
High Court of Cassation and Justice (HCCJ) 134, 135, 139–140
human rights 16–17, 55, 160; and constitutional courts 156–158, 165–167; in emergency situations 178, 188, 190, 191; international 48; protection systems 63–64; violation of 64–66, 69
Hungary 74–76, 85, 87–90, 92, 97
Hussein (King) 150

IACtHR *see* Inter-American Court of Human Rights
Iancu, B. 142
ICCPR *see* International Covenant on Civil and Political Rights
Ilaşcu v. Moldova 65
illiberal constitutionalism 4, 8, 11, 12, 14, 16, 102, 103
illiberal democracy 7–8, 10, 12, 93, 97, 102–103, 106, 122
'illiberal turn' 12, 16, 87, 101, 102, 106, 117, 122
immigration 49, 52
imprisonment 65–70

Infectious Diseases Protection Law 196–197, 200–201, 209
infringement proceedings 89–93, 97, 98
in-house attorneys 33, 35
institutional design 14
institutional positions 36
intelligence collection 136
Inter-American Court of Human Rights (IACtHR) 65
international cooperation 44
international courts 2, 9–10
International Covenant on Civil and Political Rights (ICCPR) 52, 200
internationalisation 214
international law: and constitutions 43–60; and domestic law 44–45, 49–52, 55–57, 164; mandatory provisions 48–49; public 44; self-executing 44
international norms 44
international treaties: and constitutional law 44–45, 49–53, 66–59; overriding 53, 55, 58; ratification 50–51, 52n56, 56–57, 184–186; *see also* bilateral treaties
Ireland 93
Iribarne Perez v. France 66
Israel 163
Israeli Supreme Court 98
Italian Code of Criminal Procedure 66, 70
Italian Constitutional Court 69, 70
Italian Court of Cassazione 67
Italy 10, 28, 66–73, 125; constitution 67–68
ius cogens 49

Jordan 13–14, 145–168
Journal of Laws 114
judges: active stance towards law-making 23; appointment of 117–118, 120, 125, 133–134; authority of 144; compulsory retirement 92; 'December' 113; duty of self-restraint 142, 161–164, 183, 189; 'government of' 23; 'October' 110; and power 36; remuneration of 90; retirement age 91–92, 94, 119; role of 30; specialisation 140; 'stand-in' 116, 122, 124; tenure 126
judicial activism 21–22; as defence strategy 6–7, 9, 43–60; definition 23, 45, 127–128; evolutionary 6; revolutionary 6; risks of 13; role of courts 2–3, 8, 45; and rule of law 16–17; as socio-legal phenomenon 8
judicial culture 134
judicial dialogue 3
judicial empire 2
judicial imperialism 3
judicial independence 7, 76, 90, 92, 95, 97, 145–146, 156
judicial policy-making 4, 6, 7
judicial populism 128–129
judicial power 129, 135, 139, 143, 207
judicial review 46, 78, 89, 104, 145–146, 156, 157, 160–162, 166, 206; constitutional 125, 146; Kelsenian model of 125; and parliamentary monarchy 153–154; pathology of 13, 126; in Poland 106–107; role of 43

Kelsen, Hans 25, 39, 104
Kelsenian model: of constitutional review 130, 133, 134; of judicial review 125
Kempa, Beata 114
Kieres, Leon 116
Kohl, Helmut 55
Kövesi, Laura Codruța 138–139

Landau, David 74, 78
language 41
Laska and Lika v. Albania 68
Latvia 140
Law and Justice 102, 103, 110–118, 121–123
'law-in-action' 30
'law-in-books' 30
Law on the Civil Protection System 195–197, 199–200, 209
Lebanon 146
legal actors 25, 34, 35
legal certainty 8, 10, 13, 17, 188, 190, 199, 215
legal culture 38, 39, 45, 73
legality 32–34
legal legitimacy 38
legal predictability 17
legal reasoning 34, 39
legal revolutions 2, 6
legal rules 7, 25, 27, 30, 38, 41, 48
legitimacy 32–33, 36–38, 41, 59, 122, 153, 158–161
liberal democracy 83, 102, 105
liberal-democratic consensus 103
liberal-democratic constitutionalism 1, 3, 6, 16
liberalism 4
liberal revolutions 105
liberty, right to 67
Lisbon Treaty 78–79
Listing Procedure case 81

lockdowns 187, 203
Locke, John 204–205, 210
Loewenstein, Karl 83
Lucky Dev v. Sweden 71

Maastricht Treaty 78, 81
market abuse 73
market freedoms 82
martial law 106
MENA *see* Middle East and North Africa
microconstitutionality review 141
Middle East and North Africa (MENA) 145–168
migration crisis 1, 16
militant democracy 5, 10–11, 82–88; definition 77, 82–83; and European Court of Human Rights (ECtHR) 83–84; and European Union 11, 84–97; limits of 86–88; transnational 80
Miltner judgement 58
Mohammed VI 151
monism 46, 56
Montesquieu 183
moral revival 111
Moreira Ferreira v. Portugal 66
Morocco 13–14, 146–148; constitution 146, 151–152, 154–155, 164; constitutional courts 145–168; constitutional reviews 155, 156, 164–165
'most similar case' principle 46
'Muzzle Law' 96

National Anti-Corruption Directorate (DNA) 132, 139
National Assembly 176, 178–180, 182, 184–187, 189–190, 192–193
National Broadcasting Council 118
National Charter 150
National Civil Protection Headquarters 195–198, 200–203, 210
national constitutionalism 2, 216
National Council of the Judiciary (NCJ) 94–96, 117–119
national defence 14, 172, 173, 179, 184–187, 192–193
national identity 75, 103
nationalism 4
national security 68, 136, 162, 178–179, 184–185, 207
national sovereignty 103
nation-states 78
NATO 187
NCJ *see* National Council of the Judiciary
ne bis in idem (double jeopardy) 10, 71–73
neoliberalism 4, 111
neo-nationalism 4
norm-setting 2, 7
nullum crimen sine lege 108
Nykänen v. Finland 71

obiter dicta 49, 50, 51
Öcalan v. Turkey 65, 68
'October judges' 110
'open texture' 2, 173, 174, 183, 189
Orban, Viktor 103
organisational positions 36
outcomes 37, 39–40
outputs 37–38, 40

Palestine 146
pandemic constitutionalism 5, 14
pandemics 181–182; *see also* Covid-19 pandemic
parliamentary monarchies 147–156
Parliament v. Council (the 'Chernobyl' case) 81
Pawłowicz, Krystyna 117
Piotrowicz, Stanisław 117
PKK judgement 53
Poland 12, 74–77, 85, 87–98, 101–125; constitutional review; 106–107, 109; constitutions 106–108, 111; *see also* Polish Constitutional Tribunal; Polish Supreme Court
policy-making 2, 4, 165, 214, 215; emergency 174, 177; judicial 4, 6, 7; military and defence 185, 193
Polish Constitutional Tribunal 12, 101–124; before 2015 106–109; from 2015 to 2016 112–115; from 2017 to 2018 115–117; from 2019 to 2020 117–121
Polish People's Party 109, 111
Polish Supreme Court 90–96, 118–120; Disciplinary Chamber of 94–97, 117, 119–120; Extraordinary Control and Public Affairs Chamber 119
political actors 24, 34
political constitutionalism 103
political culture 43
Political Messianism 78
political parties 24, 35, 37, 48, 109, 130, 140, 151, 155; banning of 83, 86; freedom to form 83; goals 39
political question doctrine 81
political revolutions 2
political rights 83–84, 160
popular initiatives 47–53, 55, 58

popular sovereignty 11, 14, 51, 128, 171, 183
popular vote 47
populism 11, 16, 74–75, 82, 89, 94, 97–98, 216; constitutional 4, 7, 11, 12, 214; judicial 128–129
populist backsliding 101
Portugal 125
Portuguese Judges case 90, 92
post-communist countries 126
post-modernity 2
power: balance of 132, 141, 143, 145, 158, 177; and democracy 78, 80; and judges 36; judicial 126, 129, 135, 139, 143, 207; and language 41; tripartition of 107, 108; *see also* ancillary powers; emergency powers clause; separation of powers
preliminary rulings 94–98
presidential powers 137–138
privacy, right to 108, 179, 187
private life, right to 49
private property 39
procedural acts 69
proportionality, principle of 48
Protection Against Disasters Act 180–181, 188
Przyłębska, Julia 116, 122
public good 204
public safety 73
pyramidal concept of law 44

racism 34
Raikovska, Tanya 191
rationality 29, 32, 34
Rawls, J. 84
RCC *see* Romanian Constitutional Court
refugees 76
regionalism 4
religion 179
representation, principle of 80
representative democracy 5
res judicata 9, 63–73, 139–140
restitutio in integrum 64
retirement age 91–92, 94, 119
retrial clause 68
retroactivity 107, 196–198, 200–201
revolutionary courts 4–6
revolutions 6; constitutional 104, 216; counter-constitutional 105–106, 124; legal 2, 6; liberal 104; political 2
rights: to an effective remedy 92, 95; to family life 49; individual 13, 50, 55, 82, 150, 156–158, 167; to liberty 67; to life 179; of minorities 76; political 83–84, 160; to privacy 108, 179, 187; to private life 49; restriction of 178–179, 181, 188, 190, 197; *see also* fundamental rights; human rights
Romania 125–144; constitution 129–132, 136, 138, 141; constitutional review in 13, 126, 129, 131, 133–136, 139, 140, 142; *see also* Romanian Constitutional Court (RCC)
Romanian Constitutional Court (RCC) 12–13, 90, 125–144; activism 129–142; Decision 144/2005 136; Decision 220/ 2019 135; Decision 26/2019 135–136; Decision 358/2018 138–139; Decision 417/2019 140; Decision 55/2020 135, 136; Decision 685/2018 139; Decision 727/2012 141; Decision 799/ 2011 141; Decision 874/2018 135; Decision 901/2009 136; design 129–131; Internal Ruling no. 1/2017 142; Law no. 177/2010 140; politicisation of 131–134
Rome Treaty 80–82
Roquette Frères v. Council of the European Communities 80
Ross, Alf 30
Rossiter, C.L. 205–206
Rousseau, J.J. 205, 210
rule of law 59–60, 66, 79, 87, 92; 'constructive deconstruction' of 3; crisis of 101; and democracy 89; 'emergency exceptions' 15, 204–211; and judicial activism 16–17; in Poland 109–112; and populism 75–76; primacy of 66
Rule of Law Report 76
Rzepliński, Andrzej 115

Schmitt, C. 205, 206
Schubert Praxis 53, 55
SCM *see* Superior Council of Magistracy
Sejdovic v. Italy 68
self-restraint 142, 161–164, 183, 189
semi-presidentialism 137
Semov, Atanas 191
separation of powers 3, 5, 48, 74, 78, 95, 103, 161, 189, 215
'severe natural disaster' 194–197, 199, 209–211; *see also* state of disaster
Single European Act 81
Slovenia 125
social justice 152
social solidarity 111
Solidarity 107

Somogyi v. Italy 68
Southern Europe 16
sovereignty 3, 5; European citizens' 87; of law 149, 154; national 103; of parliament 123; popular 11, 14, 51, 128, 171, 183
Spain 125, 155
Stanciu, L.-D. 136, 138
state of disaster 15, 173, 180–181, 188, 192; *see also* 'severe natural disaster'
state of emergency 173–182, 184, 187, 190, 192, 199
state of exception 15, 176, 179–181, 211
state of siege 173–182, 184, 190
statutes 25
statutory anticonstitutionalism 101
statutory law 24, 44, 47, 50–51, 53–55, 57, 67
Stoichkov v. Bulgaria 66, 67, 68
Strasbourg Court *see* European Court of Human Rights (ECtHR)
structural discrimination 33
subsidiarity, principle of 79
Superior Council of Magistracy (SCM) 138
supermajority 125, 142
supranational courts 2, 3, 6, 9–10, 14, 171, 214, 216
supranationalisation 216
supranational organisations 44
Supreme Constitutional Court of Palestine 146
Supreme Court Act 2017 94–95
supreme courts 2, 9, 214–216
surveillance 136
Swiss Federal Court *see* Federal Supreme Court of Switzerland
Switzerland: apex courts 45–54; constitution 46–47, 57–58; constitutional review in 53–54; and EU 46, 48, 50–52; the popular initiative 47–53; *see also* Federal Supreme Court of Switzerland
Szydło, Beata 115

Tănăsescu, E.-S. 128, 136, 138, 144
Tanchev, Advocate General 90–91
taxation 73
tax offences 73
technocracy 2, 215
TEU *see* Treaty on European Union
TFEU *see* Treaty on the Functioning of the European Union
torture 179
transitology 14
transplantology 14
travel ban 98
Treaty of Nice 84
Treaty on European Union (TEU) 75, 76, 85–93, 95
Treaty on the Functioning of the European Union (TFEU) 91, 93
Trump, Donald 98
Tunisia 146
Turkey 125, 155

UK Supreme Court 98
ultima ratio 51
United Kingdom 153
United Nations (UN) 48
United Nations International Law Commission (UN ILC) 65
United States 98; constitutional review in 104; Supreme Court 33, 34, 104, 141

values 34–35; European Union 75–76, 78–79, 85, 87–88, 93–97
VAT violation 73
video conferencing 203

war 173–182, 184, 190; 'on terror' 16, 204, 206
Waste Directive case *see Commission v. Ireland*
Weber, Max 32
Weiler, H. 86, 87, 88
Western legal systems 32, 34, 36
WHO *see* World Health Organization
World Health Organization (WHO) 202
World Trade Organization (WTO) 52
World War I 83
World War II 83, 103, 206
WTO *see* World Trade Organization

Ziółkowski, M. 123

www.ingramcontent.com/pod-product-compliance
Lightning Source LLC
LaVergne TN
LVHW011127300926
849160LV00008B/544
* 9 7 8 1 0 3 2 0 6 0 9 2 7 *